D1014028

Discover
Honolulu,
Waikiki
& O'ahu

Experience the best
of O'ahu

This edition written and researched by

Craig McLachlan

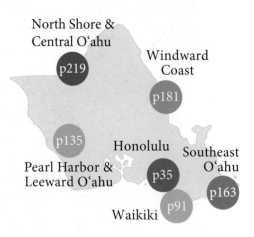

● Honolulu

● Waikiki

● Pearl Harbor & Leeward O'ahu

● Southeast O'ahu

● Windward Coast

● North Shore & Central O'ahu

Contents

Contents

Discover Honolulu, Waikiki & O'ahu

In Focus

Survival Guide

This Is O'ahu

Landing at Honolulu's airport plunges you into the urban jungle, but relax, it's still Polynesia. Even among downtown high-rises, you'll find capital-city power brokers in breezy aloha shirts. By day, inspect royal feathered capes and ancient temple carvings, then swizzle mai tais while slack key guitars play at Waikiki Beach after dark.

There's another side of the island: the 'country,' where farms and dirt roads lead deep into a Hawaiian heartland. On some wild, rugged and nearly deserted beaches, sea turtles still outnumber surfers. Set your watch to island time as you cruise past the Windward Coast's emerald valleys, rustic ranches and roadside shrimp trucks, or lose yourself on the rural Wai'anae Coast.

Don't dismiss O'ahu as a transit point en route to the Neighbor Islands. Take a closer look and you'll uncover a lifetime of adventures. Surf the Banzai Pipeline's giant waves, hike atop knife-edged *pali* (cliffs), dive in Hanauma Bay's giant fishbowl, windsurf or kayak to uninhabited islands off Kailua Bay, and be back in Waikiki for sunset hula. No worries, *brah*.

O'ahu, like Honolulu-born President Barack Obama, is proud of its multi-cultural heritage. The nerve center of the archipelago brings you face to face with Hawaii as it really is, not just a postcard fantasy. All over this island, nicknamed 'The Gathering Place,' pulses the Hawaiian lifeblood, from ancient heiau (stone temples) to sacred hula dances and chants. Boisterous festivals keep diverse traditions alive.

Spam, surfing, hula, pidgin, rubbah slippah – these are just some of the touchstones of everyday life floating in the middle of the Pacific Ocean. People are easygoing, low-key and casual, bursting with genuine aloha and fun. You'll feel welcome whether you're a surf bum, a honeymooner or part of a big *'ohana* (extended family) with grandparents and kids tagging along.

> **"**
> On some wild, rugged and nearly deserted beaches, sea turtles still outnumber surfers.
> **"**

Boats docked on Lanikai Beach (p194), near Kailua

15
Top Experiences

Kahana Bay

Windward Coast

PACIFIC OCEAN

Ka'a'awa

Ahupua'a o Kahana State Park

Kualoa Regional Park

Waikane

Waiahole

Kahalu'u

Kappa Island

Moko Manu

'Ahuimanu

Kane'ohe Bay

Mokapu Point

Kane'ohe Marine Corps Air Station

Byōdō-In

He'eia

Pu'u Kawipo'o (2441ft)

Malae

Kapoho Point

Kailua Bay

Ko'olau

Kane'ohe

Kailua

Kawai Nui Marsh

Kailua Beach Park

Lanikai

Likelike Hwy

Olomana

Wailea Point

Bellows Air Force Station

Nu'uanu Pali Lookout

Pali Hwy

Waimanalo

Waimanalo Bay

Mt Tantalus (2013ft)

Manoa Valley

Range

Manana Island

Honolulu

Makapu'u Point

Waikiki

Koko Crater (1208ft)

Kalaniana'ole Hwy

Koko Head Regional Park

Diamond Head (760ft)

Maunalua Bay

Hanauma Bay

Koko Head (642ft)

157°45'W

15 O'ahu's Top Experiences

Sunset Hula at Waikiki Beach

Every night at beachfront resorts, bars and shopping malls you can stumble upon legendary O'ahu musicians strumming their slack key guitars and ukuleles or singing *ha'i* (a style of falsetto) and Hawaiian chants, while hula dancers in swaying skirts perform subtle hand movements and patterned footsteps. After sunset, tiki torches are lit and the conch shell blown at Kuhio Beach Park, where you can watch a free show (p126) that's surprisingly not just for tourists – it's a way of keeping Hawaiian traditions alive.

1

Diamond Head

Jutting into the ocean, this extinct volcanic crater (p168) – where ancient Hawaiians once sacrificed humans to war god Ku – is Honolulu's best-known landmark. Every day hundreds of visitors stomp up the trail, leading through a 225ft-long tunnel and past concrete bunkers to the summit. The reward is panoramic views of the Pacific and Honolulu's cityscape. View from Diamond Head

Snorkeling at Hanauma Bay

With turquoise waters ringed by the remnants of an ancient volcano, this is O'ahu's most loved snorkeling spot (p175). Cradled along the island's southeast shore, legally protected Hanauma Bay offers a giant outdoor fishbowl to splash around in, plus a coral reef that's thousands of years old. Pull a snorkel mask over your eyes – you'll be amazed by the diversity of sealife visible just below the surface of the nature preserve's glimmering waters. If you're lucky, a green sea turtle will paddle by. Picasso triggerfish, Hanauma Bay

Bishop Museum

Sometimes it's a challenge to find remnants of the ancient Hawaiian ways that flowed on this island for more than 1000 years before Captain Cook arrived. That's what makes the Bishop Museum (p57) such a rich cultural and natural-history storehouse. Inspect rare artifacts such as the feathered cloak worn by Kamehameha the Great and fearsome *ki'i akua* (carved temple images), then step inside O'ahu's only planetarium and gaze at the same stars that guided the first Polynesian voyagers to this archipelago, the planet's most remote.

The Best...
Beaches

WAIKIKI BEACH
O'ahu's most buzzing all-around beach scene. (p96)

ALA MOANA BEACH PARK
Join the locals taking their morning swim. (p40)

KAILUA
Pick your beach pleasure: walking, kayaking, windsurfing or sunbathing. (p193)

KO OLINA LAGOONS
Four postcard-perfect beaches with palm trees, calm water and sunset views. (p151)

SUNSET BEACH
Watch the pros surf when the big winter waves come out to play. (p228)

Kailua Beach Park

The clouds gather on the horizon, but it's a calm morning. You put your kayak in at Ka'elepulu Canal and paddle out. As you look back over the water that fades from cobalt to azure (or is that electric blue?), you see the golden arc of sand and the ridges of the green Ko'olau Mountains in the distance. You enjoy every moment because you know by afternoon those clouds will arrive with the wind, and it will be kitesurfing time at Kailua Beach Park (p193).

ANN CECIL/GETTY IMAGES ©

The Best...
Hikes

MANOA FALLS
Family-friendly waterfall hike in the hills above Honolulu. (p59)

MAKIKI VALLEY & MANOA CLIFFS
More magical forest hikes with skyline views. (p61)

DIAMOND HEAD
Tried-and-true military trail to a volcanic summit with 360-degree views. (p169)

MAUNAWILI
Take your pick of a waterfall trail or a coastal-view trek. (p186)

KA'ENA POINT
A flat former-railbed hike between craggy cliffs and pounding shore. (p243)

END OF PAUOA FLATS TRAIL

KARL LEHMANN/GETTY IMAGES ©

6 Hiking Around Mt Tantalus

You don't have to leave Honolulu behind to find a natural escape thanks to footpaths (p59) winding into the lofty Ko'olau Range. Take the kids on a walk to Manoa Falls, or press on up a steep ladder of tree roots to Nu'uanu Valley Lookout where a gap in the peaks reveals the lush Windward Coast. No matter which trail you choose, you'll get a free lesson in Hawaiian natural history, walking past hulking banyan trees, fragrant guava and musical bamboo groves where honeycreepers flit between flowers. Hiker on Pauoa Flats Trail (p61), Nu'uanu Valley

Waimea Bay

Waimea Bay (p233) is one of the most polyglot places on O'ahu. The gorgeous deep-blue bay has attracted attention since outsiders first hit the shore in 1779. Back then the area had a large Native Hawaiian population. The valley is now a park and the beach the domain of visitors. In winter, the waves rise so high that it's international surfers and their fans who are most attracted.

USS Arizona Memorial

A hush settles over the group as you disembark onto the memorial (p141). It's hard not to be moved by the realization you are standing over the watery grave of more than 1000 sailors. Roughly half of the US servicemen who died during the Pearl Harbor attack on December 7, 1941, were killed on the USS *Arizona*. An optional audio tour recounts survivor tales, but switch it off until you get back to dry land. This sacred place is best experienced in silence.

USS *Arizona* Memorial, designed by architect Alfred Preis

Honolulu's Chinatown

An anchor's throw from Honolulu Harbor, the crowded streets of Chinatown (p49) possess more history than any other place on O'ahu. Nineteenth-century whalers whooped it up in bars and brothels, while plantation-era immigrants made their way into island society by putting down roots. Today this pan-Asian neighborhood keeps evolving, with art galleries, creative restaurants and hip nightspots. It's small enough to walk around in a morning, with a tasty break for dim sum or noodles.

SPECIAL
$1.29

The Best...
Ocean Adventures

SNORKELING AT HANAUMA BAY
Schools of tropical fish in an aquamarine preserve. (p176)

BODYSURFING AT SANDY BEACH PARK
Crashing waves for experts only. (p178)

KITESURFING AT KAILUA
Catch the wind on a sailing wakeboard. (p195)

STAND-UP PADDLING IN HALE'IWA
Ride the Anahulu River. (p235)

SURFING OFF PUA'ENA POINT
North Shore breaks for beginners. (p236)

WHALE WATCHING ON THE WAI'ANAE COAST
Spot a leviathan in winter. (p154)

Matsumoto's Shave Ice

Why would someone stand in such a long line for shave ice? Maybe it's the exotic, homemade flavors such as *li hing mui* (salty dried plum) and coconut cream. Maybe it's the ice cream and azuki beans. Or maybe it's the history. The building dates to the 1920s, but it wasn't until 1951 that Japanese immigrant Mamoru Matsumoto opened his grocery here. Shave ice quickly became the best seller when introduced in the 1960s. Today his son runs the store (p238) and, on a hot day, he sells more than 1000 serves of shave ice.

The Best...
Views

Surfing the North Shore

Phantoms, Freddyland, Backyards, Rocky Point, Log Cabins. Not only every beach, but every break on the North Shore (p294) has a name. You've heard of the Banzai Pipeline, one of the world's most perfect barrel rides, but aficionados know how the surf hits on every reef. The shore breaks around Sunset Beach are some of the most famous. Though you may get a little action in fall and spring, winter is prime time for the epic waves – several world-class competitions are held here between December and February.

Surfers on Sunset Beach (p228)

Helena's Hawaiian Food

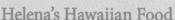

Doesn't look like much, right? Just another strip-mall storefront with a lei painted around the doors. But inside the kitchen waft the aromas of Hawaiian soul food – *kalua* (underground-pit cooked) pig, sour poi, steamed *laulau* (meat or fish wrapped in leaves) bundles, *lomilomi* (minced with tomato and onion) salmon and *pipi kaula* (beef jerky) – all made from the family recipes of Helena Chock, a James Beard Award winner. Her grandson now runs the joint (p76), and Honoluluans still crowd the tiny parking lot, ducking inside to grab takeout for an impromptu luau. Steamed *laulau* with shiitake mushrooms

Hiking to Ka'ena Point 13

Trekking along this easy ocean-side trail (p160), you'll almost certainly spot wildlife. If you're lucky you'll see an endangered monk seal bathing on the volcanic rocks below. If not, look closely for them once you hit the nature reserve at the island's tip. They'll be the black 'rocks' that are more rounded and smooth than angular and pockmarked. High above, frigates and other seabirds fly by. Keep your eyes peeled in winter: you may spot a humpback whale in the distance.

LINDA CHING/GETTY IMAGES ©

Shopping in Waikiki & Ala Moana 14

Forget hula dolls and coconut bikinis. You can pick up unique Hawaiiana and souvenirs – from handcrafted ukuleles and koa wood carvings to tropical skirts and flip-flops – in the malls and boutiques of Waikiki (p127) and Ala Moana (p84). Detour down Kapahulu Ave to Bailey's Antiques and Aloha Shirts, full of modern reproductions and vintage prints, including neon designs from the swingin' 1960s.

Shangri La

In the shadow of Diamond Head, the former mansion of billionaire tobacco heiress Doris Duke is a sight for art lovers and celebrity hounds. From its exterior this tropical hideaway (p170) looks plain and unassuming, but inside it's a treasure house of antique ceramic-tile mosaics, carved wooden screens and silk tapestries, all embraced by meditative gardens with ocean vistas. Touring Shangri La feels as intimate as reading Duke's private journal.

The Best...
Island Cuisine

ALAN WONG'S
Hawaii Regional Cuisine from a Honolulu-raised kitchen star. (p73)

LEONARD'S
Get your *malasadas* (Portuguese doughnuts) hot from the oven. (p120)

ROY'S WAIKIKI BEACH
Top-notch island bistro for evolutionary fusion food. (p119)

SIDE STREET INN
Jovial sports bar where chefs chow down after hours. (p71)

TED'S BAKERY
Classic plate-lunch fare at its finest. (p230)

POKE STOP
Take some of the island's freshest seafood to go. (p247)

O'ahu's Top Itineraries

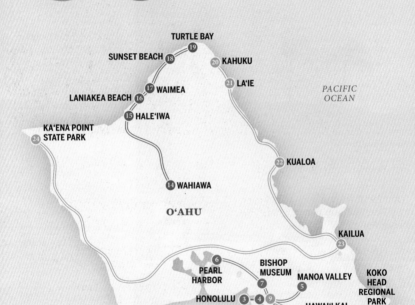

TURTLE BAY

SUNSET BEACH 18 · 19

20 KAHUKU

21 LA'IE

17 WAIMEA

LANIAKEA BEACH 16

15 HALE'IWA

KA'ENA POINT
STATE PARK 24

*PACIFIC
OCEAN*

22 KUALOA

14 WAHIAWA

O'AHU

KAILUA
23

6
PEARL
HARBOR

BISHOP
MUSEUM

7

MANOA VALLEY

5

KOKO
HEAD
REGIONAL
PARK

HONOLULU 3 · 4 9

HAWAI'I KAI

*PACIFIC
OCEAN*

WAIKIKI 1 – 2

DIAMOND HEAD

8

10

12

13

SHANGRI
LA

HANAUMA
BAY

● **Waikiki to Pearl Harbor** Four days
● **Diamond Head to Makapu'u** Two days
● **Wahiawa to Turtle Bay** Two days
● **Kahuku to Ka'ena Point** Two days

Waikiki to Pearl Harbor

4 DAYS

The Battleship *Missouri* Memorial (p143)

ANN CECIL/GETTY IMAGES ©

1 Waikiki Beach (p96)

Bronze your bod for two days on this world-famous resort strip, stretching from **Fort DeRussy Beach** to **Sans Souci Beach Park**, a secret snorkeling spot.

2 Kuhio Beach Park (p100)

After you've put up your surfboard, watch the sun sink into the Pacific and lie back on your beach mat for the free **Hawaiian music and dance show**.

3 Downtown Honolulu (p41)

On day three, take the bus to tour **'Iolani Palace**, browse the **Hawai'i State Art Museum** and ascend the **Aloha Tower**.

4 Chinatown (p49)

Walk in the steps of 19th-century whalers from Honolulu's harbor to historic Chinatown. The bustling streets are crammed with open-air markets, lei shops, art galleries, antique stores and eateries.

5 Manoa Valley (p55)

For the afternoon, shake off the urban grit and head for the hills. Wander among tropical plants in the **Lyon Arboretum**, then hike with the kids to **Manoa Falls**.

6 Pearl Harbor (p140)

On your fourth day, get up early to visit O'ahu's stirring WWII sites, starting with the sunken **USS Arizona Memorial**.

7 Bishop Museum (p57)

In the afternoon, get lost in Polynesia's top-ranked anthropological museum, where artifacts fill the **Hawaiian Hall**.

⬤ THIS LEG: 55 MILES

Coral reef at Hanauma Bay (p175)

DAVID WALL PHOTO/GETTY IMAGES ©

8 Diamond Head (p168)

Start day five with an early-morning hike up an extinct volcanic crater, scrambling through a spooky tunnel for summit views extending from *mauka* (the mountains) to *makai* (the sea).

9 Honolulu Museum of Art (p52)

Head back downtown to this exquisite, globally minded art museum. Break for lunch at the courtyard **Honolulu Museum of Art Cafe**.

10 Shangri La (p170)

With advance reservations, board a minibus back toward Diamond Head to tour Doris Duke's former mansion, today a trove of Islamic art.

11 Hanauma Bay (p175)

On the next day, if you really want to go face-to-mask with schools of rainbow-colored fish and green sea turtles, visit this crescent-shaped bay. Show up early to avoid the crowds.

12 Hawaiʻi Kai (p173)

For lunch, chow down at **Kona Brewing Company**, sample an acai bowl at **Koko-nuts Shave Ice & Snacks**, or grab an exquisite *mochi*-ice cream from Bubbie's.

13 Koko Head Regional Park (p177)

Cruise by car down Oʻahu's southeast coast. Roadside stops include **Halona Blowhole**, surf-pounded **Halona Cove**, the bodysurfers' hangout of **Sandy Beach** and the lighthouse trail up windy **Makapuʻu Point**.

THIS LEG: 35 MILES

Wahiawa to Turtle Bay

2 DAYS

Pineapple-lined Kaukonahua Rd (Hwy 803) near Wahiawa (p246)

KARL LEHMANN/GETTY IMAGES ©

14 Wahiawa (p246)

On day seven, drive from Honolulu to the North Shore via slow-and-scenic **Kunia Road**. Stop at **Dole Plantation** to get lost in the pineapple maze or go on a garden tour.

15 Hale'iwa (p235)

Spend some time that afternoon wandering among the Hale'iwa town shops at **North Shore Market Place** or taking a stand-up paddling lesson. For dinner, **Cafe Hale'iwa** has creative island cuisine starring local produce.

16 Laniakea Beach (p235)

The next morning you might have some luck spotting *honu* (sea turtles) at Laniakea Beach.

17 Waimea (p233)

Just down the road is **Waimea Valley**, where you can stretch your legs walking through an 1800-acre park filled with native flora and swim beneath **Waimea Falls**. As you leave, be sure to admire the stunning **Waimea Bay**.

18 Sunset Beach (p228)

'Ehukai Beach Park, aka Banzai Pipeline, is definitely worth a stop. As is **Ted's Bakery**, for a plate lunch and pie. Afterwards, hit **Sunset Beach** for some sunbathing and surf watching.

19 Turtle Bay (p224)

There's time for one more swim in the sheltered cove before sunset cocktails at **Turtle Bay Resort**.

THIS LEG: 42 MILES

Kahuku to Ka'ena Point

2 DAYS

Horseback riders, Kualoa Ranch (p208)

DANA EDMUNDS/GETTY IMAGES ©

 Kahuku (p214)

Turtle Bay to Kahuku is less than 5 miles, but on day nine wait to depart so you can have lunch at one of the famous Kahuku shrimp trucks like **Giovanni's**. Save room for some Kahuku-grown corn, too.

 La'ie (p212)

Unless you have an extra day to spare, skip the **Polynesian Cultural Center** on this tour. Just know that the interpretive shows and luau are worth coming back for someday.

22 Kualoa (p207)

Meander down the coast, pausing at any beaches or roadside stands of interest. Fans of *Lost* and *Jurassic Park* will want to stop at **Kualoa Ranch**, where several scenes were shot. Continue on to **Tropical Farms** to buy some flavored macadamia nuts and other Hawaiian-made products.

 Kailua (p192)

End your day in Kailua, where you'll spend two nights. You have to stop at the **Kalapawai Market**, a landmark grocery store, for a picnic to take to **Kailua Beach**. While there, watch the windsurfers and kitesurfers, or rent a kayak and take off on your own. The next morning you'll hear the guava pancakes at **Cinnamon's Restaurant** calling.

24 Ka'ena Point State Park (p242)

Those feeling in need of some downtime should stay by the beach in Kailua. Energetic sorts should take a day trip across O'ahu. The reward? A stunning coastal hike to **Ka'ena Point**, the tip of the island, with excellent animal-spotting potential en route.

 THIS LEG: 85 MILES

Get Inspired

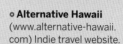

Books

Shark Dialogues (1995) Honolulu-born Kiana Davenport's multigenerational novel spans the decades from Western contact through to the plantation era.

House of Thieves (2005) Local author Kaui Hart Hemming's short stories about upper-class families in Hawaii.

Hotel Honolulu (2001) Paul Theroux's satirical tale about a washed-up writer managing a run-down Waikiki hotel.

Legends and Myths of Hawaii (1888) King David Kalakaua magically mixes history with mythology.

Best of Honolulu Fiction (1999) Sixteen years of island stories.

Films

The Descendants (2011) An O'ahu father (George Clooney) comes to terms with family after his wife's critical accident.

Blue Hawaii (1961) Elvis Presley on Waikiki.

Tora! Tora! Tora! (1971) Dramatization of the Pearl Harbor attack.

Highwater (2009) Action-filled doco about the Triple Crown surfing competition.

50 First Dates (2004) Romantic comedy filmed near Moli'i Fishpond.

 Music

Gabby (1991) Legendary slack key guitarist and vocalist Gabby Pahinui.

Hana Hou (1995) Auntie Genoa Keawe's classic Hawaiian melodies.

Generation Hawai'i (2006) Lyrical, modern Hawaiian album from Amy Hanaiali'i.

IZ in Concert: The Man and His Music (1999) O'ahu-born Israel Kamakawiwo'ole live on vocals and ukulele.

Kamahiwa (2005) A collection of Keali'i Reichel's local tunes.

 Websites

O'ahu Visitors Bureau (www.visit-oahu.com) Island's official site.

Hawaii Visitors and Convention Bureau (www.gohawaii.com) Great activity info.

Alternative Hawaii (www.alternative-hawaii.com) Indie travel website.

Honolulu Weekly (http://honoluluweekly.com) Best area event and music calendar.

Short on time?

This list will give an instant insight into the country.

Read *Growing Up Local*, an anthology from Honolulu-based Bamboo Ridge press, sheds light on what it means to be from the island.

Watch TV's *Hawaii 5-0*, the remake, offers viewers a modern-day look at Hono-lulu's sights and sounds.

Listen *Facing Forward* is the all-time best-selling album by legendary Hawaiian musician IZ (Israel Kamakawiwo'ole).

Log on The Aloha Shorts (www.hawaiipublicradio.org/alohashorts) podcast introduces you to the island's actors, playwrights, musicians and poets.

Surfing at Sandy Beach (p178), Koko Head Regional Park
ANN CECIL/GETTY IMAGES ©

O'ahu Month by Month

Top Events

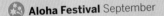

- **Aloha Festival** September

- **Triple Crown of Surfing** November

- **Prince Lot Hula Festival** July

- **Hawaii International Film Festival** October

- **'I Love Kailua' Town Party** April

January

Tourist season gets underway as mainlanders escaping less temperate climes arrive en masse. This is typically the rainiest month of the year.

Chinese New Year

Around the time of the second new moon after the winter solstice, usually between mid-January and mid-February, Chinatown in Honolulu celebrates the lunar New Year with more than a week's worth of lion dances, firecrackers, street fairs and parades.

February

Humpback whales migrate past the island from December through May, but February is one of the best times to spot them. Valentine's weekend is booked solid at resorts.

March

It's still winter elsewhere, so it's still peak season on O'ahu. Note that college students take spring break in March or April, making things even busier.

Honolulu Festival

Music, dance and drama performances at various venues in Honolulu and Waikiki take place for three days in mid-March. The Asia Pacific cultural festival also features an arts-and-crafts fair and a grand parade followed by a fireworks show.

April

Winter rains abate about the same time as the tourist crush

September Children playing saxophones at the Aloha Festival (p30), Waikiki

JOHN BORTHWICK/GETTY IMAGES ©

does. Any time after Easter is a low-key, and possibly lower-priced, time to visit the island.

Waikiki Spam Jam

One of Waikiki's wackiest street festivals is held on a day in late April. The Spam Jam celebrates the state's favorite meat product. Try Spam served as sushi, in spring rolls, atop nachos, in tacos, mixed with pasta – even as a popsicle flavoring.

'I Love Kailua' Town Party

A giant block party takes over Kailua town's main street one Sunday in April. Local bands and hula schools turn out to perform, while the community's artists vend their wares and area restaurants cook up a storm.

May

May Day, the first, is Lei Day in Hawaii, when the beautiful ancient tradition of stringing together and wearing tropical flowers, leaves and seeds is celebrated.

June

Calmer, summer currents prevail; it's relatively safe to assume you can swim instead of surf on the North Shore.

Pan-Pacific Festival

Expect outdoor hula shows and *taiko* drumming as part of the early-June Asian and Polynesian performing-arts showcase in Honolulu and Waikiki. Don't miss the huge *ho'olaule'a* (celebration) block party and parade that takes place along Kalakaua Ave.

King Kamehameha Celebrations

The state holiday, King Kamehameha Day, is June 11. A ceremony at the king's statue in Honolulu is followed by a parade and a street party. Later in the month, a hula festival is held in his majesty's honor (p62).

July

Towns around the island welcome Independence Day, July 4, with fireworks and festivities. Family summer vacation travel is at a peak around the holiday, as are lodging prices.

Prince Lot Hula Festival

On the third Saturday in July, one of O'ahu's premier Hawaiian cultural festivals features noncompetitive hula performances at Moanalua Gardens in Honolulu. The former royal retreat setting provides an even more graceful, traditional atmosphere.

August

Sunny weather continues nearly everywhere. On Statehood Day, the third Friday of the month, some celebrate, some protest – but everyone takes the day off work.

Hawaiian Slack Key Guitar Festival

Lay out a picnic blanket at Waikiki's Kapi'olani Park and enjoy free Hawaiian guitar and ukulele shows. The island's top performers take the stage, plus there are food vendors and an arts-and-crafts fair in the park.

September

Tradewinds blow in, but the temperature is still ideal, making it an excellent time for those without kids in school to explore the island – sans crowds.

October

Travel bargains abound during one of the year's slowest times for visiting O'ahu.

 Hawaii International Film Festival

Screenings of imported Pacific Rim, Asian, mainland American, European and even a few Hawaii-related films roll at venues in Honolulu and Waikiki. This highly-regarded event is popular, so book tickets ahead. For full schedules, see www.hiff.org.

 Halloween

In the days and weeks leading up to and including Halloween, October 31, look for themed performances, haunted houses, costume contests and local festivals. Attractions such as the Dole Plantation in central O'ahu, the Polynesian Cultural Center on the Windward Coast and the Hawai'i Nature Center in southeast O'ahu get into the act by hosting spooky events.

 Aloha Festival

Begun in 1946, the Aloha Festival is the state's premier cultural festival, an almost 10 day-long tribute to all things Hawaiian. The signature events are Waikiki's royal court procession, block party and floral parade. Affiliated activities may take place elsewhere across the island.

Hawai'i Food & Wine Festival

Island star chefs Roy Yamaguchi and Alan Wong co-host three days of fabulous food and wine. Events in Honolulu and beyond highlight the local bounty and may include gala dinners, farm-to-table tastings, traditional Hawaiian feasts, luncheon discussions, and wine-, chocolate- and coffee-pairing sessions.

 November

Surfers of the world descend on the North Shore at the beginning of the epic winter wave season. It can get cool at night, so bring a sweater.

 Triple Crown of Surfing

This world-class surfing competition takes place from mid-November to mid-December at the North Shore's Hale'iwa Ali'i Beach Park, Sunset Beach and 'Ehukai Beach Park. The actual start date depends on the surf. So be ready, and bring your binoculars!

December

Despite the occasional chill, Santas all over the island are putting on their best aloha shirt and shorts. Early on, locals have the place to themselves; Christmas and New Year's bring crazy-high prices and crowds.

 ## Honolulu Marathon

On the second Sunday in December, the Honolulu Marathon attracts more than 25,000 runners (more than half hailing from Japan), making it one of the world's top 10 largest marathons. Runners trace a route from downtown Honolulu to Diamond Head.

 ## Christmas

The island celebrates Christmas all month long. Many communities host parades, including a floating regatta originating at Hawai'i Kai Marina. Honolulu City Lights starts in early December with a parade and concert and finishes with fireworks for the New Year.

Far left: May Children waiting to dance on Lei Day (p29) **Above: June** King Kamehameha, who is commemorated with a state holiday (p29) **Below:** Horse wearing lei in a Honolulu parade

(FAR LEFT) JOE CARINI/ GETTY IMAGES ©; (ABOVE) JOHN BORTHWICK/GETTY IMAGES © (BELOW) ROBERT CRAVENS/GETTY IMAGES ©

Need to Know

Language
English, Hawaiian and pidgin.

ATMs
Very common.

Credit Cards
Required for vehicle rentals; widely accepted at hotels but not all other lodgings.

Visas
For Visa Waiver Program (VWP) countries, visas are not required for stays of less than 90 days.

Cell Phones
Carrier Verizon has the best network; international travelers need multiband phones.

Wi-Fi
Not all lodgings have wi-fi; some have wired connections (fees may apply). Look for wi-fi hot spots in hotel lobbies and cafes (purchase required).

Internet Access
At public libraries with a card (nonresidents $10).

Directions
Makai means 'toward the ocean'; *mauka* means 'toward the mountain.'

Tipping
Tip 18% to 20% at restaurants and bars; minimum $2 for valets, hotel maids or porters.

When to Go

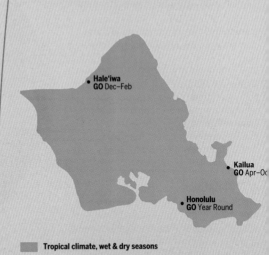

- Hale'iwa
  GO Dec–Feb
- Kailua
  GO Apr–Oc
- Honolulu
  GO Year Round

▮ Tropical climate, wet & dry seasons

High Season
(mid-Dec–mid-Apr)
- North Shore has winter waves; surf comps in full swing
- Whales migrating
- Book rooms and activities far ahead
- High lodging prices, high occupancy
- Rainiest time of the year

Shoulder
(Jun–Aug)
- Dry, hot weather
- Waves picking up in Waikiki, tame on North Shore
- Early starts best for hiking
- Visitor spike due to school summer vacations

Low Season
(mid-Apr–May & Sep–Oct)
- Lodging rates drop, bargaining may be possible
- Airfares at their lowest
- Crowds few
- Weather still temperate

Advance Planning

- **Three months before** Make flight and lodging reservations. If yo plan to travel during the winter holidays or in July and August, book at least six months ahead.

- **Two weeks before** Reserve in-demand activities such as tours, boat trips, and tickets for Valor in the Pacific National Monument, Polynesian Cultural Center and Doris Duke's Shangri La.

- **One week before** Make reservations for any top restaurants whe you hope to dine, especially in Waikiki and Honolulu.

Your Daily Budget

Budget (less than $150)
- Waikiki hostel: $25–35
- Walk to the beach
- Buses and a taxi or two to get around
- Mostly self-catering and plate lunches, occasional evening meal or drinks out

Midrange ($150–350)
- Waikiki budget hotel or Kailua vacation rental: $90–160
- Car rental for a couple of days
- Activities like surfing or stand-up paddling
- Restaurant meals as well as food-truck fare

Top End (more than $350)
- Full-service resort room
- Top chef-made meals
- Whale-watching tours, activity rentals, spa services

Exchange Rates

Australia	A$1	US$0.81
Canada	C$1	US$0.86
Europe	€1	US$1.22
Japan	¥100	US$1.20
New Zealand	NZ$1	US$0.77
UK	£1	US$1.56

For current exchange rates see www.xe.com

What to Bring

- **Light, waterproof jacket** For tropical windward showers and wind-whipped, cloud-shrouded *pali* (cliffs or mountains).
- **Shoes with traction** When trails get muddy, flip-flops (thongs) just don't cut it.
- **Dive certification** Bring card and logbooks if you're going to take the plunge. Snorkel sets are easily rented or borrowed.
- **Sunglasses and sunscreen** Come on, you know you'll be spending time at the beach.
- **Aloha spirit** This is the islands, man. Slow down and hang loose.

Arriving on Oʻahu

Honolulu International Airport (HNL)

Airport shuttle To Waikiki $12, to Kailua $40, to Haleʻiwa $80

Taxi To Waikiki $35 to $45, 25 to 45 minutes

Car Via Hwy 92 (Nimitz Fwy/Ala Moana Blvd) to Waikiki

Bus Routes 19 and 20 to Waikiki (one carry-on bag only per person) $2.50, 45 to 80 minutes

Getting Around

- **Car** Consider skipping the car if you're staying in Waikiki, otherwise a rental is almost required ($35 to $60 per day).
- **Bus** More than 100 routes, but not always convenient. Some popular parks and sights are beyond reach. Circle Isle buses (52 and 55) circumnavigate Oʻahu.
- **Bicycle** Not practical for islandwide travel; recommended for getting around the North Shore and in Kailua on the Windward Coast.

Accommodation

- **Hotels and condos** Mostly available in Waikiki, also a few in Honolulu. Price depends on location, view and room size.
- **Vacation rentals and B&Bs** This is where you'll be staying if you leave the city behind. Expect full kitchens and beach gear, but no hot breakfasts are included.
- **Resorts** Outside Waikiki, the only resorts are at Ko Olina in leeward Oʻahu and on the North Shore at Turtle Bay.

Be Forewarned

- **Swimming in wild, non-regulated waterfalls** Hazards include falling rocks and leptospirosis.
- **Car break-ins** Absolutely do not leave anything visible in a rental car. Car break-ins are common. Hiding things in the trunk is only effective if you do so before getting to your parking spot.
- **Beaches** Do not leave valuables on the beach while you swim; slippers and towels are usually left alone.

Honolulu

Here in Honolulu, away from the crowds of Waikiki, you get to shake hands with the real Hawaii.

A boisterous Polynesian capital, Honolulu delivers an island-style mixed plate of experiences. Eat your way through the pan-Asian alleys of Chinatown, where 19th-century whalers once brawled and immigrant traders thrived.

Gaze out to sea from atop the landmark Aloha Tower, then sashay past Victorian-era brick buildings, including the USA's only royal palace. Ocean breezes rustle palm trees along the harborfront, while in the cool, mist-shrouded Ko'olau Range, forested hiking trails offer postcard city views.

At sunset, cool off with an amble around Magic Island or splash in the ocean at Ala Moana Beach, a rare beauty in the middle of the concrete jungle. After dark, migrate to Chinatown's edgy art and nightlife scene. You won't even miss Waikiki, promise.

Honolulu skyline
MICHELE FALZONE/GETTY IMAGES ©

Honolulu Highlights

Ala Moana Beach Park

Surprisingly convenient and attractive, this wide, sandy beach (p40) is where Honolulu residents go for swimming, surfing, beach volleyball and picnicking. Many visitors who stay in Waikiki don't even know it's there. With plenty of facilities, this is a top place to play or even just to stroll around Magic Island, the peninsula on the eastern side of the park lining the outlet of Ala Wai Canal. Magic Island, Ala Moana Beach Park

1

2 Bishop Museum

Surely the finest Polynesian anthropological museum in the world, Bishop Museum (p57), founded in 1889, is Hawaii's version of the Smithsonian. Visit the three-story Hawaiian Hall, full of royal artifacts, walk your kids through an imaginative erupting volcano in the Science Adventure Center, then learn the traditional Polynesian ways of wayfaring and navigation at the planetarium It's all here and shouldn't be missed.

Native Books/ Nā Mea Hawai'i 3

The place to come to be inspired by everything Hawaiian. Much more than a bookstore, Nā Mea Hawaii (p84) puts you in touch with the real Hawaii. This community gathering spot hosts classes and workshops (p64) for everything from ukulele to hula to weaving to printmaking, open to everyone. There's lei-making, *lomilomi* healing and much, much more, plus the authentic, Hawaiian-made souvenirs you've been searching for. *Lauhala* weaver

Manoa Falls 4

Hawaii isn't just about the beach. Head into the lush tropical interior and take the whole family on this cool, shady forest hike (p59) at the head of the Manoa Valley. We're talking tall trees, wild orchids and red ginger on this scramble above a rocky streambed to the picturesque Manoa Falls. It's hard to believe the difference in vegetation compared to the coast not too far away.

Chinatown 5

Once the haunt of brawling, womanizing whalers, Chinatown (p49) is now ground zero for Honolulu's art, club and hipster scenes. Burning incense still wafts through Chinatown's buzzing markets and there are plenty of Asian eats, but the area also boasts a new look with nouveau art galleries, upmarket restaurants, red-hot clubs and a home-grown enthusiasm that says, 'This is not Waikiki!' Lychees for sale, Chinatown

Honolulu Itineraries

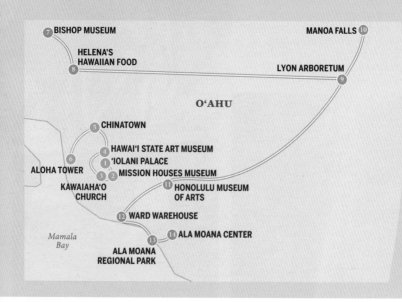

BISHOP MUSEUM ⑦

MANOA FALLS ⑩

HELENA'S HAWAIIAN FOOD
⑧

LYON ARBORETUM
⑨

O'AHU

CHINATOWN ⑤

④ HAWAI'I STATE ART MUSEUM
① 'IOLANI PALACE
⑥
ALOHA TOWER
③ ② MISSION HOUSES MUSEUM

KAWAIAHA'O CHURCH

⑪ HONOLULU MUSEUM OF ARTS

⑫ WARD WAREHOUSE

Mamala Bay

⑬ ⑭ ALA MOANA CENTER

ALA MOANA REGIONAL PARK

2 MILES
DAY ONE

Start your journey through time at the brightly restored 19th-century ① **'Iolani Palace** (p41), today also a protest symbol for Native Hawaiian sovereignty activists.

Next, tour the ② **Mission Houses Museum** (p47), Hawaii's first Protestant settlement. The ③ **Kawaiaha'o Church** (p47) is an imposing, Gothic-style church made of priceless coral rock. Look out for royal and colonial ghosts in the cemetery out back.

Sate your artistic side with visions of Hawaii's multicultural society and heritage at the ④ **Hawai'i State Art Museum** (p46), with everything from abstract paintings and landscape photographs to mixed-media and found-art collages. Then head just down the street for a gourmet island lunch at Cafe Julia.

Poke around fragrant lei stands and animated open-air markets in ⑤ **Chinatown** (p49), or join the locals for lunch at a pan-Asian kitchen. Afterwards, hound the galleries and antiques stores, or meditatively visit traditional incense-burning temples and the botanic garden.

Stroll over to the harborfront and take the elevator straight up the ⑥ **Aloha Tower** (p49), an art-deco landmark. Grab sunset drinks with ocean views at Gordon Biersch Brewery Restaurant.

2 DAYS

15 MILES
DAYS TWO & THREE

Start day two at the ⑦ **Bishop Museum** (p57), a first-rate Polynesian anthropological museum where you can marvel at ancient Hawaiian artifacts.

Taste Native Hawaiian and infused food traditions at ⑧ **Helena's Hawaiian Food** (p76), where you can custom-order your own mini luau plate for a picnic. Take a walk at the ⑨ **Lyon Arboretum** (p56), a verdant tropical reserve with a hidden waterfall at the back.

Although the Tantalus–Round Top scenic drive looks tempting, Honolulu's memorable skyline views from ⑩ **Manoa Falls** (p59) are best earned with your own two feet, so pull on those hiking shoes.

Next morning, visit the ⑪ **Honolulu Museum of Art** (p52), downtown's most prestigious art museum. It also sponsors film screenings and leads tours of Shangri La.

Stock up on island-made souvenirs, arts and crafts, and Hawaiiana books and music at ⑫ **Ward Warehouse** (p84). Swim laps or simply laze on the golden sands at ⑬ **Ala Moana Beach Park** (p40), then wander Magic Island at sunset.

At the ⑭ **Ala Moana Center** (p84), head upstairs to the boisterous Mai Tai Bar (p80) for live island-style music.

'Iolani Palace (p41)
ANN CECIL/GETTY IMAGES ©

Discover Honolulu

History

In 1793 the English frigate *Butterworth* became the first foreign ship to sail into what is now Honolulu Harbor. In 1809 Kamehameha the Great moved his royal court from Waikiki to Honolulu ('sheltered bay') to control the vigorous international trade taking place there, but it didn't replace Lahaina on Maui as the official capital of the Kingdom of Hawai'i until 1845.

In the 1820s Honolulu's first bars and brothels opened to crews of whaling ships. Hotel St, a lineup of bars and strip joints a few blocks from the harbor, became the city's red-light district. Christian missionaries began arriving around the same time, presumably for different purposes. Today, Hawaii's first missionary church still stands just a stone's throw from the royal palace.

In 1893 a small group of citizens, mostly of American missionary descent, seized control of the kingdom from Queen Lili'uokalani and declared an independent republic, imprisoning the queen in downtown Honolulu's 'Iolani Palace. After political machinations and backroom deals that reached Washington, DC, Hawaii was formally annexed by the USA in 1898.

Beaches

Ala Moana Beach Park
Beach

(Map p54; 1201 Ala Moana Blvd; P ⛹) Opposite the Ala Moana Center shopping mall, this city park boasts a broad, golden-sand beach nearly a mile long buffered from passing traffic by shade trees. Ala Moana is hugely popular, yet big enough that it never feels too crowded. This is where Honolulu residents come to go running after work, play beach volleyball and enjoy weekend picnics. The park has full facilities, including lighted tennis courts, ball fields, picnic tables, drinking water, restrooms, outdoor showers and lifeguard towers.

The peninsula jutting from the southeast side of the park is **Magic Island**. Year-round, you can take an idyllic sunset walk around the peninsula's perimeter, within an

Detail of the Queen Lili'uokalani Statue (p43)

Island Insights

The tradition of giving lei to visitors to O'ahu dates to the 19th-century steamships thalkt first brought tourists. In the heyday of cruise-ship tourism, passengers were greeted by local vendors who would toss garlands around the necks of *malihini* (newcomers, or foreigners). It was believed that if passengers threw their lei into the sea as their departing ship passed Diamond Head, and the flowers of the lei floated back toward the beach, they'd be guaranteed to return to Hawaii someday.

anchor's toss of sailboats pulling in and out of neighboring Ala Wai Yacht Harbor.

 ## Sights

Honolulu's compact downtown is just a lei's throw from the harborfront. Nearby, the buzzing streets of Chinatown are packed with food markets, antiques shops, art galleries and hip bars. Between downtown and Waikiki, Ala Moana has Hawaii's biggest mall and the city's best beach. The University of Hawai'i campus is a gateway to the Manoa Valley and the Mt Tantalus green belt. A few outlying sights, including the Bishop Museum, are worth a detour.

DOWNTOWN

This area was center stage for the political intrigue and social upheavals that changed the fabric of Hawaii during the 19th century. Major players ruled here, revolted here, worshipped here and still rest, however restlessly, in the graveyards. Today, stately Victorian-era buildings are reflected in the black glass of modern urban high-rises.

'Iolani Palace   Palace

(Map p44; info 808-538-1471, tour reservations 808-522-0832; www.iolanipalace.org; 364 S King St; grounds admission free, adult/child basement galleries $7/3, self-guided audiotour $15/6, guided tour $22/6; 9am-5pm Mon-Sat, last entry 4pm) No other place evokes a more poignant sense of Hawaii's history. The palace was built under King David Kalakaua in 1882. At that time, the

Hawaiian monarchy observed many of the diplomatic protocols of the Victorian world. The king traveled abroad meeting with leaders around the globe and received foreign emissaries here. Although the palace was modern and opulent for its time, it did little to assert Hawaii's sovereignty over powerful US–influenced business interests who overthrew the kingdom in 1893.

Two years after the coup, the former queen, Lili'uokalani, who had succeeded her brother David to the throne, was convicted of treason and spent nine months imprisoned in her former home. Later the palace served as the capitol of the republic, then the territory and later the state of Hawaii. In 1969 the government finally moved into the current state capitol, leaving 'Iolani Palace a shambles. After a decade of painstaking renovations, the restored palace reopened as a museum, although many original royal artifacts had been lost or stolen before work even began.

Visitors must take a docent-led or self-guided tour (no children under age five) to see 'Iolani's grand interior, including re-creations of the throne room and residential quarters upstairs. The palace was quite modern by Victorian-era standards. Every bedroom had its own bathroom with flush toilets and hot running water, and electric lights replaced the gas lamps years before the White House in Washington, DC, installed electricity. If you're short on time, you can independently browse the historical

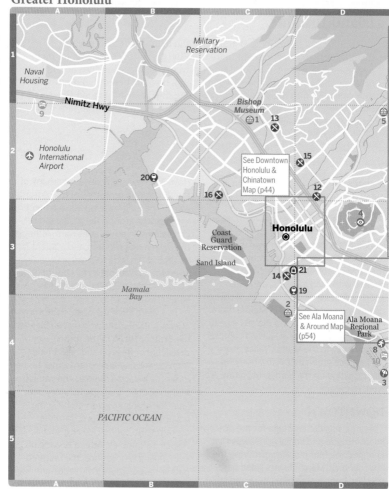

exibits in the basement, including royal regalia, historical photographs and reconstructions of the kitchen and chamberlain's office.

The palace grounds are open during daylight hours and are free of charge. The former **barracks** of the Royal Household Guards, a building that looks oddly like the uppermost layer of a medieval fort, now houses the ticket booth. Nearby, a domed **pavilion**, originally built for the coronation of King Kalakaua in 1883, is still used for state governor

inaugurations. Underneath the huge banyan tree, allegedly planted by Queen Kapi'olani, the Royal Hawaiian Band gives free concerts on most Fridays from noon to 1pm, weather permitting.

Call ahead to confirm tour schedules, and reserve tickets in advance during peak periods.

State Capitol
Notable Building
(Map p44; ☎808-586-0178; 415 S Beretania St; ⊗7:45am-4:30pm Mon-Fri) FREE Built in the architecturally interesting 1960s, Hawaii's

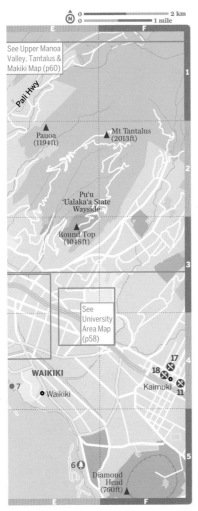

0 ——————— 2 km
0 ——————— 1 mile

See Upper Manoa
Valley, Tantalus &
Makiki Map (p60)

Pali Hwy

Pauoa
(1194ft)

Mt Tantalus
(2013ft)

Pu'u
'Ualaka'a State
Wayside

Round Top
(1048ft)

See
University
Area Map
(p58)

WAIKIKI

7

Waikiki

Kaimuki

18 17

11

6

Diamond
Head
(760ft)

Greater Honolulu

state capitol is a poster child of concep-
tual postmodernism: two cone-shaped
legislative chambers have sloping walls
to represent volcanoes; the supporting
columns shaped like coconut palms sym-
bolize the eight main islands; and a large
encircling pool represents the Pacific
Ocean surrounding Hawaii. Visitors are
free to walk through the open-air rotunda
and peer through viewing windows into
the legislative chambers. Pick up a self-
guided tour brochure on the 4th floor
from Room 415.

Queen Lili'uokalani Statue Statue
(Map p44) Pointedly positioned between
the state capitol building and 'Iolani
Palace is a life-size bronze statue of
Queen Lili'uokalani, Hawaii's last reigning monarch. She holds a copy of the
Hawaiian constitution she wrote in 1893
in an attempt to strengthen Hawaiian
rule; 'Aloha 'Oe,' a popular song she
composed; and 'Kumulipo,' the traditional
Hawaiian chant of creation.

Father Damien Statue Statue
(Map p44) In front of the capitol is a highly
stylized statue of Father Damien, the Bel-
gian priest who lived and worked with

43

Downtown Honolulu & Chinatown

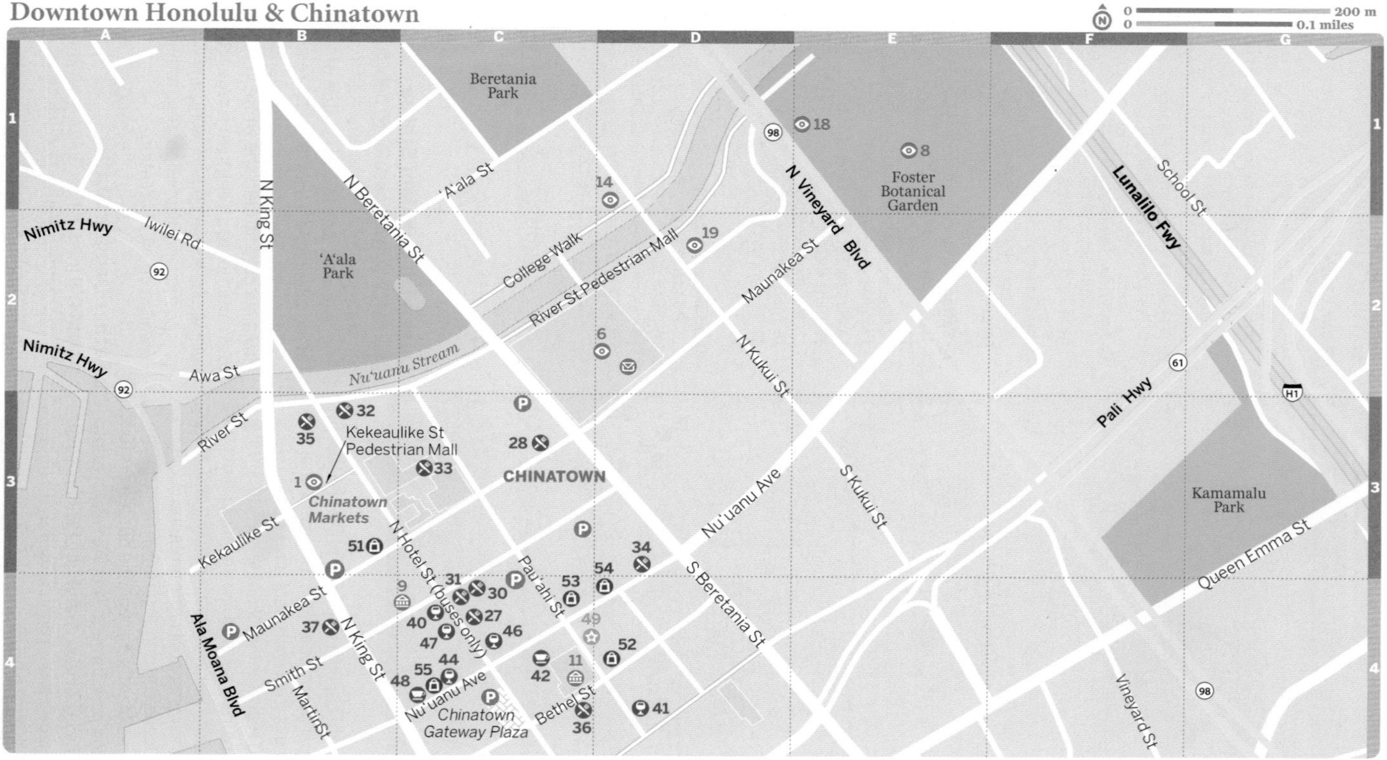

200 m
0.1 miles

N

School St

Lunalilo Fwy

Pali Hwy

Kamamalu Park

Queen Emma St

98

Vineyard St

8
Foster Botanical Garden

18

98

N Vineyard Blvd

S Kukui St

Maunakea St

N Kukui St

Nu'uanu Ave

S Beretania St

19

River St Pedestrian Mall

College Walk

9

34

S Beretania St

41

52

Beretania Park

'A'ala St

14

CHINATOWN

54

49

11

Pauahi St

53

42

36

Betel St

'A'ala Park

N Beretania St

28

30
27
46

Nu'uanu Ave

Chinatown Gateway Plaza

Nu'uanu Stream

33

31

40
47

44
55

48

Chinatown Markets

32

Kekaulike St Pedestrian Mall

N Hotel St (buses only)

9

51

N King St

Nimitz Hwy

92

Iwilei Rd

Awa St

Nimitz Hwy

92

River St

Kekaulike St

N King St

35

1

37

Maunakea St

Smith St

Martin St

Ala Moana Blvd

44

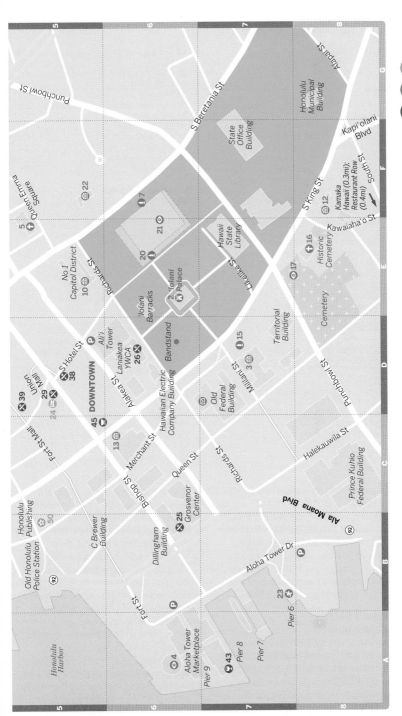

Downtown Honolulu & Chinatown

victims of Hansen's disease who were exiled to the island of Moloka'i during the late 19th century, before later dying of the disease himself. In 2009 the Catholic Church canonized Father Damien as Hawaii's first saint after the allegedly miraculous recovery from cancer in 1988 of a Honolulu schoolteacher who had prayed over Damien's original grave site on Moloka'i.

Hawai'i State Art Museum
Museum

(Map p44; ☎808-586-0900; www.hawaii.gov/sfca; 2nd fl, No 1 Capitol District Bldg, 250 S Hotel St; ⊙10am-4pm Tue-Sat, 6-9pm 1st Fri of the month) ✏ FREE With its vibrant, thought-provoking collections, this public art museum brings together traditional and contemporary art from Hawaii's multi-ethnic communities. The museum inhabits a grand 1928 Spanish Mission Revival–style building, formerly a YMCA and today a nationally registered historic site.

Upstairs, revolving exhibits of paintings, sculptures, fiber art, photography and mixed media are displayed around themes, such as the island's Polynesian heritage, modern social issues or the natural beauty of land and sea. Hawaii's complex confluence of Asian, Pacific Rim and European cultures is evident throughout, shaping an aesthetic that captures the soul of the islands and the hearts of the people. Drop by at noon on the last Tuesday of the month for free 'Art Lunch' lectures or between 11am and 3pm on the second Saturday for hands-on Hawaiian arts and crafts, often designed with kids in mind.

Ali'iolani Hale
Historic Building

(Map p44; ☑808-539-4999; www.jhchawaii. net; 417 S King St; ⊙8am-4.30pm Mon-Fri) FREE The first major government building ordered by the Hawaiian monarchy in 1874, the 'House of Heavenly Kings' was designed by Australian architect Thomas Rowe to be a royal palace, although it was never used as such. Today, it houses the Supreme Court of Hawai'i. Go through the security checkpoint and step inside the **King Kamehameha V Judiciary History Center**, where you can browse thought-provoking historical displays about martial law during WWII and the reign of Kamehameha I.

Kamehameha the Great Statue
Statue

(Map p44) Standing before the Ali'iolani Hale, a bronze statue of Kamehameha the Great faces 'Iolani Palace. Often ceremonially draped with layers of flower lei, the statue was cast in 1880 in Florence, Italy, by American sculptor Thomas Gould. The current statue is a recast, as the first statue was lost at sea near the Falkland Islands. It was dedicated here in 1883, just a decade before the Hawaiian monarchy would be overthrown.

The original statue, which was later recovered from the ocean floor, now stands in Kohala on Hawai'i, the Big Island, where Kamehameha I was born.

Kawaiaha'o Church
Church

(Map p44; ☑808-469-3000; www.kawaiahao.org; 957 Punchbowl St; ⊙usually 8:30am-4pm Mon-Fri, worship service 9am Sun) FREE Nicknamed the 'Westminster Abbey of the Pacific,' O'ahu's oldest church was built on the site where the first missionaries constructed a grass thatch church shortly after their arrival in 1820. The original structure seated 300 Hawaiians on *lauhala* mats, woven from hala (screwpine) leaves. This 1842 New England Gothic–style church is made of 14,000 coral slabs, which divers chiseled out of O'ahu's underwater reefs – a weighty task that took four years.

The clock tower was donated by Kamehameha III, and the old clock, installed in 1850, still keeps accurate time. The rear seats of the church, marked by *kahili* (feather staffs) and velvet padding, are reserved for royal descendants today.

The **tomb of King Lunalilo**, the short-lived successor to Kamehameha V, is found at the main entrance to the church grounds. The **cemetery** to the rear of the church is almost like a who's who of colonial history: early Protestant missionaries are buried alongside other important figures, including the infamous Sanford Dole, who became the first territorial governor of Hawaii after Queen Lili'uokalani was overthrown.

Hawaiian Mission Houses Historic Site and Archives
Museum

(Map p44; ☑808-447-3910; www. missionhouses.org; 553 S King St; 1hr guided tour adult/child & student $10/6; ⊙10am-4pm

Island Insights

You may notice that Hawaii's state flag is quartered, with the Union Jack in the top left corner next to the flagpole (you can see one in downtown Honolulu's historic capitol district). But Hawaii was never part of the UK. Kamehameha the Great simply thought the Union Jack would add an element of regal splendor to Hawaii's flag, so he took the liberty of adding it. The flag's eight horizontal red, white and blue stripes represent the eight main islands. Today Native Hawaiian sovereignty activists often choose to fly the state flag upside down, a time-honored symbol of distress.

Honolulu for Children

○ For grassy picnicking lawns, endless sand and calm waters, take the kids to the beach at Ala Moana Beach Park (p40), which has lifeguards and outdoor showers to wash the sand off little feet.

○ The Bishop Museum (p57) has educational diversions for kids of all ages; a planetarium chronicles the stars that guided ancient Polynesians to Hawaii, while the Science Adventure Center lets youngsters walk through an erupting model volcano.

○ In the basement of the Honolulu Museum of Art (p52), seek out the interactive arts-and-crafts center for creative families.

○ Drive up into the Manoa Valley to visit the wide-open Lyon Arboretum (p56) or make the family-friendly hike to Manoa Falls (p59).

○ Inside the woodsy Makiki Forest Recreation Area, the **Hawai'i Nature Center** (☏808-955-0100; www.hawaiinaturecenter.org; 2131 Makiki Heights Dr; program fees from $10; ♿) nonprofit community education center conducts family-oriented environmental programs and weekend hikes (reservations strongly recommended).

○ With plenty of aloha, the hands-on **Hawaii Children's Discovery Center** (Map p42; ☏808-524-5437; www.discoverycenterhawaii.org; 111 'Ohe St; adult/senior/child 1-17yr $10/6/10; ⏱9am-1pm Tue-Fri, 10am-3pm Sat & Sun; P ♿) community play space, designed for tots and young schoolchildren, is the place to go on a rainy day.

Tue-Sat, guided tours usually 11am, noon, 1pm, 2pm & 3pm) Occupying the original headquarters of the Sandwich Islands mission that forever changed the course of Hawaiian history, this modest museum is authentically furnished with handmade quilts on the beds and iron cooking pots in the stone fireplaces. You'll need to take a guided tour to peek inside any of the buildings.

Walking around the grounds, you'll notice that the first missionaries packed more than their bags when they left Boston – they brought a prefabricated wooden house, called the **Frame House**, with them around the Horn. Designed to withstand New England winter winds, the small windows instead blocked out Honolulu's cooling tradewinds, which kept the two-story house hellaciously hot and stuffy. Erected in 1821, it's the oldest wooden structure in Hawaii.

The 1831 coral-block **Chamberlain House** was the early mission's storeroom, a necessity because Honolulu had few shops in those days. Upstairs are hoop barrels, wooden crates packed with dishes, and the desk and quill pen of Levi Chamberlain. He was appointed by the mission to buy, store and dole out supplies to missionary families, who survived on a meager allowance – as the account books on his desk testify.

Mission Social Hall and Cafe, run by Chef Mark 'Gooch' Noguchi, opened in December 2014 and promises foodie delights and family fun.

Nearby, the 1841 **Printing Office** houses a lead-type press used to print the first bible in the Hawaiian language.

Washington Place   Historic Building
(Map p44; ☏808-586-0240; http://www.washingtonplacefoundation.org; 320 S Beretania St; ⏱tours by appointment only, usually at 10am

Thu) **FREE** Formerly the governor's official residence, this colonial-style mansion was built in 1846 by US sea captain John Dominis. The captain's son became the governor of O'ahu and married the Hawaiian princess who later became Queen Lili'uokalani. After the queen was released from house arrest inside 'Iolani Palace in 1896, she lived here until her death in 1917. A plaque near the sidewalk is inscribed with the lyrics to 'Aloha 'Oe,' the patriotic anthem she composed.

Cathedral of St Andrew   Church

(Map p44; ☏808-524-2822; www.saint andrewscathedral.net; 229 Queen Emma Sq; ⏰usually 8:30am-4pm Mon-Fri, tours 11:50am Sun; **P**) **FREE** King Kamehameha IV, attracted to the royal Church of England, decided to build his own cathedral and founded the Anglican Church in Hawaii in 1861. The cathedral's cornerstone was laid in 1867, four years after his death on St Andrew's Day – hence the church's name. The architecture is French Gothic, utilizing stone and stained glass shipped from England. For a free lunchtime concert, the largest pipe organ in the Pacific is sonorously played every Friday at 12.15pm.

Aloha Tower   Landmark

(Map p44; www.alohatower.com; 1 Aloha Tower Dr; ⏰9:30am-5pm; **P**) **FREE** Built in 1926, this 10-story landmark was once the city's tallest building. In the golden days when all tourists to Hawaii arrived by ship, this pre–WWII waterfront icon – with its four-sided clock tower inscribed with 'Aloha' – greeted every visitor. These days, Hawaii Pacific University has bought the Aloha Tower Marketplace and is revitalizing it for retail, dining and student

housing. Take the elevator to the top-floor tower observation deck for 360-degree views of Honolulu and the waterfront.

Honolulu Museum of Art at First Hawaiian Center   Art Gallery

(Map p44; ☏808-526-0232; www.honolulu academy.org; ⏰8:30am-4:30pm Mon-Thu, to 6pm Fri) **FREE** First Hawaiian Bank's high-rise headquarters also houses the downtown gallery of **Spalding House**, featuring fascinating mixed-media exhibits of modern and contemporary works by artists from around Hawaii. Even the building itself features a four-story-high art-glass wall incorporating 185 prisms. Free guided gallery tours typically meet at noon on the first Friday of the month while exhibitions are being held.

CHINATOWN

The location of this mercantile district is no accident. Between Honolulu's busy trading port and what was once the countryside, enterprises selling goods to city folks and visiting ship's crews

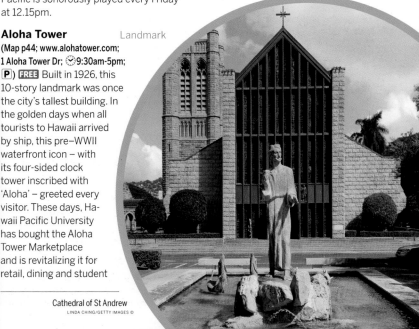

sprang up in the 19th century. Many of these shops were established by Chinese laborers who had completed their sugarcane-plantation contracts. The most successful entrepreneurial families have long since moved out of this low-rent district to wealthier suburbs, making room for newer waves of immigrants, mostly from Southeast Asia.

The scent of burning incense still wafts through Chinatown's buzzing markets, fire-breathing dragons spiral up the columns of buildings and steaming dim sum awakens even the sleepiest of appetites. Take time to explore: wander through nouveau art galleries and antiques stores, consult with a herbalist, rub shoulders with locals over a bowl of noodles, buy a lei and take a meditative botanic garden stroll.

Chinatown Markets   Market

(Map p44; www.chinatownnow.com) The commercial heart of Chinatown revolves around its markets and food shops. Noodle factories, pastry shops and produce stalls line the narrow sidewalks, always crowded with cart-pushing grandmothers and errand-running families. An

institution since 1904, the **O'ahu Market** sells everything a Chinese cook needs: ginger root, fresh octopus, quail eggs, jasmine rice, slabs of tuna, long beans and salted jellyfish. You owe yourself a bubble tea if you spot a pig's head among the stalls.

At the start of the nearby pedestrian mall is the newer, but equally vibrant, **Kekaulike Market**. At the top end of the pedestrian mall is **Maunakea Marketplace**, with its popular food court.

Foster Botanical Garden   Gardens

(Map p44; ☏ 808-522-7066; www.honolulu. gov/parks/hbg; 180 N Vineyard Blvd; adult/child 6-12yr $5/1; ☺9am-4pm, guided tours usually 1pm Mon-Sat; P) 🐾 Tropical plants you've only ever read about can be spotted in all their glory at this botanic garden, which took root in 1850. Among its rarest specimens are the Hawaiian *loulu* palm and the East African *Gigasiphon macrosiphon,* both thought to be extinct in the wild. Several of the garden's towering trees are the largest of their kind in the USA.

Oddities include the cannonball tree, the sausage tree and the double coconut palm capable of producing a 50lb nut –

Buddha statue, Foster Botanical Garden

LINDA CHING/GETTY IMAGES

watch your head! Follow your nose past fragrant vanilla vines and cinnamon trees in the spice and herb gardens, then pick your way among the poisonous and dye plants. Don't miss the blooming orchids. A free self-guided tour booklet is available at the garden entrance.

Hawaii Theater   Historic Building
(Map p44; ☎808-528-0506; www.hawaiitheatre .com; 1130 Bethel St) This neoclassical landmark first opened in 1922, when silent films were played to the tunes of a pipe organ. Dubbed the 'Pride of the Pacific', the theater ran continuous shows during WWII, but the development of Waikiki cinemas in the 1960s and '70s finally brought down the curtain. After multimillion-dollar restorations, this nationally registered historic site held its grand reopening in 1996.

Kuan Yin Temple   Temple
(Map p44; 170 N Vineyard Blvd; ⏲usually 7am-5pm) FREE With its green ceramic-tile roof and bright red columns, this ornate Chinese Buddhist temple is Honolulu's oldest. The richly carved interior is filled with the sweet, pervasive smell of burning incense. The temple is dedicated to Kuan Yin, bodhisattva of mercy, whose statue is the largest in the interior prayer hall. Devotees burn paper 'money' for prosperity and good luck, while offerings of fresh flowers and fruit are placed at the altar. Respectful visitors welcome.

Chinatown Cultural Plaza   Plaza
(Map p44; cnr Maunakea & N Beretania Sts) Inside this utilitarian modern mall, covering almost an entire city block, traditional acupuncturists, tailors and calligraphers work alongside travel agencies and dim-sum halls. In the small open-air central courtyard, elderly Chinese light incense before a **statue of Kuan Yin**. Down by the riverside, senior citizens practice tai chi after dawn and play checkers and mah-jongg all afternoon long.

Izumo Taishakyo Mission   Temple
(Map p44; ☎808-538-7778; 215 N Kukui St; ⏲usually 8am-5pm) FREE This Shintō shrine was built by Japanese immigrants in

If You Like...
Art Galleries

Chinatown overflows with art galleries.

1 **ARTS AT MARKS GARAGE**
(Map p44; ☎808-521-2903; www.
artsatmarks.com; 1159 Nu'uanu Ave; ⏰noon-5pm
Tue-Sat) Performance art and eclectic works by up-
and-coming island artists.

2 **PEGGE HOPPER GALLERY**
(Map p44; www.peggehopper.com; 1164
Nu'uanu Ave; ⏰11am-4pm Tue-Fri, to 3pm Sat)
Represents the namesake artist's distinctive prints
and paintings depicting voluptuous island women.

3 **LOUIS POHL GALLERY**
(Map p44; www.louispohlgallery.com; 1142
Bethel St; ⏰11am-5pm Tue, to 3pm Wed-Sat)
Paintings by contemporary island artists and a
former 'living treasure' of Hawaii.

1906. It was confiscated during WWII by
the city and wasn't returned to the community until the early 1960s. Ringing the
bell at the shrine entrance is considered
an act of purification for those who come
to pray. Thousands of good-luck amulets
are sold here, especially on January 1,
when the temple heaves with people from
all around O'ahu who come seeking New
Year's blessings.

Lum Sai Ho Tong   Temple
(Map p44; ☎808-536-6590; 1315 River St)
Founded in 1899, the Lum Sai Ho Tong
Society was one of more than 100 socie-
ties started by Chinese immigrants in
Hawaii to help preserve their cultural
identity. This one was for the Lum clan
hailing from west of the Yellow River. The
temple is not open to the general public,
but you can still admire the colorful exterior from the sidewalk below.

Hawai'i Heritage Center   Museum
(Map p44; ☎808-521-2749; 1040 Smith St;
adult/child 5-18yr $1/25¢; ⏰9am-2pm Mon-Sat)

Local volunteers with family ties to the
community run this friendly gallery that
displays changing historical and cultural
exhibitions about O'ahu's Chinese,
Japanese and other ethnic communities (including the Scots!).

ALA MOANA & AROUND

Ala Moana means 'Path to the Sea'
and its namesake road, Ala Moana
Blvd (Hwy 92), connects the coast
between Waikiki and Honolulu.
Although most people think of Ala
Moana only for its shopping malls,
Ala Moana Regional Park, which
happens to be O'ahu's biggest beach
park, makes a relaxing alternative to
crowded Waikiki.

**Honolulu
Museum of Art**   Museum
(Map p54; ☎808-532-8700; www.honolulu
museum.org; 900 S Beretania St; adult/child
$10/free, 1st Wed & 3rd Sun of the month free;
⏰10am-4:30pm Tue-Sat, 1-5pm Sun; [P][♿])
This exceptional fine-arts museum may
be the biggest surprise of your trip to
O'ahu. The museum, dating to 1927, has a
classical facade that's invitingly open and
airy, with galleries branching off a series
of garden and water-fountain courtyards.
Plan on spending a couple of hours at the
museum, possibly combining a visit with
lunch at the Honolulu Museum of Art Cafe
(p73). Admission tickets are also valid for
same-day visits to Spalding House.

Stunningly beautiful exhibits reflect
the various cultures that make up
contemporary Hawaii, including one of
the country's finest Asian art collections,
featuring everything from Japanese
woodblock prints by Hiroshige and
Ming dynasty–era Chinese calligraphy
and painted scrolls to temple carvings
and statues from Cambodia and
India. Another highlight is the striking
contemporary wing with Hawaiian works
on its upper level, and modern art by
such luminaries as Henri Matisse and
Georgia O'Keeffe below. Although the
collections aren't nearly as extensive
as at Honolulu's Bishop Museum, you

can still be bewitched by the Pacific and Polynesian artifacts, such as ceremonial masks, war clubs and bodily adornments.

Check the museum website for upcoming special events, including gallery tours and art lectures; film screenings and music concerts at the Doris Duke Theatre; ARTafterDARK (www.artafterdark.org) parties with food, drinks and live entertainment on the last Friday of some months; and family-friendly arts and cultural programs on the third Sunday of every month.

Parking at the Museum of Arts Center at Linekona lot, diagonally opposite the museum at 1111 Victoria St (enter off Beretania or Young Sts), costs $5. From Waikiki, take bus 2 or 13 or B CityExpress!.

Water Giver Statue   Statue
(Map p54; 1801 Kalakaua Ave, Hawaii Convention Center) Fronting the Honolulu Convention Center, this magnificent statue symbolically acknowledges the Hawaiian people for their generosity and expressions of goodwill to newcomers. Sister-statue is the Storyteller Statue in Waikiki.

UNIVERSITY AREA

In the foothills of Manoa Valley, the neighborhood surrounding the University of Hawai'i (UH) Manoa campus feels youthful, with a collection of cafes, eclectic restaurants and one-of-a-kind shops. You'll probably pass through here en route to the Manoa Falls trailhead and the university's Lyon Arboretum.

University of Hawai'i at Manoa   University
(UH Manoa; Map p58; ☎808-956-8111; www.manoa.hawaii.edu; 2500 Campus Rd; P) About 2 miles northeast of Waikiki, the main campus of the statewide university system was born too late to be weighed down by the tweedy academic architecture of the mainland. Today, its breezy, tree-shaded campus is crowded with students from islands throughout Polynesia. The university has strong programs in astronomy, oceanography and marine biology, as well as Hawaiian, Pacific and Asian studies.

From Waikiki or downtown Honolulu, take bus 4; from Ala Moana, catch buses 6 or 18.

Courtyard ceramic display, Honolulu Museum of Art

Ala Moana & Around

HONOLULU SIGHTS

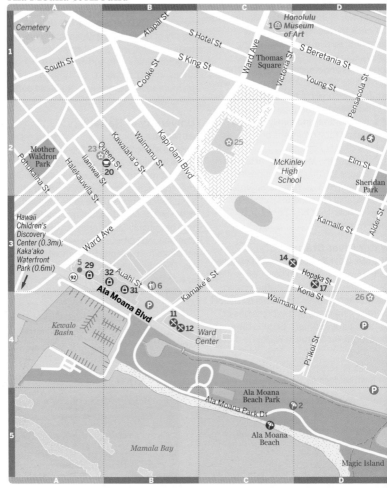

East-West Center
Cultural Center

(Map p58; ☏808-944-7111; www.eastwestcenter.
org; 1601 East-West Rd) On the eastern side
of the UH campus, the East-West Center
aims to promote mutual understanding
among the peoples of Asia, the Pacific
and the US. Changing exhibitions of art
and culture are displayed in the EWC Gallery. Spy the Japanese teahouse garden
and royal Thai pavilion outside. The center
regularly hosts multicultural programs,
including lectures, films, concerts and
dance performances.

John Young
Museum of Art
Museum

(Map p58; ☏808-956-3634; www.hawaii.edu/
johnyoung-museum; Krauss Hall, 2500 Dole
St; ⊙11am-2pm Mon-Fri, 1-4pm Sun) FREE A
short walk downhill from the UH Campus
Center, the John Young Museum of Art
features 20th-century Hawaii painter
John Young's collection of artifacts from
the Pacific islands, Africa and Asia, mostly
ceramics, pottery and sculpture. Although
it's not huge, it's worth a quick visit.

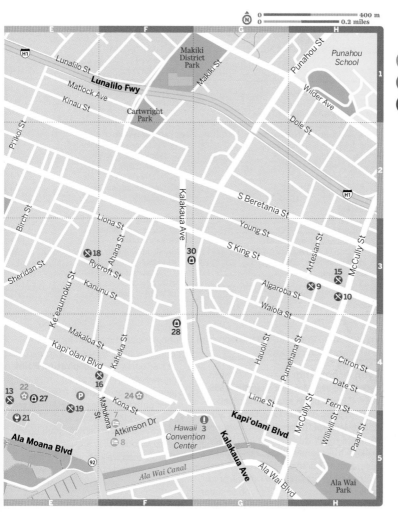

UPPER MANOA VALLEY, TANTALUS & MAKIKI

Welcome to Honolulu's green belt. Roads into the verdant Upper Manoa Valley wind north of the UH Manoa campus, passing exclusive residential homes and entering forest reserve land in the hills above downtown's high-rises. It's a peaceful place to commune with nature, especially at the arboretum and on family-friendly hikes to Manoa Falls and along Wa'ahila Ridge.

Further west lies Makiki Heights, the neighborhood where President Barack Obama spent much of his boyhood. A narrow, switchbacking road cuts its way up into more forest reserve lands in the Makiki Valley above. Offering skyline views, the 10-mile **Tantalus–Round Top scenic drive** climbs almost to the top of Mt Tantalus (2013ft), passing swank homes along the way. Although the road is one continuous loop, the west side is called Tantalus Dr and the east side,

Ala Moana & Around

Round Top Dr. Branching off the loop road is a network of hiking trails.

Lyon Arboretum
Gardens

(☎info 808-988-0456, tour reservations 808-988-0461; www.hawaii.edu/lyonarboretum; 3860 Manoa Rd; donation $5, guided tour $10; ⏰8am-4pm Mon-Fri, 9am-3pm Sat, tours usually 10am Mon-Fri; 🅿️ ♿) ⊘ Beautifully unkempt walking trails wind through this highly regarded 200-acre arboretum managed by the University of Hawai'i. It was originally founded in 1918 by a group of sugar planters growing native and exotic flora species to restore Honolulu's watershed and test their economic benefit. This is not your typical overly manicured tropical flower garden, but a mature and largely wooded arboretum, where related species cluster in a seminatural state. For a guided tour, call at least 24 hours in advance.

Key plants in the Hawaiian ethno-botanical garden are *'ulu* (breadfruit), *kalo* (taro) and *ko* (sugarcane) brought by early Polynesian settlers; *kukui,* once harvested to produce lantern oil; and *ti,* which was used for medicinal purposes during ancient times and for making moonshine after Westerners arrived.

It's a short walk to **Inspiration Point**, or keep walking uphill for about 1 mile along a jeep road, then a narrow, tree-root-ridden path to visit seasonal **'Aihualama Falls**, a lacy cliff-side cascade.

From Ala Moana Center, catch bus 5 toward Manoa Valley and get off at the last stop, then walk about half a mile uphill to the end of Manoa Rd. Limited free parking is available.

Spalding House
Museum

(☎808-526-1322; www.honoluluacademy.org; 2411 Makiki Heights Dr; adult/child 4-17yr $10/free, 1st Wed of the month free; ⏰10am-4pm Tue-Sat, noon-4pm Sun; 🅿️) Embraced by tropical sculpture gardens, this art museum occupies an estate house constructed in 1925 for O'ahu-born Anna Rice Cooke, a missionary descendant and wealthy arts patron. Inside the main galleries are changing exhibits of paintings, sculpture and other contemporary artwork from the 1940s through to today by international, national and island artists. There is a small cafe and gift shop on site. Tickets are also valid for same-day admission to the Honolulu Museum of Art.

From Waikiki, take bus 2, 13 or B CityExpress! toward downtown Honolulu and get off at the corner of Beretania and Alapaʻi Sts; walk one block *makai* (seaward) along Alapaʻi St and transfer to bus 15 bound for Pacific Heights, which stops outside Spalding House.

GREATER HONOLULU

Bishop Museum   Museum

(Map p42; ☏808-847-3511; www.bishopmu-seum.org; 1525 Bernice St; adult/child $20/15; ☉9am-5pm Wed-Mon; 🅿🚻) 🌿 Like Hawaii's version of the Smithsonian Institute in Washington, DC, the Bishop Museum showcases a remarkable array of cultural and natural history exhibits. It is often ranked as the finest Polynesian anthropological museum in the world. Founded in 1889 in honor of Princess Bernice Pauahi Bishop, a descendant of the Kamhameha dynasty, it originally housed only Hawaiian and royal artifacts. These days it honors all of Polynesia.

The recently renovated main gallery, the **Hawaiian Hall**, resides inside a dignified three-story Victorian building. Displays covering the cultural history of Hawaii include a *pili* (grass) thatched house, carved *kiʻi akua* (temple images), *kahili* (feathered royal staffs), shark-toothed war clubs and traditional *tapa* cloth made by pounding the bark of the paper mulberry tree. Don't miss the feathered cloak once worn by Kamehameha the Great, created entirely of the yellow feathers of the now-extinct *mamo* – some 80,000 birds were caught and plucked to create this single adornment. Meanwhile, upper-floor exhibits delve further into *aliʻi* (royal) history, traditional daily life and relationships between Native Hawaiians and the natural world.

The fascinating two-story exhibits inside the adjacent **Polynesian Hall** cover the myriad cultures of Polynesia, Micronesia and Melanesia. You could spend hours gazing at astounding and rare ritual artifacts, from elaborate dance masks and ceremonial costumes to carved canoes. Next door, the **Castle Memorial Building** displays changing traveling exhibitions.

Across the Great Lawn, the eye-popping, state-of-the-art multisensory **Science Adventure Center** lets kids walk through an erupting volcano, take a minisubmarine dive and play with three floors of interactive multimedia exhibits.

The Bishop Museum is also home to Oʻahu's only **planetarium**, which highlights traditional Polynesian methods of wayfaring, using wave patterns and the position of the stars to travel thousands of miles across the open ocean in traditional outrigger canoes, as well as modern astronomy and the cutting-edge telescope observatories atop Mauna Kea on the Big Island. Shows usually start at 11:30am, 1:30pm and 3:30pm daily except Tuesday, and are included in the museum admission price.

Island Insights

Oʻahu has an endemic genus of tree snail, the *Achatinella*. The island's forests were once loaded with these colorful snails, which clung like gems to the leaves of trees. They were too attractive for their own good, however; their spiral shells were collected for lei-making, and hikers also started collecting them by the handful. Even more devastating has been the deforestation of their native forest habitat and the introduction of an exotic cannibal snail and predatory nonnative rodents such as the mongoose. Of Oʻahu's 42 *Achatinella* species, less than half remain today – and all but two are endangered.

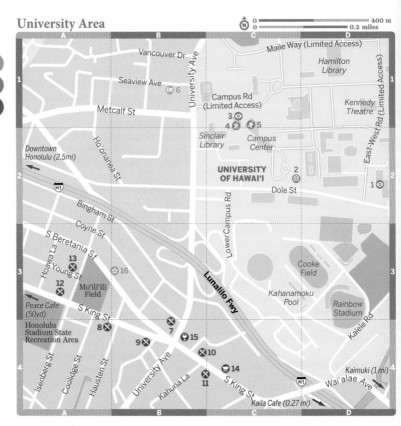

A gift shop off the main lobby sells books on the Pacific not easily found elsewhere, as well as some high-quality Hawaiian art, crafts and souvenirs. Check the museum website for special events, including popular 'Moonlight Mele' summer concerts, family-friendly Hawaiian cultural festivities and after-dark planetarium shows (buy tickets online or make reservations by calling ☎808-848-4168 in advance).

From Waikiki or downtown Honolulu, take bus 2 School St-Middle St to the intersection of School St and Kapalama Ave; walk one block *makai* on Kapalama Ave, then turn right onto Bernice St. By car, take eastbound H-1 Fwy exit 20, turn right on Houghtailing St, then take the second left onto Bernice St. Parking is free.

National Memorial Cemetery of the Pacific Cemetery

(Map p42; ☎808-532-3720; www.cem.va.gov/cems/nchp/nmcp.asp; 2177 Puowaina Dr; ⏱1, 8am-6:30pm Mar-Sep, to 5:30pm Sep-Mar; P) **FREE** Northeast of downtown Honolulu is a bowl-shaped crater, nicknamed the Punchbowl, formed by a long-extinct volcano. Hawaiians called the crater Puowaina ('hill of human sacrifices'). It's believed that at an ancient heiau here the slain bodies of kapu (taboo) breakers were ceremonially cremated upon an altar. Today the remains of ancient Hawaiians sacrificed to appease the gods share the crater floor with the bodies of nearly 50,000 soldiers, many of whom were killed in the Pacific during WWII.

The remains of Ernie Pyle, the distinguished war correspondent who was hit by machine-gun fire on Ie-shima during the final days of WWII, lie in section D, grave 109. Five stones to the left, at grave D-1, is the marker for astronaut Ellison Onizuka, the Hawai'i (Big Island) astronaut who perished in the 1986 Challenger space-shuttle disaster.

Even without the war sights, Punchbowl would be worth the drive up for the plum views of the city and Diamond Head. After entering the cemetery, bear left and go to the top of the hill, where there's a sweeping ocean-view lookout. Special events held at the cemetery include Memorial Day ceremonies to honor veterans and a traditional Easter sunrise Christian service.

From Waikiki, take bus 2, 13 or B CityExpress! toward downtown Honolulu and get off at Beretania and Alapa'i Sts. Walk one block *makai* along Alapa'i St and transfer to bus 15 Pacific Heights, which stops near the entrance at the corner of Puowaina Dr and Ho'okui St,

then walk uphill for approximately 15 minutes. If you're driving, take the H-1 Fwy westbound to the Pali Hwy – there's a marked exit on your right almost immediately as you start up the Pali Hwy. Then carefully follow the signs through winding, narrow residential streets.

Queen Emma Summer Palace
Historic Building

(Map p42; ☏808-595-3167; www.daughters ofhawaii.org; 2913 Pali Hwy; adult/child $8/1; ☺9am-4pm, last guided tour 3pm; P) In the heat and humidity of summer, Queen Emma (1836–85), the wife and royal consort of Kamehameha IV, used to slip away from her formal downtown Honolulu home to this cooler hillside retreat in Nu'uanu Valley. Gracious docents from the Daughters of Hawai'i society show off the cathedral-shaped koa cabinet that displays a set of china given by England's Queen Victoria, brightly colored feather cloaks and capes once worn by Hawaiian royalty, and more priceless antiques.

Activities

You could spend days enjoying the solitude of the forests and peaks around the city. Some of O'ahu's most popular hiking trails lead into the lush, windy Ko'olau Range just above downtown. For more details about these hikes and to find even more trails, visit the helpful government-run Na Ala Hele Hawaii Trail & Access System website (http://hawaiitrails. ehawaii.gov).

For Honolulu's best ocean swimming, head to **Ala Moana Beach Park** (p40). There are intermediate-level surf breaks just off Ala Moana, while those off **Kaka'ako Waterfront Park** are for advanced surfers and bodysurfers only.

HIKING & WALKING

Manoa Falls Trail
Hiking

(🚶) Honolulu's most rewarding short hike, this 1.6-mile round-trip trail runs above a rocky streambed before ending at a pretty little cascade. Tall tree trunks

Pali Hwy
Old Pali Rd
Nu'uanu Pali Dr
Ko'olau Range
Wa'ahi Stream

Nu'uanu
Valley
Lookout

Honolulu
Watershed
Forest Reserve

'Aihualama Trail

Manoa
Falls

END

Manoa Falls Trail

Pauoa Flats Trail

Manoa Cliffs Circuit

'Aihualama Stream

Lua'alaea Stream

Naniuapo Stream

Booth
Spring

Lyon
Arboretum

Ⓞ **START**

Pauoa
(1194ft) ▲

Kahuawai
Spring

Mt Tantalus
(2013ft) ▲

Makiki
Springs

Manoa Valley

Waiakeakua Stream

Honolulu
Watershed
Forest Reserve

END

Makiki Valley Loop Trail

Kanealole Trail

Herring
Springs

Kanealole Stream

Moleka Stream

Tantalus Dr

Pauoa Stream

Hawai'i
Nature
Center

START/ END

Makiki
Heights Dr

Maunalaha Trail

Pu'u 'Ualaka'a
State Wayside

Wai'oli
Tea Room

Pakanu St

Chinese
Cemetery

Manoa Rd
Manoa Stream

Wa'ahila Ridge Trail

Spalding
House

Round Top
(1048ft) ▲

Round Top Dr

Manoa Rd

O'ahu Ave

Lowrey Ave

E Manoa Rd

✕ Andy's Sandwiches
& Smoothies

Wa'ahila
Ridge State
Recreation
Area

START

Makiki Stream

---

line the often muddy and slippery path. Wild orchids and red ginger grow near the falls, which drop about 100ft into a small, shallow pool. It's illegal to venture beyond the established viewing area.

Falling rocks and the risk of leptospirosis (a waterborne bacterial infection) make even wading dangerous.

On public transport, take bus 5 Manoa Valley from Ala Moana Center or the university area to the end of the line; from there, it's a half-mile walk uphill to the trailhead. By car, drive almost to the end of Manoa Rd, where a privately operated parking lot charges $5 per vehicle. Free on-street parking may be available just downhill from the bus stop.

Nu'uanu Valley Lookout   Hiking

Just before Manoa Falls, the marked **'Aihualama Trail** heads up to the left and scrambles over boulders. The trail quickly enters a bamboo forest with some massive old banyan trees, then contours around the ridge, offering broad views of Manoa Valley.

Another mile of gradual switchbacks brings hikers to an intersection with the **Pauoa Flats Trail**, which ascends to the right for more than half a mile over muddy tree roots to the spectacular Nu'uanu Valley Lookout. High atop the Ko'olau Range, with O'ahu's steep *pali* (cliffs) visible all around, it's possible to peer through a gap over to the Windward Coast. The total round-trip distance to the lookout from the Manoa Falls trailhead is approximately 5.5 miles.

Makiki Valley Loop & Manoa Cliffs Circuit

Hiking

A favorite workout for city dwellers, the 2.5-mile Makiki Valley Loop links three Tantalus-area trails. The loop cuts through a diverse tropical forest, mainly composed of non-native species introduced to reforest an area denuded by the 19th-century *'iliahi* (sandalwood) trade. Keep watch for the tumbledown remains of ancient Hawaiian stone walls and a historic coffee plantation.

Starting just past the Hawai'i Nature Center, the **Maunalaha Trail** crosses a small stream and climbs over a giant staircase of tree roots, passing Norfolk pines, banyans and taro patches. Behind are views of Honolulu's skyscrapers and harbor. After 0.7 miles, you'll reach a four-way junction; continue uphill on the 1.1-mile **Makiki Valley Trail**, which traverses small gulches and gentle streams bordered by patches of ginger and guava trees while offering glimpses of the city below. The 0.7-mile **Kanealole Trail** begins as you cross Kanealole Stream, then follows the stream back to the base yard.

A more adventurous 6.2-mile hike beginning from the same trailhead leads to sweeping views of the valley and the ocean beyond. This **Manoa Cliffs Circuit**, aka the 'Big Loop,' starts on the same Maunalaha Trail. It then follows the 0.75-mile **Moleka Trail** and connects across Round Top Dr with the **Manoa Cliff Trail**, which intersects with the **Kalawahine Trail**. You can detour to the right on the **Pauoa Flats Trail** up to the **Nu'uanu Valley Lookout**. From the lookout, backtrack to the Kalawahine Trail, which connects via the **Nahuina Trail** with the

Kanealole Trail, leading back down to the forest base yard.

The starting point for both hiking loops is the **Makiki Forest Recreation Area base yard**, less than half a mile up Makiki Heights Dr from Makiki St. Where the road makes a sharp bend left, keep driving straight ahead through a green gate into the base yard. Park along the shoulder just inside the gate or in a small unpaved parking lot, then follow the signs and walk along the rolling hillside path to reach the main trailheads further inside the base yard.

From downtown Honolulu, take bus 15 Pacific Heights and get off near the intersection of Mott-Smith and Makiki Heights Drs by Spalding House, then walk half a mile southeast down Makiki Heights Dr to the base yard. From Waikiki, take bus 4 Nu'uanu to the corner of Wilder Ave and Makiki St, then walk 0.3 miles northeast up Makiki St, veering left onto Makiki Heights Dr and continuing another 0.4 miles uphill to the base yard.

Lyon Arboretum (p56)
LUCA TETTONI/GETTY IMAGES ©

Below: Golf course, O'ahu; **Right:** Humpback whale off the Hawaii coast

(BELOW) DATACRAFT CO LTD/GETTY IMAGES ©; (RIGHT) WATT JIM/GETTY IMAGES ©

Wa'ahila Ridge Trail   Hiking

Popular even with novice hikers, this boulder-strewn trail offers a cool retreat amid Norfolk pines and endemic plants, and gives ridgetop views of Honolulu and Waikiki. Rolling up and down a series of small saddles and knobs before reaching a grassy clearing, the 4.8-mile round-trip trail allows you to cover a variety of terrain in a short time, making an enjoyable afternoon's walk.

Look for the Na Ala Hele trailhead sign beyond the picnic tables inside Wa'ahila Ridge State Recreation Area, at the back of the St Louis Heights subdivision, east of Manoa Valley.

If you are traveling by car, turn left off Wai'alae Ave onto St Louis Dr at the stoplight. Heading uphill, veer left onto Bertram St, turn left onto Peter St, then turn left again onto Ruth Pl, which runs west into the park. From Waikiki, bus 14 St Louis Heights stops at the intersection of Peter and Ruth Sts, which is about a half-mile walk from the trailhead.

CYCLING

Bike Shop   Cycling

(Map p54; ☎808-596-0588; www.bikeshop hawaii.com; 1149 S King St; rental per day $20-85, car rack $5; ⏰9am-8pm Mon-Fri, to 5pm Sat, 10am-5pm Sun) Rents a variety of high-quality bicycles and can give you maps of cycling routes to match your skill level. Road cyclists looking for an athletic workout should pedal the Tantalus–Round Top scenic loop.

SURFING

Surf HNL/Girls Who Surf   Surfing, SUP

(Map p54; ☎808-772-4583; www.surfhnl.com; 1020 Auahi St; 2hr lesson from $99, rental per

hour/day SUP sets $18/47; ⊙8am-6pm) Award-winning girl-powered surf and stand up paddling (SUP) lessons are on offer in Ala Moana Beach Park and Ko Olina. Free hotel transportation to/from Waikiki for Ala Moana, $20 to Ko Olina. For surfboard, bodyboard and SUP rentals, delivery to Ala Moana Beach costs $15 and $40 to Ko Olina.

WHALE WATCHING
Atlantis Adventures   Whale-Watching
(Map p44; ☎800-381-0327; www.atlantis adventures.com/waikiki/whale-watch-cruises; Pier 6, Aloha Tower Dr; 2hr tour adult/child 7-12yr from $74/32) From mid-December through mid-April, Atlantis runs whale-watching cruises with an onboard naturalist on the *Navatek*, a high-tech catamaran designed to minimize rolling, twice daily at 9am and 12.30pm. Reservations are essential; book online for discounts, or look for coupons in free tourist magazines.

GOLF
Moanalua Golf Club   Golf
(☎808-839-2311; www.mgchawaii.com; 1250 Ala Aolani St; green fees $45; ⊙by reservation only) The oldest golf course in Hawaii was built in 1898 by a Protestant missionary family and has the distinction of once having Amelia Earhart land her aircraft on it. It's a fairly quick par-72 course with elevated greens, straight fairways and nine holes that are played twice around from different tees.

TENNIS
Ala Moana Beach Park   Tennis
(1201 Ala Moana Blvd) Municipal park has 10 free first-come, first-served public tennis courts. During the day, you can cool off with a dip in the ocean afterwards; at night, the courts are lit.

The Best...
Rainy Day Activities

 Courses

Native Books/ Nā Mea Hawai'i   Arts, Culture
(Map p54; ☎808-596-8885; www.nativebooks hawaii.com; Ward Warehouse, 1050 Ala Moana Blvd) ✦ Highly recommended community-oriented bookstore, art gallery and gift shop. Hosts free classes, workshops and demonstrations in hula dancing, Hawaiian language, traditional feather lei making and *lauhala* weaving, ukulele playing and more. Call for schedules and to check if pre-registration is required.

University of Hawai'i Recreation Services   Outdoors
(☎808-956-6468; www.manoa.hawaii.edu/ studentrec/outdoored/classes.html) The University of Hawai'i at Manoa offers a variety of inexpensive outdoor sports, 'leisure classes' and group activities that are open to the public, from hiking ($12) and kayaking ($32) excursions around O'ahu, to half-day introductory bodyboarding ($27) and learn-to-sail classes ($27). Advance sign-up is required; check class schedules online or call ahead to register.

 Tours

Guided walking tours of Chinatown are peppered with historical insights and are able to lead you to a few places you would be unable to visit by yourself. Just west of Ala Moana Regional Park, sunset sails, dinner cruises and party boats leave daily from Kewalo Basin. More expensive guided tours may include transportation to/from Waikiki and advertize various specials in the free tourist magazines available at the airport and around town.

UH Campus Walking Tour   Walking Tour
(Map p58; ☎808-956-7236; www.hawaii.edu/ campuscenter; 2465 Campus Rd; ⏰8:30am-4:30pm Mon-Fri) The UH Campus Center is your departure point for free one-hour walking tours of campus, emphasizing history and architecture. Tours usually leave at 2pm Monday, Wednesday and Friday; no reservations are necessary, but check in 10 minutes beforehand at the ticket, information and ID office upstairs.

Ask for a free Campus Art brochure, which outlines a self-guided walking tour of outdoor sculptures and other works by notable Hawaii artists.

Architectural Walking Tour   Walking Tour
(☎808-628-7243; www.aiahonolulu.org; tours $10; ⏰usually 9-11:30am Sat) Led by professional architects, these historical-minded walking tours will literally change your perspective on downtown Honolulu's capitol district. Reservations required – register online.

Hawaii Food Tours   Tour
(☎808-926-3663; www.hawaiifoodtours. com; tours from $119) These guys offer two extremely popular tours. The five-hour 'Hole-in-the-Wall' tour hits all sorts of spots around Honolulu such as Chinatown, island plate-lunch stops, beloved bakeries, crack-seed candy shops and more. The seven- to eight-hour 'North Shore Food Tour' heads to the other side of the island. Tours include food, fun and transportation. Reservations are essential.

Festivals & Events

Some of Honolulu's biggest festivals spill over into Waikiki.

Chinese New Year   Cultural
(www.chinatownhonolulu.org; ⏱late Jan–mid-Feb) Between late January and mid-February, Chinatown's swirling festivities include a parade with lion dances and crackling firecrackers.

Great Aloha Fun Run   Sports
(www.greataloharun.com; ⏱Feb) This popular 8.15-mile race sees participants run from the harborfront Aloha Tower to Aloha Stadium on the third Monday in February.

Honolulu Festival   Cultural
(www.honolulufestival.com; ⏱Mar) Three days of Asian-Pacific cultural exchange with music, dance and drama performances, an arts-and-crafts fair, a parade and fireworks, all in early to mid-March.

Lantern Floating Hawaii   Cultural
(www.facebook.com/lanternfloatinghawaii; ⏱May) On the last Monday in May, the souls of the dead are honored with a Japanese floating-lantern ceremony after sunset at Magic Island in Ala Moana Beach Park.

Pan-Pacific Festival   Art, Cultural
(www.pan-pacific-festival.com; ⏱early Jun) This festival brings three days of Japanese, Hawaiian and South Pacific entertainment to Honolulu in early to mid-June, with music, dancing and *taiko* (traditional Japanese drumming) performances at Waikiki and the Ala Moana Center.

King Kamehameha Hula Competition   Dance
(www.hulacomp.webstarts.com; ⏱Jun) One of Hawaii's biggest hula contests, with hundreds of dancers competing at downtown's Neal S Blaisdell Center in late June.

Queen Liliʻuokalani Keiki Hula Competition   Dance
(www.kpcahawaii.com/Site/Queen_Liliuokalani_Keiki_Hula_Comp.html; ⏱Jul) Children's hula troupes from throughout Hawaii take over the stage at the Neal S Blaisdell Center in mid-July.

Prince Lot Hula Festival   Dance
(www.mgf-hawaii.org; ⏱Jul) The state's oldest and largest noncompetitive hula event invites Hawaii's leading hula *halau* (schools) to the royal Moanalua Gardens on the third Saturday in July.

Hawaii Dragon Boat Festival   Sports, Music
(www.dragonboathawaii.com; ⏱Jul) Colorful Chinese dragon boats race to the beat

Hiker on the Manoa Falls Trail (p59)
KARL LEHMANN/GETTY IMAGES ©

The Best...
Annual Festivals & Celebrations

of island drummers at Ala Moana Beach Park in late July.

Hawai'i Food & Wine Festival
Food

(www.hawaiifoodandwinefestival.com; ☺Sep) Star chefs, sustainable farms and food lovers come together for a weekend of wining and dining in early September.

Talk Story Festival
Literature

(☺Oct; 👪) Storytellers gather at Ala Moana Beach Park over a long weekend in mid-October; Friday is usually spooky stories.

Hawaii International Film Festival
Film

(www.hiff.org; ☺Oct) This celebration of celluloid packs the city's movie theaters with homegrown and imported Pacific Rim, Asian, mainland American and European films for 11 days from late October.

King Kalakaua's Birthday
Music, Cultural

(www.iolanipalace.org; ☺Nov) Festive Victorian-era decorations and a concert of traditional monarchy-era music by the Royal Hawaiian Band at 'Iolani Palace on November 16.

Sleeping

Almost a dead zone after dark, downtown Honolulu doesn't have much in the way of accommodations. Most visitors sleep by the beach at Waikiki.

Hostelling International (HI) Honolulu
Hostel $

(Map p58; 🕿808-946-0591; www.hostels aloha.com; 2323-A Seaview Ave; dm $22, r $85; ☺reception 8am-noon & 4pm-midnight; 🅿@🛜) Along a quiet residential side street near the UH Manoa campus, this tidy, low-slung house just a short bus ride from Waikiki has same-sex dorms and basic private rooms kept cool by the tradewinds. Some students crash here while looking for apartments, so it's often full. It has a kitchen, a laundry room, lockers and two free parking spaces.

Central Branch YMCA
Hostel $

(Map p54; 🕿808-941-3344; www.ymcahonolulu. org; 401 Atkinson Dr; s/d $55/75, with shared bathroom $45/65; @🛜🏊) Opposite the Ala Moana Center, the ol' Y lets unfussy budget travelers book basic, well-worn rooms with shared bathrooms or slightly larger en suite rooms on single-sex or co-ed floors. Perks include an Olympic-sized swimming pool and a gym. Traffic noise, a general lack of cleanliness and an institutional atmosphere are downers.

Ala Moana Hotel
Hotel $$

(Map p54; 🕿808-955-4811, 866-956-4262; www. alamoanahotelhonolulu.com; 410 Atkinson Dr; r/ ste from $139/285; 🅿✳@🛜🏊) Looming over the Ala Moana Center mall and convenient to the convention center, this high-rise offers bland hotel rooms without island flavor. Upper floors may have straight-on views of the beach – request the Waikiki Tower for a lanai (balcony). Parking costs $20.

Airport Honolulu Hotel
Hotel $$

(Map p42; 🕿818-836-0661, 866-956-4262; www.outrigger.com; 3401 N Nimitz Hwy; r from $110; 🅿✳@🛜🏊) If you need to be next to the airport (although Waikiki hotels are only a 20-minute taxi ride away), this nondescript hotel sleeps underneath the noisy freeway. Rates include infrequent 24-hour airport-shuttle service and free wi-fi.

Aston at the Executive Centre Hotel
Hotel $$$

(Map p44; ☏808-539-3000; www.resort-questhawaii.com; 1088 Bishop St; ☎) Honolulu's only downtown hotel is geared for business travelers and extended stays. Large, modern suites with floor-to-ceiling windows get kitchenettes, while one-bedroom condos add a full kitchen and washer/dryer. A fitness center, heated lap pool and complimentary continental breakfast round out the executive-class amenities. Free wi-fi.

 Eating

You might sleep and play in Waikiki, but you should definitely eat in Honolulu. In fact, if O'ahu weren't so far away from the US mainland, you'd hear a lot more buzz about this multiethnic chowhound capital. During Restaurant Week Hawaii (www.restaurantweekhawaii.com), usually happening in mid-November,

dozens of locally owned restaurants offer serious discounts for dining out, including prix-fixe dinner menus.

DOWNTOWN

Weekday cafes for office workers and students abound downtown. The Aloha Tower Marketplace has breezy waterfront tables for sunset drinks and *pupu* (appetizers). Heading toward Ala Moana, Restaurant Row has hot spots that come and go.

Bishop St Cafe
Japanese, Italian $

(Map p44; ☏808-537-6951; www.facebook.com/bishopstreetcafe; 725 Bishop St; mains $7-15; ⏰11am-3pm Mon-Fri) Offering up lunches to downtown workers in an extremely convivial setting, Bishop St Cafe is one of those lovely fusion places, serving equally good Japanese and Italian cuisine. There's outside courtyard seating in the historic Dillingham Transportation Building. Choices range from Japanese udon or soba noodles to paninis and pastas.

Vita Juice
Health Food $

(Map p44; ☏808-526-1396; www.freewebs.com/vitajuice; 1111-C Fort St Mall; items $3-7;

Lantern Floating Hawaii (p65), off Magic Island

NAOMI HAYES OF ISLAND MEMORIES PHOTOGRAPHY/GETTY IMAGES ©

Detour:
Pu'u 'Ualaka'a State Wayside

For a remarkable panorama of Honolulu, take a scenic drive or cycle up into the mountains to find this tiny roadside **park** (www.hawaiistateparks.org; ⏰7am-7:45pm Apr-Aug, to 6:45pm Sep-Mar; P). Atop a volcanic cinder cone now taken over by the forest, sweeping views extend from Kahala and Diamond Head on the far left, across Waikiki and downtown Honolulu to the Wai'anae Range on the far right. To the southeast is the University of Hawai'i, easily recognizable by its sports stadium; to the southwest you can peek into the green mound of Punchbowl Crater. The airport is visible at the edge of the coast, and Pearl Harbor beyond. The park entrance is about 2.4 miles up Round Top Dr from Makiki St, then another half-mile to the lookout, bearing left at the fork.

⏰7am-5pm Mon-Fri; 🖋) Flooded with Hawai'i Pacific University students, this orange-walled juice and smoothie bar takes the concept of 'brain food' seriously. Healthy ingredients range from Amazonian acai and Tibetan goji berries to green tea and ginseng.

'Umeke Market & Deli
Supermarket $

(Map p44; 📞808-522-7377; www.umekemarket. com; 1001 Bishop St; mains $4-10; ⏰7am-4pm Mon-Fri; 🖋) 🍃 Fresh, organic island produce, natural-foods groceries and a vegetarian- and vegan-friendly takeout deli counter for healthy pick-me-ups such as kale and quinoa salads, hummus sandwiches, hoisin turkey meatloaf and iced kombucha fermented tea.

Cafe Julia
Cafe $$

(Map p44; 📞808-533-3334; http://cafejulia-hawaii.com; 1040 Richards St; mains $10-28; ⏰11am-2pm Mon-Fri, 4-9pm Wed-Fri, 9am-1pm & 4-9pm Sun) In the charming old YWCA Laniakea building opposite 'Iolani Palace, Cafe Julia is a gem. It is named after Julia Morgan, one of America's first female architects, who designed the building. The service and cuisine is superb, as is the open-air setting. Perfect for *poke* tacos or garlic ahi for lunch; or for settling in for a few cocktails in the evening.

Hiroshi Eurasian Tapas
Fusion $$

(Map p42; 📞808-533-4476; www.hiroshihawaii. com; Waterfront Plaza, 500 Ala Moana Blvd; shared plates $9-17, mains $26-29; ⏰5:30-9:30pm; P) A serious player on the Honolulu culinary scene, chef Hiroshi Fukui puts a Japanese twist on Pacific Rim fusion style, from crab cannelloni swirled with miso sauce to smoked *hamachi* (yellow-tail) with a garlicky habanero pepper kick. Order foamy tropical martinis and fresh-fruit sodas at the bar. Make reservations for dinner.

Hukilau
Hawaiian $$

(Map p44; 📞808-523-3460; www.dahukilau. com/honolulu; Executive Centre, 1088 Bishop St; mains $11-20; ⏰11am-2pm & 3-9pm Mon-Fri) Underground at downtown's only high-rise hotel, this sports bar and grill serves an aloha-shirt-wearing business crowd. Huge salads, sandwiches and burgers aren't as tempting as only-in-Hawaii specialties such as miso butterfish, kimchi (Korean seasoned vegetable pickle dish) and *kalua* (cooked in an underground pit) pig *saimin* (noodle soup), and ahi *poke*. Live music on most Friday nights.

CHINATOWN

Chinese restaurants are plentiful, but the cavalcade doesn't stop there – dishes from all across Asia and around the Pacific Rim are cooked in this historic downtown neighborhood, packed with hole-in-the-wall kitchens, dim-sum palaces and trendy fusion eateries for art scenesters.

Maunakea Marketplace
Fast Food $

(Map p44; 1120 Maunakea St; meals from around $6; ⏰5.30am-4pm; 🚻) In the food court of this open-air marketplace, you'll find about 20 stalls dishing out authentic Chinese, Filipino, Thai, Vietnamese and Korean fare. Chow down at tiny wooden tables crowded into the walkway. Cash only.

Downbeat Diner & Lounge
Diner $

(Map p44; ☎808-533-2328; www.downbeatdiner.com; 42 N Hotel St; mains $5-15; ⏰11am-midnight Mon, to 3am Tue-Thu, to 4am Fri & Sat, to 10pm Sun; 🅿🚻) Shiny late-night diner with lipstick-red booths posts a vegetarian- and vegan-friendly menu of salads, sandwiches, grilled burgers and heaping island-style breakfasts such as *loco moco* (rice, fried egg and hamburger patty) and Portuguese sweet-bread French toast. The lounge, running a full bar, features live music three to four times per week.

Pho To-Chau
Vietnamese $

(Map p44; ☎808-533-4549; 1007 River St; mains $7-10; ⏰8:30am-2:30pm) Always packed, this Vietnamese restaurant holds fast to its hard-earned reputation for serving Honolulu's best *pho* (Vietnamese noodle soup). With beef, broth and vegetables, the dish is a complete meal in itself. It's so popular that you may have to queue underneath the battered-looking sign outside to score one of a dozen or so rickety wooden tables.

Bangkok Chef
Thai $

(Map p42; ☎808-585-8839; http://bangkok chefexpress.com; 1627 Nu'uanu Ave; mains $8-10; ⏰10:30am-9pm Mon-Sat, noon-8pm Sun) It feels strangely like you're eating out of someone's garage, but who cares when the Thai curries, noodle dishes and savory salads taste exactly like those from a Bangkok street cart? Dessert is either mango ice cream over warm sticky rice topped with salty peanuts, or tapioca pudding cups in a rainbow of flavors.

Mei Sum
Chinese $

(Map p44; ☎808-531-3268; 1170 Nu'uanu Ave; dim-sum dishes $2-4, mains $8-23; ⏰8am-9pm

Woman burning offerings, Kuan Yin Temple (p51)

Mon-Fri, 7am-9pm Sat & Sun) Where else can you go to satisfy that crazy craving for dim sum in the afternoon or evening (though maybe not as fresh as it is in the morning)? For over a decade, this no-nonsense corner stop has been cranking out a multitude of cheap little plates and a full spread of Chinese mains.

Mabuhay Cafe & Restaurant
Filipino $

(Map p44; ☎808-545-1956; 1049 River St; mains $6-13; ⏰10am-9pm Mon-Sat) The tablecloths, well-worn counter stools and jukebox should clue you in that this is a mom-and-pop joint. They've been cooking pots of succulent, garlic-laden pork *adobo* (meat marinated in vinegar and garlic) and *kare-kare* (oxtail stew) on this corner by the river since the 1960s.

The Pig & the Lady
Asian, Fusion $$

(Map p44; ☎808-585-8255; http://thepig andthelady.com; 83 N King St; mains $10-25; ⏰10.30am-2pm Mon-Sat, 5.30-9.30pm Tue-Thu, to midnight Fri & Sat) An award-winning Vietnamese fusion restaurant that you'll need to reserve in the evening, The Pig & the Lady is one of the hottest new places to dine on the island. Imaginative lunch sandwiches come with shrimp chips or *pho* broth, while delicious dinner options include Laotian fried chicken and dipping-style *pho tsukumen*.

Lucky Belly
Asian, Fusion $$

(Map p44; ☎808-531-1888; www.luckybelly. com; 50 N Hotel St; mains $8-14; ⏰11am-2pm & 5pm-midnight Mon-Sat) Where Japanese pop art hangs over sleek bistro tables packed elbows-to-shoulders, this arts-district noodle bar crafts hot and spicy Asian fusion bites, knock-out artisanal cocktails and amazingly fresh, almost architectural salads that the whole table can share. A 'Belly Bowl' of ramen soup topped with buttery pork belly, smoked bacon and pork sausage is carnivore heaven.

Duc's Bistro
Fusion $$

(Map p44; ☎808-531-6325; www.ducsbistro .com; 1188 Maunakea St; mains $16-26; ⏰11am-2pm Mon-Fri, 5-10pm daily) Honolulu's bigwigs hang out after work at this swank French-Vietnamese bistro with a tiny bar. Ignore the surrounding seedy streets and step inside this culinary oasis for buttery escargot, *bánh xèo* (Vietnamese crepes), pan-fried fish with green mango relish, and fire-roasted eggplant. A small jazz combo serenades diners some evenings. Reservations recommended.

Little Village Noodle House
Chinese $$

(Map p44; ☎808-545-3008; 1113 Smith St; mains $8-22; ⏰10:30am-10:30pm Sun-Thu, to midnight Fri & Sat) Forget about chop suey. If you live for anything fishy in black-bean sauce, this is Honolulu's gold standard. On the eclectic pan-Chinese menu, regional dishes are

Dim sum steamers
STUART MCCALL/GETTY IMAGES ©

served up garlicky, fiery or with just the right dose of saltiness. For a cross-cultural combo, fork into sizzling butterfish or roasted pork with island-grown taro. Reservations recommended.

Soul de Cuba
Cuban $$

(Map p44; ☎808-545-2822; www.souldecuba. com; 1121 Bethel St; mains $10-24; ⏲11am-10pm Mon-Thu, to 11pm Fri & Sat, to 9pm Sun) Nowhere else in Honolulu can you sate your craving for Afro-Cuban food and out-of-this-world *mojitos* except at this hip resto-lounge near Chinatown's art galleries. Stick with family-recipe classics such as *ropa vieja* (shredded beef in tomato sauce), *bocadillos* (sandwiches, served until 5pm) and black-bean soup. Reservations recommended.

ALA MOANA & AROUND

Shopping-mall food courts are ground zero for this neighborhood, but surprisingly many star chef's kitchens are spread out along trafficked thoroughfares or on dumpy-looking side streets.

Kaka'ako Kitchen
Fast Food $

(Map p54; ☎808-596-7488; http://kakaako kitchen.com; Ward Center, 1200 Ala Moana Blvd; meals $7-15; ⏲10am-9pm Mon-Thu, to 10pm Fri & Sat, to 5pm Sun; P 🍴) As 'ono (delicious) as always, this popular counter joint still dishes up healthy-minded plate lunches with brown rice and organic greens. For a local deli twist, get the tempura mahimahi sandwich on a homemade taro bun. Anticipate lines at lunchtime.

Yataimura
Japanese $

(Map p54; www.shirokiya.com; 2nd fl, Shirokiya, Ala Moana Center, 1450 Ala Moana Blvd; items $2-12; ⏲10am-10pm) Head to the upper level of the Ala Moana Center's Japanese department store Shirokiya to unlock a beer garden and boisterous food-stall marketplace that's a gold mine of takeout meals, from bento boxes to hot *takoyaki* (fried minced-octopus balls).

Kua 'Aina
Fast Food $

(Map p54; ☎808-591-9133; www.kua-aina.com; Ward Center, 1200 Ala Moana Blvd; burgers &

The Best...
Local Plate Lunches

sandwiches $5-10; ⏲10:30am-9pm Mon-Sat, to 8pm Sun; P 🍴) Shopping-mall outpost of Hale'iwa's gourmet burger joint serves crispy matchstick fries, pineapple and avocado beef burgers, and grilled ahi and veggie sandwiches to hungry crowds. Also in Kapolei.

Makai Market
Fast Food $

(Map p54; 1st fl, Ala Moana Center, 1450 Ala Moana Blvd; mains $6-12; ⏲8am-8pm; 🍴) Let your preconceptions about mall food courts fly out the window at these Asian-fusion-flavored indoor food stalls. Dig into Yummy Korean BBQ, Donburi Don-Don for Japanese rice bowls, or the island-flavored Lahaina Chicken Company and Ala Moana Poi Bowl.

Honolulu Farmers Market
Market $

(Map p54; http://hfbf.org/markets; Neal S Blaisdell Center, 777 Ward Ave; ⏲4-7pm Wed; 🍴🍴) ✎ Pick up anything from aquacultured seafood and O'ahu honey to fresh fruit and tropical flowers, all trucked into the city by Hawaii Farm Bureau Federation members. Graze food stalls set up by island chefs, food artisans and Kona coffee roasters, too.

Side Street Inn
Hawaiian $$

(Map p54; ☎808-591-0253; http://sidestreetinn. com; 1225 Hopaka St; mains $7-20; ⏲2pm-midnight Sun-Thu, to 1am Fri & Sat) This late-night mecca is where you'll find Honolulu's

Mr Obama's Neighborhood

During the 2008 race to elect the 44th president of the United States, Republican vice-presidential candidate Sarah Palin kept asking the country, 'Who is Barack Obama?' It was Obama's wife, Michelle, who had an answer ready: 'You can't really understand Barack until you understand Hawaii.'

Obama, who grew up in Honolulu's Makiki Heights neighborhood, has written that 'Hawaii's spirit of tolerance...became an integral part of my world view, and a basis for the values I hold most dear.' The local media and many *kama'aina* (those who were born and grew up in Hawaii) agree that Hawaii's multiethnic social fabric helped shape the leader who created a rainbow coalition during the 2008 election.

Obama has also said Hawaii is a place for him to rest and recharge, as he has done with his family every winter after assuming office. Back in 1999 he wrote: 'When I'm heading out to a hard day of meetings and negotiations, I let my mind wander back to Sandy Beach, or Manoa Falls... It helps me, somehow, knowing that such wonderful places exist and I'll always be able to return to them.'

If you want to walk in Obama's boyhood and presidential footsteps on O'ahu, here are some places you can visit:

Manoa Falls (p59)

Alan Wong's (p73)

Kapi'olani Beach Park (p100)

Rainbow Drive-In (p121)

Waiola Shave Ice (p120)

Hanauma Bay (p175)

Sandy Beach (p178)

National Memorial Cemetery of the Pacific (p58)

Nu'uanu Pali State Wayside (p186)

Olomana Golf Links (p190)

top chefs hanging out after their own kitchens close, along with partying locals who come for hearty portions of *kalbi* and pan-fried pork chops. Make reservations and bring friends, or join the construction-worker crews ordering plate lunches at the takeout counter. Warning: big portions!

Sorabol Korean $$
(Map p54; 808-947-3113; www.sorabolhawaii.com; 805 Ke'eaumoku St; set meals $11-38; 24hr) Sorabol feeds lunching Korean

ladies by day and bleary-eyed clubbers before dawn. Detractors often sniff that its reputation is undeserved, but the rest of the city has undying gratitude for this around-the-clock joint, often visited after midnight in a drunken stupor. Marinated *kalbi* and steamed butterfish are specialties. Watch out for a late-night service charge (20%).

Shokudo Japanese $$
(Map p54; 808-941-3701; www.shokudo japanese.com; 1585 Kapi'olani Blvd; shared plates

$5-25; ⏱11:30am-midnight Sun-Thu, to 1am Fri & Sat) Knock back lychee sake-tinis at this sleek, modern Japanese restaurant (*shokudō* means 'dining room') that's always filled to the rafters. A mixed-plate traditional Japanese and island-fusion menu depicts dozens of dishes, from *mochi* (rice cake) cheese gratin to lobster dynamite rolls, more traditional noodles and sushi, and silky house-made tofu. Reservations recommended.

Honolulu Museum of Art Cafe   Modern American $$

(Map p54; ☎808-532-8734; www.honoluluacademy.org; Honolulu Museum of Art, 900 S Beretania St; mains $11-22; ⏱11:30am-1:30pm Tue-Sat) Market-fresh salads and sandwiches made with O'ahu-grown ingredients, a decent selection of wines by the glass and tropically infused desserts make this an indulgent way to support the arts. Romantic tables facing the sculpture courtyard fountain and underneath a monkeypod tree are equally well suited to dates or power-broker lunches. Reservations recommended.

Alan Wong's   Hawaii Regional Cuisine $$$

(Map p54; ☎808-949-2526; www.alanwongs.com; 1857 S King St; mains $35-60; ⏱5-10pm) 🍴 One of O'ahu's big-gun chefs, Alan Wong offers his creative interpretations of Hawaii Regional Cuisine with emphasis on fresh seafood and local produce. Order Wong's time-tested signature dishes such as ginger-crusted *onaga* (red snapper), Kona lobster seafood stew and twice-cooked *kalbi* (short ribs). Make reservations for in-demand tables weeks in advance. Valet parking $5.

Nanzan Girogiro   Japanese $$$

(Map p54; ☎808-521-0141; www.guiloguilo.com; 560 Pensacola St; chef's tasting menu $50-60; ⏱6pm-midnight Thu-Mon) Traditional *kaiseki ryōri* (seasonal small-course) cuisine infused with Hawaii-grown fruits and vegetables, fresh seafood and, frankly, magic. Inside an art gallery, bar seats ring the open kitchen. Ceramic turtles hide savory custard in their shells and pottery bowls harbor tea-soaked rice topped with delicately poached fish. Reservations essential.

Ala Moana Beach Park (p40)

Chef Mavro
Fusion $$$

(Map p54; ☎808-944-4714; www.chefmavro.com; 1969 S King St; multicourse tasting menus from $95; ⏱6-9pm Wed-Sun) At Honolulu's most avant-garde restaurant, maverick chef George Mavrothalassitis creates conceptual dishes, all paired with Old and New World wines. Unfortunately the cutting-edge experimental cuisine, like the half-empty atmosphere, sometimes falls flat, although some will swear they've had the meal of a lifetime. Reservations essential.

UNIVERSITY AREA

Internationally flavored restaurants that'll go easy on your wallet cluster south of the UH Manoa campus near the three-way intersection of University Ave and S King and Beretania Sts. It's just a short bus ride from Waikiki.

Bubbies
Ice Cream $

(Map p58; www.bubbiesicecream.com; Varsity Center, 1010 University Ave; items $1.50-6; ⏱noon-midnight Mon-Thu, to 1am Fri & Sat, to 11:30pm Sun; 🚼) Homemade ice cream in tropical flavors such as papaya-ginger, plus unique bite-sized frozen *mochi* (Japanese pounded-rice cakes) ice-cream treats. Very, very difficult to walk past without going in once you've tried a mango *mochi* ice cream!

Kokua Market Natural Foods
Supermarket $

(Map p58; ☎808-941-1922; www.kokua.coop; 2643 S King St; ⏱8am-9pm; 🍴) 🌱 Hawaii's only natural-food co-op has an organic hot-and-cold salad bar and a vegetarian- and vegan-friendly deli for takeout meals on S King St near UH. Free parking off Kahuna Lane behind the store.

Down to Earth Natural Foods
Supermarket $

(Map p58; ☎808-947-7678; www.downtoearth.org; 2525 S King St; ⏱7:30am-10pm; 🍴) 🌱 Emphasizing organic and natural foods, this always-busy grocery store has a vegetarian- and vegan-friendly salad bar, a deli for made-to-order sandwiches, a

juice and smoothie bar, and a few sidewalk tables for chowing down. Free garage parking on the 2nd floor.

Sweet Home Café   Taiwanese $
(Map p58; ☎808-947-3707; 2334 S King St; shared dishes $2-8; ⊙4-10pm) You won't believe the lines snaking outside this strip-mall eatery's door. On long wooden family-style tables squat heavily laden, steaming-hot pots filled with lemongrass beef, sour cabbage, mixed tofu or Asian pumpkin squash, plus spicy dipping sauces and extra lamb, chicken or tender beef tongue as side dishes. Bonus: complimentary shave ice for dessert!

Da Spot   International $
(Map p58; ☎808-941-1313; http://daspot.net; 2469 S King St; smoothies $3-5, plate lunches $6-10; ⊙10:30am-9:30pm Mon-Sat) An enterprising duo of chef-owners set up kiosks at farmers markets and on the UH Manoa campus, but this converted auto mechan-

ic's garage is home base for their world fusion and island-flavored plate lunches, plus dozens of smoothie combinations. Egyptian chicken, Southeast Asian curries and homemade baklava will leave you as stuffed as a dolma.

Peace Cafe   Health Food $
(☎808-951-7555; www.peacecafehawaii.com; 2239 S King St; mains $8-10; ⊙11am-9pm Mon-Sat, to 3pm Sun; ☀) Vegan home cooking is the theme at this strip-mall kitchen, where daily dishes get handwritten on the chalkboard. Pick up a Popeye spinach or cilantro hummus sandwich to go, or a substantial lunch box with Moroccan stew. Mochi (Japanese pounded-rice cakes) and soy ice creams are dairy-free delights.

Yama's Fish Market   Seafood, Fast Food $
(Map p58; www.yamasfishmarket.com; 2332 Young St; mains $5-10; ⊙9am-7pm Mon-Sat, to

5pm Sun; P) Swing by this side-street sea-food market for heaping island-style plate lunches (eg *kalua* pig, *mochiko* chicken, *lomilomi* salmon) and freshly mixed *poke* by the pound with sour poi (fermented taro paste) and sweet *haupia* (coconut pudding) on the side.

Kaila Cafe
Cafe $$

(☏808-732-3330; www.cafe-kaila-hawaii.com; 2919 Kapi'olani Blvd, Market City Shopping Center; mains $8-18; ☺7am-3pm) This place has racked up Best Breakfast gold medals in local culinary awards and Kaila is so successful that she has opened her second shop...in Tokyo! Expect to wait to get in for the legendary line-up of incredibly well-presented breakfast specials. A tad out of the way, but well worth the effort.

Pint & Jigger
Pub Food $$

(Map p54; ☏808-744-9593; http://pintandjigger.com; 1936 S King St; shared plates $4-13; ☺4:30pm-midnight Sun-Wed, to 2am Thu-Sat) Red-brick walls and high-top tables make this gastropub, not too far west of the UH Manoa campus, trendy enough for aspiring 20- and 30-something foodies, who mix-and-match craft beers and cocktails with creative noshes such as guava wood-smoked sausage sliders and Scotch eggs.

Imanas Tei
Japanese $$$

(Map p58; ☏808-941-2626; 2626 S King St; shared dishes $5-30; ☺5-11:30pm Mon-Sat) Look for the orange sign outside this long-standing *izakaya*, where staff shout their welcome ('*Irrashaimase!*') as you make your way to a low-slung tatami-mat booth. Sake fans come here for the liquid version of rice, then graze their way through a seemingly endless menu of sushi and epicurean and country-style Japanese fare.

GREATER HONOLULU

Kaimuki is making its mark on Honolulu's cuisine scene by sprouting trendy restaurants along Wai'alae Ave, east of the university area. More casual and classic homegrown joints worth going out of your way for are scattered between downtown and the airport.

Helena's Hawaiian Food
Hawaii Regional Cuisine $

(Map p42; ☏808-845-8044; http://helenashawaiianfood.com; 1240 N School St; dishes $3-8; ☺10am-7:30pm Tue-Fri) Walking through the door is like stepping into another era. Even though long-time owner Helen Chock has passed away, her relatives still command the family kitchen, which opened in 1946. Most people order à la carte and Helena's is good! It's just a few blocks southeast of the Bishop Museum.

Andy's Sandwiches & Smoothies
Sandwiches $

(☏808-988-6161; www.andyssandwiches.com; 2904 E Manoa Rd; items $4-12; ☺7am-

Dancers, Prince Lot Hula Festival (p65)
JOE CARINI/GETTY IMAGES ©

5pm Mon-Thu, to 4pm Fri, to 2.30pm Sun) Andy's is a hidden gem up the Manoa Valley that doesn't see too many tourists. Opposite the Manoa Shopping Centre, it's a squeeze to get in, but worth the effort. The sandwiches, smoothies and salads are superb, especially the Bird's Nest salad.

Tamura's Poke
Seafood $

(Map p42; ☏808-735-7100; www.tamuras finewine.com; 3496 Waialae Ave, Kaimuki; ⏰11am-8.45pm Mon-Fri, 9.30am-8.45pm Sat, to 7:45pm Sun; P) Arguably the best *poke* on the island is up on Waialae Rd in undistinguished-looking Tamura's Fine Wines & Liquors. Head inside, turn right, wander down to *poke* corner and feast your eyes. The 'spicy *ahi*' and the smoked marlin is to die for. Ask for tasters before you buy and take away.

Crack Seed Store
Sweets $

(Map p42; ☏818-737-1022; 1156 Koko Head Ave; ⏰9.30am-6pm Mon-Sat, noon-4pm Sun; ♿) Mom-and-pop candy store on a side street in Kaimuki vends overflowing glass jars of made-from-scratch crack seed, plus addictive frozen slushies spiked with *li hing mui* (salty dried plums).

Liliha Bakery
Bakery $

(Map p42; ☏808-531-1651; www.lilihabakery hawaii.com; 515 N Kuakini, cnr Liliha St; items from $2, mains $6-10; ⏰6am-5.30am Tue-Sat, to 8pm Sun) Not far northwest of Chinatown, this old-school island bakery and diner causes a neighborhood traffic jam for its cocopuff and green-tea cream pastries. Still hungry? Grab a counter seat and order a hamburger steak or other hearty lumberjack faves in Liliha's retro coffee shop.

12th Avenue Grill
Modern American $$

(Map p42; ☏808-732-9469; http://12thavegrill. com; 1120 12th Ave; mains $18-36; ⏰5:30-10pm Sun-Thu, to 11pm Fri & Sat) Hidden in a side road off Waialae Ave, this Kaimuki grill has been picking up a number of best-restaurant awards of late. Combining the efforts of an impressive team and using as much local produce as possible, 12th Ave Grill has the locals drooling.

♥ If You Like…
Brewpubs

If you're searching for that perfect pint glass from the USA's westernmost state, you can round out your souvenir collection at the Big Island's Kona Brewing Company (p174) in Hawai'i Kai, or stop by these two Honolulu brewpubs.

1 HONOLULU BEERWORKS
(Map p42; ☏808-589-2337; www. honolulubeerworks.com; 328 Cooke St; ⏰11am-10pm Mon-Thu, to midnight Fri & Sat) This new kid on the microbrewery scene is fast building up a following with 12 brews on tap and barrel-aged beers. Based in a warehouse with recycled wooden walls, chairs and benches, the menu of 'beer food' may be limited, but it certainly hits the spot as you work your way through the beers on offer.

2 GORDON BIERSCH BREWERY RESTAURANT
(Map p44; ☏808-599-4877; www.gordonbiersch. com; 1st fl, 1 Aloha Tower Dr; ⏰10am-11pm Sun-Thu, to midnight Fri & Sat) Down fresh lagers made according to Germany's centuries-old purity laws, often with live music by the waterfront.

Town
Fusion $$

(Map p42; ☏808-735-5900; www.townkaimuki .com; 3435 Wai'alae Ave; mains breakfast & lunch $5-16, dinner $16-26; ⏰7am-2:30pm daily, 5:30-9:30pm Mon-Thu, to 10pm Fri & Sat) 🌿 At this hip modern coffee shop and bistro hybrid in Kaimuki, the motto is 'local first, organic whenever possible, with aloha always.' On the daily-changing menu of boldly flavored cooking are burgers and steaks made from North Shore free-range cattle and salads that taste as if the ingredients were just plucked from a backyard garden.

Nico's at Pier 38
Seafood $$

(Map p42; ☏808-540-1377; www.nicospier38. com; 1133 N Nimitz Hwy; breakfast & lunch plates $6-13, dinner mains $13-16; ⏰6:30am-9pm Mon-Sat, 10am-9pm Sun) Chef Nico was inspired by the island-cuisine scene to merge his

The Best...
Low-Key Locals' Hangouts

classical French training with Hawaii's humble plate lunch. French standards such as *steak frites* appear alongside market-fresh fish sandwiches and local belly-fillers such as *furikake*-crusted ahi and hoisin BBQ chicken. Tables with chairs are positioned near the waterfront and Honolulu's fish auction. Happy hour 4pm to 6pm daily.

Mitch's Fish Market & Sushi Bar
Seafood $$$

(☎808-837-7774; www.mitchsushi.com; 524 Ohohia St; small plates $5-35, set meals $25-40, chef's tasting menu $110; ⏰11:30am-8:30pm) A hole-in-the-wall sushi bar near the airport for cashed-up connoisseurs, who come for the chef's superbly fresh *omakase* tasting menu and rarely seen fishy delicacies shipped in from around the globe. Reservations essential; BYOB.

 Drinking & Nightlife

For what's going on after dark this week, from live-music and DJ gigs to theater, movies and cultural events, check the TGIF section (www.honolulupulse.com) of the *Honolulu Star-Advertiser*, which comes out every Friday, and the free alternative tabloid *Honolulu Weekly* (http://honoluluweekly.com), published every Wednesday.

CAFES

Manifest
Bar, Cafe

(Map p44; http://manifesthawaii.com; 32 N Hotel St; ⏰8am-2am Mon-Fri, 10am-2am Sat; 🛜) Smack in the middle of Chinatown's art scene, this lofty apartment-like space adorned with provocative photos and paintings doubles as a serene coffee shop by day and a cocktail bar by night, hosting movie and trivia nights and DJ sets (no cover). Foamy cappuccinos and spicy chais are daytime perfection.

Beach Bum Cafe
Cafe

(Map p44; ☎808-521-6699; www.beachbumcafe.com; 1088 Bishop St; ⏰6:30am-5pm Mon-Fri; 🛜) 🍃 Right in downtown's high-rise financial district, this connoisseur's coffee bar serves 100% organic, grown-in-Hawaii beans, roasted in small batches and hand-brewed just one ideal cup at a time. Chat up the baristas while you sip the rich flavors of the Big Island, Maui, Kaua'i and even Moloka'i. Also has an outpost at the First Hawaiian Center down the road.

Fresh Cafe Downtown
Cafe

(Map p44; ☎808-953-7374; www.freshcafehi.com; 1121 Nu'uanu Ave; ⏰7am-11pm Mon-Sat) Fresh Cafe's new bright and breezy Chinatown place is proving just as popular as its original location. With everything from breakfast to lunch to dinner and bar, with options to sit inside or out, Fresh hits the spot with its 'garden-fresh and local' attitude to food. Dedicated to promote local music, culture and art, too!

Honolulu Coffee Company
Coffee Shop

(Map p44; ☎808-521-4400; www.honolulucoffee.com; 1001 Bishop St; ⏰6am-5:30pm Mon-Fri, 7am-noon Sat; 🛜) Overlooking Tamarind Sq with city skyline views, here you can take a break from tramping around Honolulu's historical sites for a java jolt brewed from handpicked, hand-roasted 100% Kona estate-grown beans. Also at Ala Moana Center and in Waikiki.

Glazers Coffee
Cafe

(Map p58; ☎808-391-6548; www.glazerscoffee.com; 2700 S King St; ⏰7am-11pm Mon-Thu, to 9pm Fri, 8am-11pm Sat & Sun; 🛜) They're serious about brewing strong espresso drinks and batch-roasted coffee at this university students' hangout, where you can kick back on comfy living-room sofas next to jazzy artwork and plentiful electrical outlets.

Fresh Cafe Cafe
(Map p54; 📞808-688-8055; http://freshcafehi.com; 831 Queen St; 🕗8am-11pm Mon-Sat, 9am-6pm Sun; 🛜) At this alternative coffeehouse in an industrial warehouse area just west of Ala Moana Center, artists, bohemians and hipster hangers-on sip Vietnamese coffee, pikake iced tea, and Thai or *haupia*-flavored lattes. Evening special events vary.

Wai'oli Tea Room Teahouse
(📞808-988-5800; www.thewaiolitearoom.com; 2950 Manoa Rd; 🕗8am-2pm) If 19th-century author Robert Louis Stevenson were still hanging around Honolulu today, this is where you'd find him. Set in the verdant Manoa Valley, this open-air teahouse overlooks gardens of red ginger and birds-of-paradise and serves excellent breakfasts and lunches. Afternoon high tea by reservation only.

Tea at 1024 Teahouse
(Map p44; 📞808-521-9596; www.teaat1024.net; 1024 Nu'uanu Ave; 🕗11am-2pm Tue-Fri, to 3pm Sat) Tea at 1024 takes you back in time to another era. Cutesy sandwiches, scones and cakes accompany your choice of tea as you relax and watch the Chinatown crowd rush by the window. There are even bonnets for you to don to add to the ambience. Set menus run from $20.95 per person and reservations are recommended.

BARS, LOUNGES & CLUBS

Every self-respecting bar in Honolulu has a *pupu* menu to complement the liquid sustenance, and some bars are as famous for their appetizers as their good-times atmosphere. A key term to know is *pau hana* (literally 'stop work'), Hawaiian pidgin for 'happy hour.' Chinatown's edgy nightlife scene revolves around N Hotel St, which was the city's notorious red-light district not so long ago.

La Mariana Sailing Club Bar
(Map p42; 📞808-848-2800; www.lamariana sailingclub.com; 50 Sand Island Access Rd; 🕗11am-9pm) Time warp! Who says all the

Fresh scones and tea at the Wai'oli Tea Room

LINDA CHING/DESIGN PICS/GETTY IMAGES ©

Friday Nights in Chinatown

Chinatown's somewhat seedy Nu'uanu Ave and Hotel St have become surprisingly cool places for a dose of urban art and culture, socializing and bar-hopping during **First Friday Honolulu** (www.firstfridayhawaii.com), held from 5pm to 9pm on the first Friday of each month. What was once a low-key art walk has become almost too big for its britches, according to local naysayers. A giant block party now rocks out to live music and DJs, with food trucks and over-21 wristbands required for getting into Chinatown's most popular bars and clubs – be prepared to queue behind velvet ropes. Aiming to lure back more chilled crowds, some art galleries, shops, cafes and restaurants have banded together to jump-start a newer event called **Slow Art Friday** (www.artsdistricthonolulu.com), happening from 6pm to 9:30pm on the third Friday of every month, featuring more local food, live music and art.

great tiki bars have gone to the dogs? Irreverent and kitschy, this 1950s joint by the lagoon is filled with yachties and long-suffering locals. Classic mai tais are as killer as the other signature tropical potions, complete with tiki-head swizzle sticks and tiny umbrellas. Grab a waterfront table and dream of sailing to Tahiti.

Hank's Cafe
Bar

(Map p44; ☎808-526-1410; http://hankscafe hawaii.com; 1038 Nu'uanu Ave; ⏰7am-2am) You can't get more low-key than this neighborhood dive bar on the edge of Chinatown. Owner Hank is a jack-of-all-trades when it comes to the barfly business: the walls are decorated with Polynesian-themed art, live music rolls in some nights and regulars practically call it home.

Next Door
Club, Lounge

(Map p44; ☎808-852-2243; www.facebook. com/nextdoorhi; 43 N Hotel St; ⏰7pm-2am Wed-Sat) Situated on a skid-row block of N Hotel St where dive bars are still the order of the day, this svelte cocktail lounge is a brick-walled retreat with vivid red couches and flickering candles. DJs spin house, hip hop, funk, mash-ups and retro sounds, while on other nights loud, live local bands play just about anything.

Tropics Tap House
Sports Bar

(Map p58; ☎808-955-5088; www.tropicstap house.com; 1019 University Ave; ⏰2pm-2am Mon-Fri, 11am-2pm Sat & Sun) Relive your college days at this open-air sports bar on University Ave that couldn't be called fancy, but gets the job done. Standard sports-bar fare, but lots of beers to choose from and even beer cocktails. Lots of big screens for game-watching.

Mai Tai Bar
Bar

(Map p54; ☎808-947-2900; www.maitaibar.com; Ho'okipa Tce, 3rd fl, Ala Moana Center, 1450 Ala Moana Blvd; ⏰11am-1am; 🛜) A happening bar in the middle of a shopping center? We don't make the trends, we just report 'em. During sunset and late-night happy hours, this enormous circular tropical bar is packed with a see-and-flirt crowd. Island-style live music plays nightly.

Fix Sports Lounge & Nightclub
Club

(Map p44; ☎808-728-4416; http://thefix sportsloungeandnightclub.com; 80 S Pau'ahi St; ⏰11am-2am Mon-Fri, 5pm-2am Sat) These guys have got the bases covered with a cavernous sports lounge full of large flatscreens offering the standard sports-lounge fare...morphing into a raging nightclub later on with DJs and dancing. One of the largest venues on O'ahu.

M Nightclub
Club, Lounge

(Map p42; 808-529-0010; http://mnlhnl.com; Waterfront Plaza, 500 Ala Moana Blvd; admission after 10pm Fri & Sat $10; 4:30pm-2am Tue-Thu, to 4am Fri, 8pm-4am Sat) Flickering votive candles, bartenders who juggle bottles of Grey Goose and Patrón, and table service at sexy white couches backlit with purple hues – this restaurant-nightclub hybrid is as close as Honolulu gets to Vegas. An insider crowd of dressed-to-kill locals bumps shoulders on the dance floor ruled by electronica DJs.

Bar 35
Bar

(Map p44; 808-537-3535; www.bar35hawaii. com; 35 N Hotel St; 4pm-2am Mon-Fri, 6pm-2am Sat) Filled with aloha, this indoor-outdoor watering hole has a dizzying 100 domestic and international bottled beers to choose from, plus addictive chef-made gourmet fusion pizzas to go with all the brews. There's live music or DJs some weekend nights.

 # Entertainment

LIVE MUSIC

If traditional and contemporary Hawaiian music is what you crave, don't look any further than Waikiki. But if it's jazz, alt-rock and punk sounds you're after, venture outside the tourist zone into Honolulu's other neighborhoods.

Dragon Upstairs
Live Music

(Map p44; 808-526-1411; http://thedragonupstairs. com; 2nd fl, 1038 Nu'uanu Ave; usually 7pm-2am) Right above Hank's Cafe in Chinatown, this claustrophobic hideaway with a sedate older vibe and lots of funky artwork and mirrors hosts a rotating lineup of jazz cats, blues strummers and folk singers, usually on Thursday, Friday and Saturday nights. Occasional $5 cover charge.

Republik
Live Music

(Map p54; 808-941-7469; http://jointherepublik.com; 1349 Kapi'olani Blvd; lounge 6pm-2am Mon-Sat, concert schedules vary) Honolulu's most intimate concert hall for touring and local acts – indie rockers, punk and metal bands, and more – has a graffiti-bomb vibe and backlit black walls that trippily light up. Buy tickets for shows in advance to make sure you get in and also to save a few bucks.

Anna O'Brien's
Live Music

(Map p58; 808-946-5190; http://annaobriens.com; 2440 S Beretania St; 2pm-2am) A college dive bar, part roadhouse and part art-house, the reincarnation of Anna Bannanas, goes beyond its retro-1960s 'Summer of Love' atmosphere to book alt-rock, punk and metal bands. Regular DJs, comedy nights and Sunday reggae.

Hawaii Theatre (p82)
LINDA CHING/GETTY IMAGES ©

HONOLULU ENTERTAINMENT

Check the online calendar for what's on and cover charges.

Jazz Minds Art & Café   Live Music

(Map p54; ☎808-945-0800; www.honolulu jazzclub.com; 1661 Kapiʻolani Blvd; cover charge $10; ⏰9pm-2am Mon-Sat) Don't let the nearby strip clubs turn you off this place. This tattered brick-walled lounge with an almost speakeasy ambience pulls in the top island talent – fusion jazz, funk, bebop, hip hop, surf rock and minimalist acts. However, you will need to be prepared for a stiff two-drink minimum.

PERFORMING ARTS

Hawaii's capital city is home to a symphony orchestra, an opera company, ballet troupes, chamber orchestras and more, while more than a dozen community theater groups perform everything from David Mamet satires to Hawaiian pidgin fairy tales.

Hawaii Theatre   Performing Arts

(Map p44; ☎808-528-0506; www.hawaiitheatre. com; 1130 Bethel St) 🍃 Beautifully restored, this grande dame of Oʻahu's theater scene is a major venue for dance, music and theater. Performances include top Hawaii musicians, contemporary plays, international touring acts and film festivals. The theater also hosts the annual Ka Himeni Ana competition of singers in the traditional *nahenahe* style, accompanied by ukuleles.

Neal S Blaisdell Center   Performing Arts

(Map p54; ☎808-768-5252; www.blaisdellcenter. com; 777 Ward Ave) A cultural linchpin, this modern performing-arts complex stages symphony and chamber-music concerts, opera performances and ballet recitals, prestigious hula competitions, Broadway shows and more. Occasionally big-name pop and rock touring acts play here instead of at Aloha Stadium. Parking costs from $6.

Left: Neil S Blaisdell Center; **Below:** Detail of coconut and orchid lei
(LEFT) BARRY WINIKER/GETTY IMAGES ©; (BELOW) LINDA CHING/GETTY IMAGES ©

ARTS at Marks Garage
Performing Arts

(Map p44; ☎808-521-2903; www.artsatmarks.
com; 1159 Nu'uanu Ave; ☉11am-6pm Tue-Sat)
On the cutting edge of the Chinatown
arts scene, this community gallery and
performance space puts on a variety
of live shows, from stand-up comedy,
burlesque cabaret nights and conversa-
tions with island artists to live jazz and
Hawaiian music.

Kumu Kahua Theatre
Performing Arts

(Map p44; ☎808-536-4441; www.kumukahua.
org; 46 Merchant St) ✐ In the restored
Kamehameha V Post Office building, this
little 100-seat treasure is dedicated to
premiering works by Hawaii's playwrights, with themes focusing on contemporary multicultural island life, often
richly peppered with Hawaiian pidgin.

Ala Moana Centertainment
Performing Arts

(Map p54; ☎808-955-9517; www.alamoana-
center.com; ground fl, Center Court, 1450 Ala
Moana Blvd; ♿) FREE The mega Ala Moana
shopping center's courtyard area is the
venue for all sorts of island entertainment, including performances by O'ahu
musicians and the Royal Hawaiian Band.
Japanese *taiko* drumming and Sunday-
afternoon *na keiki* (children's) hula
shows also take place.

HawaiiSlam
Performing Arts

(Map p54; www.hawaiislam.com; Fresh Cafe,
831 Queen St; admission before/after 8:30pm
$3/5; ☉8:30pm 1st Thu of the month) One
of the USA's biggest poetry slams, here
international wordsmiths, artists, musicians, MCs and DJs share the stage. For
aspiring spoken-word stars, sign-up starts
at 7:30pm.

The Best...
Made-in-Hawaii Shops

CINEMAS

For more theater locations, show times and ticketing, check **Fandango** (📞800-326-3264; www.fandango.com).

Doris Duke Theatre   Cinema

(Map p54; 📞808-532-8768; www.honolulu museum.org; Honolulu Museum of Art, 900 S Beretania St; tickets $10) Shows a mind-bending array of experimental, alternative, retro-classic and art-house films, especially ground-breaking documentaries, inside the Honolulu Museum of Art. For weekday matinees, validated parking costs $3 (evenings and weekends free).

Movie Museum   Cinema

(Map p42; 📞808-735-8771; www.kaimukihawaii. com; 3566 Harding Ave; tickets $5; 🕐noon-9pm Thu-Mon) In the Kaimuki neighborhood, east of the UH Manoa campus, this sociable spot screens classic oldies, foreign flicks and indie films, including some Hawaii premieres, in a tiny theater equipped with digital sound and just 20 comfy Barca-loungers. Reservations recommended.

🔒 Shopping

Although it's not a brand-name mecca like Waikiki, Honolulu has unique shops and multiple malls offering plenty of local flavor. Check out traditional flower lei stands, ukulele factories, Hawaiiana souvenir shops, contemporary island-style clothing boutiques, and vintage and antiques stores.

Native Books /Nā Mea Hawaii   Books, Gifts

(Map p54; 📞808-597-8967; www.nativebooks hawaii.com; Ward Warehouse, 1050 Ala Moana Blvd; 🕐10am-8:30pm Mon-Thu, to 9pm Fri & Sat, to 6pm Sun) So much more than just a bookstore stocking Hawaiiana tomes, CDs and DVDs, this cultural gathering spot also sells beautiful silk-screened fabrics, koa-wood bowls, Hawaiian quilts, fish-hook jewelry and hula supplies. Call or check online for special events, including author readings, live local music and cultural classes.

Ala Moana Center   Mall

(Map p54; www.alamoanacenter.com; 1450 Ala Moana Blvd; 🕐9.30am-9pm Mon-Sat, 10am-7pm Sun; 🚻) This open-air shopping mall and its nearly 300 department stores and mostly chain stores could compete on an international runway with some of Asia's famous megamalls. A handful of Hawaii specialty shops such as Crazy Shirts for tees, Reyn Spooner for aloha shirts, Loco Boutique for swimsuits, Local Motion surfwear and Na Hoku jewelry are thrown into the mix.

Ward Warehouse   Mall

(Map p54; www.wardcenters.com; 1050 Ala Moana Blvd; 🕐10am-9pm Mon-Sat, to 6pm Sun) Situated across the street from Ala Moana Beach, this mini-mall has many one-of-a-kind island shops and eateries. There is a possibility that it will all be bowled over to make way for glitzy towers, but at the time of writing, Ward Warehouse survives!

Island Slipper — Shoes

(Map p54; www.islandslipper.com; Ward Warehouse, 1050 Ala Moana Blvd; ⏱10am-9pm Mon-Sat, to 8pm Sun) Across Honolulu and Waikiki, scores of stores sell flip-flops (aka 'rubbah slippah'), but nobody else carries such ultracomfy suede and leather styles – all made in Hawaii since 1946 – let alone such giant sizes (as one clerk told us, 'We fit *all* the island people.'). Try on as many pairs as you like until your feet really feel the *aloha*.

Manuheali'i — Clothing

(Map p54; ☎808-942-9868; www.manuhealii.com; 930 Punahou St; ⏱9:30am-6pm Mon-Fri, 9am-4pm Sat, 10am-3pm Sun) Look to this island-born shop for original and modern designs. Hawaiian musicians often sport Manuheali'i's bold-print silk aloha shirts. Flowing synthetic print and knit dresses and wrap tops take inspiration from the traditional muumuu, but are transformed into spritely contemporary looks. Also in Kailua.

Kamaka Hawaii — Music

(Map p42; ☎808-531-3165; www.kamakahawaii.com; 550 South St; ⏱8am-4pm Mon-Fri) 🍃 Skip right by those tacky souvenir shops selling cheap plastic and wooden ukuleles. Kamaka specializes in handcrafted ukuleles made on O'ahu since 1916, with prices starting at around $500. Its signature is an oval-shaped 'pineapple' ukulele, which has a more mellow sound. Call ahead for free 30-minute factory tours, usually starting at 10:30am Tuesday through Friday.

Tin Can Mailman — Antiques, Books

(Map p44; http://tincanmailman.net; 1026 Nu'uanu Ave; ⏱11am-5pm Mon-Thu, to 9pm Fri, to 4pm Sat) If you're a big fan of vintage tiki wares and 20th-century Hawaiiana books, you'll fall in love with this little Chinatown antiques shop. Thoughtfully collected treasures include jewelry and ukuleles, silk aloha shirts, tropical-wood furnishings, vinyl records, rare prints and tourist brochures from the post–WWII tourism boom. No photos allowed.

Nohea Gallery — Arts, Crafts

(Map p54; www.noheagallery.com; Ward Warehouse, 1050 Ala Moana Blvd; ⏱10am-9pm Mon-Sat, to 6pm Sun) A meditative space amid the shopping-mall madness, this

Ala Moana Center

LINDA CHING/GETTY IMAGES ©

high-end gallery sells handcrafted jewelry, glassware, pottery and woodwork, all of it made in Hawaii. Local artisans occasionally give demonstrations of their crafts on the sidewalk outside.

Cindy's Lei Shoppe   Arts, Crafts

(Map p44; ☎808-536-6538; www.cindyslei shoppe.com; 1034 Maunakea St; ☺usually 6am-6pm Mon-Sat, to 5pm Sun) At this inviting little shop, a Chinatown landmark, you can watch aunties craft flower lei made of orchids, plumeria, twining maile, lantern 'ilima (flowering ground-cover) and ginger. Several other lei shops clustered nearby will also pack lei for you to carry back home on the plane.

Lion Coffee   Gifts, Souvenirs

(☎808-847-3600; www.lioncoffee.com; 1555 Kalani St; ☺6am-5pm Mon-Sat; ☎) In an out-of-the-way warehouse west of downtown en route to the airport, this discount grown-in-Hawaii coffee giant roasts myriad flavors from straight-up strong (100% Kona 24-Karat and Diamond Head espresso blend) to outlandishly wacky (chocolate mac-nut, toasted coconut). Friendly baristas pour free tastes.

Fabric Mart   Arts, Crafts

(Map p54; ☎808-947-4466; www.fmart.com; 1631 Kalakaua Ave; ☺9am-7pm) This fabric store has masses of Hawaiian print materials that can be used for everything from cushion covers to dresses to aloha shirts. Buy them at best prices by the yard. The only place on the island with more fabric is the main store out in Aiea.

Madre Chocolate   Food

(Map p44; ☎808-377-6440; http://madrechoc olate.com; 8 N Pau'ahi St; ☺11am-6pm Mon, to 8pm Tue-Sat) The Honolulu outpost of this Kailua chocolate company is serving up a storm in Chinatown with free samplings of innovative chocolate flavors such as Lili'koi passionfruit, and coconut milk and caramelized ginger. A must for chocolate-lovers, but it doesn't come cheap! If you're really keen, Madre also offers a five-day 'Experience Hawaiian Cacao and

Left: Aloha Tower (p49) and Honolulu harbor at sunset; **Below:** Traditional-style jewelry at a Honolulu shop
(LEFT) SHANEFF CARL/GETTY IMAGES ©; (BELOW) MUNTASIR MAMUN/GETTY IMAGES ©

Chocolate Bootcamp' on
O'ahu.

ℹ Information

Dangers & Annoyances

Drug dealing and gang activity are prevalent on the north side of Chinatown, particularly along Nu'uanu Stream and the River St pedestrian mall, which should be avoided after dark. Chinatown's skid rows include blocks of Hotel St.

Emergency

Police, Fire & Ambulance (☎911) For all emergencies.

Honolulu Police Department (☎808-529-3111; www.honolulupd.org; 801 S Beretania St) For nonemergencies (eg stolen property reports necessary for insurance claims).

Internet Access

Cheaper cybercafes on King St near the UH Manoa campus stay open late.

FedEx Office (www.fedex.com/us/office; per hr $12; 🛜) Ala Moana (1500 Kapi'olani Blvd; ⊙7:30am-9pm Mon-Fri, 10am-6pm Sat, noon-6pm Sun); Downtown (590 Queen St; ⊙7am-11pm Mon-Fri, 9am-9pm Sat & Sun); University Area (2575 S King St; ⊙24hr; 🛜) Self-serve computer terminals (20¢ to 30¢ per minute), pay-as-you-go digital photo-printing and CD-burning stations, and free wi-fi.

Hawaii State Library (☎808-586-3500; www.librarieshawaii.org; 478 S King St; ⊙10am-5pm Mon & Wed, 9am-5pm Tue, Fri & Sat, 9am-8pm Thu; 🛜) Free wi-fi and internet terminals (temporary nonresident library card $10) downtown that may be reserved by calling ahead.

Media

Newspapers & Magazines

Honolulu Magazine (www.honolulumagazine.com) Glossy monthly magazine covering arts, culture, fashion, shopping, lifestyle and cuisine. Also with online edition.

Honolulu Star-Advertiser (www.staradvertiser.com) Honolulu's daily newspaper; look for 'TGIF,'

Friday's special events and entertainment pull-out section. Also with online edition.

Honolulu Weekly (www.honoluluweekly.com) Free weekly arts-and-entertainment tabloid. Has a local events calendar that lists museum and gallery exhibits, cultural classes, outdoor activities, farmers markets, volunteering meetups and 'whatevas.'

Radio & TV

KHET (Oceanic cable channel 10) Hawaii public TV (PBS).

KHON (Oceanic cable channel 3) Evening news broadcast ends with slack key guitar music by Keola and Kapono Beamer and clips of people waving the *shaka* (Hawaii hand greeting) sign.

KHPR (88.1FM) Hawaii Public Radio (NPR); classical music and news.

KIKU (channel 9) Multicultural community TV programming.

KINE (105.1FM) Classic and contemporary Hawaiian music.

KIPO (89.3FM) Hawaii Public Radio; news, jazz and world music.

KQMQ (93.1FM) 'Da Pa'ina' island-style music and Hawaiian reggae.

KTUH (90.3FM) Quirky University of Hawai'i student-run radio.

Medical Services

Longs Drugs (www.cvs.com/longs) Convenient 24-hour drugstores with pharmacies in a number of locations.

Queen's Medical Center (☎808-691-7000; www.queensmedicalcenter.net; ⏰24hr) O'ahu's biggest, best-equipped hospital has a 24-hour emergency room downtown.

Straub Clinic & Hospital (☎808-522-4000; www.straubhealth.org; 888 S King St; ⏰24hr) Operates a 24-hour emergency room downtown and a nonemergency clinic open weekdays (call ahead to check hours).

ℹ Getting There & Around

Bus

Just northwest of Waikiki, the Ala Moana Center mall is the central transfer point for TheBus, O'ahu's public-transportation system.

Useful Bus Routes

ROUTE	DESTINATION
2	Waikiki, Honolulu Museum of Art, 'Iolani Palace, downtown Honolulu, Chinatown, Bishop Museum
4	Waikiki, University of Hawai'i, 'Iolani Palace, downtown Honolulu, Chinatown, Queen Emma Summer Palace
8	Waikiki, Ala Moana Center, Ward Centers, downtown Honolulu, Chinatown
13	Waikiki, Honolulu Convention Center, Honolulu Museum of Art, 'Iolani Palace, downtown Honolulu, Chinatown
19 & 20	Waikiki, Ala Moana Center, Ward Centers, Restaurant Row, Aloha Tower Marketplace, downtown Honolulu, Chinatown, Honolulu International Airport*; also Pearl Harbor (route 20 only)
42	Waikiki, Ala Moana Center, Ward Centers, downtown Honolulu, Chinatown, Pearl Harbor
B (CityExpress!)	Waikiki, Honolulu Museum of Art, 'Iolani Palace, downtown Honolulu, Chinatown, Bishop Museum
E (CountryExpress!)	Waikiki, Ala Moana Center, Restaurant Row, Aloha Tower Marketplace, downtown Honolulu

*One piece of hand-held carry-on baggage only per person; luggage prohibited.

Aerial view of the H-3 Fwy between Pearl Harbor and Kailua

ROYCE BAIR/GETTY IMAGES ©

Note that to reach Honolulu's various neighborhoods from Waikiki there are several direct bus routes that don't require transferring at Ala Moana Center.

Car

Major car-rental companies are found at Honolulu International Airport and in Waikiki.

Traffic jams up during rush hours, roughly from 7am to 9am and 3pm to 6pm weekdays. Expect heavy traffic in both directions on the H-1 Fwy during this time, as well as on the Pali and Likelike Hwys headed into Honolulu in the morning and away from the city in the late afternoon.

Two major thoroughfares run the length of Honolulu: Ala Moana Blvd (Hwy 92) skirts the coast from the airport to Waikiki, while the H-1 Fwy runs east–west between the beach and the mountains. To/from Waikiki, King St (one-way heading southeast) and Beretania St (one-way heading northwest) are alternate surface streets into and out of downtown. Chinatown is full of confusing one-way streets, and N Hotel St is open to buses only.

Parking

Downtown and Chinatown have on-street metered parking; it's reasonably easy to find an empty space on weekends, but nearly impossible on weekdays. Bring lots of quarters.

Pay parking is also available at several municipal garages and there are a lot scattered around Chinatown and downtown. On the outskirts of the downtown core, the private Neal S Blaisdell Center offers all-day parking from $6, depending on special events.

Most shopping centers, including the Ala Moana Center, provide free parking for customers. The Aloha Tower Marketplace offers a pay self-parking lot (three hours for $3 before 4pm Monday to Friday, or $5 flat rate after 4pm weekdays and all day on weekends). Restaurant patrons get three hours of free parking with validation.

Waikiki

Once a Hawaiian royal retreat, Waikiki is riding high on a new wave of effortlessly chic style these days.

No longer just a plasticky beach destination for package tourists, this famous strand of sand is flowering, starting with a renaissance of Hawaiian music at beachfront hotels and resorts. In this concrete jungle of modern high-rises, you can, surprisingly, still hear whispers of Hawaii's past, from the chanting of hula troupes at Kuhio Beach to the legacy of Olympic gold medalist Duke Kahanamoku.

Take a surfing lesson from a bronzed beach-boy, then spend a lazy afternoon lying on Waikiki's golden sands. Before the sun sinks below the horizon, hop aboard a catamaran and sail off toward Diamond Head. Sip a sunset mai tai and be hypnotized by the lilting harmonies of slack key guitar, then mingle with the locals, who come here to party after dark, too.

Duke Kahanamoku statue by Jan Gordon Fisher (p101)

Waikiki Highlights

Surfing

Could there be a better place to learn to surf (p106) than virtually right under the nose of Duke Kahanamoku, the father of modern surfing? *Malihini* (newcomers) learn to stand up on their boards at Kuhio Beach, while experts join the lineups at Queens, Canoes and Populars. The 'Surfer on a Wave' statue down at Queen's Surf Beach says it all – surfing is part of the culture in Waikiki. Surfers at Waikiki Beach (p96)

1

2 House Without a Key

Swizzle sunset cocktails such as House Without a Key's signature mai tai while slack key guitars play island lullabies and former Miss Hawaiis dance gracefully before you (p126). Throw in panoramic ocean views and the century-old kiawe tree that extends its branches above you and it might seem like the whole thing's straight out of a movie.

ANN CECIL/GETTY IMAGES ©

Sans Souci Beach Park

3

Also known among locals as Kaimana Beach, Sans Souci (p101), at the Diamond Head end of Waikiki, offers a different feel from the crowded sands of downtown Waikiki, only a short stroll away. Locals come here for their daily swims, and with the laid-back atmosphere, you too can enjoy your own private little sandy hideaway without having to venture too far. Saltwater pool, Sans Souci Beach Park

RICHARD NEWSTEAD/GETTY IMAGES ©

4

Kuhio Beach Torch Lighting & Hula Show

When the conch shell blows in the evening on Kuhio Beach (p126), everyone knows they are in for something special. This is not some corny, kitsch version of Hawaiian culture; this is the authentic, real thing. These are proud Hawaiians sharing their aloha and love of everything Hawaiian. Hula dancers reach toward the sky, elders strum on ukuleles and guitars and everyone is captivated.

5

Bailey's Antiques & Aloha Shirts

First impressions may be that you've walked into a jumble sale, but with racks crammed with thousands upon thousands of aloha shirts, this is the equivalent of the holy grail for aloha shirt enthusiasts (p127). Prices range from five bucks to several thousand for collectibles. If you've ever wondered where musician Jimmy Buffet spends his 'Margaritaville' royalties, you've found it!

Waikiki Itineraries

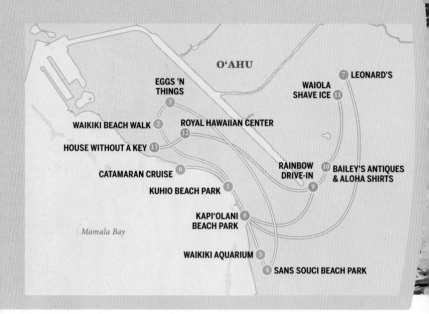

O'AHU

LEONARD'S ⑦

EGGS 'N THINGS ③

WAIOLA SHAVE ICE ⑪

WAIKIKI BEACH WALK ②

ROYAL HAWAIIAN CENTER ⑫

HOUSE WITHOUT A KEY ⑬

CATAMARAN CRUISE ⑥

RAINBOW DRIVE-IN ⑨

BAILEY'S ANTIQUES & ALOHA SHIRTS ⑩

KUHIO BEACH PARK ①

KAPI'OLANI BEACH PARK ⑧

Mamala Bay

WAIKIKI AQUARIUM ⑤

SANS SOUCI BEACH PARK ④

4 MILES
DAYS ONE & TWO

Pay your respects to iconic surfer Duke Ka-hanamoku's statue at ❶**Kuhio Beach Park** (p100) before taking a morning surfing lesson from one of Waikiki's modern-day beachboys. Head out on an outrigger-canoe ride or laze away until the torch lighting and hula show.

After dark, ❷**Waikiki Beach Walk** is the most buzzing place to be. Change out of your rubbah slippah and treat yourself to stellar Hawaii Regional cuisine at Roy's Waikiki Beach, a star island chef's bistro.

Sometimes all the tourists really are headed in the right direction; at ❸**Eggs 'n Things** (p118) dig into Portuguese sausage and fluffy pancakes topped with guava or coconut syrup at this always-busy diner early on day two.

After breakfast, stroll, cycle or catch a bus down toward the Diamond Head side of Waikiki to the seldom-crowded strand of ❹**Sans Souci Beach Park** (p101). When morning waters are calm, snorkeling here is a joy. Learn about all those fish you just snorkeled by at ❺**Waikiki Aquarium** (p102), an eco-conscious educational center.

Amble back to Waikiki's main strip and climb aboard one of the ❻**catamaran cruise** (p109) party boats that pull up right on the beach, catering sunset mai tais shaken by the waves.

5 MILES

DAY THREE

Nothing says aloha like a sugary, sweet *malasada* (Portuguese-style doughnut), still warm and straight from the ovens of ❼ **Leonard's** (p120), a 1950s vintage bakery.

Kick back with local families laying out picnic blankets on the grass shaded by palm trees at ❽ **Kapi'olani Beach Park** (p100). Join the local surfers and working folks on their lunch break at ❾ **Rainbow Drive-In** (p121), an authentic spot that dishes up mixed-plate lunches covered in good gravy.

Get yourself a stylin' aloha shirt at vintage ❿ **Bailey's Antiques & Aloha Shirts** (p127). Detour further up Kapahulu Ave to ⓫ **Waiola Shave Ice** (p120) to sample one of O'ahu's

tastiest contenders for rainbow-colored icy goodness, layered with azuki beans or topped off with *liliko'i* (passion fruit) cream.

⓬ **Royal Hawaiian Center** (p127) is Waikiki's biggest shopping mall, where you can browse for island-made surfwear, or learn how to make a lei at free drop-in cultural classes, offered on many afternoons.

Sashay inside ⓭ **House Without a Key** (p126), Waikiki's classiest resort, and grab an ocean-view table outdoors by the century-old kiawe tree. Sip tropical cocktails while watching graceful hula dancers.

Outrigger canoes on Waikiki Beach (p96)
JOSS JOSS/GETTY IMAGES ©

Discover Waikiki

History

Looking at Waikiki today, it's hard to imagine that less than 150 years ago this tourist mecca was almost entirely wetlands filled with fishponds and *lo'i kalo* (taro fields). Fed by mountain streams from the Manoa Valley, Waikiki (Spouting Water) was once one of O'ahu's most fertile farming areas. In 1795 Kamehameha I became the first *ali'i* (chief) to successfully unite the Hawaiian Islands under one sovereign's rule, bringing his royal court to Waikiki.

By the 1880s, Honolulu's more well-to-do citizens had started building gingerbread-trimmed cottages along the narrow beachfront. Tourism started booming in 1901 when Waikiki's first luxury hotel, the Moana, opened its doors on a former royal compound. Tiring quickly of the pesky mosquitoes that thrived in Waikiki's wetlands, early beachgoers petitioned to have the 'swamps' brought under control. In 1922 the Ala Wai Canal was dug to divert the streams that flowed into Waikiki and to dry out the wetlands. Tourists quickly replaced the water buffaloes.

In the 'Roaring '20s,' the Royal Hawaiian hotel opened to serve passengers arriving on luxury ocean liners from San Francisco. The Depression and WWII put a damper on tourism, but the Royal Hawaiian was turned into an R&R playground for sailors on shore leave. From 1935 to 1975, the classic radio show *Hawaii Calls*, performed live at the Moana hotel, broadcast dreams of a tropical paradise to the US mainland and the world. As late as 1950, surfers could still drive their cars right up to the beach and park on the sand – hard to imagine nowadays!

 ## Beaches

The 2-mile stretch of white sand that everyone calls Waikiki Beach runs from Hilton Hawaiian Village all the way to Kapi'olani Beach Park. Along the way, the beach keeps changing names and personalities. In the early morning, quiet seaside paths belong to walkers and runners, and strolling toward Diamond Head at dawn can be a meditative experience. By midmorning

Surfers on Waikiki Beach
SEIDEN ALLAN/GETTY IMAGES ©

Island Insights

Near the police substation at Waikiki Beach Center, four ordinary-looking boulders are actually the legendary **Wizard Stones of Kapaemahu**, said to contain the secrets and healing powers of 16th-century Tahitian sorcerers. Just east is a **bronze statue of Duke Kahanamoku** standing with one of his long-boards, often with fresh flower lei hanging around his neck. Considered the father of modern surfing, Duke made his home in Waikiki. Many local surfers have taken issue with the placement of the statue – Duke is standing with his back to the sea, a position they say he never would've taken in real life. Stop to wave the *shaka* (Hawaiian hand greeting sign) to all the folks back home via the Duke's live-streaming webcam (www.honolulu.gov/cameras/waikiki.html).

it looks like any resort beach – packed with water-sports concession stands and lots of tourist bodies. By noon it's a challenge to walk along the packed beach without stepping on anyone.

Waikiki is good for swimming, bodyboarding, surfing, sailing and other water sports most of the year, and there are lifeguards, restrooms and outdoor showers scattered along the beachfront. Between May and September, summer swells make the water a little rough for swimming, but great for surfing. For snorkeling, head to Sans Souci Beach Park or Queen's Surf Beach.

The beaches are listed geographically from northwest to southeast.

Kahanamoku Beach   Beach

(Map p42) Fronting the Hilton Hawaiian Village, Kahanamoku Beach is Waikiki's westernmost beach. It takes its name from Duke Kahanamoku (1890–1968), the legendary Waikiki beachboy whose family once owned the land where the resort now stands. Hawaii's champion surfer and Olympic gold medal winner learned to swim right here. The beach offers calm swimming conditions and a gently sloping, if rocky, bottom. Public access is at the end of Paoa Pl, off Kalia Rd.

Fort DeRussy Beach   Beach

(Map p98; 🛝) Seldom crowded, this often-overlooked beauty extends along the shore of a military reservation. Like all beaches in Hawaii, it's free and open to the public. The water is usually calm and good for swimming, but it's shallow at low tide. When conditions are right, windsurfers, bodyboarders and board surfers all play here. Usually open daily, beach-hut concession stands rent bodyboards, kayaks and snorkel sets. A grassy lawn with palm trees offers some sparse shade, an alternative to frying on the sand.

Gray's Beach   Beach

(Map p98) Nestled up against the Halekulani luxury resort, Gray's Beach has suffered some of the Waikiki strip's worst erosion. Because the seawall in front of the Halekulani hotel is so close to the waterline, the beach sand fronting the hotel is often totally submerged by the surf, but the offshore waters are shallow and calm, offering decent swimming conditions. Public access is along a paved walkway. It was named after Gray's-by-the-Sea, a 1920s boarding house that stood here.

Kahaloa & Ulukou Beaches   Beach

(Map p98) The beach between the Royal Hawaiian and Moana Surfrider hotels is Waikiki's busiest section of sand and surf, great for sunbathing, swimming and people-watching. Most of the beach has a shallow bottom with a gradual slope. The only drawback for swimmers is its popularity with beginning surfers, and the occasional catamaran landing hazard. Queens and Canoes, Waikiki's best-known

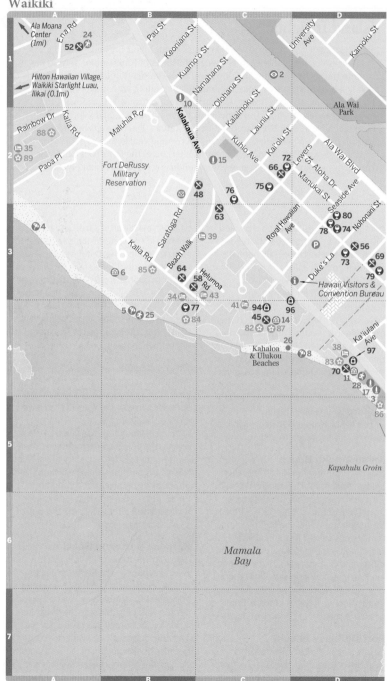

WAIKIKI

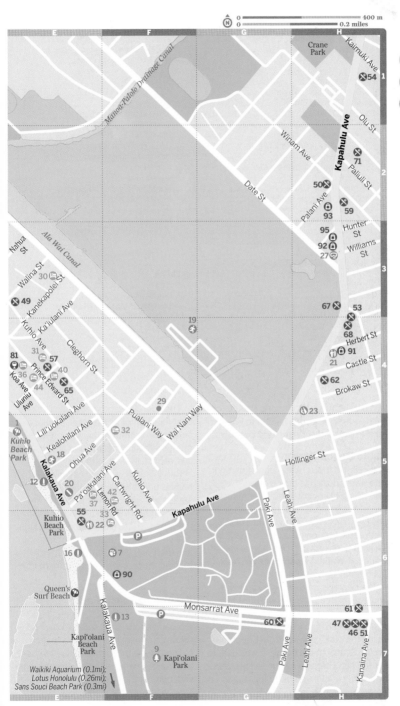

Crane Park

Kaimuki Ave

Olu St

Kapahulu Ave

Paiului St

Winam Ave

Date St

Palani Ave

Hunter St

Williams St

Nahua St

Walina St

Kanekapolei St

Ka'iulani Ave

Kuhio Ave

Cleghorn St

Herbert St

Castle St

Brokaw St

Prince Edward St

Koa Ave

Uluniu Ave

Lili'uokalani Ave

Kealohilani Ave

Ohua Ave

Pualani Way

Wai Nani Way

Hollinger St

Kuhio Beach Park

Pa'oakalani Ave

Lemon Rd

Cartwright Rd

Kuhio Ave

Kapahulu Ave

Paki Ave

Leahi Ave

Kalakaua Ave

Kuhio Beach Park

Queen's Surf Beach

Kapi'olani Beach Park

Kalakaua Ave

Monsarrat Ave

Paki Ave

Leahi Ave

Kanaina Ave

Kapi'olani Park

Waikiki Aquarium (0.1mi);
Lotus Honolulu (0.26mi);
Sans Souci Beach Park (0.3mi)

Manoa-Palolo Drainage Canal

Ala Wai Canal

400 m
0.2 miles

Waikiki

surf breaks, are just offshore. Paddle further offshore over a lagoon to Populars (aka 'Pops'), a favorite of long-boarders.

Kuhio Beach Park   Beach
(Map p98; 👟) If you're the kind of person who wants it all, this beach offers everything from protected swimming to canoe rides, and even a free sunset-hula and Hawaiian-music show. You'll find restrooms, outdoor showers, a snack bar, surfboard lockers and beach-gear-rental stands at **Waikiki Beach Center**, near the friendly police substation.

The beach is marked on its opposite end by Kapahulu Groin, a walled storm drain with a walkway on top that juts out into the ocean. A low stone breakwater, called the Wall, runs out from Kapahulu Groin, parallel to the beach. It was built to control sand erosion and, in the process, two nearly enclosed swimming pools were formed.

The pool closest to Kapahulu Groin is best for swimming. However, because circulation is limited, the water gets murky with a noticeable film of sunscreen oils, especially later in the day.

Kapahulu Groin is one of Waikiki's hottest bodyboarding spots. If the surf's right, you can find a few dozen bodyboarders, mostly teenagers, riding the waves. These experienced local kids ride straight for the groin's cement wall and then veer away at the last moment, thrilling the tourists watching them from the little pier above.

Kapi'olani Beach Park   Beach
(Map p98) Where did all the tourists go? From Kapahulu Groin south to the Natatorium, this peaceful stretch of beach, backed by a green space of banyan trees and grassy lawns, offers a relaxing niche with none of the frenzy found on the beaches fronting the Waikiki hotel strip.

Facilities include restrooms and outdoor showers. Kapi'olani Beach is a popular weekend picnicking spot for local families, who unload the kids to splash in the ocean while adults fire up the BBQ.

The widest northern end of Kapi'olani Beach is nicknamed **Queen's Surf Beach**. The stretch in front of the pavilion is popular with Waikiki's gay community. Its sandy bottom offers decent swimming. Long-boarders favor the offshore left-handed surf break Publics.

Sans Souci Beach Park   Beach
(Map p99) At the Diamond Head edge of Waikiki, Sans Souci is a prime sandy stretch of oceanfront that's far from the frenzied tourist scene. It's commonly called Kaimana Beach, as it's next door to the New Otani Kaimana Beach Hotel. Local residents often come here for their daily swims. A shallow reef close to shore makes for calm, protected waters and provides good snorkeling.

 Sights

Let's be honest: you're probably just here for the beach. Honolulu's most important museums and historic sites are all outside Waikiki, but minor oceanfront diversions found here include two historical hotels, an ecofriendly aquarium, a military museum and a kiddie zoo.

Duke Kahanamoku Statue   Statue
(Map p98) On the waterfront on Kalakaua Ave, this wonderful statue of Duke Kahanamoku is always draped in colorful lei. The Duke was a real Hawaiian hero, winning numerous Olympic swimming medals, breaking the world record for the 100yd freestyle in his first competitive event, and becoming known as 'the father of modern surfing.' He even had stints as sheriff of Honolulu and as a Hollywood actor. Duke also pioneered the Waikiki Beachboys, teaching visitors how to surf.

Below: Waikiki Aquarium; **Right:** Kalakaua Ave, in front of Waikiki Beach
(BELOW) LINDA CHING/GETTY IMAGES ©; (RIGHT) MICHELE FALZONE/GETTY IMAGES ©

Wizard Stones of Kapaemahu
Statue

(Map p98) Near the police substation at Waikiki Beach Center, four ordinary-looking boulders are actually the legendary Wizard Stones of Kapaemahu, said to contain the mana (power) of four wizards who came to O'ahu from Tahiti around 400 AD. According to ancient legend, the wizards helped the island residents by relieving their aches and pains and their fame became widespread. As tribute when the wizards left, the islanders placed the four boulders where the wizards had lived.

King David Kalakaua Statue
Statue

(Map p98) Born in 1836, King David Kalakaua ruled Hawaii from 1874 until his death in 1891. With his wife, Queen Kapi'olani, Kalakaua traveled the world extensively. This statue, designed by Native Hawaiian sculptor Sean Browne, greets visitors coming into Waikiki and was donated in 1985 by the Japanese–American Community of Hawaii to mark 100 years of Japanese immigration. Kalakaua was instrumental in the signing of a Japan–Hawaii Labor Convention that brought 200,000 Japanese immigrants to Hawaii between 1885 and 1924.

Waikiki Aquarium
Aquarium

(Map p99; 808-923-9741; www.waquarium.org; 2777 Kalakaua Ave; adult/child $12/5; 9am-5pm, last entry 4:30pm;) Located on Waikiki's shoreline, this university-run aquarium features dozens of tanks that re-create diverse tropical Pacific reef habitats. Check the website or call ahead to make reservations for special family-friendly events and fun educational programs for kids such as Aquarium After Dark adventures. It's about a 15-minute walk southeast of the main Waikiki beach strip.

You'll see rare fish species from the Northwestern Hawaiian Islands, as well as moon jellies and flashlight fish that

host bioluminescent bacteria. Especially hypnotizing are the Palauan chambered nautiluses with their unique spiral shells – in fact, this is the world's first aquarium to breed these endangered creatures in captivity, a groundbreaking achievement. An outdoor pool is home to rare and endangered Hawaiian monk seals.

Kapiʻolani Park Park

(Map p98; off Kalakaua & Paki Aves) **FREE** In its early days, horse racing and band concerts were the biggest attractions at Waikiki's favorite green space. Although the racetrack is long gone, this park named after Queen Kapiʻolani is still a beloved outdoor venue for live music and local community gatherings, from farmers markets to arts-and-crafts fairs to festivals to rugby matches. The tree-shaded Kapiʻolani Bandstand is ideal for catching a concert by the time-honored Royal Hawaiian Band, which performs classics here on many Sunday afternoons.

Queen Kapiʻolani Statue Statue

(Map p98) This bronze statue depicts Queen Kapiʻolani, the wife of King David Kalakaua – his statue at the other end of Waikiki greets visitors to Waikiki. The Queen was a beloved philanthropist, known as the queen who loved children. Among other accomplishments, she founded a maternity home in 1890 for disadvantaged Hawaiians and today you'll hear her name often – the park, a hospital, a major boulevard and a community college are all named for her.

Moana Surfrider Hotel Historic Building

(Map p98; ☎ 808-922-3111; www.moana-surfrid-er.com; 2365 Kalakaua Ave; ⏱ tours 11am Mon, Wed & Fri) **FREE** Christened the Moana Hotel when it opened in 1901, this beaux-arts plantation-style inn was once the haunt of Hollywood movie stars, aristocrats and business tycoons. The historic hotel embraces a seaside courtyard with a big banyan tree and a wraparound verandah, where island musicians and hula dancers perform in the evenings.

103

Island Insights

Tourism at Waikiki Beach took off in the 1950s, after the age of jet travel arrived. As the beachfront developed, landowners haphazardly constructed seawalls and offshore barriers (called groins) to protect their properties, blocking the natural forces of sand accretion, which makes erosion a serious problem. Some of Waikiki's legendary white sands have had to be barged in from Papohaku Beach on the island of Moloka'i. In 2012, a massive hydraulic sand-pumping project was carried out off-shore in an attempt to restore Waikiki's shrinking beaches using an estimated 24,000 cubic yards of reclaimed sand.

Upstairs from the lobby you'll find displays of memorabilia from the early days: everything from scripts of the famed *Hawaii Calls* radio show broadcast live from the courtyard here between 1935 and 1975 to woolen bathing suits, historical period photographs and a short video of Waikiki back in the days when the Moana was the only hotel on the oceanfront horizon.

Royal Hawaiian Hotel
Historic Building

(Map p98; ☎808-923-7311; www.royal-hawaiian. com; 2259 Kalakaua Ave; ⊙tours 2pm Tue & Thu) FREE With its Moorish-style turrets and archways, this gorgeously restored 1927 art-deco landmark, dubbed the 'Pink Palace,' is a throwback to the era when Rudolph Valentino was *the* romantic idol and travel to Hawaii was by Matson Navigation luxury liner. Its guest list read like a who's-who of A-list celebrities, from royalty to Rockefellers, along with luminaries such as Charlie Chaplin and Babe Ruth. Today, historic tours explore the architecture and lore of this grande dame.

Ask the concierge for a self-guided walking-tour brochure.

Honolulu Zoo
Zoo

(Map p98; ☎808-971-7171; www.honoluluzoo. org; cnr Kapahulu & Kalakaua Aves; adult/ child 4-12yr $14/6; ⊙9am-4:30pm; P🚼) Honolulu Zoo does a great job on limited finances of showcasing tropical animals from around the globe. There are 40-plus acres of tropical greenery, happy-looking animals and a petting zoo for kids. Hawaii has no endemic land mammals, but in the aviary near the entrance you can see some native birds, including the nene (Hawaiian goose) and 'apapane, a bright-red Hawaiian honeycreeper. Make reservations for family-oriented twilight tours, dinner safaris, zoo campouts and stargazing nights.

Prince Kuhio Statue
Statue

(Map p98) This statue of Prince Jonah Kuhio Kalaniana'ole sits at Kuhio Beach in Waikiki. It celebrates the man who was prince of the reigning House of Kalakaua when the Kingdom of Hawaii was overthrown in 1893. When Hawaii was annexed as territory of the United States, Kuhio was elected as Hawaii's congressional delegate for 10 consecutive terms. Kuhio was often called Ke Ali'i Makaainana (Prince of People), and is well known for his efforts to preserve and strengthen the Hawaiian people and their culture.

Hawai'i Army Museum
Museum

(Map p98; www.hiarmymuseumsoc.org; 2161 Kalia Rd; donations welcome, audiotour $5; ⊙9am-5pm Tue-Sat, last entry 4:45pm; P) FREE At Fort DeRussy, this museum showcases an almost mind-numbing array of military paraphernalia as it relates to Hawaii's history, starting with shark-tooth clubs that Kamehameha the Great used to win control of the island more than two centuries ago. Fascinating old photographs and stories help bring an understanding of the influence of the US military presence in Hawaii.

Extensive exhibits include displays on the 442nd, the Japanese American regiment that became the most decorated regiment in WWII, and on Kaua'i-born Eric Shinseki, a retired four-star army general who spoke out against the US invasion of Iraq and has served as President Barack Obama's Secretary of Veterans Affairs.

Surfer on a Wave Statue   Statue
(Map p98) Opposite the entrance to Honolulu Zoo and right on the beach, the 'Surfer on a Wave' statue celebrates surfing as a major part of the culture of Waikiki. Cast in bronze by Robert Pashby, it was unveiled in 2003.

Ala Wai Canal   Canal
(Map p98) The Ala Wai Canal was created in 1922 to drain the rice paddies, marshes and swamps that would become present-day Waikiki. Running from Kapahulu Ave, the waterway runs in a straight line down the back of Waikiki before turning left and out to sea between the Ala Wai Yacht Harbor and Ala Moana Beach Park's Magic Island. The canal is a popular spot with kayakers and outrigger-canoe teams.

Storyteller Statue   Statue
(Map p98) This bronze statue just off Kalakaua Ave represents 'The Storytellers,' the keepers of Hawaiian culture. For centuries, women have been at the top of Hawaiian oral traditions, and the storytellers preserve the identity of their people and land by reciting poems, songs, chants and genealogies. The Storyteller's brother-statue is the Water Giver statue at the Hawaiian Convention Center.

🏃 Activities

Waikiki's beaches steal the spotlight, but landlubbers can also find plenty of fun in the sun. In the early mornings and late afternoons, runners pound the pavement next to Ala Wai Canal, where outrigger-canoe teams paddle. Just inland from the beach, Kapi'olani Park has tennis courts and sports fields for soccer and softball, and even cricket.

Waikiki Ocean Club   Water Sports
(Map p42; ☎808-539-9481; www.waikikiocean club.com; 1651 Ala Moana Blvd; adult/child $39/30; 🚐) Zip on a shuttle over from Ala Wai Yacht Harbor to this aquatic theme park moored offshore. Bounce on the ocean trampoline, swivel down the water slide or test the triple-level diving deck, then go snorkeling or swimming in the Pacific. Add-on activities such as banana-boating, jet-skiing, scuba-diving and parasailing all cost extra. Reservations are advised.

Hawaiian hawk at Honolulu Zoo
BOB ABRAHAM/GETTY IMAGES ©

24-Hour Fitness

Gym

(Map p98; 808-923-9090; www.24hourfitness. com; 2490 Kalakaua Ave; daily/weekly pass $25/75; 24hr) For an indoor workout in Waikiki, 24-Hour Fitness is a modern gym with cardio and weight machines and group classes.

SURFING, STAND UP PADDLING, BODYBOARDING & OUTRIGGER-CANOE RIDES

Waikiki has good surfing year-round, with the largest waves rolling in during winter. Gentler summer surf breaks are best for beginners. Surfing lessons (from $75 for a two-hour group class) and surfboard, stand up paddling (SUP) and bodyboard rentals (from $10 to $80 per day) can be arranged at the concession stands along the sand at Kuhio Beach Park, near the bodyboarding hot spot of Kapahulu Groin. Some surf outfits offer outrigger-canoe rides ($75 for two people) that take off from the beach and ride the tossin' waves home – kids especially love those thrills. **Girls Who Surf** (p62) in nearby Ala Moana offer women-only surf lessons.

Hawaiian Watersports

Surfing, SUP

(Map p98; 808-739-5483; www.hawaiianwatersports.com; 415 Kapahulu Ave; 9am-5pm) Inland on Kapahulu Ave, this shop offers surfing and SUP rentals and lessons away from the crowds at Diamond Head beaches (transportation to/from Waikiki included for lessons, $10 surcharge for rental delivery).

Hans Hedemann Surf

Surfing

(Map p98; 808-924-7778; www.hhsurf.com; Park Shore Waikiki, 2586 Kapahulu Ave; 2hr group/semiprivate/private lesson $75/125/150; 8am-5pm) You can take baby steps and learn to board or paddle surf at this local pro surfer's well-established school, which is conveniently opposite the main beach strip in the lobby of the Park Shore Hotel. Rentals are also available.

Hawaii Surfboard Rentals

Surfing, SUP

(808-672-5055; www.hawaiisurfboardrentals. com) Free surfboard, SUP, bodyboard and car-rack delivery and pick-up with a two-day minimum rental; weekly rates are an especially good deal.

Royal Hawaiian Hotel (p104)

Waikiki for Children

Start at the beach. In just an hour or so, the older kids can learn how to stand up on a board and surf, or they can rent a bodyboard and ride on their bellies. Another fun way to play is to take an outrigger-canoe ride and then paddle back into shore afterwards.

Want to see the world from beneath the waves? Don a snorkel and take a look at the colorful fish at Queen's Surf Beach or take a ride on the Atlantis Submarine (p110) and see it all through a porthole.

At the beach at the north end of Kapi'olani Park, Waikiki Aquarium (p102), with its kaleidoscopic array of tropical fish and reef sharks, has lots of fun just for *na keiki* (children). Check online for the schedule of family programs such as 'Marine Munchies' feedings for ages five and up, or wet-and-wild 'Exploring the Reef at Night' field trips for ages six and up (reservations required).

The small Honolulu Zoo (p104) has a petting zoo where children can get eye to eye with tamer creatures and weekend 'twilight tours' geared to children aged five and older. Buy special program tickets in advance, including for 'snooze in the zoo' campouts and 'breakfast with the animals.'

Families sprawl with beach mats on the grass to watch Kuhio Beach Park's free torch lighting and hula show (p126). And then there are Waikiki's luau and dinner shows, all with a lively drum beat and hip-shakin' hula and fire dancing. The Hilton Hawaiian Village puts on a kid-friendly poolside Polynesian song and dance show on Friday night, topped off with a grand fireworks display that's visible from the beach for free.

Diamond Head Surfboards Surfing (Map p98; 808-691-9599; http://diamond-headsurfboards.com; 525 Kapahulu Ave; 10am-6pm Mon-Wed, to 7pm Thu-Sat, 9am-1pm Sun) Check out Ben's place on Kapahulu for all your surfing requirements. As well as renting out surfboards, stand up paddleboards and bodyboards by the hour, day or week, it has excellent personalized surfing lessons based out of its well-stocked and attractive shop.

SNORKELING & SCUBA DIVING

Waikiki's crowded central beaches are not particularly good for snorkeling, so pick your spot carefully. Two top choices are Sans Souci Beach Park and Queen's Surf Beach, where you'll find some live coral and a decent variety of tropical fish. But to really see the gorgeous stuff – coral gardens, manta rays and more exotic tropical fish – head out on a boat. You can easily rent snorkel sets (from $10 to $20 per day) and scuba-diving equipment (from $35), or book ahead for boat trips (from $110) and PADI open-water certification courses (from $350).

AquaZone Diving, Snorkeling (Map p98; 808-923-3483, 866-923-3483; www.aquazonescuba.com; Marriott Waikiki Beach Resort, 2552 Kalakaua Ave) Dive shop and tour outfitter on Kalakaua Ave behind the Harley Davidson shop in the front of the Waikiki Beach Marriott. Sign up for a beginner's scuba-diving pool lesson (no PADI certification required), a sea-turtle snorkeling tour or a morning deep-water boat dive, including out to WWII shipwrecks. Rental snorkel and diving gear available.

O'ahu Diving Diving (808-721-4210; www.oahudiving.com) Specializes in first-time experiences for beginning divers without certification, as well as deep-water boat dives offshore and PADI refresher classes if you're

Island Insights

When land is developed in Hawaii, more than earth and plants may be disturbed. Construction workers may dig up the *iwi* (bones) and *moepu* (funeral objects) of ancient Hawaiian burial sites. Locals tell 'chicken skin' (goose flesh) stories of machinery breaking down and refusing to operate until the bones are removed and prayers are said. It's common practice for a Hawaiian priest to bless ground-breaking at construction sites. A memorial in Kapi'olani Park contains the skeletal remains of around 200 Native Hawaiians unearthed over the years by construction projects in Waikiki. Some say that the foundations of all of Waikiki's resort hotels contain *iwi,* simply because the sand used to make the concrete also contained it.

already certified and have some experience under your diving belt.

Snorkel Bob's Snorkeling
(Map p98; ☎808-735-7944; www.snorkelbob. com; 702 Kapahulu Ave; ⏲8am-5pm) A top spot to get your gear. Rates vary depending on the quality of the snorkeling gear and accessories packages, but excellent weekly discounts are available and online reservations taken. You can even rent gear on O'ahu, then return it on another island.

KAYAKING & WINDSURFING

Fort DeRussy Beach has fewer swimmers and catamarans to share the water with than Waikiki's central beaches, although most local windsurfers sail near Diamond Head.

**Hawaiian
Watersports** Windsurfing, Kayaking
(Map p98; ☎739-5483; www.hawaiianwatersports.com; 415 Kapahulu Ave; ⏲9am-5pm) Inland from the beach, this pro shop offers windsurfing and kayak rentals and lessons at Kailua Beach on the Windward Coast, a short drive over the Pali Hwy from Honolulu. Transportation to/from Waikiki is complimentary if you're taking lessons.

HIKING

Hiking Hawaii Hiking
(Map p98; ☎855-808-4453; hikinghawaii808. com; 1910 Ala Moana Blvd; per person from $40)

Based out of Hiking Hawaii Cafe, these guys offer a number of hiking options daily all over O'ahu, from a Makap'u Lighthouse walk ($40) to a hike to Manoa Falls ($45) to a full-day trip to the North Shore ($165). Check out the options online. Hotel pick-ups, transportation and guides are included.

GOLF

Ala Wai Golf Course Golf
(Map p98; ☎reservations 808-296-2000; www. honolulu.gov/des/golf/alawai.html; 404 Kapahulu Ave; green fees $22-55) With views of Diamond Head and the Ko'olau Range, this flat 18-hole, par-70 layout scores a Guinness World Record for being the world's busiest golf course. Local golfers are allowed to book earlier in the week and grab most of the starting times, leaving few for visitors (who may call to reserve up to three days in advance).

TENNIS

If you've brought your own rackets, the Diamond Head Tennis Center, at the Diamond Head end of Kapi'olani Park, has 10 courts. For night play, go to the Kapi'olani Park Tennis Courts, opposite the aquarium; all four courts are lit. All of these public courts are free and first-come, first-served. A few Waikiki condos and hotels offer tennis courts and equipment rentals for guests.

Courses

Waikiki Community
Center
Hawaiiana, Arts & Crafts

(Map p98; 808-923-1802; www.waikikicommunitycenter.org; 310 Pa'oakalani Ave; most classes $5-15) Try your hand at mah-jongg, the ukulele, hula, tai chi or a variety of island arts and crafts. Instructors at this homespun community center are brimming with aloha. Although most students are locals, visitors are welcome too. Pre-registration may be required.

Royal Hawaiian
Center
Hawaiiana, Arts & Crafts

(Map p98; 808-922-2299; www.royalhawaiiancenter.com; 2201 Kalakaua Ave) FREE Gargantuan shopping mall that offers free cultural classes and demonstrations in Hawaiian arts and crafts, such as quilting and flower lei making, plus hula dancing, ukulele playing and even *lomilomi* traditional body massage.

Tours

Several catamaran cruises leave right from Waikiki Beach – just walk down to the sand, step into the surf and hop aboard. A 90-minute, all-you-can-drink 'booze cruise' will typically cost you $25 to $40 per adult. Reservations are especially recommended for sunset sails, which sell out fast.

Maita'i Catamaran
Cruise

(Map p98; 808-922-5665; www.leahi.com; adult/child from $28/14;) Ahoy! Pulling up on the beach between the Halekulani and Sheraton hotels, this white catamaran with green sails offers the biggest variety of boat trips. Reserve ahead for a 90-minute daytime or sunset booze cruise (children allowed) or a moonlight sail to take in the Hilton's Friday fireworks show. Looking for something a bit different? On weekdays, family-friendly reef-snorkeling tours include an onboard picnic lunch.

Na Hoku II Catamaran
Cruise

(Map p98; 808-554-5990; www.nahokuii.com; incl drinks $30) With its unmistakable yellow-and-red striped sails, this catamaran is so famous you'll see a photo of it on the Waikiki edition of the Monopoly board game. These hard-drinkin' tours set sail four times daily (11.30am, 1.30pm, 3.30pm and 5:30pm), shoving off from in

Outrigger canoes at Waikiki, with Diamond Head (p168) in the background

CAVATAIO VINCE/GETTY IMAGES ©

Below: Blue Hawaii cocktail; **Right:** Hula performance at House Without a Key (p126)

(BELOW) ANN CECIL/GETTY IMAGES ©; (RIGHT) ANN CECIL/GETTY IMAGES ©

front of Duke's Waikiki bar. The sunset sail usually sells out, so book early.

Atlantis Submarine

Tour

(Map p43; ☎800-548-6262; www.atlantissub-marines.com; ⏱90min tour adult/child under 13yr & taller than 36in $124/53) See the world from a porthole aboard the sub that dives to a depth of 100ft near a reef off Waikiki, offering views of sea life otherwise reserved for divers – though honestly, it's not nearly as exciting as it sounds. There are several sailings daily; you should book ahead online for discounts. Check-in is at the Hilton Hawaiian Village's pier in front of the Ali'i Tower.

✦ Festivals & Events

Waikiki loves to party all year round. Every Friday night, usually starting around 7:45pm, the Hilton Hawaiian Village shoots off a big ol' **fireworks show**, which is visible from Kahanamoku Beach and sounds like thunder inside hotel rooms all across Waikiki.

Duke Kahanamoku Challenge

Cultural, Sports

(http://waikikicommunitycenter.org/Events. html; ⏱Mar; 👪) Outrigger-canoe and stand up paddling races, island-style local food, traditional Hawaiian games, arts-and-crafts vendors and live entertainment all happen on a Sunday in early March at Kahanamoku Beach.

Honolulu Festival

Art, Cultural

(www.honolulufestival.com; ⏱Mar) Free Asian and Pacific arts and cultural performances are staged at Waikiki Beach Walk and Waikiki Shopping Plaza, with a festive parade along Kalakaua Ave followed by a fireworks show in early March.

Waikiki Spam Jam

Food

(www.spamjamhawaii.com; 👪) On a Saturday in late April or early May, join thousands of Spam aficionados celebrating at this

street festival devoted to Hawaii's favorite tinned meat product.

Pan-Pacific Festival   Art, Cultural
(www.pan-pacific-festival.com; ⊘mid-Jun) In mid-June, this Asian and Polynesian cultural festival puts on a performing-arts showcase at the Royal Hawaiian Center, outdoor hula shows at Kuhio Beach Park, and a huge *ho'olaule'a* (celebration) block party and parade along Kalakaua Ave.

Na Hula Festival   Art, Cultural
(www.facebook.com/pages/Na-Hula-Festival/157159837738728; ⊘Aug) Local hula *halau* (schools) gather for a full day of music and dance celebrations at Kapi'olani Park in early August.

Hawaiian Slack Key Guitar Festival   Music, Art
(www.slackkeyfestival.com; ⊘mid-Aug) A day-long celebration of traditional Hawaiian slack key guitar and ukulele music with food vendors and an arts-and-crafts fair at Kapi'olani Park in mid-August.

Aloha Festivals   Art, Cultural
(www.alohafestivals.com; ⊘mid-Sep) During Hawaii's premier statewide cultural festival. Waikiki is famous for its royal court ceremonies and also its *ho'olaule'a* evening block party and float parade along Kalakaua Ave, which feature food vendors, live music and hula dancers.

Na Wahine O Ke Kai   Sports, Cultural
(www.nawahineokekai.com; ⊘Sep) Hawaii's major annual women's outrigger-canoe race is held near the end of September. It starts at sunrise on the island of Moloka'i and ends 42 miles later at Waikiki's Kahanamoku Beach.

Moloka'i Hoe   Sports, Cultural
(www.molokaihoe.com; ⊘mid-Oct) In mid-October, the men's outrigger-canoe world-championship race starts just after sunrise on Moloka'i and then finishes at Waikiki's Kahanamoku Beach less than five hours later.

The Best...
Family-Friendly Hotels

Honolulu Marathon   Sports

(www.honolulumarathon.org; ⊙Dec) The USA's third-largest marathon runs from downtown Honolulu to Diamond Head on the second Sunday of December.

 ## Sleeping

Waikiki's main beachfront strip, along Kalakaua Ave, is lined with hotels and sprawling resorts. Some of them are true beauties with quiet gardens, seaside courtyards and either historic or boutique atmosphere, while others are generic high-rises, which cater to the package-tour crowd.

If stepping out of your room and digging your toes in the sand isn't a must, look for inviting small hotels on Waikiki's backstreets. Some hotels off Kuhio Ave and near Ala Wai Canal have rooms as lovely as many of the beachfront hotels, but at half the price. If you don't mind walking to the beach, you can save a bundle.

Be aware that 'ocean view' and its cousins 'ocean front' and 'partial ocean view' are all liberally used and may require a periscope to spot the waves. 'City,' 'garden' or 'mountain' views may be euphemisms for rooms that overlook the parking lot. When making a reservation, you should first check the hotel's property map online or call a reservations agent directly to find out about the different views. Generally, the higher the floor, the higher the price, and oceanfront rooms may cost over 50% more.

Book rooms as far in advance as possible for the best rates and availability; last-minute bookings are tough and generally expensive. Parking usually costs $15 to $30 per night, whether for valet or self-parking (the latter is sometimes off-site). Increasingly, Waikiki's bigger hotels are also charging mandatory 'resort fees,' which could tack another $20 or more per day onto your final bill. Resort fees may cover internet connections, local and toll-free phone calls and fitness-room entry, or no extra perks at all, but regardless, you're gonna have to pay.

All rates listed below are standard rates for high season (mid-December through late March or mid-April, depending on when Easter spring break falls). Substantial discounts are usually available online through the hotels' own websites, via travel booking and airline websites, or for flight and rental-car package deals, especially during the low season.

Waikiki Beachside Hostel   Hostel $

(Map p98; ☑808-923-9566, 866-478-3888; www.waikikibeachsidehostel.com; 2556 Lemon Rd; dm $25-35, semiprivate r from $70; P@☎) This private hostel attracts an international party crowd and offers plenty of perks, from an internet cafe to surfboard and moped rentals. Like most hostels on sketchy, back-alley Lemon Rd, this one occupies an older apartment complex. Each dorm has its own kitchen, bathroom and telephone, but no air-con.

Royal Grove Hotel   Hotel $

(Map p98; ☑808-923-7691; www.royalgrovehotel.com; 161 Uluniu Ave; r from $60; ❄@☎) No frills but plenty of aloha characterize this kitschy, candy-pink hotel that attracts so many returning snowbirds it's nearly impossible to get a room in winter without advance reservations. Retro motel-style rooms in the main wing are basic but do have lanai. All rooms have kitchenettes.

Inquire about discounted weekly off-season rates. Great budget option.

Hostelling International (HI) Waikiki
Hostel $

(Map p98; ☎808-926-8313; www.hostelsaloha.com; 2417 Prince Edward St; dm/r from $28/60, all with shared bath; ⏱reception 7am-midnight; 🅿@📶) Occupying a converted low-rise apartment building, this tidy hostel is just a few blocks from the beach. Inside are fan-cooled single-sex dormitories and simple private rooms, a self-catering kitchen, coin-op laundry and free bodyboards to borrow. No smoking or alcohol allowed, but no daytime lockout or curfew either. Reservations are strongly recommended (seven-night maximum stay). Limited self-parking ($5 per night).

Waikiki Prince
Hotel $

(Map p98; ☎808-922-1544; www.waikikiprince.com; 2431 Prince Edward St; r from $79; 🅿❄📶) Forget about ocean views and never mind the cramped check-in office at this six-story, 1970s-era apartment complex on an anonymous side street. Inside this standout budget option are two dozen compact yet cheery rooms with kitchenettes that feel fresh and reasonably modern. Free wi-fi and weekly rates available year-round. A good option if you are on a budget.

Aston at the Waikiki Banyan
Hotel $$

(Map p98; ☎808-922-0555, 855-718-9908; www.astonwaikikibanyan.com; 201 Ohua Ave; 1br from $145; 🅿❄@📶♿) Perfect for families, this all-suites high-rise hotel is a short walk from the aquarium, the zoo and, of course, the beach. Roomy if sometimes beat-up suites have a handy sofabed in the living room. The pool deck has a playground, as well as a tennis and basketball court. A mandatory nightly resort fee of $18 includes in-room wi-fi.

Castle Waikiki Grand
Hotel $$

(Map p98; ☎808-923-1814; www.waikikigrandcondos.com; 134 Kapahulu Ave; r with/without kitchenette from $130/103; 🅿❄@📶♿) This small, gay-friendly condo hotel is best known as the home of Hula's Bar & Lei Stand (p124). Standard-issue rooms are compact, with limited kitchenette rooms available. Each vacation-rental condo is individually owned, so they can vary in quality – view online photos with some skepticism. Free in-room wi-fi. Ask about

Kapi'olani Park (p103)

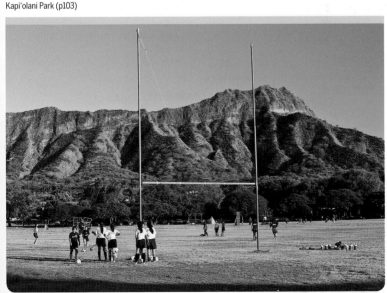

ANN CECIL/GETTY IMAGES ©

Below: Swimmers at Waikiki Beach (p96); **Right:** Floral lei (p304)

(BELOW) RICHARD I'ANSON/GETTY IMAGES ©; (RIGHT) JOHN ARNOLD IMAGES LTD /ALAMY ©

weekly and low-season discounts. There is limited self-parking available on-site.

Aqua Aloha Surf Waikiki
Boutique Hotel $$

(Map p98; 808-923-0222, 866-970-4160; www.alohasurfhotelwaikiki.com; 444 Kanekapolei St; r from $107; @ 📶) If you don't mind a shoebox-size room, or being next to Ala Wai Canal, this youthful hotel can be a real bargain. The lobby is lively, with surf videos playing an endless-summer loop and surfboards hanging on the walls. The $15 hospitality fee includes wi-fi in lobby, wired internet in rooms, and complimentary breakfast, coffee and beach gear.

Aqua Bamboo
Boutique Hotel $$

(Map p98; 808-954-7412, 866-326-8423; www.aquabamboo.com; 2425 Kuhio Ave; r from $149, studio/1 bedroom ste from $169/199; P ❄ @ 📶 🏊) Looking for a meditative retreat in Waikiki's concrete jungle? This refreshed boutique hotel with an intimate cabana spa has a small saltwater pool, should you tire of the ocean. Stylishly minimalist rooms include suites with kitchenettes or full kitchens. A $15 amenity fee includes wi-fi, coffee, beach gear and newspaper.

Hilton Hawaiian Village
Resort $$

(Map p98; 808-949-4321; www.hiltonhawaiianvillage.com; 2005 Kalia Rd; r from $215; P ❄ @ 📶 🏊) On the Fort DeRussy side of Waikiki, the Hilton is Waikiki's largest resort hotel – practically a self-sufficient tourist fortress of towers, restaurants, bars and shops. It's geared almost entirely to families and package tourists, offering standard-issue hotel rooms, swimming pools and a lagoon, and tons of kid-centric activities by the beach, including kayak and surfboard rentals.

Hotel Renew — Boutique Hotel $$

(Map p98; ☎808-687-7700, 888-485-7639; www.hotelrenew.com; 129 Pa'oakalani Ave; r from $180; P✳@🛜) ✐ At this fabulous find, just a half-block from the beach, a $25 per room 'amenity fee' brings a slew of services, from chilled drinks upon arrival to daily continental breakfast to free beach mats and bodyboards to borrow. Design-savvy, ecofriendly accommodations come with mod platform beds, projection-screen TVs, spa robes, earth-toned furnishings and Japanese-style *shōji* (sliding paper-screen doors).

Outrigger Regency on Beachwalk — Hotel $$

(Map p98; ☎808-922-3871, 866-956-4262; www.outrigger.com; 255 Beach Walk; 1/2 bedroom from $199/269; P✳@) This sleek, modern high-rise has more than respectable family-size rooms, with earth-toned furnishings, marble baths and bold, modern artwork. Spacious condo-style suites have full kitchens and some have private lanai with peek-a-boo ocean views. Step outside the downstairs lobby and you're right on Waikiki Beach Walk – then keep walking five minutes to the beach or the off-site swimming pool.

Royal Hawaiian — Resort $$$

(Map p98; ☎866-716-8110, 808-923-7311; www.royal-hawaiian.com; 2259 Kalakaua Ave; r from $400; P✳@🛜🏊) Waikiki's original luxury hotel, this pink Spanish-Moorish-style landmark is loaded with charm, especially since recent splendid, multimillion-dollar renovations. The historic section of the aristocratic 'Pink Palace' maintains its classic appeal, although you may prefer the modern high-rise tower for its ocean views.

Moana Surfrider — Historic Hotel $$$

(Map p98; ☎866-716-8112, 808-922-3111; www.moana-surfrider.com; 2365 Kalakaua Ave; r from $350; P✳@🛜🏊) Waikiki's most historic beachfront hotel, this grand, colonial-style establishment has been painstakingly restored. A line of rocking chairs beckons on the front porch and

Hawaiian artwork hangs on the walls, while wedding parties sweep through the bustling lobby every 10 minutes. Graceful yet compact guest rooms no longer retain much of their period look, having been upgraded with 21st-century amenities and style.

Halekulani   Resort $$$

(Map p98; ☏808-923-2311; www.halekulani. com; 2199 Kalia Rd; r from $490; P ❄ @ 🛜 🏊) Evincing modern sophistication, this resort hotel lives up to its name, which means 'House Befitting Heaven.' It's an all-encompassing experience of gracious living, not merely a place to crash. Meditative calm washes over you immediately as you step onto the lobby's cool stone tiles.

Sheraton Waikiki   Resort $$$

(Map p98; ☏808-922-4422, 866-716-8109; www.sheraton-waikiki.com; 2255 Kalakaua Ave; r from $325; P ❄ @ 🛜 🏊) Looming over the Royal Hawaiian, this high-rise has plenty of room to accommodate families, package-tour groups and conferences.

No-surprises rooms are clean and crisp, with a well-equipped gym and drop-off day-care center downstairs. By the beach, an amphibious playground keeps kids entertained with a 'superpool' and 70ft-long waterslide, while adults retreat to the infinity pool.

Waikiki Parc   Boutique Hotel $$$

(Map p98; ☏808-921-7272; www.waikiki-parc.com; 2233 Helumoa Rd; r from $295; P ❄ @ 🛜 🏊) Epitomizing new-wave Waikiki, this hip hangout mixes nostalgic touches such as plantation-shuttered windows with minimalist contemporary furnishings. The staff are top-class, and although guest rooms are cool and modern, they're not nearly as spacious or as chic as Nobu Waikiki lounge and restaurant downstairs. For serenity, swim in the rooftop pool with oceanview cabanas.

Lotus Honolulu   Boutique Hotel $$$

(Map p99; ☏808-922-1700, 866-970-4166; www.lotushonoluluhotel.com; 2885 Kalakaua Ave; r from $215; ❄ 🛜) This hip boutique hotel is a lovely sanctuary by Sans Souci Beach, at the calm southern edge of Waikiki. Mingle with honeymooners looking for a romantic escape at wine social hours in a lobby that's more like a living room. Included in the $25 boutique fee are complimentary morning coffee, afternoon wine, wi-fi, beach gear and cruiser bicycle use.

Modern Honolulu   Boutique Hotel $$$

(Map p42; ☏808-943-5800, 866-970-4161; www.themodern honolulu.com; 1775 Ala Moana Blvd; r $345-525; P ❄ @ 🛜 🏊) Terraced oceanview rooms and suites are elementally chic, showing off teak doors, Frette linens and marble baths. The lanai deck pool overlooks Ala Wai Yacht Harbor, as does an Iron Chef's sushi bar,

Halekulani resort
STUART WESTMORLAND/GETTY IMAGES ©

Morimoto Waikiki (p120). The only downside to staying at this mod spa oasis is the 10-minute walk to a sandy beach.

New Otani Kaimana Beach   Boutique Hotel $$$

(☎808-923-1555; www.kaimana.com; 2863 Kalakaua Ave; r $170-505; P ❄ @ 🛜) Location, location, location. Right? Small rooms will leave you wanting more space, but the soothing setting right on Sans Souci Beach makes this 1960s-era hotel special. There's no pool, but with a beach this gorgeous, who needs one?

Eating

Warning for foodies: many of Waikiki's middle-of-the-road restaurants are overpriced and not worth eating at, no matter how enticing the ocean views look. For a more vibrant cuisine scene, check out downtown Honolulu, Chinatown and around the Ala Moana Center mall.

BY THE BEACH

Along Kalakaua Ave, suburban chains such as the Cheesecake Factory overflow with hungry tourists, while a few stellar beachfront hotel restaurants are overseen by Hawaii's top chefs. A block further inland, Kuhio Ave is great for cheap grazing, especially at multi-ethnic takeout joints.

Marukame Udon   Japanese $

(Map p98; ☎808-931-6000; www.facebook.com/marukameudon; 2310 Kuhio Ave; mains $2-8; ⏰7am-9am & 11am-10pm; 👪) Everybody loves this Japanese noodle shop, which is so popular there is often a line stretching down the sidewalk. Watch those thick udon noodles being rolled, cut and boiled fresh right in front of you, then stack mini plates of giant tempura and *musubi* (rice balls) stuffed with salmon or a sour plum on your cafeteria tray.

Hiking Hawaii Cafe   Cafe $

(Map p98; ☎855-808-4453; http://hikinghawaii808.com; 1910 Ala Moana Blvd; ⏰7am-9pm Tue-Sat, to 3pm Sun & Mon; 🛜) This downstairs eco-cafe serves up healthy meals such as

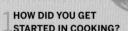
1 HOW DID YOU GET STARTED IN COOKING?

When I worked as a restaurant manager in Waikiki, I enrolled in a local culinary school. I found myself making salad dressing and bread, which I thought only came out of a bottle or package. After that, I never left the kitchen.

2 HOW HAS HAWAII'S FOOD SCENE EVOLVED?

When the food supply changes, the menu changes. Twenty years ago when Hawaii Regional Cuisine started, we didn't have as many farmers markets as today. We also talk more about sustainability now.

3 WHERE CAN VISITORS LEARN ABOUT HAWAII'S FOOD CULTURE?

Hawaii's Plantation Village. Three migrations of people came to Hawaii: Polynesians in canoes, tall ships of missionaries and whalers, and immigrant laborers who worked in the plantation fields. Those plantation immigrants were poor, but they brought with them their food, ingredients and culture. They ate what they had. Today, it's our island soul food.

4 ANY COMMON MISCONCEPTIONS ABOUT HAWAII'S FOOD?

A lot of people don't understand that there's an ethnic cuisine, a Native Hawaiian people. What is *laulau*? What is kalua pig? These are traditional Hawaiian dishes, and they're not to be confused with local food, which is an ethnic melting pot.

5 HOW DO VISITORS FIND GREAT LOCAL FOOD?

Hole-in-the-wall kitchens. That's where you find the real essence of Hawaii. Every Saturday there's a farmers market at Kapi'olani Community College. Look for restaurants that serve locally grown fruit and vegetables, or locally caught seafood.

paninis, wraps and smoothies using fresh local produce. Worth trying is the Pitaya (Dragonfruit) Bowl for $8.95. There's complimentary wi-fi and the cafe serves as base for Hiking Hawaii's various daily tours on O'ahu. A great spot to hang out.

Me's BBQ   Hawaiian, Korean $
(Map p98; ☎808-926-9717; 151 Uluniu Ave; mains $5-12; ☺7am-8:45pm Mon-Sat; 🚻) The street-side takeout counter may be a tad short on atmosphere, but there are plastic tables sitting in the sunshine where you can chow down on Korean standards such as *kimchi* and *kalbi* (marinated short ribs). The wall-size picture menu offers a mind-boggling array of mixed-plate combos including chicken *katsu* (batter-fried chicken), Portuguese sausage and eggs, and other only-in-Hawaii tastes.

Veggie Star Natural Foods   Health Food $
(Map p98; ☎808-922-9568; 417 Nahua St; ☺10am-6pm Mon-Sat; 🖉) For organic, all-natural and health-conscious groceries, plus tropical smoothies and monster-sized vegetarian burritos, fake-meat burgers, salads and 'airplane ready' sandwiches wrapped to go, visit this little

side-street shop. It's the vegan chili that makes the most people rave.

Musubi Cafe Iyasume   Japanese $
(Map p98; www.tonsuke.com/eomusubiya; 2427 Kuhio Ave, Pacific Monarch Hotel; menu items $2-8; ☺6:30am-8pm) This hole-in-the-wall keeps busy making fresh *onigiri* (rice balls) stuffed with seaweed, salmon roe, sour plums and even Spam. Other specialties include salmon-roe rice bowls, bizarre Japanese curry and island-style *mochiko* fried chicken. In a hurry? Grab a bento (boxed lunch) to go.

Ruffage Natural Foods   Health Food $
(Map p98; ☎808-922-2042; www.facebook.com/ruffage.naturalfoods; 2443 Kuhio Ave; mains $4-8; ☺9am-9pm; 🖉) This pint-sized health-food store whips up taro burgers, veggie burritos, deli sandwiches with fresh avocado, and real-fruit smoothies that will revitalize your whole body. At night, the grocery shop shares space with a tiny, backpacker-friendly sushi bar run by a Japanese expat chef.

Food Pantry   Supermarket $
(Map p98; 2370 Kuhio Ave; ☺6am-1am) It's more expensive than chain supermarkets found elsewhere in Honolulu, but cheaper than buying groceries at Waikiki's convenience stores; look for a Coffee Bean & Tea Leaf coffee bar inside.

Eggs 'n' Things   Breakfast $$
(Map p98; www.eggsnthings.com; 343 Saratoga Rd; mains $9-18; ☺6am-2pm & 4-10pm; 🚻) This never-empty, bustling diner dishes straight-up comfort food: banana–mac nut pancakes with tropical syrups (guava, honey or coconut), sugary crepes topped with fresh fruit, or fluffy omelets scrambled with Portuguese sausage. You'll fit right in with the early-morning crowd of jet-lagged tourists lined up outside the door – and sometimes around the block.

Ramen Nakamura   Japanese $$
(Map p98; ☎808-922-7960; 2141 Kalakaua Ave; mains $9-14; ☺11am-11:30pm) Hit this urban connoisseurs' noodle shop at lunchtime

and you'll have to strategically elbow aside Japanese tourists toting Gucci and Chanel bags just to sit down. Once seated, however, you're free to dig into hearty bowls of oxtail or *tonkatsu* (breaded and fried pork cutlets) or *kimchi* ramen soup served with crunchy fried garlic slices on top. Cash only.

LuLu's Surf Club American $$

(Map p98; 808-926-5222; www.luluswaikiki.com; Park Shore Waikiki, 2586 Kalakaua Ave; mains breakfast $6-15, dinner $10-24; 7am-2am;) The surfboards hanging on the wall and an awesome ocean view set the mood at this gregarious open-air restaurant, bar and nightclub. Lulu's filling breakfasts – complete with 'dawn patrol' omelets, eggs Benedict, stuffed French toast, *loco moco* and fruit bowls – are legendary. Sunset Happy Hour runs every day between 3pm and 5pm.

Siam Square Thai $$

(Map p98; 808-923-5320; 2nd fl, 408 Lewers St; mains $11-16; 11am-10.30pm;) It's Waikiki's most authentic Thai restaurant, although that's not saying much. You want it spicy? You won't have to work too hard to convince your waitress that you can handle the heat when you order *larb* pork salad or fried fish with chili sauce. The service can be standoffish, but the kitchen works so fast and furiously that you probably won't mind.

Sansei Seafood Restaurant & Sushi Bar Japanese, Fusion $$

(Map p98; 808-931-6286; www.sanseihawaii.com; 3rd fl, Marriott Waikiki Beach Resort, 2552 Kalakaua Ave; most shared plates $5-20, mains $16-35; 5:30-10pm Sun-Thu, to 1am Fri & Sat) From the mind of one of Hawaii's hottest chefs, DK Kodama, this Pacific Rim menu rolls out everything from 'new look' fusion sushi and sashimi to Dungeness crab ramen with black-truffle broth – all to rave reviews. Tables on the torch-lit verandah equal prime sunset views.

Veranda Cafe $$$

(Map p98; 808-921-4600; www.moana-surfrider.com; Moana Surfrider, 2365 Kalakaua Ave; afternoon tea from $34; 6-11am & noon-3pm;) For colonial atmosphere that harks back to early 20th-century tourist traditions, traditional afternoon tea comes complete with finger sandwiches, scones with pillowy Devonshire cream and tropically flavored pastries. Portions are small, but the oceanfront setting and house-blended teas are memorable. Make reservations and come prepared to shoo away those pesky beggar birds.

Roy's Waikiki Hawaii Regional Cuisine $$$

(Map p98; 808-923-7697; www.royshawaii.com; 226 Lewers St; mains $30-60; 11am-9:30pm Mon-Thu, to 10pm Fri-Sun) This contemporary

Sunset on the Beach

On some starry nights, most often on Saturdays, Queen's Surf Beach (p101) turns into a festive scene. Dubbed Sunset on the Beach, it's more fun than a gimmicky luau and almost everything is free – except for the food sold by local vendors, and even that's a bargain. Tables and chairs are set up on the sand and live Hawaiian music acts perform on a beachside stage for about two hours before show time. When darkness falls, a huge screen is unscrolled above the stage and a feature movie is shown, starting around 7pm. Sometimes it's a film with island connections, such as *Blue Hawaii* (the 1961 classic starring Elvis Presley), while other nights it's a Hollywood blockbuster. For more info, visit www.sunsetonthebeach.net.

The Best...
Breakfast & Brunch

incarnation of Roy Yamaguchi's island-born chain is perfect for a flirty date or for just celebrating the good life. The ground-breaking chef doesn't actually cook in the kitchen here, but his signature *misoyaki* butterfish, blackened ahi (yellowfin tuna) and macadamia-nut-encrusted *mahimahi* are always on the menu (vegans and vegetarians have options, too). Molten-chocolate soufflé for dessert is a must.

Azure   Seafood **$$$**
(Map p98; ☎808-921-4600; www.azurewaikiki.com; Royal Hawaiian, 2259 Kalakaua Ave; mains from $38, 5-course tasting menu $79; ☺5:30-9pm) 🌱 Azure is the signature restaurant at the Royal Hawaiian Hotel. Seafood fresh from the pier, such as Kona abalone, red snapper and *ono* (white-fleshed mackerel), are all exquisitely prepared island-style, with finishing touches such as red Hawaiian sea salt and Moloka'i purple sweet potatoes on the side.

Morimoto Waikiki   Asian, Fusion **$$$**
(Map p43; ☎808-943-5900; www.morimotowaikiki.com; Modern Honolulu, 1775 Ala Moana Blvd; mains lunch $18-35, dinner $22-50; ☺11am-2:30pm & 5-10pm; P) In Modern Honolulu boutique hotel, Iron Chef Morimoto's

oceanfront dining room seduces with coconut cocktails and yacht-harbor views from a sunny poolside patio. Sink back against a mod sea-green pillow banquette and fork into cubic seafood *poke* and sushi rolls, ginger-soy braised black cod, wagyu beef *loco moco* or curried whole roasted lobster. Complimentary valet parking with restaurant validation.

Nobu   Japanese, Fusion **$$$**
(Map p98; ☎808-237-6999; www.noburestaurants.com/waikiki; Waikiki Parc, 2233 Helumoa Rd; shared dishes $5-48, mains $30-40; ☺restaurant 5:30-10pm Sun-Thu, to 10:30pm Fri & Sat, lounge 5pm-midnight daily) Nobu Matsuhisa's first Japanese-fusion restaurant and sushi bar in Hawaii has made a big splash, and his elegant seafood tapas tastes right at home by the beach. Broiled black cod with miso sauce, new-style sashimi with spicy sauce drizzled on top and Japanese-Peruvian *tiradito* (ceviche) rank among Nobu's signature tastes. A low-lit cocktail lounge serves appetizing small bites and 'sake-tinis.'

INLAND – KAPAHULU AVE

On the outskirts of Waikiki, Kapahulu Ave is always worth a detour for its standout neighborhood eateries, drive-ins and bakeries, cooking up anything from Hawaiian soul food to Japanese country fare.

Waiola Shave Ice   Desserts **$**
(Map p98; ☎808-949-2269; www.waiolashaveice.com; 3113 Mokihana St; shave ice $2-5; ☺11am-5:30pm Mon-Thu, to 6pm Fri-Sun; P👪) This clapboard corner shop has moved locations but still makes the same superfine shave ice as it did back in 1940, and we'd argue that it's got the formula exactly right. Get yours doused with 20-plus flavors of syrup and topped by azuki beans, *liliko'i* cream, condensed milk, Hershey's chocolate syrup or spicy-sweet *li hing mui* (crack seed).

Leonard's   Bakery **$**
(Map p98; ☎808-737-5591; www.leonardshawaii.com; 933 Kapahulu Ave; snacks from $1; ☺5:30am-10pm Sun-Thu, to 11pm Fri &

Sat; 👪) It's almost impossible to drive by the Leonard's eye-catching vintage 1950s neon sign without stopping in. This bakery is famous on O'ahu for its *malasadas,* sweet fried dough rolled in sugar, Portuguese-style – like a doughnut without the hole. Order ones with *haupia* (coconut cream) or *liliko'i* (passion fruit) filling, and you'll be hooked for life.

Ono Seafood Seafood **$**

(Map p98; ☎808-732-4806; 747 Kapahulu Ave; mains $7-12; ⏲9am-6pm Mon-Sat, 10am-3pm Sun) Arrive early at this addictive, made-to-order *poke* shop, before it runs out of fresh fish marinated in *shōyu* (soy sauce), house-smoked *tako* (octopus), spicy ahi rice bowls or boiled peanuts spiked with star anise. Limited free parking.

Rainbow Drive-In Hawaiian **$**

(Map p98; ☎808-737-0177; www.rainbowdrivein.com; 3308 Kanaina Ave; meals $4-9; ⏲7am-9pm; 👪) Started by an island-born US army cook after WWII, this classic Hawaii drive-in wrapped in rainbow-colored neon is a throwback to another era. Construction workers, surfers and gangly teens order all their down-home favorites such as burgers, mixed-plate lunches, *loco moco* and Portuguese sweet-bread French toast from the takeout counter.

Haili's Hawaiian Foods Hawaiian **$$**

(Map p98; ☎808-735-8019; http://hailishawaiianfood.com; 760 Palani Ave; meals $11-16; ⏲10am-7pm Tue-Thu, to 8pm Fri & Sat, 11am-3pm Sun) 🍃 Haili's has been cooking up homegrown Hawaiian fare since the 1950s. Locals cheerfully shoehorn themselves into kid-friendly booths and tables, then dig into heaping plates of *kalua* pig, *lomilomi* salmon and *laulau* (meat wrapped in ti leaves and steamed) served with poi or rice.

Uncle Bo's Pupu Bar & Grill Asian, Fusion **$$**

(Map p98; ☎808-735-8311; www.unclebosrestaurant.com; 559 Kapahulu Ave; shared plates $8-15, mains $19-27; ⏲5pm-1am) Inside this chic storefront, boisterous groups devour the inventive chef's encyclopedic list of fusion *pupu* (appetizers) crafted with island flair, such as *kalua* pig nachos with wonton chips and Maui onions or baby back ribs basted in pineapple BBQ sauce. For dinner, focus on market-fresh seafood such as baked *opah* (moonfish) or steamed *'opakapaka* (pink snapper). Reservations recommended.

Irifune Japanese **$$**

(Map p98; ☎808-737-1141; 563 Kapahulu Ave; mains $10-15; ⏲11:30am-1:30pm & 5:30-9:30pm Tue-Sat) This bustling kitchen decorated with Japanese country kitsch may look very odd, especially when they turn off the lights so you can see those glow-in-the-dark stars on the ceiling. But it's

Box of *malasadas* from Leonard's
LINDA CHING/GETTY IMAGES ©

locally beloved for garlic ahi and crab dinners. With bargain-priced bento-box lunches and combo dinner plates, you'll never walk away hungry. BYOB.

Side Street Inn on Da Strip
Hawaiian $$

(Map p98; 📞808-739-3939; http://sidestreetinn. com; 614 Kapahulu Ave; shared plates $7-15, mains $12-25; ⏰3pm-midnight Mon-Fri, 1pm-midnight Sat & Sun; P👪) This Hawaiian-style sports bar serves up meal portions so huge that virtually everyone walks out with a bag containing what they couldn't eat. The good news is that the food is great. Pan-fried pork chops, *kimchi* fried rice and 'Side' soba are all tops, but you might have to wait a while for a table. Valet parking costs $5.

INLAND – MONSARRAT AVE

The strip malls of Monsarrat Ave are great spots to search out locals-only cafes.

Diamond Head Cove Health Bar
Cafe $

(Map p98; www.diamondheadcove.com; 3045 Monsarrat Ave, Ste 5; ⏰10am-8pm Mon & Sat,

9am-11pm Tue-Thu, to 8pm Fri, 10am-11pm Sun) This place specialises in acai bowls, fruit smoothies, healthy wraps, fresh *poke* and sashimi. ome here to chill out with a coconut-husk dose of 'awa (kava), Polynesia's mildly intoxicating elixir, and enjoy a relaxed vibe on 'awa nights, when local musicians play until late.

Bogart's Cafe
Cafe $

(Map p98; 📞808-739-0999; http://boga-rtscafe.webs.com; 3045 Monsarrat Ave, Ste 3; ⏰6am-6.30pm Mon-Fri, to 6pm Sat & Sun) The taro-banana pancakes get rave reviews at Bogart's. This cafe uses fresh local produce to keep the locals happy with a full menu served from breakfast right through to the early evening.

People's Open Market
Farmers Market $

(Map p98; www.honolulu.gov/parks/dprpom; cnr Monsarrat & Paki Aves, Kapi'olani Park; ⏰10-11am Wed; 🖋) 🖉 The city-sponsored farmers market in Kapi'olani Park trades in fresh bounty from *mauka* to *makai*. It's just a short walk from Waikiki.

Typical Hawaiian food, including *kalua* pork (cooked in an underground pit) and butterfish

Pioneer Saloon
Japanese, Fusion $

(Map p98; 📞808-732-4001; www.facebook.
com/pages/pioneer-saloon/339130739445778;
3046 Monsarrat Ave; ⏰11am-8pm Tue-Sun)
It's simple stuff, but the locals can't get
enough of Pioneer Saloon's Japanese fusion plate lunches, with everything from
grilled ahi to fried baby octopus to *yak-
isoba* (fried noodles). On the opposite
side of the road from Waikiki School.

Hawaii Sushi
Sushi $

(Map p98; 3045 Monsarrat Ave, Ste 1;
⏰10am-8pm Mon-Sat, to 6pm Sun) This
new place up Monsarrat Ave in the
strip mall just past Waikiki School
is a winner for Hawaiian-style fresh
sushi with rolls and bowls such as the
Spicy Ahi Bowl for $11. There's parking
outside and a few seats inside.

🍷 Drinking & Nightlife

Waikiki is tourist central with all the
kitschy-fun telltale signs: fruity cocktails
with paper umbrellas and coconut
bikini bras. Almost all of the hip bars and
nightclubs have migrated to Chinatown
in downtown Honolulu. But if you crave
spring-break-style dance clubs and tiki
bars, hit Waikiki Beach Walk or rock on
down Kuhio Ave after dark.

RumFire
Bar

(Map p98; www.rumfirewaikiki.com; Sheraton
Waikiki, 2255 Kalakaua Ave; ⏰noon-midnight)
The collection of vintage rum is mighty
tempting at this lively hotel bar at the
Sheraton Waikiki, with flirty fire pits
looking out onto the beach and live
contemporary Hawaiian (or jazz) music.
Or wander over to the resort's cabana-like
Edge of Waikiki Bar for knockout views,
designer cocktails and more live Hawaiian
and pop-rock music poolside.

Addiction Nightclub & Lobby Bar
Club, Bar

(Map p43; 📞808-943-5800; www.addiction
nightclub.com; Modern Honolulu, 1775 Ala
Moana Blvd; ⏰nightclub 10:30pm-3am Thu-Sun,
beach club noon-4pm Sat, lobby bar 6pm-late
daily) Superstar mainland DJs and island
dynamos spin at this boutique hotel's

If You Like...
Luau & Dinner Shows

Choose from a hotel production right on
the beach or a big bash outside town. Just
don't expect anything too authentic – all of
this fanfare is strictly for tourists.

1 'AHA 'AINA
(Map p98; 📞808-921-4600; www.royal-
hawaiian.com/dining/ahaaina; Royal Hawaiian, 2259
Kalakaua Ave; adult/child 5-12yr from $179/101;
⏰5:30-8pm Mon) This oceanfront sit-down dinner
show is like a three-act musical play narrating the
history of Hawaiian *mele* (songs) and hula. The food
is top-notch and there's an open bar.

2 WAIKIKI STARLIGHT LUAU
(Map p98; 📞808-947-2607; www.
hiltonhawaiianvillage.com/luau; Hilton Hawaiian
Village, 2005 Kalia Rd; adult/child 4-11yr from
$99/50; ⏰5:30-8pm Sun-Thu, weather permitting;
👶) Enthusiastic pan-Polynesian show, with buffet
meal, outdoor seating, Samoan fire dancing and
hapa haole (literally, 'half foreign') hula.

chic nightspot with an upscale dress
code (no shorts, flip-flops or hats). On
special weekends, Addiction's daytime
beach club lets you hang out on the pool
deck with the sounds of electronica and
techno grooves.

Lulu's Waikiki
Bar, Club

(Map p98; 📞808-926-5222; www.luluswaikiki.
com; Park Shore Waikiki, 2586 Kalakaua Ave;
⏰7am-2am) Brush off your sandy feet at
Kuhio Beach, then step across Kalakaua
Ave to this surf-themed bar and grill with
2nd-story lanai views of the Pacific Ocean
and Diamond Head. Lap up sunset happy
hours (3pm to 5pm daily), then chill out
to acoustic acts and local bands later
most evenings. DJs crank up the beats
after 10pm on Saturday.

Five-O Bar & Lounge
Sports Bar

(Map p98; 📞808-922-0550; www.five-o-bar.
com; 2nd fl, Bldg B, Royal Hawaiian Center, 2233

Gay & Lesbian Waikiki

Waikiki's queer community is tightly knit, but it's full of aloha for visitors. Free monthly magazine *Odyssey* (www.odysseyhawaii.com) covers the admittedly small but active scene.

If you're new to Waikiki, make your first stop **Hula's Bar & Lei Stand** (Map p98; 808-923-0669; www.hulas.com; 2nd fl, Castle Waikiki Grand, 134 Kapahulu Ave; 10am-2am;). This friendly, open-air bar, Waikiki's main gay venue, is a great place to make new friends, boogie and have a few drinks. Hunker down at the pool table, or gaze at the spectacular vista of Diamond Head.

On a side street, **Wang Chung's** (Map p98; 808-921-9176; http://wangchungs.com; 2424 Koa Ave; 5pm-2am) is a happy-go-lucky, living-room-sized karaoke bar, just a block inland from Kuhio Beach. Or drop by svelte **Bacchus** (Map p98; 808-926-4167; www.bacchus-waikiki.com; 2nd fl, 408 Lewers St; noon-2am), an intimate wine bar and cocktail lounge, with happy-hour specials and a Sunday-afternoon beer bust.

Not far away, **Fusion Waikiki** (Map p98; 808-924-2422; www.fusionwaikiki.com; 2260 Kuhio Ave; 10pm-4am) is a high-energy nightclub hosting weekend drag shows and go-go boys after midnight; women welcome. Next door **Lo Jax Waikiki** (Map p98; www.lojaxwaikiki.com; 2256 Kuhio Ave; noon-2am;) is a raucous gay sports bar that ramps it up with pool tournaments and weekend DJs.

Tiki-themed **Tapa's Restaurant & Lanai Bar** (Map p98; 808-921-2288; www.tapaswaikiki.com; 2nd fl, 407 Seaside Ave; 2pm-2am Mon-Sat, 9am-2am Sun) is a more laid-back spot, with bear-y talkative bartenders, pool tables, a jukebox and a karaoke machine. **In Between** (Map p98; 808-926-7060; www.facebook.com/inbetween.waikiki; 2155 Lau'ula St; noon-2am), a rubbah-slippah neighborhood bar, attracts an older crowd with 'the happiest of happy hours.'

For daytime diversions, Queen's Surf Beach is the darling of the sun-worshipping gay crowd. Further afield near the lighthouse, Diamond Head Beach is another popular gay gathering spot, with some (technically illegal) clothing-optional sunbathing going on. Gay-oriented **Like Hike** (http://gayhawaii.com/likehike) organizes twice-monthly trips around O'ahu, but you must call or email the trip leader before joining up (check the website for details and schedules).

Where to sleep? The Castle Waikiki Grand (p113), home to Hula's, and the boutique Hotel Renew (p115) are not exclusively gay, but rank highly with LGBTQ visitors, as do Waikiki's **Aqua Hotels** (www.aquaresorts.com), especially the chic Modern Honolulu (p116) and tranquil Aqua Lotus branches.

Kalakaua Ave; noon-midnight Mon-Thu, to 2am Fri & Sat, 11am-11pm Sun) You won't spot any *Hawaii 5-0* stars hiding out among the tropical lanai greenery inside this shopping-mall bar, but it's still loads of fun with friends. Boogie down on the dance floor or twirl the swizzle stick in your mai tai while listening to live bands. When you're hungry, belly up to the polished native-wood bar for *kalua* pork sliders.

Lewers Lounge   Lounge
(Map p98; www.halekulani.com/dining/lewers-lounge-bar; 2199 Kalia Rd, Halekulani; 7:30pm-1am) The nostalgic dream of Waikiki as an aristocratic playground is kept alive

at this Halekulani hotel bar. We're talking contemporary and classic cocktails, tempting appetizers and desserts, and smooth jazz combos that serenade after 8:30pm nightly.

Genius Lounge   Lounge

(Map p98; 📞808-626-5362; www.geniusloungehawaii.com; 3rd fl, 346 Lewers St; ⏰6pm-2am) Like a Japanese speakeasy, this glowing candlelit hideaway is a chill retreat for ultracool hipsters and lovebird couples. East–West tapas bites will have you nibbling on squid tempura, *loco moco* or banana cake while you sip made-in-Japan sake brews, and your ears are tickled by the sounds of retro jazz or cutting-edge electronica.

Da Big Kahuna   Bar

(Map p98; 📞808-923-0033; www.dabigkahuna.net; 2299 Kuhio Ave; ⏰10:30am-3am) Do you dream of a kitschy tiki bar where fruity, Kool Aid–colored drinks are poured into ceramic mugs carved with the faces of Polynesian gods? To get soused fast, order Da Fish Bowl – just don't try picking up a pool cue or shimmying on the small dance floor once you've drained it. A full food menu is served until 3am.

Nashville Waikiki   Bar, Club

(Map p98; www.nashvillewaikiki.com; 2330 Kuhio Ave; ⏰4pm-4am) Like Waikiki's own little honkytonk, this country-and-western dive bar can get as rowdy as a West Texas brawl. Homesick Southerners show up for sports TV, billiards, darts, pool tournaments, and free line-dancing and two-steppin' lessons. The afternoon, evening and late-night happy hours seem endless.

⭐ Entertainment

Whether you want to linger over one of those cool, frosty drinks with the little umbrellas or are craving live Hawaiian music and hula dancing, you're in the right place. For what's going on tonight, from DJ and live-music gigs to special events, check the *Honolulu Star-Advertiser's TGIF* section (www.honolulupulse.com), which comes out every Friday, and the free alternative tabloid *Honolulu Weekly* (http://honoluluweekly.com), published every Wednesday.

Traditional and contemporary Hawaiian music calls all up and down the beach in Waikiki, from the rhythmic drums and *ipu* (gourds) accompanying hula dancers to

Tiki torches on the beach, Waikiki

MICHELE FALZONE/GETTY IMAGES ©

mellow duos or trios playing slack key guitars and ukuleles and singing with *leo ki'eki'e* (male) or *ha'i* (female) high falsetto voices. All performances are free, unless otherwise noted.

Kuhio Beach Torch Lighting & Hula Show   Live Music

(Map p98; 808-922-5331; www.honolulu. gov/moca; Kuhio Beach Park; 6.30-7.30pm Tue, Thu & Sat Feb-Oct, weather permitting, 6-7pm Nov-Jan;) It all begins at the Duke Kahanamoku statue with the sounding of a conch shell and the lighting of torches after sunset. At the nearby hula mound, lay out your beach towel and enjoy the authentic Hawaiian music and dance show. It's full of aloha!

House Without a Key   Live Music, Hula

(Map p98; 808-923-2311; www.halekulani. com; Halekulani, 2199 Kalia Rd; 7am-9pm) Named after a 1925 Charlie Chan novel set in Honolulu, this genteel open-air hotel lounge sprawled beneath a century-old kiawe tree simply has no doors to lock. A sophisticated crowd gathers here for sunset cocktails, Hawaiian music and solo hula dancing by former Miss Hawaii pageant winners. Panoramic ocean views are as intoxicating as the tropical cocktails.

Mai Tai Bar   Live Music, Hula

(Map p98; 808-923-7311; www.royal-hawaiian. com; Royal Hawaiian, 2259 Kalakaua Ave; 10am-midnight) At the Royal Hawaiian's low-key bar (no preppy resort wear required), you can catch some great acoustic island music acts and graceful solo hula dancers some nights. Even if you don't dig who's performing, the signature Royal Mai Tai still packs a punch and romantic views of the breaking surf extend down to Diamond Head.

Beach Bar   Live Music, Hula

(Map p98; 808-922-3111; www.moana-surfrider.com; Moana Surfrider, 2365 Kalakaua Ave; 10:30am-midnight) Inside this historic beachfront hotel bar, soak up the sounds of classical and contemporary Hawaiian musicians playing underneath the old banyan tree where the *Hawaii Calls* radio program was broadcast nationwide during the mid-20th century. Live-music schedules vary, but hula soloists dance from 6pm to 8pm most nights.

Tapa Bar   Live Music

(Map p98; 808-949-4321; www. hiltonhawaiianvillage.com; ground fl, Tapa Tower, Hilton Hawaiian Village, 2005 Kalia Rd; 10am-11pm) It's worth navigating through the gargantuan Hilton resort complex to this Polynesian-themed open-air bar just to see some of the best traditional and contemporary Hawaiian groups performing on O'ahu today. There is live music nightly from 7.30pm or 8pm.

Mai Tai Bar
ANN CECIL/GETTY IMAGES ©

Moana Terrace
Live Music

(Map p98; ☎808-922-6611; 2nd fl, Marriott Waikiki Beach Resort, 2552 Kalakaua Ave; ☺11am-11pm; 👪) If you're in a mellow mood, come for sunset happy-hour drinks at this casual, poolside bar, just a lei's throw from Kuhio Beach. Slack key guitarists, ukulele players and *ha'i* falsetto singers make merry for a family-friendly crowd.

Kani Ka Pila Grille
Live Music

(Map p98; ☎808-924-4990; www.outriggerreef.com; Outrigger Reef on the Beach, 2169 Kalia Rd; ☺11am-10pm) Once happy hour ends, the Outrigger's lobby bar sets the scene for some of the most laid-back live-music shows of any of Waikiki's beachfront hotels, with traditional and contemporary Hawaiian musicians playing their hearts out and cracking jokes.

Royal Grove
Live Music, Hula

(Map p98; ☎808-922-2299; www.royalhawaiiancenter.com/info/entertainment; ground fl, Royal Hawaiian Center, 2201 Kalakaua Ave; ☺schedules vary) This shopping mall's open-air stage may lack oceanfront views, but Hawaiian music and hula performances by top island talent happen here almost every evening, along with twice-weekly lunchtime shows by performers from the Windward Coast's Polynesian Cultural Center and concerts by the Royal Hawaiian Band.

🔒 Shopping

Hundreds of shops in Waikiki are vying for your tourist dollars. Catwalk designers such as Armani, Gucci and Pucci have boutiques inside the DFS Galleria at the northwest end of Kalakaua Ave. On beachfront Kalakaua Ave, Waikiki's shopping centers are mostly chock-full of the brand-label stores you'd find in any US mainland city. But a handful of only-in-Hawaii stores line Waikiki Beach Walk and round out the multistory Royal Hawaiian Center. For even more shopping, Ala Moana Center, Hawaii's largest mall, and the eclectic open-air Ward Centers strip malls are a short bus ride from Waikiki.

Not feeling flush? You'll never be far from Waikiki's ubiquitous ABC Stores,

The Best...

Sunset Drinks with Music & Ocean Views

1 House Without a Key (p126)

2 Mai Tai Bar (p126)

3 RumFire (p123)

4 Lulu's Waikiki (p123)

5 Beach Bar (p126)

WAIKIKI SHOPPING

conveniently cheap places to pick up vacation essentials such as beach mats, sunblock, snacks and sundries, not to mention plastic flower and shell lei, 'I got lei'd in Hawaii' T-shirts, and motorized, grass-skirted hula girls for the dashboard of your car back home. For offbeat, vintage and antique, and one-of-a-kind shops stocking island-style clothes and beachwear, handmade jewelry, arts and crafts, souvenirs and surfboards, walk inland along Kuhio Ave and locals' Kapahulu Ave.

Bailey's Antiques & Aloha Shirts
Clothing, Antiques

(Map p98; http://alohashirts.com; 517 Kapahulu Ave; ☺10am-6pm) Bailey's has, without a doubt, the finest aloha-shirt collection on O'ahu, possibly the world! Racks are crammed with thousands of collector-worthy vintage aloha shirts in every conceivable color and style, from 1920s kimono-silk classics to 1970s polyester specials to modern offerings. Prices dizzyingly vary from five bucks to several thousand dollars. 'Margaritaville' musician Jimmy Buffett is Bailey's biggest fan.

Royal Hawaiian Center
Mall

(Map p98; www.royalhawaiiancenter.com; 2201 Kalakaua Ave; ☺10am-10pm) Not to be

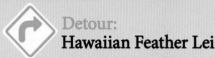

Detour:
Hawaiian Feather Lei

Aunty Mary Louise Kaleonahenahe Kekuewa and her daughter Paulette co-wrote Hawaii's celebrated handbook *Feather Lei as an Art,* which encouraged a revival of this indigenous art starting in the late 1970s. That was the heyday of the Hawaiian Renaissance, when indigenous arts, culture and language were being reborn. Although Aunty has since passed away, Paulette and her own daughter and granddaughter keep alive the ancient Hawaiian craft of feather lei making at **Na Lima Mili Hulu No'eau** (Map p98; 808-732-0865; 762 Kapahulu Ave; usually 9am-4pm Mon-Sat) . This homespun little shop's name translates as 'the skilled hands that touch the feathers,' and it can take days to produce a single lei, prized by collectors. Call ahead to make an appointment for a personalized lei-making lesson.

confused with the Royal Hawaiian resort hotel next door, Waikiki's biggest shopping center has four levels and houses more than 80 breezily mixed stores. Look for Hawaii-born labels such as Noa Noa for Polynesian-print sarongs, sundresses and shirts. Art galleries display high-quality koa carvings, while jewelers trade in Ni'ihau shell lei necklaces, and flower lei stands sell fresh, wearable art.

Reyn Spooner
Clothing

(Map p98; 808-923-7896; www.reynspooner.com; Sheraton Waikiki, 2259 Kalakaua Ave; 8am-10:30pm) Since 1956, Reyn Spooner's subtly designed, reverse-print preppy aloha shirts have been the standard for Honolulu's businessmen, political power brokers and social movers-and-shakers. Reyn's Waikiki flagship is a bright, mod and clean-lined store, carrying colorful racks of men's shirts and board shorts, too. Also at Kahala Mall and Ala Moana Center. Ask about Reyn's Rack downtown for discounts on factory seconds.

Ukulele PuaPua
Music

(Map p98; 808-924-2266; www.hawaiianukuleleonline.com; Sheraton Waikiki, 2255 Kalakaua Ave; 9am-10pm) Avoid those flimsy souvenir ukuleles and head to one of Pua-Pua's two locations, one at the Sheraton Waikiki, the other at the Moana Surfrider

(p115), to find the real thing. These guys are passionate and offer free group beginner lessons every day.

Newt at the Royal
Clothing

(Map p98; www.newtattheroyal.com; Royal Hawaiian, 2259 Kalakaua Ave; 9am-9pm) With stylish flair and panache, Newt specializes in Montecristi Panama hats – classic men's fedoras, plantation-style hats and women's *fino*. It also has fine reproductions of aloha shirts using 1940s and '50s designs. Everything's tropical, neat as a pin and top-drawer quality.

Genius Outfitters
Arts, Crafts

(Map p98; 808-922-2822; www.geniusoutfitters.net; 346 Lewers St; 10.30am-10pm) This cutesy arts, crafts and clothing store on Lewers specializes in locally made goods. It covers the first two floors of an attractive three-story building with Genius Lounge on top.

Peggy's Picks
Souvenirs

(Map p98; 808-737-3297; www.facebook.com/PeggysPicks; 732 Kapahalu Ave; 11am-7pm Mon-Sat) Peggy's Picks on Kapahulu Ave is the place to go for Hawaiiana, treasures and collectibles from all over the world. It's a bit ramshackle and can get a tad crowded, but well worth it for the collectors among us.

Island Paddler — Clothing

(Map p98; 📞 808-737-4854; www.islandpaddler hawaii.com; 716 Kapahulu Ave; 🕙10am-6pm) Besides having a great selection of paddles and paddling gear, these guys have T-shirts, aloha shirts, beachwear and everything you might need for a day at the beach – along with a friendly and relaxed atmosphere.

Art on the Zoo Fence — Arts, Crafts

(Map p98; www.artonthezoofence.com; Monsarrat Ave, opposite Kapi'olani Park; 🕙9am-4pm Sat & Sun) Dozens of artists hang their works along the fence on the south side of the Honolulu Zoo every weekend, weather permitting. Browse the contemporary watercolor, acrylic and oil paintings and colorful island photography as you chat with the artists themselves.

ℹ Information

Dangers & Annoyances

Never leave your valuables unattended on the beach. At night, it's risky to walk on the beach or along Ala Wai Canal. After dark, prostitutes stroll Kuhio Ave, preying on naive-looking male tourists.

The hustlers who push time-shares and con deals on Waikiki's street corners are not totally gone either. Some have deceptively metamorphosed into 'activity centers' where time-share salespeople will offer you all sorts of deals, from a free luau and sunset cruises to $5-a-day car rentals, if you'll just come to hear their 'no obligation' pitch. *Caveat emptor.*

Emergency

Waikiki Police Substation (📞808-723-8562; www.honolulupd.org; 2405 Kalakaua Ave; 🕙24hr) If you need nonemergency help, or just friendly directions, stop here next to Kuhio Beach Park.

Internet Access

Most Waikiki hotels have wired internet connections in guest rooms (a surcharge may apply), with wi-fi only in the lobby or poolside. Cybercafes on Kuhio and Kalakaua Aves provide pay-as-you-go internet terminals, charging $6 to $12 per hour, but few places offer wi-fi.

Waikiki Beachside Hostel (Map p98; www.waikikibeachsidehostel.com; 2556 Lemon Rd; per hr $7; 🕙24hr; 📶) Internet cafe terminals available to nonguests.

Waikiki-Kapahulu Public Library (📞808-733-8488; www.librarieshawaii.org; 400 Kapahulu

Main shopping strip, Waikiki

Ave; ◷10am-5pm Tue, Wed, Fri & Sat, noon-7pm Thu; 📶) Free wi-fi and internet terminals (temporary nonresident library card $10) that may be reserved by calling ahead.

Laundry

Many accommodations provide coin-operated laundry facilities for guests.

Waikiki Laundromat (📞808-351-5331; http://waikikilaundromathi.com; 2450 Prince Edward St; ◷6am-8pm) Clean and simple in the heart of Waikiki.

Campbell Highlander Laundry (3340 Campbell Ave; ◷6:30am-9pm) Self-serve washers and dryers; same-day laundry service available. Inland off Kapahulu Ave.

Medical Services

Doctors on Call (www.straubhealth.org) North Waikiki (📞808-973-5250; 2nd fl, Rainbow Bazaar, Hilton Hawaiian Village, 2005 Kalia Rd; ◷8am-4:30pm Mon-Fri); South Waikiki (📞808-971-6000; ground fl, Sheraton Princess Kaiulani, 120 Ka'iulani Ave; ◷24hr) Nonemergency walk-in medical clinics located in north and south Waikiki. Some travel health-insurance policies are accepted.

Money

There are 24-hour ATMs located all over Waikiki, including at these full-service banks near Waikiki Beach Walk.

Bank of Hawaii (www.boh.com; 2155 Kalakaua Ave; ◷8:30am-4pm Mon-Thu, to 6pm Fri, 9am-1pm Sat) International banking and currency exchange.

First Hawaiian Bank (www.fhb.com; 2181 Kalakaua Ave; ◷8:30am-4pm Mon-Thu, to 6pm Fri) Lobby displays Hawaii history murals by French artist Jean Charlot.

Tourist Information

Freebie tourist magazines containing discount coupons such as *This Week O'ahu* and *101 Things to Do* can be found in street-corner boxes and hotel lobbies and at Honolulu's airport.

Hawaii Visitors & Convention Bureau (📞800-464-2924, 808-923-1811; www.gohawaii.com; ste 801, Waikiki Business Plaza, 2270 Kalakaua Ave; ◷8am-4:30pm Mon-Fri) This business office hands out free tourist maps and brochures.

Hilton Hawaiian Village (p114)

❶ Getting There & Around

Technically, Waikiki is a district of the city of Honolulu. It's bounded on two sides by Ala Wai Canal, on another by the ocean and on the fourth by Kapi'olani Park. Three parallel roads cross Waikiki: one-way Kalakaua Ave alongside the beach; Kuhio Ave, the main drag inland for pedestrians and buses; and Ala Wai Blvd, which borders Ala Wai Canal.

Bicycle

You can rent beach cruisers and commuter bikes all over Waikiki. For top-quality mountain and road bikes, visit downtown Honolulu's Bike Shop (p62).

Big Kahuna Motorcycle Tours & Rentals (☎808-924-2736; www.bigkahunarentals.com; 407 Seaside Ave; per 4hr/9hr/24hr/week $10/15/20/100) Rents commuter-style mountain bikes only.

Hawaiian Style Rentals (☎866-916-6733; www.hawaiibikes.com; Waikiki Beachside Hostel, 2556 Lemon Rd; per day $20-30) Multiday and monthly discounts on both beach cruiser and 'comfort bike' rentals.

EBikes Hawaii (☎808-722-5454; www.ebikeshawaii.com; 3318 Campbell Ave; 4/7hr $40/50) These guys are passionate about E-bikes and are based just off Kapahulu Ave. Half-, full- and multiday rentals available.

Bus

Most public bus stops in Waikiki are found inland along Kuhio Ave. The Ala Moana Center mall, just northwest of Waikiki, is the island's main bus-transfer point.

Be careful to catch the bus that's going in your direction. Each route can have different destinations, and buses generally keep the same number whether inbound or outbound. For instance, bus 2 can take you either to the aquarium or downtown Honolulu, so take note of both the number and the written destination before you jump on – or you can just ask the driver.

Useful Bus Routes

ROUTE	DESTINATION
2	Honolulu Museum of Art, 'Iolani Palace, downtown Honolulu, Chinatown, Bishop Museum; also Waikiki Aquarium, Honolulu Zoo
4	University of Hawai'i, 'Iolani Palace, downtown Honolulu, Chinatown, Queen Emma Summer Palace; also Honolulu Zoo
8	Ala Moana Center, Ward Centers, downtown Honolulu, Chinatown; also Kapi'olani Park, Honolulu Zoo
13	Honolulu Convention Center, Honolulu Museum of Art, 'Iolani Palace, downtown Honolulu, Chinatown; also Kapahulu Ave
19 & 20	Ala Moana Center, Ward Centers, Restaurant Row, Aloha Tower Marketplace, downtown Honolulu, Chinatown, Honolulu International Airport*
22	Honolulu Zoo, Kapi'olani Park, Diamond Head, Kahala Mall, Koko Marina Center, Hanauma Bay (no service Tuesday), Sea Life Park; also Ala Moana Center, Pearl Harbor
23	Honolulu Zoo, Kapi'olani Park, Diamond Head, Kahala Mall, Hawai'i Kai Towne Center, Sea Life Park; also Ala Moana Center
42	Ala Moana Center, Ward Centers, downtown Honolulu, Chinatown, Pearl Harbor; also Kapi'olani Park, Honolulu Zoo
B (CityExpress!)	Honolulu Museum of Art, 'Iolani Palace, downtown Honolulu, Chinatown, Bishop Museum
E (CountryExpress!)	Ala Moana Center, Restaurant Row, Aloha Tower Marketplace, downtown Honolulu

*One piece of hand-held carry-on baggage only per person; luggage prohibited.

It's hardly worth checking timetables for various routes, which run frequently throughout the day and evening, with most operating until around 9pm or 10pm daily.

Car

Major car-rental companies have branches in Waikiki. If you're renting a car for the entire time you're on O'ahu, you may be better off picking up and dropping off at Honolulu's airport, where rates are usually cheaper, but then you'll also have to pay for parking at your hotel (averaging $15 to $30 per night).

Independent rental agencies in Waikiki:

808 Smart Car Rentals (☎808-735-5000; http://smartcartours.com; 444 Niu St) Rents smart cars with convertible roofs that get over 40mpg on island highways; being smaller, they're also easier to park.

Paradise Rent-a-Car (☎808-946-7777; www.paradiserentacar.com; 1837 Ala Moana Blvd; ⏰8am-5pm) Rents sedans, SUVs, jeeps and convertibles; drivers aged 18 to 24 accepted with a hefty cash deposit (no credit card required).

VIP Car Rental (☎808-922-4605; http://vipcarrentalhawaii.com; 234 Beach Walk; ⏰7am-5pm) Rents compacts, sedans, jeeps, minivans and convertibles; drivers aged 18 to 24 accepted with hefty cash deposit (no credit card required).

Parking

Most hotels charge $15 to $30 per night for either valet or self-parking. The **Waikiki Trade Center Parking Garage** (2255 Kuhio Ave, enter off Seaside Ave) and next-door **Waikiki Parking Garage** (333 Seaside Ave) usually offer Waikiki's cheapest flat-rate day, evening and overnight rates. At the less-trafficked southeast end of Waikiki, there's a free parking lot along Monsarrat Ave beside Kapi'olani Park with no time limit. Waikiki's cheapest metered lot (25¢ per hour, four-hour limit) is along Kapahulu Ave next to the zoo. But neither of these last two places are particularly safe for rental cars, which are marked with bar-code stickers that make them easy targets for smash-and-grab thieves.

Motorcycle & Moped

You can tool around on a motorcycle or moped, but don't expect to save any money that way –

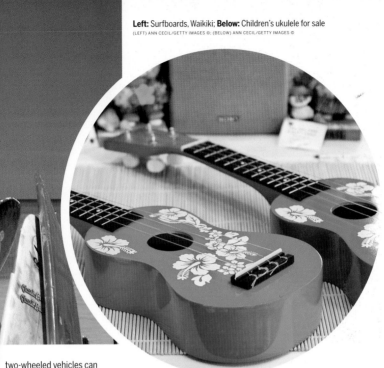

Left: Surfboards, Waikiki; **Below:** Children's ukulele for sale

two-wheeled vehicles can be more expensive to rent than a car. They're not necessarily safe – drivers should have some prior experience navigating in city traffic.

Chase Hawaii Rentals (808-942-4273; www.chasehawaiirentals.com; 355 Royal Hawaiian Ave) Rents Harley-Davidson, Kawasaki and Honda motorcycles and Vespa scooters (over-21s with valid motorcycle license and credit card only).

Cruzin Hawaii (808-945-9595, 877-945-9595; http://cruzinhawaii.com; 444 Niu St) Rents mostly Harley-Davidson motorcycles (over-21s with valid motorcycle license and credit card only).

Taxi

Taxi stands are found at Waikiki's bigger resort hotels and shopping malls. Elsewhere, you'll probably need to call for a taxi.

Trolley

The motorized **Waikiki Trolley** (808-593-2822; www.waikikitrolley.com; adult/child 4-11yr 4-day pass $54/37, 7-day pass $59/41) runs three color-coded lines designed for tourists that connect Waikiki with the Ala Moana Center, downtown Honolulu, Chinatown, Diamond Head and Kahala Mall. Passes allow you to jump on and off the trolley as often as you like, but they don't offer much in the way of value compared with buses. Purchase trolley passes at **DFS Galleria** (330 Royal Hawaiian Ave) or **Royal Hawaiian Center** (2201 Kalakaua Ave), or buy them online in advance at a discount.

Pearl Harbor & Leeward Oʻahu

The WWII–era rallying cry 'Remember Pearl Harbor!' that once mobilized an entire nation dramatically resonates on Oʻahu.

It was here that the surprise Japanese attack on December 7, 1941, hurtled the US into war in the Pacific. Every year about 1.5 million tourists visit Pearl Harbor's unique collection of war memorials and museums, all clustered around a quiet bay where oysters were once farmed. Head further west and you're into an area that isn't on the tourist trail unless you're staying at the Ko Olina resorts.

Leeward Oʻahu's land is dry and brown, and much of the region's population subsists at the lower end of the economic scale. Intrepid travelers will find undeveloped beaches and unvarnished communities full of cultural pride – more Native Hawaiians live on the Waiʻanae Coast than anyplace else island-wide.

Ko Olina lagoon (p151)
PETER FRENCH/GETTY IMAGES ©

Pearl Harbor & Leeward Oʻahu Highlights

USS Arizona Memorial

A solemn tribute to the more than 1000 sailors who lost their lives during the Pearl Harbor attack, the USS *Arizona* Memorial (p141) was built over the midsection of the sunken ship with deliberate geometry to represent initial defeat, ultimate victory and eternal serenity. This is one of the USA's most significant WWII sites and it certainly feels that way.

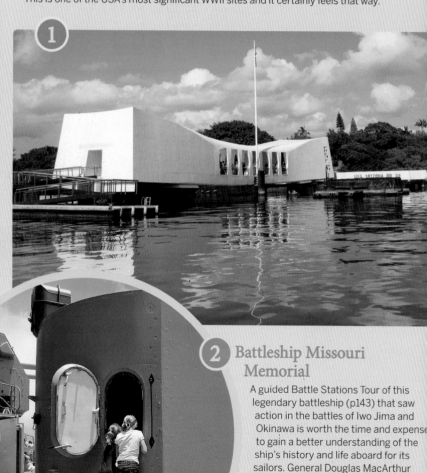

1

2 ## Battleship Missouri Memorial

A guided Battle Stations Tour of this legendary battleship (p143) that saw action in the battles of Iwo Jima and Okinawa is worth the time and expense to gain a better understanding of the ship's history and life aboard for its sailors. General Douglas MacArthur accepted the Japanese surrender on board the 'Mighty Mo' on September 2, 1945, in Tokyo Bay.

SHELDON LEVIS/GETTY IMAGES ©

Makaha Beach Park

Big-wave surfing got its start at Makaha (p157) when Hawaii's first international surfing competition was hosted here in the 1950s. These days surfers still turn up in winter, but this beautifully arching golden beach is a real beauty for snorkeling and swimming in summer. Except for weekends and big surf days you'll likely have the place to yourself.

RIDDHISH CHAKRABORTY/GETTY IMAGES ©

KARL LEHMANN/GETTY IMAGES ©

Aloha Stadium Swap Meet

In the parking lot of Hawaii's largest outdoor sports venue you'll find the island's biggest flea market (p148) operating three mornings per week. More than 400 stalls will vie for your attention with rows and rows of discounted island souvenirs and clothing at this open swap meet and marketplace. There are plenty of refreshment options on hand as you sift your way through the endless bargains.

Ka'ena Point Trail

Until the mid-1940s the O'ahu Railway ran all the way from Honolulu, around Ka'ena Point and on to Hale'iwa on the North Shore. These days the tracks are gone, but the old railbed serves as an excellent family-friendly hiking trail (p160) out to the point with the sea on your left and craggy cliffs on your right. Most head out to Ka'ena Point, then back the same way. Laysan albatross, Ka'ena Point

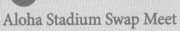

137

Pearl Harbor & Leeward O'ahu Itineraries

BUZZ'S STEAKHOUSE

Pearl Harbor

USS BOWFIN SUBMARINE MUSEUM & PARK

WWII VALOR IN THE PACIFIC NATIONAL MONUMENT

BATTLESHIP MISSOURI MEMORIAL

PACIFIC AVIATION MUSEUM

DAY ONE

6 MILES

Arrive early for the ❶**WWII Valor in the Pacific National Monument** (p140), even if you've made advance reservations. Thousands of people per day come to take the tour that includes a moving theater presentation about the attack on Pearl Harbor and a boat ride to the USS *Arizona* Memorial, the watery grave for the sailors who fell here. The monument also has two captivating museums.

Accessed through the monument are several other, paid, Pearl Harbor sights. At the ❷**USS Bowfin Submarine Museum & Park** (p144), the moored WWII–era submarine *Bowfin* is worth exploring both above and below deck. Take the shuttle bus to see the USS *Missouri* at the ❸**Battleship Missouri Memorial** (p143). This historic battleship not only served in two of WWII's final naval battles, Iwo Jima and Okinawa, but aboard its deck is where General MacArthur accepted the Japanese surrender.

From there the shuttle bus continues out to the ❹**Pacific Aviation Museum** (p144), a military aircraft museum that investigates the period from WWII through the US–Vietnam conflict. Sunset views over Pearl Harbor attract quite the crowd at ❺**Buzz's Steakhouse** (p148); make a reservation in advance.

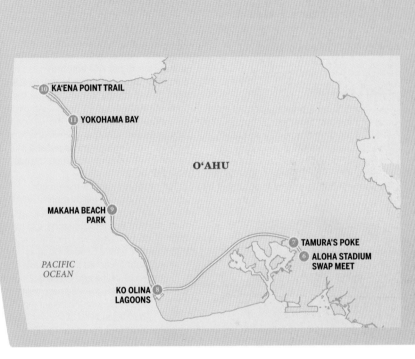

45 MILES

DAY TWO

Kitschy carved signs, tropical-print muu-muus and island-style quilts at ⑥ **Aloha Stadium Swap Meet** (p148) are all you could want for your Hawaiian souvenirs! Open Wednesday, Saturday and Sunday.

As one customer put it, 'If I was on death row and could choose my last meal, it would be 'spicy ahi' *poke* from Tamura's.' ⑦ **Tamura's Poke** (p148) is simply that good. Pick some up on your way west. Drop in to Ko Olina and head directly to the postcard-perfect ⑧ **Ko Olina Lagoons** (p151) for a swim and snorkel. The calm blue waters, palm-lined beaches and colorful fish are everything paradise is meant to be.

Stop for a swim at sandy ⑨ **Makaha Beach Park** (p157). Summer swimming is good, and if you're a wave-rider, the break here can be epic when the winter conditions are right.

Hike along the dramatic ⑩ **Ka'ena Point Trail** (p160) for fine views the entire way with the ocean crashing against dark volcanic rocks on one side and the Wai'anae Range's craggy cliffs on the other.

Finish up your day by watching the sun go down from the west-facing scenic mile-long sandy beach at ⑪ **Yokohama Bay** (p160). It's said to be the best sunset spot on O'ahu.

Discover Pearl Harbor & Leeward Oʻahu

PEARL HARBOR AREA

Pearl Harbor

December 7, 1941 – 'a date which will live in infamy,' President Franklin D Roosevelt later said – began at 7:55am with a wave of more than 350 Japanese planes swooping over the Koʻolau Range headed toward the unsuspecting US Pacific Fleet in Pearl Harbor. The battleship USS *Arizona* took a direct hit and sank in less than nine minutes, trapping most of its crew beneath the surface. The average age of the 1177 enlisted men who died in the attack on the ship was just 19 years. It wasn't until 15 minutes after the bombing started that American anti-aircraft guns began to shoot back at the Japanese warplanes. Twenty other US military ships were sunk or seriously damaged and 347 airplanes were destroyed during the two-hour attack.

The offshore shrine at the sunken USS *Arizona* doesn't tell the only story. Nearby are two other floating historical sites: the USS *Bowfin* submarine, aka the 'Pearl Harbor Avenger,' and the battleship USS *Missouri,* where General Douglas MacArthur accepted the Japanese surrender at the end of WWII.

Together, for the US, these military sites represent the beginning, middle and end of the war. To visit all three, as well as the Pacific Aviation Museum, dedicate at least a day.

Sights

WWII Valor in the Pacific National Monument Park

(Map p145; www.nps.gov/valr) FREE
One of the USA's most significant WWII sites, this National Park Service monument narrates the history of the Pearl Harbor attack and commemorates fallen service members. The monument is entirely wheelchair accessible. The main entrance also leads to Pearl Harbor's other parks and museums.

The monument grounds are much more than just a boat dock for the USS *Arizona* Memorial. Be sure to stop at the two museums, where multimedia and

US flag, with the Battleship *Missouri* Memorial (p143) in the background

HOLGER LEUE/GETTY IMAGES ©

interactive displays bring to life the Road to War and the Attack & Aftermath through historic photos, films, illustrated graphics and taped oral histories. A shoreside walk passes signs illustrating how the attack unfolded in the now-peaceful harbor.

The bookstore sells just about every book and movie ever produced on the Pearl Harbor attack and WWII's Pacific theater, as well as informative illustrated maps of the battle. If you're lucky, the few remaining, 90-plus-year-old Pearl Harbor veterans who volunteer might be out front signing autographs and answering questions.

Admission to the monument is free but there are various ticket packages available for the three attractions that have admission fees. The best deal is the seven-day Passport to Pearl Harbor (adult/child $65/35), which includes admission to all attractions. Tickets are sold online at www.pearlharborhistoricsites.org, at the main monument ticket counter, and at each attraction.

USS Arizona Memorial
Museum, Memorial

(Map p145; ☎808-422-3300; www.nps.gov/valr; 1 Arizona Memorial Pl; admission free, boat-tour reservation fee $1.50; ☺7am-5pm, boat tours 8am-3pm) FREE One of the USA's most significant WWII sites, this somber monu-ment commemorates the Pearl Harbor attack and its fallen service members with an offshore shrine reachable by boat.

The USS Arizona Memorial was built over the midsection of the sunken USS Arizona, with deliberate geometry to represent initial defeat, ultimate victory and eternal serenity. In the furthest of three chambers inside the shrine, the names of crewmen killed in the attack are engraved onto a marble wall. In the central section are cutaways that allow visitors to see the skeletal remains of the ship, which even now oozes about a quart of oil each day into the ocean. In its rush to recover from the attack and prepare for war, the US

1 **WHAT QUESTIONS DO YOU THINK SOMEONE MIGHT TAKE AWAY FROM A VALOR IN THE PACIFIC NATIONAL MONUMENT VISIT?**

One leaves the monument with lingering questions about our military at that time. There were numerous warning signs that should have alerted the military to the impending attack.

2 **WHAT IS THE MOST IMPORTANT WWII–RELATED ISLAND EXPERIENCE BESIDES PEARL HARBOR?**

A visit to the National Memorial Cemetery of the Pacific (Punchbowl) should be a mandatory spot to visit on O'ahu. There is a 200ft-long, 20ft-high panorama of all the Pacific theater battles during the war. It is in 3-D and in color with the names and dates of each battle. It is free to the public.

3 **ANY OTHER LESSER-KNOWN SITES?**

There are numerous bunkers ['pillboxes'] all around O'ahu that housed large guns during and after the attack on Pearl Harbor [including at Lanikai]. Perhaps the most visited are those on the peaks of Diamond Head. The Hawai'i Army Museum in Waikiki has a lot of information about the island before, during and after the attack. Some may want to visit the memorial at the Opama radar site near the entrance to the Turtle Bay Resort on the North Shore.

Navy exercised its option to leave the servicemen inside the sunken ship; they remain entombed in its hull, buried at sea. Visitors are asked to maintain respectful silence at all times.

Boat tours to the shrine depart every 15 minutes from 8am until 3pm (weather permitting). For the 75-minute tour program, which includes a 23-minute

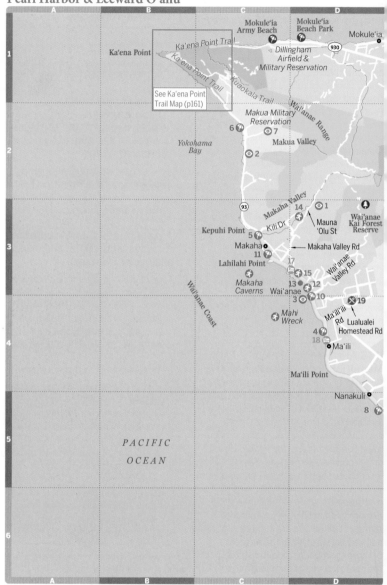

documentary film on the attack, make reservations online (fee per ticket $1.50) at www.recreation.gov at least a few days before your visit. Free first-come, first-serve tickets are also available in person at the visitor center's Aloha Court,

but during peak season when more than 4000 people take the tour daily, the entire day's allotment of tickets may be gone by 10am and waits of a few hours are not uncommon, so arrive early.

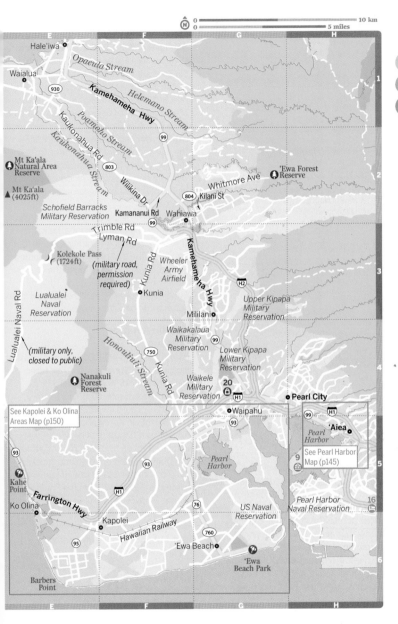

Battleship Missouri Memorial

Museum, Memorial

(Map p145; ☎808-455-1600; www.ussmissouri.com; 63 Cowpens St, Ford Island; admission incl tour adult/child from $25/13; ⏱8am-4pm

Sep-May, to 5pm Jun-Aug) The last battleship built at the end of WWII, the USS *Missouri* provides a unique historical 'bookend' to the US campaign in the Pacific during WWII. Nicknamed the 'Mighty Mo', this decommissioned battleship saw action during the decisive WWII battles of Iwo Jima and Okinawa.

The USS *Missouri* is now docked on Ford Island, just a few hundred yards from the sunken remains of the USS *Arizona*. During a self-guided audiotour, you can poke about the officers' quarters, browse exhibits on the ship's history and stride across the deck where General MacArthur accepted the Japanese surrender on September 2, 1945. Guided battle-station tours, which are sometimes led by knowledgeable US military veterans, are worth the extra time and expense.

To visit the memorial, board the mandatory Ford Island visitor shuttle bus (bring photo ID) outside the visitor center's Aloha Court.

USS Bowfin Submarine Museum & Park
Museum, Park

(Map p145; ☏808-423-1341; www.bowfin.org; 11 Arizona Memorial Dr; museum adult/child $5/3, incl self-guided submarine tour $12/5; ⏲7am-5pm, last entry 4:30pm) If you have to wait an hour or two for your USS *Arizona* Memorial tour to begin, this adjacent park harbors the moored WWII–era submarine USS *Bowfin* and a museum that traces the development of submarines from their origins to the nuclear age, including wartime patrol footage. Undoubtedly, the highlight is clambering aboard a historic submarine.

Launched on December 7, 1942, one year after the Pearl Harbor attack, the USS *Bowfin* sank 44 enemy ships in the Pacific by the end of WWII. A self-guided audiotour explores the life of the crew – watch your head below deck! Children under age four are not allowed aboard the submarine for safety reasons.

Pacific Aviation Museum
Museum

(Map p142; ☏808-441-1000; www.pacificaviation museum.org; 319 Lexington Blvd, Ford Island; adult/child $25/15, incl guided tour $35/25; ⏲9am-5pm, last entry 4pm) This military aircraft museum covers WWII through the US conflicts in Korea and Vietnam. The first aircraft hangar has been outfitted with exhibits on the Pearl Harbor attack, the Doolittle Raid on mainland Japan in 1942 and the pivotal Battle of Midway, when the tides of WWII in the Pacific turned in favor of the Allies.

Authentically restored planes on display here include a Japanese Zero and a Dauntless navy dive bomber. Walk next door to explore the MiG Alley Korean War exhibit or take a guided tour to look behind the scenes at restoration work in Hangar 79's replica WWII–era maintenance shop.

To visit the museum, board the mandatory Ford Island visitor shuttle bus (bring photo ID) outside the visitor center's Aloha Court.

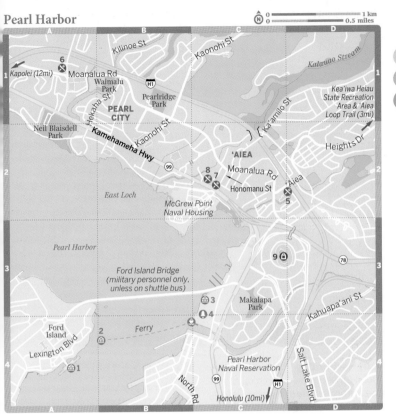

Tours

Private tours of Pearl Harbor from Wai-kiki don't add much, if anything, to the experience of visiting the memorials and museums. Besides, tourist boats aren't allowed to disembark at the USS *Arizona* Memorial.

Festivals & Events

Memorial Day   Commemoration
(☉May) On the last Monday in May, this national public holiday honors military personnel killed in battle. The USS *Arizona* Memorial, dedicated on Memorial Day in 1962, has a special ceremony.

Veterans Day   Commemoration
(☉Nov) Held on November 11 each year, this national public holiday honors US

Pearl Harbor

⊙ Sights
1 Battleship Missouri Memorial.............A4
2 USS Arizona Memorial.......................B4
3 USS Bowfin Submarine
   Museum & Park..................................C3
4 WWII Valor in the Pacific
   National Monument...........................C3

⊗ Eating
5 Alley Restaurant Bar & Grill.................D2
6 Buzz's Steakhouse A1
7 Forty Niner Restaurant C2
8 Tamura's Poke C2

⊕ Shopping
9 Aloha Stadium Swap Meet &
   Marketplace.......................................C3

military veterans. As part of the occasion, the USS *Missouri* hosts a sunset ceremony and tribute.

145

Pearl Harbor Day Commemoration

(🕐Dec) On December 7, ceremonies at Pearl Harbor include a Hawaiian blessing and heartfelt accounts from survivors of the 1941 Japanese attack.

Eating

All four sights have concession stands or snack shops. The cafe at the Pacific Aviation Museum is the biggest, with the best selection; the hot dogs at Bowfin Park are the cheapest. For a full meal, detour to nearby 'Aiea or go a little further to the Kapolei area on the Leeward Coast.

Information

Strict security measures are in place at Pearl Harbor. You are not allowed to bring in *any* items that allow concealment (eg purses, camera bags, fanny packs, backpacks, diaper bags). Personal-sized cameras and camcorders are allowed. Don't lock valuables in your car. Instead use the storage facility outside the main park gate.

ⓘ Getting There & Away

The entrance to the Valor in the Pacific Monument and the other Pearl Harbor historic sites is off the Kamehameha Hwy (Hwy 99), southwest of Aloha Stadium. From Honolulu or Waikiki, take H-1 west to exit 15A (Arizona Memorial/Stadium), then follow the highway signs for the monument, not the signs for Pearl Harbor (which lead onto the US Navy base). There's plenty of free parking.

From Waikiki, bus 42 ('Ewa Beach) is the most direct, running twice hourly between 6am and 3pm, taking just over an hour each way. The 'Arizona Memorial' stop is right outside the main memorial entrance.

'Aiea

Just north of Pearl Harbor lies the town of 'Aiea. Beyond Aloha Stadium and its famous flea market, the crowded old community climbs the hill to a historic heiau (stone temple).

Left: Traditional Hawaiian *poke* with macadamia nuts and *limu* (seaweed);
Below: Firedancer performing at a luau

◎ Sights

Kea'iwa Heiau State Recreation Area
Park

(www.hawaiistateparks.org; off 'Aiea Heights Dr, 'Aiea; ⊙7am-7:45pm Apr-Sep, to 6:45pm Sep-Mar) **FREE** Situated in the mountains north of Pearl Harbor, this state park protects Kea'iwa Heiau, an ancient *ho'ola* (healing or medicinal) temple. Today people wishing to be cured may still place offerings here. The 4ft-high terraces are made of stacked rocks that enclose an approximately 16,000-sq-ft platform; the construction may date to the 16th century.

The scenic, 4.8-mile (2½-hour) 'Aiea Loop Trail starts from the top of the park's paved loop road. There are some steep, sometimes muddy, switchbacks, but you'll enjoy sweeping vistas of Pearl Harbor, Diamond Head and the Ko'olau Range. About two-thirds of the way along the trail, the wreckage of a plane that crashed in 1944 can be spotted through the foliage on the east ridge.

The park has picnic tables, covered pavilions with barbecue grills, restrooms, showers, a payphone and drinking water. The four tent sites at the campground (tent sites by permit $5; 8am Friday to noon Wednesday) are well tended, but don't have much privacy. Permits must be obtained in advance. Be sure to bring waterproof gear; rains are frequent at this elevation. There's a resident caretaker by the front gate, which is locked at night.

To get to the park from Honolulu, take exit 13A 'Aiea off Hwy 78 onto Moanalua Rd. Turn right onto 'Aiea Heights Dr at the third traffic light. The road winds up through a residential area for more than 2.5 miles to the park. From downtown Honolulu, bus 11 ('Aiea Heights; 35 minutes, hourly) stops about 1.3 miles downhill from the park's entrance.

Island Insights

In ancient times, *kahuna lapaʻau* (herbalist healers) used hundreds of medicinal plants that grew on the grounds surrounding a Hawaiian heiau (temple). Among the plants were *noni,* whose pungent yellow fruits were used to treat heart disease; *kukui,* the nuts of which are an effective laxative; and *ti* leaves, which were wrapped around a sick person to break a fever. Not only did the herbs have curative value, but the heiau was believed to possess life-giving energy that could be channeled by the kahuna.

Eating

Locally Kamehameha Hwy has numerous hole-in-the-wall and ethnic eateries.

Forty Niner Restaurant Diner $
(Map p145; ☎808-484-1940; 98-110 Honomanu St, ʻAiea; mains $4-9; ⊙7am-8pm Mon-Thu, to 9pm Fri & Sat, to 2pm Sun) Don't judge a book by its cover. This little 1940s diner may look abandoned, but its old-fashioned saimin (local-style noodle soup) is made with a secret-recipe broth. The garlic chicken and hamburgers aren't half bad either; ask the locals.

Tamura's Poke Seafood $
(Map p145; ☎808-488-7444; http://tamuras-finewine.com; 98-302 Kamehameha Hwy, Aiea; poke per pound $8-16; ⊙9.30am-9pm Mon-Sat, to 8pm Sun) The sign may read Tamura's Fine Wine & Liquor, but what you're really here for is the huge selection of tasty *poke,* claimed by many to be the best on the island. It's strictly takeout, so pick some up on the way to the beach.

Alley Restaurant Bar & Grill Hawaiian $$
(Map p145; ☎808-486-3499; www.aieabowl.com; 99-115 ʻAiea Heights Dr; breakfast $5-10, mains $9-17; ⊙7am-9:30pm Sun-Wed, to 10pm Thu-Sat) A bowling-alley-attached restaurant seems an unlikely place to get great food, but that's what makes it so fun. You can dig into a scrumptious *furikake ʻahi*

sandwich with supercrispy fries, or Asian braised pork with brown rice, and then bowl a few rounds. Head to Tasty Tuesday for a $42 five-course tasting menu! There is a full bar available.

Buzz's Steakhouse Steak $$$
(Map p145; ☎808-487-6465; http://buzzsoriginalsteakhouse.com; 98-751 Kuahoa Pl, Pearl City; mains $18-36; ⊙5-9pm) Located just west of ʻAiea, Buzz's classic island surf-and-turf steakhouse sits atop a bluff off Moanalua Rd, with sunset views of Pearl Harbor. Buzz's salad bar is as popular as the steaks. You will need to make reservations.

🔒 Shopping

Aloha Stadium Swap Meet & Marketplace Market
(Map p145; www.alohastadiumswapmeet.net; 99-500 Salt Lake Blvd, Aiea; adult/child $1/free; ⊙8am-3pm Wed & Sat, 6.30am-3pm Sun) Aloha Stadium's parking lot contains the island's biggest flea market. Don't expect to find any antiques or vintage goods, but there are endless stalls of cheap island-style souvenirs, including Hawaiian-style quilts.

To get here by car, take the H-1 west to Stadium/Halawa exit 1E. **VipTrans** (☎808-836-0317; www.viptrans.com; round trip $14) runs shuttle buses from Waikiki hotels by reservation, every 30 minutes on meet days.

LEEWARD OʻAHU

Kapolei Area

Times they are a-changin' in the southwestern corner of Oʻahu, once the stomping ground of sugarcane plantations and the US Navy. You'll still find a few run-down beach houses, but this is the fastest-growing residential area on the island today, with housing and super megamarts on the build. If you're looking for activities, scattered about are a water park, a go-kart track, a Sunday railroad and an old plantation living-history village. Plan ahead if you day-trip out or are stopping en route to the Ko Olina resorts; though it's less than a 10-mile drive from Honolulu, rush-hour traffic through established Waipahu, beachfront 'Ewa and suburban Kapolei is a real slow go.

Beaches

'Ewa Beach Park   Beach
(Map p150; 91-050 Fort Weaver Rd) A huge grassy lawn and sizable pavilion attract large Hawaiian families to this pleasant western beachfront on weekends. There's always a spare table or two for a picnic, and a good view of Honolulu from the spit of sand.

Sights & Activities

Hawaii's Plantation Village   Museum
(Map p150; ☏ 808-677-0110; www.hawaiiplantationvillage.org; Waipahu Cultural Garden Park, 94-695 Waipahu St; 90min tours adult/child 4-11yr $13/5; ⊙ tours hourly 10am-2pm Mon-Sat) Waipahu was one of Oʻahu's last plantation

towns and this outdoor museum tells the story of life on the sugar plantations. Though the village is definitely showing its age, you can still learn plenty about the lives of plantation workers on the 90-minute tour.

Hawaiian Railway   Historic Site
(Map p150; www.hawaiianrailway.com; 91-1001 Renton Rd, 'Ewa; adult/child $12/8; ⊙ 1pm & 3pm Sun) For half a century from 1890 to 1940 a railroad carried sugarcane and passengers from Honolulu all the way around the coast through to Kahuku. The railway closed and the tracks were torn up after WWII and the automobile boom in Hawaii. Thanks to the historical society, trains run again along a segment of restored track between 'Ewa and Kahe Point. The 90-minute round-trip chugs along through sometimes pastoral, sometimes industrial scenery, and past the Ko Olina resorts.

Wet 'n' Wild Hawaii   Amusement Park
(Map p150; ☏ 808-674-9283; www.wetnwild hawaii.com; 400 Farrington Hwy, Kapolei; adult/

Wet 'n' Wild Hawaii
ANN CECIL/GETTY IMAGES ©

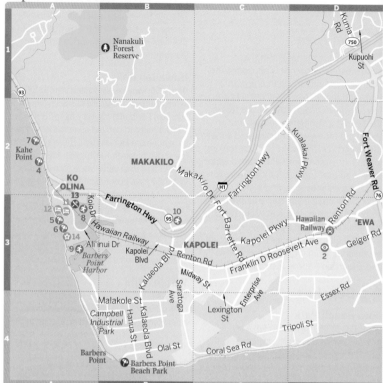

child $48/38; ⏱10:30am-3:30pm Mon, Thu & Fri, to 4pm Sat & Sun) Every temperament from timid to thrill-seeking is served at this 25-acre water park. Float on a lazy river or brave a seven-story waterslide and the football-field-sized wave pool with bodysurfable rides. Such splashy fun doesn't come cheap; parking ($10) and some activities are extra.

Bus 40 takes 1¼ hours to get here from the Ala Moana Center in Honolulu; it runs every half hour between 8:30am and 6:30pm.

🔒 Shopping

Waikele Premium Outlets
Shopping Centre

(Map p142; ☎808-676-5656; www.premium outlets.com/waikele; 94-790 Lumiania Street, Waipahu; ⏱9am-9pm) The mother lode in terms of outlet stores. Lots of big brands are here and the place is so popular that there is direct transport from Waikiki. Prepare to battle the shopper crowds for the deals.

Ko Olina

Four perfect, sunset-facing coves with palm-lined sand and sea as calm as bathwater...is this too good to be true? Well, yes and no. Before this resort went under development, a key feature was missing – the beaches. After a bit of lateral thinking, a lot of construction and a couple of thousand tons of imported soft white sand – voilà, the lagoons were born. The JW Marriott Ihilani and luxury condominiums originally anchored the complex, but the recent addition of Disney's Aulani, its first

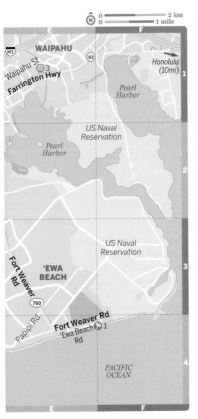

Kapolei & Ko Olina Areas

and serviced lagoon fronts the Four Seasons Resort and Disney Aulani.

Both resorts offer daytime beach-equipment rentals of snorkeling gear and such. The rocks that block the open sea from the lagoons are great places for spotting fish. Keep an eye on the kiddies, though – the current picks up near the opening. At dusk a Disney outrigger canoe enters the cove as a conch shell sounds the end to the day. The nearest free parking is north of the Ihilani. The hotels each charge $30 a day for valet parking, but will validate if you spend at least an equivalent amount at one of their restaurants – easy to do.

The southern two lagoons are probably our favorite. Though they're smaller, the water and the sand are just as beautiful, and there are fewer people to contend with. The nearby free public parking is just before the marina at the end of the drive.

Hawaiian resort, has made quite a splash. By law, the waterfront must be accessible to the public, and these human-made beaches are well worth a visit whether or not you're staying at the hotels. Water sports, golf, a marina and restaurants all add to the upscale attraction. Ko Olina is 25 miles (about 35 minutes) from downtown Honolulu, off the southern side of the Farrington Hwy near Kapolei.

Beaches

Lagoons
Beach

(Map p150; off Ali'inui Dr) A wide, paved recreational path connects all four lagoons, inviting a lazy stroll from beach to beach. Extremely limited free public beach-access parking can be found at each. The largest and most elaborately landscaped

🤸 Activities

Though most facilities are reserved for guests, hotel grounds are open to the public during the daytime. Just wandering around the lush landscaping of Aulani or checking out the saltwater marine-life pools at Four Seasons can be interesting.

The Best...
Family Activities

1 Ko Olina Lagoons (p151)

2 Poka'i Bay Beach Park (p154)

3 Ka'ena Point Trail (p000)

4 Fia Fia Luau (p153)

5 Wet 'n' Wild Hawaii (p149)

6 Hawaiian Railway (p149)

Both have incredible spas and activities desks that book boat tours and water sports.

Ko Olina Marina
Fishing, Cruise

(Map p150; ☎808-853-4300; www.koolina marina.com; 92-100 Waipahe Pl, Kapolei; cruises adult/child 2-13yr from $119/99) The marina will hook you up with snorkeling tours, sunset cruises, whale-watching (December through March) and sport-fishing charters. A five-hour boat tour ranges from $120 to $150 per person.

Ko Olina Golf Club
Golf

(Map p150; ☎808-676-5300; www.koolinagolf. com; 92-1220 Ali'inui Dr, Kapolei; green fees $139-199; ⊙by reservation only) Both the LPGA and the senior PGA tour have held tournaments at this highly acclaimed course and driving range. Mere golf mortals can also enjoy the landscaped oasis of green among the barren brown hills. Check online for special rates and packages; free transportation from Waikiki available.

Sleeping

Vacation rentals around Ko Olina are generally not small studios; they include villas, multibedroom beachfront condos, and golf-course homes. A two-bedroom

place runs between $250 and $500, three bedrooms will set you back $400 to $800 a night. Check **VRBO** (www.vrbo.com) and other agencies.

Aulani
Resort $$$

(Map p150; ☎808-674-6200, reservations 714-520-7001; http://resorts.disney.go.com/ aulani-hawaii-resort; 92-1185 Ali'inui Dr, Kapolei; r from $450; ❄@☎☎) The daily activity list at Aulani is mind-boggling. Tone up at beach-body boot camp, take a Hawaiian craft class or hula the day away. All the while the little ones will be listening to Hawaiian tales at Aunty's House kids club and the older kids will be off on a treasure hunt or tasting a treat at the teen spa.

Four Seasons Resort Oahu at Ko Olina
Resort $$$

(Map p150; www.fourseasons.com; 92-1001 Olani St, Kapolei; ❄@☎☎) Formerly the JW Marriott Ihilani Resort, the newly renovated Four Seasons resort is expected to open in late 2015. Right on the beach, it should be popular with those wanting to avoid the Waikiki scene, but still have all the trappings of top-end luxury.

Eating

Though both the Four Seasons and Aulani have dining outlets, don't expect cheap eats at a resort. There are a few more reasonable places in the Ko Olina Station shopping center, including a small market. Otherwise, to save costs drive a few miles east to Kapolei. A free shuttle scoots you between all places in Ko Olina proper.

Pizza Corner
Pizza $$

(Map p150; ☎808-380-4626; http://pizza-cornerhawaii.com; Ko Olina Station, 92-1047 Olani St; pizzas from $24; ⊙11am-9pm) These innovators are earning raves from locals for their new Hawaiian-style pizzas. We're talking about their Poke Pizza with spicy ahi and *lomilomi* chopped tomato and red onions on a thin-crust hand-tossed base, and the Kalua Pork pizza with mango salsa and chutney. There's takeout and they deliver to the Ko Olina resorts.

Entertainment

Live music is occasionally staged at the hotel bars of both Disney's Aulani and Marriott's Four Seasons.

Fia Fia Luau   Luau
(Map p150; 🎵808-679-4700; http://chiefsielu. com/fia-fia-show/; Marriott's Ko Olina Beach Club, 92-161 Waipahe Pl, Kapolei; adult/child $65/50; ⏱5pm Tue; 👪) Though it's one of the least-known island luau, Fia Fia is among the most entertaining. The Polynesian performances lean heavily toward the Samoan, because that's where the hilarious Chief Sielu Avea, who MCs the evening, hails from. Kids love the preshow games and the fire and knife dances. The buffet's not bad either. Reserve in advance.

Kahe

If few nonislanders make it to southwest O'ahu, fewer still round the corner and follow the Farrington Hwy (Hwy 93) north up the Wai'anae Coast. Touring around here is best done by car and your first potential stop is Kahe. A hulking power plant complete with towering smoke stacks isn't the best neighbor for a beach – but, as they say, you can't pick your neighbors.

 # Beaches

Kahe Point Beach Park   Beach
(Map p150; 92-301 Farrington Hwy) At a rocky point that's popular with snorkelers and anglers. There are also great coastal views, as well as running water, picnic tables and restrooms.

Tracks Beach Park   Beach
(Map p150; off Farrington Hwy (Hwy 93)) Just north of Kahe Point Beach Park and sometimes called Hawaiian Electric Beach, Tracks Beach Park has sandy shores that are good for swimming in the summer and great for surfing in the winter. Its name stems from the train-transported beachgoers who frequented the beach prior to WWII.

Nanakuli

It's hard to find much that qualifies as aesthetic in this seaside town, which is essentially a strip of fast-food joints along the highway. There's so little opportunity

Ko Olina Golf Club

SHANEFF CARL/GETTY IMAGES ©

to experience the culture, you probably won't even realize there's a Hawaiian Homesteads settlement here with one of the largest native populations on Oʻahu.

Beaches

Nanakuli Beach Park
Beach

(Map p142; 89-269 Farrington Hwy) This beach park lines the town in a broad, sandy stretch that offers swimming, snorkeling and diving during the summer. In winter, high surf can create rip currents and dangerous shorebreaks. The park has a playground, sports fields and beach facilities. To get to the beach park, turn *makai* at the traffic lights on Nanakuli Ave.

Maʻili

Beaches

Maʻili Beach Park
Beach

(Map p142; 87-021 Farrington Hwy) This attractive beach has the distinction of being one of the longest stretches of snow-white sand on the island. The grassy park that sits adjacent to the beach is popular with families having weekend barbecues and island-style parties. Like other places on the Waiʻanae Coast, the water conditions are often treacherous in winter, but usually calm enough for swimming in summer. The park has a lifeguard station, a playground, beach facilities and a few coconut palms that provide limited shade.

Sleeping

Maʻili Cove
Condo

(Map p142; ☎808-696-4186; www.mailicove. org; 87-561 Farrington Hwy; 1-bedroom per week $675; ☎✿) Walk out the patio door and right onto the beach if you stay at a one-bedroom Maʻili Cove condo. The two condos for rent are clean, comfortable and eclectically decorated. There is a BBQ available for your use. One-week minimum stays.

Waiʻanae

POPULATION 10,525

The coast's hub for everyday needs, Waiʻanae has more grocery stores and eateries than anyplace else leeward. A nice family beach, a large harbor popular with nautical folks, and an ancient heiau (stone temple) make this a good stop. The town is a little rough around the edges, but new shops and more services keep emerging.

Beaches

Pokaʻi Bay Beach Park
Beach

(Map p142; 85-037 Waiʻanae Valley Rd; 🚻) Protected by Kaneʻilio Point and a long breakwater, the beach is a real beauty. Waves seldom break inside the bay, and

Tropical fruits at a luau
LINDA CHING/GETTY IMAGES ©

Homeless in Paradise

Living on the beach sounds like paradise, right? Even if you have no other choice? Estimates indicate that around 4500 homeless people live on O'ahu. There are shelters and temporary encampments all over the island, but it is thought that one-third of that number reside on the Wai'anae Coast. Locals say this is because there are fewer rich residents and tourists here, and there's a not-in-my-backyard mentality on other parts of the island.

The homeless issue is a complex one. Though many think that mainland states send their homeless to Hawaii with a one-way ticket, the fact is that most of the disenfranchised are local. The skyrocketing housing prices during the real-estate bubble, and woefully inadequate public housing, forced many out into their cars or camps. But the homeless numbers remained relatively steady during the subsequent recession. Contrary to the lone-male stereotype, the homeless of the Wai'anae Coast overwhelmingly live in family groups. Many of those groups have at least one member who is employed. There are also some with drug-addiction problems, some with mental illness, and a few who choose this lifestyle, in the mix.

If citing a reason for the high number of homeless on the coast is challenging, coming up with a solution is even more problematic. In the past, periodic 'clean-ups' in both Waikiki and Wai'anae have forced the homeless to move from concentrations along beach parks and public rights-of-way. But adequate assistance has not always been provided during these actions and officials have been accused of caring more about appearances during international conferences than about the people.

In the past few years, new homeless shelters have opened up and now number 19 in the Wai'anae area. The state has a long-term goal of ending homelessness in Hawaii by 2021. To date, numerous agencies are involved, but little in the way of new monies has been allocated for the project. Only time will tell whether good intentions will lead to constructive solutions in this corner of paradise.

the sandy beach slopes gently. Calm, year-round swimming conditions make it perfect for children, as evidenced by the number of Hawaiian families here on weekends. The park has showers, restrooms and picnic tables, and a lifeguard is on duty daily.

◉ Sights

Ku'ilioloa Heiau   Temple
(Map p142) Along the south side of the bay, Kane'ilio Point is the site of a terraced-stone platform temple, partly destroyed by the army during WWII, then later reconstructed by local conservationists. The site was used in part as a teaching and blessing place for navigation and fishing. Wai'anae was one of the last places on the island to accept Christianity, and the heiau continued to be used after the kapu system was overthrown in 1819.

Today the area around the terraces still affords superb coastal views all the way to Makaha in the north. To get here, start at the parking lot of Poka'i Bay Beach Park, walk straight across the lawn with the outrigger canoes at your right and take the path half a mile out to the point.

Leeward Farmers Markets

Farmers markets in central and leeward Oʻahu are short-and-sweet affairs, sometimes lasting less than an hour. But they can be great, especially in areas where eating options are limited. Most are People's Open Markets; for more, log on to www.honolulu.gov/parks/dprpom. Our favourites include the following:

ʻEwa Beach Park (91-955 North Rd, ʻEwa Beach; ⏱9-10am Fri)

Kapolei Community Park (91-1049 Kamaʻaha Loop, Kapolei; ⏱7-8:30am Sun)

Waiʻanae Farmers' Market (www.waianaefarmersmarket.org; Waiʻanae Mall, 86-120 Farrington Highway; ⏱9am-1pm Sat)

Pokaʻi Bay Beach Park (Map p142; 85-037 Pokaʻi Bay Rd, Waiʻanae; ⏱11-11:45am Fri)

Activities

Hawaii Nautical
Boat Tour

(Map p142; ☎808-234-7245; www.hawaiinautical.com; Waianae Harbor, 85-491 Farrington Hwy; tours adult/child $79/109) Set sail on a deluxe catamaran to look at marine life and go snorkeling on the southwest coast. You can either upgrade to snuba, or opt for a scuba-dive trip, but don't expect to be frolicking with Flipper; this is a Dolphin Smart–certified boat that cares about all of the ocean's inhabitants. There are shuttle rides available from both Ko Olina and Waikiki.

Wild Side Specialty Tours
Whale-Watching, Cruise

(Map p142; ☎808-306-7273; http://sailhawaii.com; Waiʻanae Boat Harbor, 85-371 Farrington Hwy; tours from $175; 🚸) Recognized by the Hawaiian Ecotourism Association, Wild Side Tours caters to the naturalist in you. For respectful snorkeling, take a morning wildlife cruise and stay near the shore, or go further to less-frequented sites with the Best of the West excursion for more dolphin and whale-watching.

Paradise Isle
Water Sports

(Map p142; ☎808-695-8866; 84-1170 Farrington Hwy; rentals per day $15-50; ⏱9am-5pm) Across from the beach, this island shop rents all things water-sport related: surfboards, stand up paddling setups,

kayaks, snorkels...plus it sells local crafts and dispenses free area information.

Hale Nalu Surf & Bike
Water Sports, Cycling

(Map p142; ☎808-696-5897; www.halenalu.com; 85-876 Farrington Hwy; ⏱10am-5pm) This sports shop sells and rents mountain bikes, surfboards, snorkel sets and such.

🍴 Eating

Waiʻanae has numerous fast-food outlets, both chains and walk-up burger and barbecue joints. All are along Farrington Hwy.

Coquitos Latin Cuisine
Latin American $$

(Map p142; ☎808-888-4082; 85-773 Farrington Hwy; mains $8-18; ⏱11am-9pm Tue-Sat, to 4pm Sun) Inside a breezy green plantation-style house that looks like it belongs in the Caribbean or Key West, this Puerto Rican kitchen has hooked locals with its *mofongo* (mashed plantains with garlic and bacon), grilled Cuban sandwiches, shredded beef empanadas and tall *tres leches* (sponge cake) for dessert.

Kahumana Cafe
Health Food $$

(Map p142; ☎808-696-8844; www.kahumana.org; 86-660 Lualualei Homestead Rd; mains $10-15; ⏱11.30am-2pm & 6-8pm Tue-Sat; 🌱) 🌿 Way off the beaten track, this organic farm's cafe inhabits a cool, tranquil hardwood-floored dining room with green-field views. Fork into fresh daily specials, bountiful salads and sandwiches or macadamia-nut pesto pasta with fish or fowl. Don't forget the homemade *liliko'i* (passion fruit) and mango cheesecake. The cafe is about 2 miles inland from Farrington Hwy via Ma'ili'ili Rd.

Sleeping

VRBO (www.vrbo.com) and other vacation-rental consolidators list few options in Wai'anae. Most of the condo rentals on this coast are a few miles further north in Makaha. Otherwise the closest lodgings are the Ko Olina resorts, 10 miles (20 minutes) south.

Information

Wai'anae has several banks and ATMs along the main drag, Farrington Hwy.

Makaha

POPULATION 7750

Big-wave surfing actually got its start here in the 1950s, when Makaha hosted Hawaii's first international surfing competition. Not that you would know it, as the oceanfront highway is blissfully free from the gawking tourists of the North Shore. It is worth a visit for the beautiful sandy beach alone – and the incredible sea views from the area condos. Most services are 3 miles south in Wai'anae. As in other places along this coast, Makaha has its rugged edges. North out of town, the tree-lined beaches are home to a large homeless community.

Beaches

Makaha Beach Park   Beach

(Map p142; 84-369 Farrington Hwy) This beautifully arching beach invites you to spread out your towel and spend the day. Except for weekends and big surf days, you'll likely have the place to yourself. Snorkeling is good during the calmer summer months. There are showers and restrooms, and lifeguards on duty daily. Winter brings big swells that preclude swimming.

In December 1969 legendary surfer Greg Noll rode what was thought to be the biggest wave in surfing history (to that point) at Makaha. Speculation still rages as to exactly how big the monster wave was, but it is commonly accepted

Hawaiian monk seal, Ka'ena Point State Park (p160)

KARL LEHMANN/GETTY IMAGES ©

that it was at least a 30ft face – a mountain of water for the era. The long point break at Makaha still produces waves that inspire big-wave surfers.

Turtle Beach   Beach
(Map p142) Another beautiful, mostly deserted half-mile of sand sits behind the Hawaiian Princess and Makaha Beach Cabana condos. If you're lucky, you may see green sea turtles in the surf early mornings or late evenings. There are sea caves and rocks they use as a cleaning station offshore. Though the area is protected somewhat by Lahilahi Point to the south, be cautious if you have kids – the beach's sandy bottom has a quick and steep drop-off.

Activities

Makaha Valley
Riding Stables   Horseback Riding
(Map p142; ☎808-779-8904; http://makahastables.com; 84-1042 Maunaolu St; rides from $50) Saddle up at this historic ranch for a sunset trail ride with a BBQ dinner and s'mores by the firepit, or an afternoon horseback ramble through the valley as

you learn about Hawaiian culture, including traditional games and crafts. Advance reservations required.

Sleeping

Makaha has the majority of the vacation rentals available on the Wai'anae Coast; check out **VRBO** (www.vrbo.com), **Home Away** (www.homeaway.com), **Airbnb** (www.airbnb.com) and others. Gated beachside condos are the most popular (one bedrooms run from $100 to $200, two bedrooms from $250 to $350). You should be wary of house rentals as they could be in sketchier neighborhoods. Three-night minimums are usually required.

Affordable Oceanfront
Condos   Accommodation Services $$
(www.hawaiibeachcondos.com) Rents condos at both Makaha Cabanas and Hawaiian Princess on Turtle Beach; 30-day bookings available at lower-lying Makaha Surfside.

Inga's Realty,
Inc   Accommodation Services $$
(Map p142; ☎808-696-1616; www.ingasrealty.com; 85-910 Farrington Hwy, Wai'anae) Has

Yokohama Bay (p160), Ka'ena Point State Park

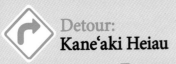

Detour:
Kaneʻaki Heiau

Kaneʻaki Heiau (Map p142; ☎808-695-8174; end of Maunaolu St; ⊙call for hours)
Hidden within a gated residential community in Makaha Valley, this quietly impressive heiau is one of Oʻahu's best-restored sacred sites. Originally an agricultural temple dedicated to Lono, the Hawaiian god of agriculture and fertility, the site was later used as a *luakini*, a temple dedicated to the war god Ku and a place for human sacrifices.

Kamehameha the Great worshipped here and the temple remained in use until his death in 1819. Restorations by the Bishop Museum added two prayer towers, a *kapu* house, drum house, altar and *kiʻi* (deity statues), while the heiau was reconstructed using traditional ohia tree logs and *pili* grass.

To get here, turn *mauka* off Farrington Hwy (Hwy 93) onto Makaha Valley Rd. Just over a mile later, follow Huipu Dr as it briefly curves left, then right. Turn right again onto Maunaolu St, which enters Mauna Olu Estates. Sign in at the security gatehouse (bring your driver's license and car-rental contract).

At the time of writing, public access was closed indefinitely due to vandalism. Call ahead to ask if the site has since reopened.

vacation rentals at Makaha Shores, Makaha Beach Cabanas and at Maʻili Cove further down the coast.

Eating

Basic places to eat are 3 miles south in Waiʻanae. Drive on to Ko Olina (13 miles, 25 minutes) for fine dining.

Makaha to Kaʻena Point

As you travel north of Makaha, you leave development behind. You won't find gas stations, restaurants – or even towns. A couple of beach parks have grassy strips or short stretches of sand, but there can be large numbers of homeless people camped permanently on the beach edge or in the surrounding trees. Though serious trouble is rarely reported, be mindful of petty theft such as car break-ins and bags disappearing while you swim.

Sights

Kaneana Cave   Historic Site
(Map p142) The waves that created this giant stone amphitheater receded long ago. Now the highway sits between the ocean and this cave, about 2 miles north of Keaʻau Beach. Kahuna (priests) performed rituals inside the cave's inner chamber, which was the legendary abode of a vicious shark-man, a shapeshifter who lured human victims into the cave before devouring them. Hawaiians consider it a sacred place and won't enter the cave for fear that it's haunted by the spirits of deceased chiefs.

Makua Valley   Valley
(Map p142) The scenic Makua Valley opens up wide and grassy, backed by a fan of sharply fluted mountains. It serves as the ammunition field of the Makua Military Reservation. The seaside road opposite the southern end of the reservation leads to a little graveyard that's shaded by yellow-flowered be-still trees. This site is all that remains of the valley community that was forced to evacuate during WWII when the US military took over the entire valley for war games.

After several ground fires, and lawsuits charging that not enough environmental-impact studies had been done, live-fire exercises were discontinued in 2011.

Ka'ena Point State Park

You don't have to be well versed in Hawaiian legends to know that something mystical occurs at this dramatic convergence of land and sea in the far northwestern corner of the island. Powerful ocean currents altered by O'ahu's landmass have been battling against each other for millennia here. The watery blows crash onto the long lava-bed fingers, sending frothy explosions skyward. All along this untamed coastal slice, nature is at its most furious and beautiful.

Running along both sides of the westernmost point of O'ahu, Ka'ena Point State Park is a completely undeveloped 853-acre coastal strip with a few beaches. Until the mid-1940s the O'ahu Railway ran up here from Honolulu and continued around the point, carrying passengers on to Hale'iwa on the North Shore. Now the railbed serves as an excellent hiking trail.

Incidentally, those giant, white spheres that are perched on the hillsides above the park belong to the air force's Ka'ena Point Satellite Tracking Station. The satellite tracking station was originally built in the 1950s for use in the USA's first reconnaissance-satellite program, but now those giant white golf balls support weather, early-warning, navigation and communications systems.

 Beaches

Makua Beach
Beach

(Map p142) Way back in the day, this beach was a canoe-landing site for interisland travelers. In the late '60s it was used as the backdrop for the movie *Hawaii,* which starred Julie Andrews. Today there is little here beyond a nice, gated stretch of sand and trees opposite the Makua Military Reservation.

Yokohama Bay
Beach

(www.hawaiistateparks.org; Farrington Hwy (Hwy 930); ☾sunrise-sunset) Some say this is the best sunset spot on the island. It certainly has the right west-facing orientation and a blissfully scenic mile-long sandy beach. You'll find rest rooms, showers and a lifeguard station at the park's southern end. Swimming is limited to the summer and then only when calm. When the water's flat, it's also possible to snorkel. The best spot with the easiest access is on the south side of the bay.

Activities

Ka'ena Point Trail
Hiking, Mountain Biking

(www.hawaiistateparks.org; end of Farrington Hwy (Hwy 930)) An extremely windy, mostly level coastal trail runs along the old railbed for 2.5 miles from Yokohama Bay to Ka'ena Point, then continues another 2.5 miles around the point to the North Shore. Most hikers take the trail from the end of the

Island Insights

Ancient Hawaiians believed that when people went into a deep sleep or lost consciousness, their souls would wander. Souls that wandered too far were drawn west to Ka'ena Point. If they were lucky, they were met here by their *'aumakua* (guardian spirit), who led their souls back to their bodies. If unattended, their souls would be forced to leap from Ka'ena Point into the endless night, never to return.

Ka'ena Point Trail

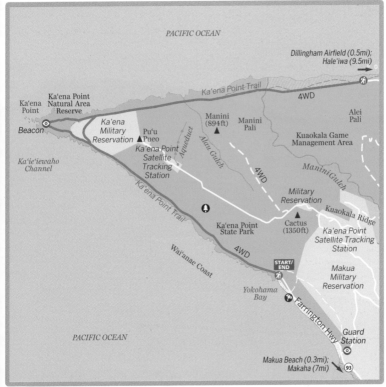

paved road at Yokohama Bay as far as the point, then return the same way.

This hike offers fine views the entire way, with the ocean on one side and craggy cliffs on the other. Along the trail are tidepools, sea arches and blowholes that occasionally come to life on high surf days. In addition to native and migratory seabirds, you might spot Hawaiian monk seals hauled out on the rocks or the sand – but do not approach or otherwise disturb these endangered creatures.

The trail is extremely exposed and lacks any shade, so take sunscreen and plenty of water, and hike during the cooler parts of the day. Be cautious near the shoreline, as there are strong currents, and rogue waves can reach extreme heights.

Kuaokala Trail
Hiking, Mountain Biking

(https://hawaiitrails.ehawaii.gov; off Farrington Hwy (Hwy 930)) Hawaii's Division of Forestry & Wildlife issues advance permits for the hiking and mountain-biking trail system surrounding Ka'ena Point's satellite tracking station. From a dirt parking lot, the dusty 2.5-mile one-way Kuaokala Trail climbs a high ridge into Mokule'ia Forest Reserve. On a clear day you can see Mt Ka'ala (4025ft), O'ahu's highest peak.

Check in with your hiking permit at the station guardhouse opposite Yokohama Bay. Without a permit, the Kuaokala Trail can still be accessed via the Kealia Trail, starting from the North Shore's Dillingham Airfield.

Southeast O'ahu

Cue the *Hawaii Five-0* theme music and pretend to be the star of your own TV show or Hollywood blockbuster on O'ahu's most glamorous stretch of coastline.

It looks a lot like Beverly Hills by the beach, with cherry-red convertibles cruising past private mansions with drop-dead ocean views. But you'll also find more natural thrills that are open to the public on these scenic shores; the snorkeling hot spot of Hanauma Bay, hiking trails to the top of Diamond Head and the wind-blown lighthouse at Makapu'u Point, and O'ahu's most famous bodysurfing and bodyboarding beaches are all just a short ride east of Waikiki.

Save time for this coast's more hidden delights, such as Doris Duke's former estate, filled with Islamic art; a fragrant botanical garden sheltering inside a volcanic crater; and O'ahu's biggest farmers market every Saturday morning.

Hanauma Bay (p175)
ANN CECIL/GETTY IMAGES ©

Southeast Oʻahu Highlights

Hanauma Bay

Hanauma Bay (p175) is a gem. This is undoubtedly one of the world's top spots for inexperienced snorkelers to get an up-close look at spectacular sea life. Protected by a 7000-year-old coral reef that stretches across the width of the bay, snorkelers can paddle about and come face-to-face with an amazingly colorful array of Hawaiian tropical fish. Confident swimmers and scuba divers can head further out.

Diamond Head

Is there a more recognizable backdrop in Hawaii? Named when British sailors thought they'd found diamonds here in 1825, this volcanic tuff cone and crater was used by ancient Hawaiians for human sacrifices. These days, even families with kids in tow can tackle the military-built trail (p168) with tunnels and staircases up to the windy summit for fantastic 360-degree views.

Shangri La

3

Doris Duke, the tobacco heiress who was once nicknamed 'the richest little girl in the world', inherited an immense fortune in 1925 when her father died. Ten years later, on her honeymoon, she fell in love with O'ahu and subsequently built a dazzling oceanfront hideaway and stocked it with priceless Islamic art. Shangri La (p170) can be visited on a guided tour run by the Honolulu Museum of Art.

4

Sandy Beach

Sandy Beach (p178) may be wide and long, but it's no place to frolic. O'ahu's wildest waves for bodyboarders and bodysurfers pound the beach, and if you're not experienced, it's best to stay out of the water. Admiring crowds of awestruck onlookers watch the daredevils being tossed about. Not all the action is in the water though. The grassy strip inland is a favorite spot with hang-gliders and kite-flyers.

5

Makapu'u Point

For stunning views of the deep blue ocean from O'ahu's easternmost tip, walk up the mile-long paved road that is the Makapu'u Lighthouse Trail (p178). Those little islands close to the north are Manana Island (aka Rabbit Island) and Kaohikaipu Island, bird sanctuaries. Look out east and you may see whales in winter, and possibly the islands of Lana'i, Maui and Moloka'i.

Southeast Oʻahu Itineraries

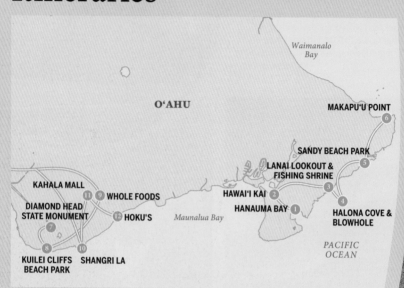

6 MILES

DAY ONE

On your first day it's worth getting out of bed early to beat the hordes of day trippers to gorgeous crescent-shaped ❶**Hanauma Bay** (p175), with its tropical fishbowl waters and coral kingdoms. Scuba divers have the bay's least-trammeled nooks practically all to themselves. After you've sunned yourself on the beach, head inland to ❷**Hawaiʻi Kai** (p173) for lunch with views of Hawaiʻi Kai's marina from waterfront restaurant decks.

In the afternoon, cruise along the Kalanianaʻole Hwy (Hwy 72) to ❸**Lanai Lookout & Fishing Shrine** (p177) stopping at photo-worthy roadside lookouts. When the surf is blasting, you're almost guaranteed a good show at the lava-rock

❹**Halona Cove & Blowhole** (p177). The short cliff-side trek down to Halona Cove is worth the scramble: this gorgeous pocket of sand cameoed in the steamy love scene from the classic flick *From Here to Eternity*.

Even if you're not an expert bodyboarder, you can still get your thrills vicariously at ❺**Sandy Beach Park** (p178) as local bodysurfing and bodyboarding experts test their skills against skull-crushing waves. Finally, trek up toward the lighthouse to ❻**Makapuʻu Point** (p178) from where you can capture panoramic photos. In winter, you might spot migrating whales cruising down below.

28 MILES

DAY TWO

Tackle the summit at ⑦**Diamond Head State Monument** (p169) – it helps to get to the trailhead early on day two for fewer crowds and cooler temperatures. When the surf's up, join the locals getting in a few waves before work at the rocky ⑧**Kuilei Cliffs Beach Park** (p168) in the shadow of Diamond Head. Or come when the cooling tradewinds are blowing and do a little windsurfing.

Keep it local with a healthy made-to-order lunch from ⑨**Whole Foods** (p172), a natural-foods supermarket at Kahala Mall, which specializes in organic grown-in-Hawaii produce – and plenty of aloha! Backtrack west to downtown's Honolulu Museum of

Art, the departure point for an afternoon tour (you've made advance reservations, right?) of Doris Duke's private mansion ⑩**Shangri La** (p170) scenically set on Black Rock.

Not just another shopping mall, eclectic ⑪**Kahala Mall** (p172) packs in boutique shops with authentic island flavor, whether you're searching for an aloha shirt or a sundress splashed with a tropical print.

In the evening, aspire to the lifestyles of the rich and famous with a feast of Hawaii Regional cuisine at ⑫**Hoku's** (p172), Kahala's most romantic restaurant.

Lana'i Lookout (p177)
ANNA GORIN/GETTY IMAGES ©

Discover Southeast O'ahu

DIAMOND HEAD

A dramatic backdrop for Waikiki Beach, Diamond Head is one of the best-known landmarks in Hawaii. The mountain is actually a tuff cone and crater formed by a violent steam explosion long after most of O'ahu's other volcanic activity stopped. Ancient Hawaiians called it Le'ahi and at its summit they built a *luakini* heiau (temple) dedicated to the war god Ku and used for human sacrifices.

Ever since 1825, when British sailors found calcite crystals sparkling in the sun and mistakenly thought they'd struck it rich, the sacred peak has been called Diamond Head. In the early 1900s the US Army began building Fort Ruger at the crater's edge. They also constructed a network of tunnels and topped the rim with cannon emplacements, bunkers and observation posts. Reinforced during WWII, the fort today is a silent sentinel whose guns have never been fired.

Beaches

From Waikiki, bus 14 stops nearby the following beaches once or twice every hour.

Kuilei Cliffs Beach Park
Beach

(3450 Diamond Head Rd) In the shadow of Diamond Head, this rocky beach draws experienced wind-surfers when the tradewinds are blowing. When the swells are up, surfers take over the waves. The little beach has outdoor showers but no other facilities. You'll find paved parking lots off Diamond Head Rd, just east of the lighthouse.

Diamond Head Beach Park
Beach

(3300 Diamond Head Rd) Bordering the lighthouse, this rocky beach occasionally draws surfers, snorkelers and tide-poolers, plus a few picnickers. The narrow strand nicknamed Lighthouse Beach is popular with gay men, who pull off Diamond Head Rd onto short, dead-end Beach Rd, then walk east along the shore to find a little seclusion and (illegally) sunbathe au naturel.

Slopes of Diamond Head volcanic cone
LYNN GAIL/GETTY IMAGES ©

Sights & Activities

Diamond Head State Monument
Hiking

(www.hawaiistateparks.org; off Diamond Head Rd btwn Makapu'u & 18th Aves; admission per pedestrian/car $1/5; ⏱6am-6pm, last trail entry 4:30pm; ♿) The extinct crater of Diamond Head is now a state monument, with picnic tables and a hiking trail up to the 760ft-high summit. The trail was built in 1908 to service military observation stations located along the crater rim. Although a fairly steep trail, it's partly paved and only 0.8 miles to the top, taking about an hour round-trip. Plenty of people of all ages make the hike.

The trail, which passes through several tunnels and up head-spinning staircases, is mostly open and hot, so wear a hat and sunscreen and bring plenty of water. The windy summit affords fantastic 360-degree views of the southeast coast to Koko Head and the Leeward Coast to the Wai'anae Range.

The state park has restrooms, drinking fountains, vending machines and a picnic area. From Waikiki, catch bus 23 or 24; from the closest bus stop, it's about a 20-minute walk to the trailhead. By car, take Monsarrat Ave to Diamond Head Rd and turn right immediately after passing Kapi'olani Community College (KCC).

Eating

KCC Farmers Market
Market $

(http://hfbf.org/markets; parking lot C, Kapi'olani Community College, 4303 Diamond Head Rd; ⏱7:30-11am Sat; 🚭♿) 🌿 At O'ahu's premier gathering of farmers and their fans, everything sold is locally made or grown and has a loyal following, from Nalo greens to Kahuku shrimp and corn. Restaurants and vendors sell all kinds of tasty takeout meals, with Hawaii coffee brewed fresh, and cold coconuts cracked open on demand. Get there early for the best of everything.

The Best...
For Kids

1 Hanauma Bay (p175)

2 Diamond Head State Monument (p169)

3 Bubbie's (p174)

4 Halona Blowhole (p177)

5 Makapu'u Lighthouse (p179)

⭐ Entertainment

Diamond Head Theatre
Theater

(📞808-733-0277; www.diamondheadtheatre.com; 520 Makapu Ave) Opened in 1915 and known as 'the Broadway of the Pacific,' this lovely old theater is the third-oldest continuously running community theater in the USA. Runs a variety of high-quality shows throughout the year, presenting everything from *Mary Poppins* to *Spamalot* to *South Pacific*. Also runs acting, dancing and singing classes.

KAHALA

The affluent seaside suburb of Kahala is home to many of Honolulu's wealthiest residents, the island's most exclusive resort hotel and the Waialae Country Club, a PGA tournament golf course. The coastal road, Kahala Ave, is lined with expensive waterfront homes that block out virtually any ocean views. In between the mansions, a few shoreline access points provide public rights-of-way to the beach, but swimming here ain't grand – it's mostly shallow and rocky.

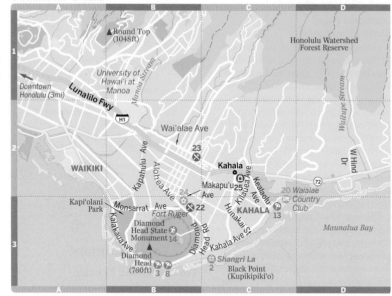

Beaches

Wai'alae Beach Park   Beach
(4925 Kahala Ave) At this picturesque sandy
beach, a gentle stream meets the sea.
Local surfers challenge Razors, a break
off the channel's west side. Swimming
conditions are usually calm, though
not the best due to the shallow reef. A
favorite of wedding parties, the beach
park has shady picnic tables, restrooms
and outdoor showers. The parking lot is
often full.

Sights

Shangri La   Historic Building
(☎ 808-532-3853; www.shangrilahawaii.org;
2½hr tour incl transportation $25; ☉ tours 9am,
10:30am & 1:30pm Wed-Sat, closed early Sep-early
Oct) Celebrity Doris Duke had a lifelong
passion for Islamic art and architecture,
inspired by a visit to the Taj Mahal during
her honeymoon voyage to India at the
age of 23. During that same honeymoon
in 1935, she stopped at O'ahu, fell in love
with the island and decided to build Shangri La, her seasonal residence, on Black
Point in the shadow of Diamond Head.

Over the next 60 years she traveled
the globe from Indonesia to Istanbul,
collecting priceless Islamic art objects.
Duke appreciated the spirit more than
the grand scale of the world wonders
she had seen, and she made Shangri
La into an intimate sanctuary rather
than an ostentatious mansion. One of
the true beauties of the place is the
way it harmonizes with the natural
environment.

Finely crafted interiors open to
embrace gardens and the ocean, and
one glass wall of the living room looks
out at Diamond Head. Throughout
the estate, courtyard fountains spritz
Duke's extensive collection of Islamic
art includes vivid gemstone-studded
enamels, glazed ceramic paintings
and silk *suzanis* (intricate needlework
tapestries). Art often blends with
architecture to represent a theme or
region, as in the Damascus Room, the
restored interior of an 18th-century
Syrian merchant's house.

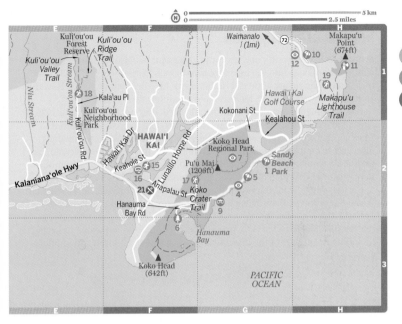

Southeast O'ahu

Shangri La can only be visited on a guided tour departing from downtown's Honolulu Museum of Art, where you'll watch a brief background video first, then travel as a group by minibus to the estate. Tours often sell out weeks ahead of time, so make reservations as far ahead as possible. Children under eight are not allowed.

Secrets of Shangri La

Shangri La is captivating not just for its collection but also for the unique glimpse it provides into the life of tobacco heiress Doris Duke (1912–93), once nicknamed 'the richest little girl in the world.' Like her contemporary Howard Hughes, she was eccentric, reclusive and absolutely fascinating.

Duke's immense fortune, which she inherited after her father died in 1925, when she was just 12 years old, granted her freedom to do as she pleased. Among other things, that meant two very public divorces and a scandalous marriage to an international playboy. While living in Hawaii, she became the first white woman to surf competitively and, naturally, she learned from the best: Olympic gold medalist Duke Kahanamoku and his brothers.

Curious to know more? Watch the HBO movie *Bernard and Doris,* starring Susan Sarandon as Doris Duke and Ralph Fiennes as her butler Bernard Lafferty. Upon her death, Doris appointed her butler as the sole executor of her fortune. She directed it to be used to further her philanthropic projects, including in support of the arts and against cruelty to children and animals.

Sleeping

Kahala Hotel & Resort   Resort $$$
(📞808-739-8888; www.kahalaresort.com; 5000 Kahala Ave; r from $495; ❄@🛜🏊) Facing a private beach, this luxury resort is a favorite of celebs, royalty and other rich-and-famous types who crave Kahala's paparazzi-free seclusion. The grande dame still maintains an appealing island-style casualness: staff who have been working here for decades and guests who return every year know each other by name, and it's that intimacy that really separates it from the Waikiki pack.

A lei greeting at check-in, Hawaiian cultural classes, rental bicycles and stand up paddling lessons are all complimentary, but overnight parking costs $25.

Eating

Whole Foods   Supermarket $
(www://wholefoodsmarket.com/stores/honolulu; Kahala Mall, 4211 Wai'alae Ave; ⏱7am-10pm; 🚗) 🌿 Fill your picnic basket with organic produce and locally made specialty foods, hot and cold deli items, takeout sushi and salads, made-to-order hot pizzas and imported wines.

Hoku's   Pacific Rim $$$
(📞808-739-8760; www.kahalaresort.com; Kahala Hotel & Resort, 5000 Kahala Ave; Sun brunch adult/child 6-12yr $65/33, dinner mains $30-65; ⏱10am-2pm Sun, 5:30-10pm Wed-Sun) Chef Wayne Hirabayashi is revered for his elegant East-West creations such as braised short ribs with avocado tempura and wok-fried market-fresh fish paired with a world-ranging wine list. The Sunday brunch buffet stars a seafood raw bar piled high with all-you-can-eat king-crab legs and a chocolate dessert fountain. Make reservations; collared shirts and slacks for men and evening attire for women are required.

⭐Entertainment

Kahala Mall   Cinema
(📞movie infoline 808-593-3000; www.kahala-mallcenter.com; 4211 Wai'alae Ave) The eight-screen multiplex frequently screens independent art-house and foreign films.

Shopping

Kahala Mall   Mall
(www.kahalamallcenter.com; 4211 Wai'alae Ave; ⏱10am-9pm Mon-Sat, to 6pm Sun) It's no competition for the Ala Moana Center, but this neighborhood mall has a noteworthy mix of only-in-Hawaii shops, including Cinnamon Girl clothing boutique, Reyn Spooner and Rix Island Wear for aloha shirts, and Sanrio Surprises selling collectible, hard-to-find imported Hello Kitty toys and logo gear.

HAWAI'I KAI

Claiming a yacht-filled marina and breezy canals surrounded by mountains, bays and gentle beach parks, this meticulously planned suburb designed by the late steel tycoon Henry J Kaiser (he's the Kai in Hawai'i Kai) is a nouveau-riche scene. All the action revolves around the three shopping centers off Kalaniana'ole Hwy (Hwy 72) and Keahole St. If you're driving around southeast O'ahu, Hawai'i Kai is mostly just a convenient stop for a bite to eat or sunset drinks.

Activities

The marina is flush with tour operators and water-sports outfitters that can hook you up with jet skis, banana and bumper boats, parasailing trips, wakeboarding, scuba dives, speed sailing – whatever will get your adrenaline pumping – but it'll cost you plenty. Up in the mountains of the Ko'olau Range, which makes a cinematic backdrop for Hawai'i Kai, some wonderful, and often overlooked, hiking trails await for you to get your boots on.

Kuli'ou'ou
Ridge Trail   Hiking, Mountain Biking
(https://hawaiitrails.ehawaii.gov) West of town, this 5-mile round-trip route is open to both hikers and mountain bikers. The trail winds up forest switchbacks before making a stiff but ultimately satisfying climb along a ridgeline to a windy sum-

mit offering 360-degree views of Koko Head, Makapu'u Point, the Windward Coast, Diamond Head and downtown Honolulu.

The trail is not always well maintained and may be partly overgrown with vegetation. Start from the Na Ala Hele trailhead sign at the end of Kala'au Pl, which branches right off Kuli'ou'ou Rd, just over 1 mile north of the Kalaniana'ole Hwy (Hwy 72).

Island Divers   Diving, Snorkeling
(☏808-423-8222; www.oahuscubadiving.com; Hawai'i Kai Shopping Center, 377 Keahole St) Five-star PADI operation offers boat dives for all levels, including expert-level wreck dives. If you're a novice, staff can show you the ropes and take you to calm, relatively shallow waters. Snorkelers can ride along on the dive boats ($40 per person, including equipment rental), which visit all sides of the island.

H²O Sports Hawaii   Water Sports
(☏808-396-0100; www.h2osportshawaii.com; Hawai'i Kai Shopping Center, 377 Keahole St) This water sports outfit can hook you up with jet packs – the first commercial operation of H²O jet packs in the US – water skis, banana boats, bumper tubes, parasailing trips, wakeboarding, scuba dives or speed sailing to get your adrenaline running. Just be prepared to pay for it; check online for advance booking discounts.

Koko Crater Trail   Hiking
This nerve-rattling trail is not for anyone with a fear of heights! The fully exposed route leads for almost a mile along an abandoned wooden-tie railbed to reach the summit of Pu'u Mai (1206ft). There's no shade, but don't worry: the panoramic views from atop the extinct crater's rim are worth your sweat.

Turn north off the Kalaniana'ole Hwy (Hwy 72) onto Lunalilo Home Rd, which borders the east side of Koko Marina Center, then turn right onto Anapalau St, which leads into the community park where you'll find the trailhead.

Eating & Drinking

Kokonuts Shave Ice & Snacks
Sweets $

(☎808-396-8809; Koko Marina Center, 7192 Kalaniana'ole Hwy; ⏰10.30am-9pm) After a tough day at Hanauma Bay, do as President Obama has done (attested to by photos of Obama in a Kokonuts Shave Ice T-shirt!) and drop into Kokonuts at Koko Marina for some tasty refreshments. The acai and pitaya bowls are top notch, the shave ice really hits the spot, and the welcome is friendly. Good aloha here!

Bubbie's
Ice Cream $

(☎808-396-8722; www.bubbiesicecream.com; Koko Marina Center, 7192 Kalaniana'ole Hwy; items $1.50-6; ⏰10am-11pm; 👪) Could it possibly get any better than a Bubbie's *mochi* ice cream? We don't think so! There are so many great flavors to try that it will be hard to stop, especially after a day at the beach.

Fatboy's
Hawaiian $

(☎808-394-2373; http://fatboyshawaii.com; Koko Marina Center, 7192 Kalaniana'ole Hwy; mains $7-12; ⏰8am-8pm) Slightly indelicately named, Fatboy's handle says it all. If you're into Hawaiian-style plate lunches, then Fatboy's at Koko Marina ticks all the boxes. The garlic chicken gets rave reviews, but it's the Fatboy's bento that has sold more than 500,000 plates through the Fatboy's O'ahu stores. The full tables are testament to Fatboy's popularity.

Kona Brewing Company
Pub

(☎808-396-5662; www.konabrewingco.com; Koko Marina Center, 7192 Kalaniana'ole Hwy; mains $12-28; ⏰11am-10pm; 👪) On the docks of Koko Marina, this Big Island import is known for its microbrewed beers, especially the Longboard Lager, the Pipeline Porter and the Big Wave Golden Ale. There's live Hawaiian music some nights, and the brewpub's island-style *pupu* (appetizers), wood-fired pizzas, burgers,

Left: Aerial view of Hanauma Bay; **Below:** Koko Crater Botanical Garden (p178)
(LEFT) LYNN GAIL/GETTY IMAGES ©; (BELOW) ANN CECIL/GETTY IMAGES ©

seafood and salads are filling. But it's the beer that makes this place!

🛍 Shopping

Island Treasures at the Marina
Arts, Crafts

(☎808-396-8827; Koko Marina Center, 7192 Kalaniana'ole Hwy; ⊙10am-6pm Mon-Sat, 11am-4pm Sun) Near the waterfront at Koko Marina, this locally owned shop displays high-quality artisan handiwork such as koa wood carvings, etched glass, pottery and island paintings. Handmade soaps, lotions and jewelry make memorable gifts.

ℹ Getting There & Away

From Waikiki, bus 22 stops at Koko Marina Center (30 minutes, every 30 to 60 minutes) en route to Hanauma Bay. Running daily, bus 23 from Waikiki turns inland at Keahole St, stopping near the Hawai'i Kai Towne Center and Hawai'i Kai Shopping Center (35 minutes, every 30 to 60 minutes).

HANAUMA BAY

A wide, curved bay of sapphire and turquoise waters protected by a rugged volcanic ring, Hanauma is a gem. You come here for the scenery, you come here for the beach, but above all you come here to snorkel – and if you've never been snorkeling before, it's a perfect place to start.

From the overlook, you can peer into crystal waters and view the 7000-year-old coral reef that stretches across the width of the bay. You're bound to see schools of glittering silver fish, the bright-blue flash of parrotfish and perhaps sea turtles so used to snorkelers they're ready to go eyeball-to-mask with you. Feeding the fish is strictly prohibited, to preserve the delicate ecological balance of the bay. Despite its protected status as a marine life conservation district, this beloved bay is still a threatened ecosystem, constantly in danger of being loved to death.

175

Island Insights

Once a favorite Hawaiian fishing spot, Hanauma Bay saw its fish populations nearly depleted by the time it was designated a marine life conservation district in 1967. After they were protected instead of being hunted, fish swarmed back by the thousands – and the bay's ecological balance went topsy-turvy. Compounding the problem, as many as 10,000 snorkelers started arriving at Hanauma Bay each day, many trampling on the coral and leaving human waste in the bay. Snorkelers feeding the fish led to a burst in fish populations beyond naturally sustainable levels and radically altered the variety of species. Now here's the good news: since 1990, scientific ecology management programs have begun to bring the bay's natural balance back.

Past the entrance ticket windows is an award-winning educational center run by the University of Hawai'i. Interactive, family-friendly displays teach visitors about the unique geology and ecology of the bay. Everyone should watch the 12-minute video, intended to stagger the crowds and inform you about environmental precautions before snorkeling. Down below at beach level are snorkel and beach gear rental concessions, lockers, lifeguards and restrooms.

Activities

The bay is well protected from the vast ocean by various reefs and the inlet's natural curve, making conditions favorable for **snorkeling** year-round. The fringing reef closest to shore has a large, sandy opening known as the Keyhole Lagoon, which is the best place for novice snorkelers. It's also the most crowded part of the bay and later in the day visibility can be poor. The deepest water is 10ft, though it's very shallow over the coral. Be careful not to step on the coral or to accidentally knock it with your fins. Feeding the fish is strictly prohibited.

For confident snorkelers and strong swimmers, it's better on the outside of the reef, where there are large coral heads, bigger fish and fewer people; to get there follow the directions on the signboards or ask the lifeguard at the southern end of the beach. Because of the channel currents on either side of the bay, it's generally easier getting outside the reef than it is getting back in. Don't attempt to swim outside the reef when the water is rough or choppy. Not only are the channel currents too strong, but the sand will be stirred up and visibility poor.

If you're **scuba diving**, you'll have the whole bay to play in, with crystal-clear water, coral gardens and sea turtles. Beware of currents when the surf's up, especially those surges near the shark-infested Witches Brew, on the bay's right-hand side, and the amusingly named Moloka'i Express, a treacherous current on the left-hand side of the bay's mouth.

Information

Hanauma Bay is both a county beach park and a nature preserve. To beat the crowds, arrive as soon as the park opens, and avoid Monday and Wednesday, both very popular days because the park is closed every Tuesday.

Getting There & Away

Car

Hanauma Bay is about 10 miles east of Waikiki via the Kalaniana'ole Hwy (Hwy 72). Self-parking costs $1. As soon as the parking lot fills (sometimes before noon), drivers will simply be turned away, so get there early or take the bus.

Bus

Bus 22 (the 'Beach Bus') runs between Waikiki and Hanauma Bay (50 minutes, every 30 to 60 minutes). Buses leave Waikiki between approximately 8am and 4pm (4:45pm on weekends and holidays); the corner of Kuhio Ave and Namahana St is the first stop, and the bus fills up quickly. Buses back to Waikiki pick up at Hanauma Bay roughly from 10:45am until 5:20pm (5:50pm on weekends and holidays).

KOKO HEAD REGIONAL PARK

With mountains on one side and a sea edged by bays and beaches on the other, the drive along this coast rates among O'ahu's best. The highway rises and falls as it winds around the eastern tip of the Ko'olau Range, looking down on stratified rocks, lava sea cliffs and other fascinating geological formations. Ah, yes – you've definitely left the city behind at last.

◉ Sights & Activities

Lana'i Lookout   Lookout
 Less than a mile east of Hanauma Bay, roadside Lana'i Lookout offers a panorama on clear days of several Hawaiian islands: Lana'i to the right, Maui in the middle and Moloka'i to the left. It's also a good vantage point for getting a look at lava-rock formations that form the sea cliffs along this coast.

Fishing Shrine   Shrine
(Kalaniana'ole Hwy) As you drive east, make sure to keep your eyes toward the ocean. At the highest point, you should spot a templelike mound of rocks. The rocks surround a statue of Jizō, a Japanese Buddhist deity and a guardian of

fishers. The fishing shrine is often decked out in flower lei and surrounded by sake cups. There is a little roadside pull-off in front of the shrine, about a half-mile east of the Lana'i Lookout.

Halona Blowhole   Lookout
 Just watch where all the tour buses are turning off to find this one. Here, ocean waves surge through a submerged tunnel in the rock and spout up through a hole in the ledge. It's preceded by a gushing sound, created by the air that's being forced out of the tunnel by rushing water. The action depends on water conditions – sometimes it's barely discernible, while at other times it's a real showstopper.

Halona Cove   Beach
Take your lover down for a roll in the sand at this sweet pocket cove made famous in the steamy love scene between Burt Lancaster and Deborah Kerr in the 1953 movie *From Here to Eternity*. You can peer down at the cove from the Halona Blowhole parking lot, from where you'll just be able to make out a path leading down to the beach.

Stairs down from Diamond Head crater (p169)
ANN CECIL/GETTY IMAGES ©

Sandy Beach Park
Beach

(8800 Kalaniana'ole Hwy) Here the ocean heaves and thrashes like a furious beast. This is one of O'ahu's most dangerous beaches, with a punishing shorebreak, powerful backwash and strong rip currents. Expert bodysurfers and bodyboarders spend hours trying to mount the skull-crushing waves, as crowds gather to watch the daredevils being tossed around. Sandy Beach is wide, very long and, yes, sandy, but this is no place to frolic for the inexperienced – dozens of people are injured every year.

Koko Crater Botanical Garden
Gardens

(www.honolulu.gov/parks/hbg.html; end of Kokonani St; ☺9am-4pm, closed Dec 25 & Jan 1) **FREE** According to Hawaiian legend, Koko Crater is the imprint left by the magical flying vagina of Kapo, sent from the Big Island to lure the pig-god Kamapua'a away from Kapo's sister Pele, the Hawaiian goddess of fire and volcanoes. Inside the crater today is a quiet, county-run botanical garden abloom with flowering aloe plants and *wiliwili* trees, fragrant plumeria, spiny cacti and other native and exotic dryland species. Connecting loop trails lead through the lonely garden.

To get here, turn inland on Kealahou St off the Kalaniana'ole Hwy (Hwy 72), opposite Sandy Beach. After about 0.5 miles, turn left onto Kokonani St. From Waikiki, bus 23 stops every hour or so near the intersection of Kealahou and Kokonani Sts, just over 0.3 miles from the garden entrance.

MAKAPU'U POINT

Makapu'u Point and its coastal lighthouse mark the easternmost point of O'ahu. On the north side of the point, a roadside **lookout** gives you an exhilarating view down onto Makapu'u Beach Park, its aqua-blue waters outlined by diamond-white sand and jet-black lava. It's an even more spectacular sight when hang gliders take off from the cliffs above.

From the lookout you can see two offshore islands, the larger of which is **Manana Island** (aka Rabbit Island). Once

Makapu'u Beach Park, and Manana and Kaohikaipu Islands

populated by feral rabbits, this aging volcanic crater now harbors burrowing wedge-tailed shearwaters. Curiously, it looks vaguely like the head of a rabbit with its ears folded back. In front is smaller, flat **Kaohikaipu Island**, another seabird sanctuary.

◎ Sights & Activities

Makapuʻu Point Lighthouse Trail   Hiking
(www.hawaiistateparks.org; off Makapuʻu Lighthouse Rd; ⏰7am-7:45pm Apr-1st Mon in Sep, 7am-6:45pm 1st Tue in Sep-Mar) South of the lookout on the *makai* side of the road, a mile-long paved service road climbs toward the red-roofed Makapuʻu Lighthouse. You can park in the lot just off the main road. Although not difficult, the uphill walk can be hot and extremely windy – take drinks and hang onto your hat!

Along the way stop to take in the stellar coastal views of Koko Head and Hanauma Bay and, in winter, migrating whales who might just happen to be swimming by below. The trail itself is part of the Ka Iwi State Scenic Shoreline.

Makapuʻu Beach Park   Beach
(41-095 Kalanianaʻole Hwy) Opposite Sea Life Park, Makapuʻu Beach is one of Oʻahu's top winter bodyboarding and bodysurfing spots, with waves reaching 12ft and higher. It also has the island's best shorebreak. As with Sandy Beach Park, Makapuʻu is strictly the domain of experts who can handle rough water and dangerous currents. In summer, when the wave action disappears, calmer waters allow swimming. The beach park has restrooms, outdoor showers, drinking water and lifeguards.

Sea Life Park   Theme Park
(☎808-259-2500; www.sealifeparkhawaii.com; 41-202 Kalanianaʻole Hwy; adult/child 3-11yr $30/20; ⏰10:30am-5pm; 🚼) Hawaii's only marine-life park offers a small mixed bag of rundown attractions. The theme-park entertainment features animals that aren't found in Hawaiian waters, though it also maintains a breeding colony of

1 WHAT DREW YOU TO SCUBA DIVING IN HAWAII?
I became a dive master in San Diego, then traveled around the world, ran out of money and ended up in Hawaii. My first job was with a sailing club, and as a part of their crew, I sailed to all of the Hawaiian Islands except Niʻihau.

2 WHAT MAKES DIVING IN HAWAII STAND OUT?
More than anything else, an abundance of green sea turtles. Your chances of seeing a sea turtle while diving are about 85%. Because Hawaii is the most isolated inhabited island chain on earth, it's a unique ecosystem. For example, one third of the endemic fish are found nowhere else in the world.

3 ANYTHING DIVERS SHOULD BE AWARE OF?
The water here is almost always clear, with an average visibility of 80ft to 100ft, but it's a misconception that it's warm. A lot of people find 76°F surprisingly chilly after being immersed underwater for 45 minutes. You'll want to wear a 3mm-thick wetsuit.

4 ADVICE FOR SOMEONE WHO'S NEVER TRIED SCUBA DIVING BEFORE?
If you're nervous, find a dive operation that gives you a swimming-pool session first – that's the safest way to learn.

5 WHAT ARE SOME GREAT DIVE SITES ON OʻAHU?
Hanauma Bay is an excellent dive, but it's logistically challenging. For first-timers, try a shallow reef dive. For experts, Oʻahu is famous for its shipwrecks and also the *Corsair*, a WWII plane sunk over 100ft below the ocean's surface.

green sea turtles, releasing young hatchlings back into the wild every year.

Windward Coast

Welcome to Oʻahu's lushest, most verdant coast, where turquoise waters and light-sand beaches share the dramatic backdrop of misty cliffs in the Koʻolau Range.

Cruise over the *pali* (mountains) from Honolulu and you first reach Kailua, aka adventure central. Many repeat visitors make this laid-back community their island base, whether they intend to kayak, stand up paddle, snorkel, dive, drive around the island or just laze on the sand.

To the south, more beautiful beaches await in Waimanalo. North up the coast, Kamehameha Hwy narrows into a winding two-lane road with a dramatic oceanfront on one side and small rural farms and towns on the other. Along the way there are good local eats, hiking diversions and a couple of major sights. So never mind the frequent tropical rain showers that guarantee everything stays green. Get going: the Windward Coast is only a half hour from Waikiki, but a world apart.

Kualoa Ranch (p208)

Windward Coast Highlights

Kailua Beach Park

A white sandy beach perfect for swimming year-round, Kailua (p193) offers wonderful opportunities for wind-powered watersports like windsurfing or kitesurfing, or people-powered kayaking, outrigger-canoeing or stand up paddleboarding. You'll find plenty of people making the most out of all these activities. The arc of golden sand extends for 4 miles and is made for strolling.

① ...

② Waimanalo Bay Beach Park

You know you're somewhere special when you glance up from dozing on your towel on one of the world's most stunning beaches (p189) to find weddings going on barely 200ft away – both up and down the strip of sand you're lying on. Two weddings! A testament to the beauty of this virtually untouched 5½-mile stretch of paradise that lures you back time and again.

ROBERT CRAVENS/GETTY IMAGES ©

Kahuku's Shrimp Trucks

This is relaxed Hawaiian eating at its best (p216) and a favorite stop on a circle-island tour. We're talking classic food-truck fare made from shrimp raised in local ponds. Chow down on shrimp drowning in delicious, garlicky butter and two-scoop rice at outdoor picnic tables. There are plenty of trucks to choose from and other options if you don't like garlic.

Nu'uanu Pali State Wayside

A drive over the Pali Hwy is a highlight in itself, but make sure to take a time-out at this spectacular viewpoint (p186). From a height of 1200ft you'll discover sweeping vistas of the corrugated Ko'olau Range, Kailua and Kane'ohe Bay. This is where more than 500 O'ahuan warriors plunged to their deaths when chased by the forces of King Kamehameha the Great in 1795.

A Drive up the Windward Coast

The drive (p217) from Kane'ohe along the coast to the North Shore is an experience not to be missed. From the moment you spot the spectacular Kualoa mountains you'll be drawn north. How did the island of Mokoli'i, better known as Chinaman's Hat, attain that amazing shape? You're in the country now, so slow down and keep an eye out for those small treasures you might otherwise miss.

Windward Coast Itineraries

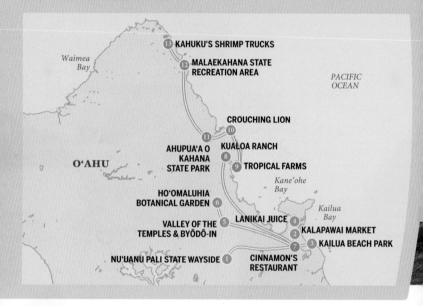

PACIFIC OCEAN

Waimea Bay

⑬ KAHUKU'S SHRIMP TRUCKS

⑫ MALAEKAHANA STATE RECREATION AREA

CROUCHING LION

⑪ ⑩

AHUPUA'A O KAHANA STATE PARK

⑧ KUALOA RANCH

O'AHU

⑨ TROPICAL FARMS

Kane'ohe Bay

HO'OMALUHIA BOTANICAL GARDEN ⑥

Kailua Bay

LANIKAI JUICE ④

VALLEY OF THE TEMPLES & BYŌDŌ-IN ⑤

② KALAPAWAI MARKET

⑦ ③ KAILUA BEACH PARK

NU'UANU PALI STATE WAYSIDE ①

CINNAMON'S RESTAURANT

30 MILES

DAY ONE

As you drive over the mountains from Honolulu on day one, stop at the windy ❶**Nu'uanu Pali State Wayside** (p186) viewpoint and walk a little ways down the Old Pali Hwy for panoramas of the Windward Coast. If you're inspired by the view, you can keep going along the Maunawili Trail, which winds in and out of lush, stream-fed gulches.

Next head to ❷**Kalapawai Market** (p200). Belly up to the espresso bar as you wait for sandwiches made for your picnic at the beach. While there, browse the local foodstuffs and gifts inside this beloved 1930s general store and deli. Don't miss the Windward Coast's most beautiful whites and beach at ❸**Kailua Beach Park** (p193)

with gentle waves ideal for taking a dip. Swimmers, make sure you get here before afternoon breezes kick up (to the delight of windsurfers).

The healthy-minded ❹**Lanikai Juice** (p201) is the best place to hang after surf and sun.

Although its location inside a cemetery is odd, ❺**Valley of the Temples & Byōdō-in** (p204), an exquisite replica of an ancient Japanese temple backed by craggy *pali* (cliffs), is a rare beauty.

Before sunset, take a wander through ❻**Ho'omaluhia Botanical Garden** (p204), with fragrant groves of tropical trees and an artificial reservoir on soft, grassy paths.

DAY TWO

35 MILES

Follow the one-day itinerary, then rise early for a drive through the 'country.' Before you hit the Kamehameha Hwy, though, stop at ⑦ **Cinnamon's Restaurant** (p201), a local classic for breakfast. Ever wonder where the set designers for *Jurassic Park* and *Lost* found such incredible locations? Right here at the historic ⑧ **Kualoa Ranch** (p208), which offers several adventure tours; book ahead.

Snack on free samples of freshly roasted macadamia nuts at the huge ⑨ **Tropical Farms** (p207) shop, filled with made-in-Hawaii products. Everyone pulls off the highway to see the natural rock formation known as the ⑩ **Crouching Lion** (p209).

At ⑪ **Ahupua'a o Kahana State Park** (p210), hike up the hill past an ancient fishing shrine to an overlook with knock-out views of Kahana Bay. Don't miss a stop at ⑫ **Malaekahana State Recreation Area** (p214), the northern Windward Coast's most inviting swimming and snorkeling beach. When the waters are calm and low, you can wade across to an offshore island.

Stop to devour a dozen crustaceans at ⑬ **Kahuku's shrimp trucks** (p216). Dipped in garlic butter, doused in hot-and-spicy sauce or coconut fried – it's your choice.

Byōdō-in temple (p204)
BARON REZNIK/GETTY IMAGES ©

Discover
Windward Coast

PALI HIGHWAY

Slicing through the spectacular emerald Ko'olau Range, the Pali Hwy (Hwy 61) runs between Honolulu and Kailua. True, the H-3 Fwy is quicker, but the Pali wins hands down for beauty and scenic stops. If it's been raining heavily, every fold and crevice in the jagged cliffs will have a fairyland waterfall streaming down it.

Once upon a time, an ancient Hawaiian footpath wound its way perilously over these cliffs. In 1845 the path was widened into a horse trail and later into a cobblestone carriage road. In 1898 the Old Pali Hwy (as it's now called) was built along the same route but was abandoned in the 1950s after tunnels were blasted through the Ko'olau Range.

⊙ Sights & Activities

Nu'uanu Pali
State Wayside   Lookout
(Map p188; www.hawaiistateparks.org; per car $3; ☉sunrise-sunset) About 5 miles northeast of Honolulu, turn as indicated to the popular ridge-top lookout with a sweeping vista of Windward O'ahu from a height of 1200ft. Standing at the edge, Kane'ohe lies below straight ahead, Kailua to the right, Mokoli'i Island and the coastal fishpond at Kualoa Point to the far left. The winds that funnel through the *pali* here are so strong you can sometimes lean against them; it's usually so cool that you'll want a jacket.

Maunawili
Falls Trail   Hiking
(Map p187; http://hawaiitrails.ehawaii.gov) The most popular, and populated, trail on Windward O'ahu ascends and descends flights of wooden stairs and crosses a stream several times before reaching the small, pooling Maunawili Falls amid the tropical vegetation. When the trail forks, veer left; straight ahead is the connector to the much longer **Maunawili Trail**.

Even with the moderate elevation change, this 2.5-mile round-trip is kid-friendly and you'll see lots of families on the trail at weekends. Just be prepared, as the way can be muddy and mosquitoes are omnipresent.

Hiker near Kailua (p192)
/GETTY IMAGES ©

Maunawili Trail System

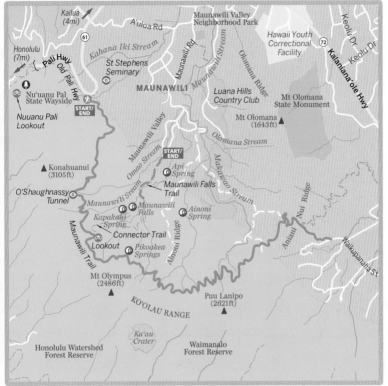

To reach the trailhead, driving east on the Pali Hwy from Honolulu, take the second right-hand exit onto A'uloa Rd. At the first fork, veer left onto Maunawili Rd, which ends in a residential subdivision; look for a gated trailhead-access road on the left. Note that this road is accessible only to pedestrians (and by residents' vehicles); nonresidents may not drive or park along this road. Instead, park along nearby residential streets that aren't gated.

WAIMANALO

POPULATION 3660

Squeezed between the knife-edged Ko'olau Range and the crystal waters of Waimanalo Bay, this little bitty town has O'ahu's longest continuous stretch of beach. Five and a half miles of white sand spreads southeast all the way to Makapu'u Point in southeast O'ahu. A long coral reef protects much of the shore from big waves and the thick stands of ironwood pines can protect you from the sun. Though only 5 miles south of Kailua, you can definitely feel the rural vibe here. Small, hillside farms in 'Nalo, as it's called by locals, grow many of the fresh leafy greens served in Honolulu's top restaurants.

🏖 Beaches

As elsewhere at O'ahu's beaches, don't leave any valuables in your car; petty theft is not uncommon.

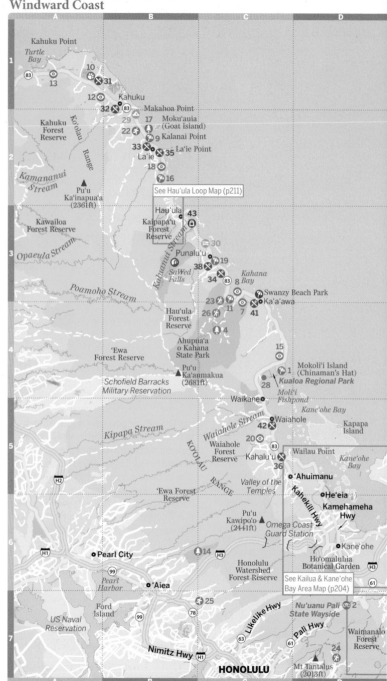

Kahuku Point

Turtle Bay

Kahuku

Makahoa Point

Moku'auia (Goat Island)

Kalanai Point

La'ie Point

La'ie

Kahuku Forest Reserve

Ko'olau Range

Kamananui Stream

Pu'u Ka'inapua'a (2361ft)

Kawailoa Forest Reserve

Opaeula Stream

Poamoho Stream

See Hau'ula Loop Map (p211)

Hau'ula

Kaipapa'u Forest Reserve

Punalu'u

Sacred Falls

Kahana Bay

Swanzy Beach Park

Ka'a'awa

Hau'ula Forest Reserve

Ahupua'a o Kahana State Park

'Ewa Forest Reserve

Pu'u Ka'aumakua (2681ft)

Schofield Barracks Military Reservation

Mokoli'i Island (Chinaman's Hat)

Kualoa Regional Park

Moli'i Fishpond

Waikane

Kane'ohe Bay

Kapapa Island

Kipapa Stream

Waiahole Stream

Waiahole

Wailau Point

Kane'ohe Bay

Waiahole Forest Reserve

Kahalu'u

'Ahuimanu

KO'OLAU RANGE

Valley of the Temples

He'eia

Kamehameha Hwy

Kahekili Hwy

Pu'u Kawipo'o (2441ft)

Omega Coast Guard Station

Kane'ohe

Ho'omaluhia Botanical Garden

'Ewa Forest Reserve

Pearl City

Honolulu Watershed Forest Reserve

See Kailua & Kane'ohe Bay Area Map (p204)

'Aiea

Pearl Harbor

Ford Island

Nu'uanu Pali State Wayside

Likelike Hwy

US Naval Reservation

Nimitz Hwy

HONOLULU

Pali Hwy

Mt Tantalus (2013ft)

Waimanalo Forest Reserve

PACIFIC
OCEAN

Moku
Manu

Mokapu
Peninsula   Mokapu
              Point
Kane'ohe Marine
Corps Air Station

Kapoho
Point

Kailua Bay

Kailua● ●Kailua
          Beach Park
          ●Lanikai
● Olomana *Bellows
           Air Force
           Station*
 72 27   6   *Waimanalo*
               Bay
      ● 5 3 *Waimanalo Bay*
Waimanalo ●   *Beach Park*
   ● 40   ● 37
      39   ● ● 21

See Maunawili Trail
System Map (p187)

Waimanalo Bay Beach Park   Beach

(Map p188; Kalaniana'ole Hwy (Hwy 72)) A wide
forest of ironwoods hides a broad sandy
beach with little development in sight. This
75-acre county park has Waimanalo Bay's
biggest waves and is popular with board
surfers and bodyboarders. Even if you're
not planning to hit the water, just take a
walk along the cream-colored sand and
try to imagine the feeling of old Hawaii.
Countless weddings take place on this
enchanting beach. There are lifeguards,
campsites and restrooms. Entrance is
opposite the Honolulu Polo Club.

Waimanalo Beach Park   Beach

(Map p188; Kalaniana'ole Hwy (Hwy 72)) By the
side of the roadway south of the main
business area, this sloping strip of soft
white sand has little puppy waves that are
excellent for swimming. Manana Island and
Makapu'u Point are visible to the south.
The facilities include a huge grassy picnic
area, restrooms, ball-sports courts, a playground and a rather unappealing campground. Lifeguards are on watch here.

Bellows Field Beach Park   Beach

(Map p188; Tinker Rd, off Kalaniana'ole Hwy
(Hwy 72); ⏰open to the public noon Fri-8am
Mon, gates closed 8pm-6am) With fine
sand and a natural setting backed by
ironwood trees in places, this is a great
beach. The only problem is that the park
is only open to civilians on weekends
(and national holidays) because it fronts
Bellows Air Force Station. The small
shorebreak waves are good for beginning bodyboarders and board surfers.
Lifeguards, showers, restrooms, drinking
water and camping are all available on-
site. The park entrance is just north of
Waimanalo Bay Beach Park.

◎ Sights

Akebono Statue   Statue

(Map p188) Posed in fighting form outside
East Honolulu Clothing Company in
Waimanalo Town Center is one of
Waimanalo's most famous sons. Chad
Rowan was born here in 1969 and went
on to make history by becoming the first

non-Japanese-born sumo wrestler ever to reach *yokozuna*, the highest rank in sumo. At 6ft 8in (203cm) in height and a hefty 514lb (233kg) in weight, Akebono was a *yokozuna* for eight years, winning 11 championships before his retirement in 2001.

Activities

Olomana Golf Links   Golf
(☏808-259-7926; www.pacificlinks.com/oloma-na; 41-1801 Kalaniana'ole Hwy; green fees $100) LPGA star Michelle Wie got her start here, and President Obama regularly swings through these two challenging nine-hole courses on his holidays. Played together they form a regulation 18-hole, par-72 course beneath the dramatic backdrop of the Ko'olau Range. The facilities include a driving range and a restaurant.

Sleeping

There are fewer private house and apartment-suite vacation rentals around Waimanalo than near Kailua; check with consolidators such as **VRBO** (www.vrbo. com) and **Home Away** (www.homeaway.com) and others. All three Waimanalo beach parks have campsites.

Bellows Field
Beach Park   Campground $
(Map p188; tent sites by permit free; ☾noon Fri-8am Mon) The nearby army base guard shack makes this the most secure of area campgrounds. Some of the 40 sites are beneath the ironwood trees, some by the beach. Barbecue grills, showers and restrooms available. Note that buses stop

in front of the entrance road, about 1.5 miles from the beach itself.

Waimanalo Bay Beach Park
Campground $

(Map p188; tent sites by permit free; ⏰8am Fri-8am Wed) The 10 tree-shaded sites are a good choice if Bellows isn't open. It has BBQ grills and restrooms with showers.

Beach House Hawaii
Accommodation Services $$

(☎808-224-6213, 866-625-6946; www.beach-househawaii.com) Has a number of properties in Waimanalo ranging from studios to five-bedroom estates. Check out the website and see what is available.

Eating

There isn't much to Waimanalo town, but a few food trucks usually hang out past the convenience store, on the *mauka* (inland) side of the road.

Serg's Mexican Kitchen Nalo
Mexican $

(Map p188; ☎808-259-7374; 41-865 Kalaniana'ole Hwy; mains $6-11; ⏰10am-8pm) Whether you're heading to the beach or are cruising on a round-island trip, Serg's offers an excellent roadside option for takeout or eat-in Mexican favorites. Try the fish tacos.

Tersty Treats
Seafood $

(Map p188; ☎808-259-3474; 41-1540 Kalaniana'ole Hwy; mains $6-12; ⏰10am-7pm Mon-Thu, to 8pm Fri & Sat, to 5pm Sun) This locally owned fish market allows you to sample a dozen flavors of freshly made *poke,* including old-school luau options such as crab, squid and 'opihi (Hawaiian limpet). Fill your beach cooler with deli faves such as *char siu* pork and seared ahi belly.

Sweet Home Waimanalo
Hawaiian $

(Map p188; ☎808-259-5737; http://sweethome-waimanalo.com; 41-1025 Kalaniana'ole Hwy; mains $8-13; ⏰9:30am-6.30pm Wed-Mon) 🍴 Taste local Waimanalo's back-to-the-earth farm goodness from this family kitchen, where local chicken gets

1 WHAT MAKES HULA SPECIAL?

The hula is so much more than a dance form; it encompasses the history and philosophy of a culture. Even without understanding the words, there is an emotional connection on a cellular level, in my way of thinking. I don't think you can have a true and meaningful view of Hawai'i without experiencing the hula.

2 WHERE DOES YOUR HULA *HALAU* (SCHOOL) PERFORM THROUGHOUT THE YEAR?

We participate in meaningful public celebrations such as 'I Love Kailua Town Party,' the annual Ulupo Heiau celebration and various outer-island celebrations.

3 WHERE ELSE MIGHT VISITORS SEE LOCAL HULA AND TRADITIONAL MUSIC?

There are special programs and hula competitions all over this island. The King Kamehameha Hula Competition is certainly one. Honolulu's World Invitational Hula Festival in November offers not only dance but many classes. I love the Moanalua Gardens gathering in July. Everything that Robert Cazimero or Keali'i Reichel produce is outstanding. The Kalihi-Palama [Queen Lili'uokalani] *keiki* [children] hula competition is the Merry Monarch for children's hula.

4 DO YOU RECOMMEND ANY OF THE TOURIST-ORIENTED SHOWS?

I don't think anything can equal the evening show at the Polynesian Cultural Center. The magnificence of the stage, the huge cast and the authentic dances are beyond the scope of any other venue.

The Battle of Nu'uanu

O'ahu was the lynchpin conquered by Kamehameha the Great during his campaign to unite the Hawaiian Islands under his rule. In 1795, on the quiet beaches of Waikiki, Kamehameha landed his fearsome fleet of canoes to battle Kalanikupule, the *mo'i* (king) of O'ahu.

Heavy fighting started around Puowaina ('Hill of Sacrifice,' now nicknamed Punchbowl), and continued up Nu'uanu Valley. O'ahu's spear-and-stone warriors were no match for Kamehameha's troops, which included a handful of Western sharpshooters. O'ahu's defenders made their last stand at the narrow ledge near the current-day Nu'uanu Pali lookout. Hundreds were driven over the top to their deaths. A century later, during the construction of the Old Pali Hwy, more than 500 skulls were found at the base of the cliffs.

Some O'ahu warriors, including their king, escaped into the forest. When Kalanikupule surfaced a few months later, he was sacrificed by Kamehameha to the war god Ku. Kamehameha's taking of O'ahu marked the last battle ever fought between Hawaiian warriors.

---

sauced with honey and citrus, and fresh corn tortillas wrap lime cream and grilled fish for tacos. Even the island standards get a twist: the *kalua* pork sandwich is topped with bok choy slaw.

 Shopping

Naturally Hawaiian Gallery
Arts, Crafts

(www.patrickchingart.com; 41-1025 Kalaniana'ole Hwy; ⊙9:30am-5:30pm) Since it shares space inside a converted gas station with Sweet Home Waimanalo, you can browse island artists' paintings and handmade crafts while you wait for a kale smoothie. Naturalist Patrick Ching's prints are especially good.

Waimanalo Market Co-op
Market

(☑808-690-0390; www.waimanalomarket.com; 41-1029 Kalaniana'ole Hwy; ⊙9am-6pm Thu-Sun) A local cooperative selling everything from art to kitchenware to fruit and vegetables. Next to Sweet Home Waimanalo.

East Honolulu Clothing Company
Clothing, Souvenirs

(Map p188; www.doublepawswear.com; Waimanalo Town Shopping Center, 41-537 Kalaniana'ole Hwy; ⊙9am-5pm) The striking, graphic one-color tropical prints on the clothing here are all designed and silk screened in-house. This company provides many local hula schools with their costumes. There's plenty of local artwork to peruse as well.

ⓘ Getting There & Away

Waimanalo is about a 35-minute drive (17 miles) from Waikiki via Hwy 61; it's 10 minutes (6 miles) down the coast from Kailua.

Bus 57 travels between Honolulu's Ala Moana Center and Waimanalo (one hour) via Kailua (25 minutes), running every 15 to 30 minutes. It makes stops along the Kalaniana'ole Hwy (Hwy 72) through town. A few continue on to Sea Life Park (five minutes).

KAILUA

POPULATION 38,635

A long, graceful bay protected by a coral reef is Kailua's claim to fame. The nearly 4-mile-long shoreline stretch of ivory sand is made for strolling, and the weather and wave conditions can be just about perfect for swimming, kayaking, windsurfing and kitesurfing. None of this has gone unnoticed. Decades ago expatriates from the mainland bought up cottages crowded into the little neighborly lanes; the ones near the beachfront were often replaced with megahouses. South along the shore lies the exclusive enclave of Lanikai, with million-dollar views – and mansions that may be valued at 10 times that much.

In ancient times Kailua (meaning 'two seas') was a home to Hawaiian chiefs, including briefly Kamehameha the Great after he conquered O'ahu. Today it's the Windward Coast's largest suburban town, where you'll find the vast majority of the coast's restaurants and retail. Eclectic boutiques and independent eateries predominate, but lately more chains have moved in. Many repeat travelers to O'ahu leapfrog over touristy Waikiki (only 15 miles and 30 minutes away) and stay in this laid-back, residential community. It's a great place to pretend you live.

 # Beaches

Kailua Beach Park   Beach
(Map p194) A wide arc of sand drapes around the jewel-colored waters of Kailua Bay, with formidable volcanic headlands bookending either side and interesting little islands rising offshore. It's ideal for long, leisurely walks, family outings and all kinds of aquatic activities. The beach has a gently sloping sandy bottom with usually calm waters; it's good for swimming year-round, especially in the morning. The wind can blow any time but generally kicks up in the afternoon.

Kalama Beach Park   Beach
(248 N Kalaheo Ave) Kalama Beach Park, 1 mile north of Kailua Beach Park on Kalaheo Ave, is the best place to park for a great walk. Climb over the grassy lawn to a much more residential stretch of sand. Weekdays there's hardly a soul besides tan, fit locals walking their dogs and the occasional group of mums with their infants. Restrooms and outdoor shower available. No lifeguards.

Lanikai Beach (p194), with the Mokulua Islands (p195) in the background

/GETTY IMAGES ©

Kailua

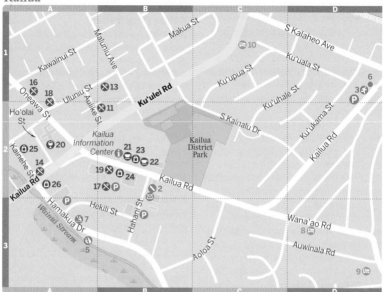

Kailua

Lanikai Beach   Beach

(off Mokolua Dr) Just southeast of Kailua, Lanikai is an exclusive residential neighborhood fronting a gorgeous stretch of powdery white sand overlooking two postcard-perfect islands, known locally as the Mokes. Today the beach is shrinking: nearly half the sand has washed away as a result of retaining walls built to protect the neighborhood's multimillion-dollar mansions. There are 11 narrow public beach-access walkways off Mokulua Dr. There are no bathrooms and no lifeguards.

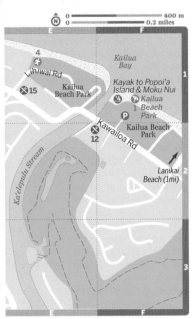

Sights

Note that sights in the nearby Kane'ohe Bay area are also easily accessible.

Ulupo Heiau
State Monument   Temple
(Map p204; www.hawaiistateparks.org; ☉sunrise-sunset) 🅿 **FREE** Rich in stream-fed agricultural land, abundant fishing grounds and protected canoe landings, Kailua was an ancient economic center that supported at least three temples. Ulupo, once bordered by 400 acres of cultivated fishponds and taro fields, is the only one left to visit.

Activities

WATER SPORTS

See those pretty little uninhabited islands off in Kailua Bay? Those are inside a protective reef, making this a great place to pick up a paddle. Kayak and stand up paddle landings are allowed on Popoi'a Island (Flat Island), off the southern end of Kailua Beach Park. Beginner pad-dle boarders practice on the Kaelepulu Stream, in the middle of the beach park, before heading out into the currents.

The magical twin Mokulua Islands, nicknamed 'the Mokes,' lie off Lanikai Beach. Landings are prohibited on the smaller, Moku Iki, a nature reserve. But it's fine to kayak over to Moku Nui, which has a beautiful beach for sunbathing and snorkeling. If you hike around to the back side of the island, there is an ideal 50ft-wide swimming hole the locals call Shark's Cove; just don't tell them that we told you about it.

The northwestern end of Kailua Beach Park is designated a kite- and windsurfing launch zone. Thanks to strong onshore winds, you can raise sail year-round here. Summer tradewinds average 10mph to 15mph, with stronger bursts in spring. Different parts of the bay have different water conditions, some good for jumps and wave riding, others for flat-water sails. Kitesurfing (also called kiteboarding), especially, requires a lot of muscle, stamina and coordination, but all you really need to start is the ability to swim.

Board surfers will find less love on this side of the island. Kalama Beach Park has one of the largest shorebreaks in the bay. When the waves are up, board surfers and bodyboarders can find decent conditions there.

Local outfitters suggest itineraries to match all skill levels for self-rental of kayaks ($49 to $65 per day), paddleboard set-ups ($45 to $60 per day) and surfboards ($30 per day), with beach delivery an option. Lodgings generally have snorkeling gear and bodyboards available free for guest use, but if not, you can rent those, too ($15 to $20 per day). Two-hour, small-group stand up paddle lessons average $100. Guided kayak tours (two/four hours $95/125) include a picnic, and give you time for snorkeling and swimming. Windsurfing lessons ($130) usually provide two hours of training, two hours of sailing. Three-hour private kitesurfing lessons run about $250. Discounts are often available if you book ahead online.

Kailua Sailboards & Kayaks, Inc
Water Sports

(Map p194; 📞808-262-2555; www.kailuasailboards.com; Kailua Beach Center, 130 Kailua Rd; ⏱8:30am-5pm) Good all-purpose outfitter with energetic staff and great kayak tours, near the beach. Lots of options such as kayaking, windsurfing, SUP, surfing and kite-surfing. Free parking, showers, lockers and dressing room on site.

Naish Hawaii
Windsurfing, Kitesurfing

(Map p194; 📞808-262-6068; www.naish.com; 155-C Hamakua Dr; ⏱9am-5:30pm) Owned by the family of one of the sport's local pioneers, Robbie Naish, this is *the* place to go for windsurfing. In addition to wind- and kitesurfing lessons, it also has the gear for rent.

Aaron's Dive Shop
Diving

(Map p194; 📞808-262-2333; www.hawaii-scuba.com; 307 Hahani St; ⏱7am-7pm Mon-Fri, to 6pm Sat, to 5pm Sun) Sea caves, lava tubes, coral gardens and WWII–era shipwrecks can all be explored with this five-star PADI operation that has dives all over the island. Certification also offered.

Twogood Kayaks Hawaii
Kayaking

(Map p194; 📞808-262-5656; www.twogoodkayaks.com; 134-B Hamakua Dr; ⏱9am-6pm Mon-Fri, 8am-6pm Sat & Sun) Focusing on kayaks: take a tour, rent your own, or book an advanced lesson and learn to surf the waves or race in the craft. Snorkel gear and SUPs also available.

HIKING

Ka'iwa Ridge (Lanikai Pillboxes) Trail
Hiking

(Map p204; http://hawaiitrails.ehawaii.gov; off Kaelepulu Dr) Though officially named for Ka'iwa Ridge, this 1.25-mile (one-way), half-hour trek is better known for the several WWII 'pillboxes,' aka concrete bunkers, it passes. The barren trail is steep and often slippery. Make it to the top and you're rewarded with head-spinning views of the Mokulua Islands in Kailua Bay, Lanikai and the Ko'olau Range.

The trailhead is in Lanikai: turn right off A'alapapa Dr onto Ka'elepulu Dr; park uphill just beyond the country club. On the side road across the street, you'll see a trail marker and a dirt track beginning next to a chain-link fence.

Kailua Beach Park (p193)

/GETTY IMAGES ©

Detour:
Likeke Falls

Ready for a hidden waterfall, and maybe even being lucky enough to have it to yourself? The family-friendly **Likeke Falls Trail** winds through a forest of native and exotic trees into the lush Ko'olau Range. It starts out unspectacularly, uphill along a paved maintenance road. Veering left before a water tank, the trail enters the forest, ascending a set of steps alternating with moss-covered rocks and gnarled tree roots. This shady path eventually emerges briefly onto a cobblestone road (part of the Old Pali Hwy) that continues climbing. Keep a sharp eye out for the (often muddy) side trail leading to the right toward the waterfall. You'll do some more forest climbing before you reach the lacy 20ft-high cascade, where often the only sounds are of tumbling water and tropical birdsong. The water is too shallow to take a dip, but you can get your feet wet. Be sure to continue up the short hill past the falls to see some great valley views. You can keep going for about another mile, but you'll have to turn around to return. The 2-mile round-trip to the falls takes about an hour.

Do not attempt this hike if dark clouds are in the sky and rain is forecast; there is the danger of flash floods along the stream. Be aware that this trail accesses a frequently used but informal right of way on private land. While there were no 'Kapu' or 'No Trespassing' signs posted at the time of writing, these could appear at any time. If so, then consider this trail closed to the public. It is illegal (not to mention unsafe) to trespass in Hawaii.

To get to the trail head, en route from Kailua to Kane'ohe, turn off on Kionaole Rd, just west of Kamehameha Hwy (Hwy 83) near the H-3 Fwy junction. The trail starts past a chain-link gate at the uphill end of the Ko'olau Golf Club parking lot, in the furthest corner from the clubhouse.

BIRD WATCHING

The area historically was known for its marshes and you still may see rare water birds in their natural habitat, including the *koloa maoli* (Hawaiian duck), *ae'o* (Hawaiian stilt), *'alae kea* (Hawaiian coot) and *kolea* (Pacific golden plover).

Kawai Nui Marsh   Park
(Map p204; www.kawainuimarsh.com; off Kaha St; ⊘7am-7pm) FREE One of Hawaii's largest fresh-water marshes, Kawai Nui provides flood protection for the town, a habitat for endangered waterbirds, and is also one of the largest remaining fishponds used by ancient Hawaiians. You may see rare birds including the *koloa maoli* (Hawaiian duck), *ae'o* (Hawaiian stilt), *'alae kea* (Hawaiian coot) and *kolea* (Pacific golden plover). Several local groups work to preserve and restore the marsh.

To access the area, park in the lot at the end of Kaha St, off Oneawa St, just over a mile northwest of Kailua Rd.

Segway Hawaii-Kailua   Tour
(Map p194; ☏808-262-5511; www.segwayof-hawaii-kailua.com; Kailua Beach Center, 130 Kailua Rd; tours $59-129; ⊘9am-5pm) Quiet and electric-powered, Segway provides an ecofriendly open-air ride. Take a tour along Kailua Beach, into Lanikai, out to Ulupo Heiau or through Kawanui Marsh.

Festivals & Events

I Love Kailua Town Party   Cultural
(www.lanikailuaoutdoorcircle.org/index/Kailua_Town_Party; Kailua Rd; ⊘Apr) One Sunday in April the whole community turns out for a giant block party, with hula schools and bands performing, local artists selling

WINDWARD COAST KAILUA

wares and local restaurants feeding the masses.

I Love Hula
Cultural

(http://castlefoundation.org/ilovehula; **Kailua Rd**) See a rotating schedule of area hula schools perform the second Sunday of every month at 3pm, behind Long's Drugs in Kailua Town.

 ## Sleeping

A soul-soothing alternative to hectic Waikiki, Kailua has no hotels, but what it does have is O'ahu's biggest selection of vacation-rental houses, cottages, apartment suites and B&B-style rooms in private homes. Note that licensing stopped in 1989 (even then no hot breakfast is allowed without a commercial kitchen), so most of the places are unofficial, whether listed at the local agencies below or with national consolidators such as **VRBO**

(www.vrbo.com) and others. What to expect locally:

○ *'Ohana* (family), or mother-in-law suites, are very common as Kailua rentals. These will have private entrances, but may share walls with the main house. Noise can be an issue, as anywhere on O'ahu; people live close together here.

○ Licensed B&Bs will have off-street parking, other rentals may not (all those we recommend in Kailua do).

○ Unless otherwise noted all have a kitchenette or kitchen and beach chairs, snorkels and beach towels available for guest use.

Manu Mele Bed & Breakfast
B&B $$

(Map p204; ☎808-262-0016; www.manumele. net; 153 Kailuana Place, Kailua; d $110-130; ❄🛜🏊) Just 100 steps from the beach, Manu Mele enjoys a peaceful location west from town. The simple, island-contemporary guest rooms feel light and bright. Creature comforts include private

entrances, Hawaiian quilts, plush seven-layer beds, and a pool available for guest use – very rare. Free wi-fi, beach accessories and complimentary baked goods and fruit on your first morning.

Kailua Guesthouse
B&B $$

(Map p194; ☎808-261-2637, 888-249-5848; www.kailuaguesthouse.com; d $139-159; 🛜)
Not far from downtown, two large apartment studio-style suites feel bright and breezy. Helpful amenities include flat-screen TVs with DVD players, free wi-fi, digital in-room safes and shared washer and dryer access. The owner is an excellent source of local lore. It's a healthy 10-minute walk to the beach. Coffee only provided.

Sheffield House
B&B $$

(Map p194; ☎808-262-0721; www.hawaiisheffieldhouse.com; d $139-169; 🛜🐕) Bring the family: the two private-entrance apartment-suites here welcome kids. The beach is an easy, 10-house walk down the road. And the suitably cottagey decor fits

right in with the lush tropical gardens created by landscape designer and architect owners. Pastries and fruit for the first day included.

Papaya Paradise Bed & Breakfast
B&B $$

(Map p194; ☎808-261-0316; www.kailuaoahuhawaii.com; d incl breakfast from $100; ❄🛜♿) The giant covered patio with comfortable sofas, reading nook and a dining table is more like a living room than a lanai – with views of Mt Olomana. The quiet atmosphere here is best suited to more mature travelers. Rooms are simple, with free wi-fi and a self-catered breakfast. Shared kitchen available.

🍴 Eating

In addition to the eateries that are recommended below, numerous hole-in-the-wall Asian food joints and BBQ drive-ins – heck, lots of restaurants in general – are scattered among the town's mini-strip malls. The grocery stores in town include Whole Foods and Foodland.

Kalapawai Market
Supermarket, Deli $

(Map p194; www.kalapawaimarket.com; 306 S Kalaheo Ave; items $2-12; ⏱6am-9pm) This don't-miss 1930s landmark market near the beach stocks picnic supplies and serves the same fancy, made-to-order sandwiches and market-fresh salads as its in-town sister. Good coffee, too.

Tamura's Poke
Seafood $

(Map p205; ☎808-254-2000; www.tamuras-finewine.com; 25 Kaneʻohe Bay Dr; per lb $7-15; ⏱10:30am-7:45pm) The wine is fine, but you're really here for the *poke*. Tucked into the back of Tamura's Fine Wines & Liquors is a deli with a top *poke* selection. Some say this is the best on the island!

Rai Rai Ramen
Japanese $

(Map p194; ☎808-230-8208; 124 Oneawa St; mains $7-10; ⏱11am-8:30pm Wed-Mon) Look for the red-and-white banner written in Kanji outside this brightly lit noodle shop.

The menu of ramen styles ranges from Sapporo south to Hakata, all with rich broth and topped with tender pork, if you like. The *gyōza* (dumplings) are grilled or steamed bundles of heaven.

Whole Foods
Supermarket $

(Map p194; ☎808-263-6800; www.wholefoodsmarket.com/stores/kailua; Kailua Town Center, 629 Kailua Rd; ⏱7am-10pm; ☐) ⊘ Emphasizing organic, natural and locally sourced food, this supermarket offers deliciously healthy options. Grab a hot meal from the full-service deli – sandwiches, BBQ meats or tacos, anyone? – or graze the pizza, *poke*, sushi and salad bars. Island-made gelato is sold at the coffee kiosk up front. Come for happy-hour drinks and *pupu* at the supermarket's Windward Bar.

Thursday Farmers Market
Market $

(Map p194; http://hfbf.org/markets/markets/kailua; 609 Kailua Rd; ⏱5-7:30pm Thu) An incredible spread of vendors sell not only fruit and veggies but also a bevy of hot meals to take out: organic pizza, Portuguese stew, BBQ, Filipino dishes, Thai curries – you name it. Located in the parking lot by Longs Drugs.

Kalapawai Cafe
Bistro, Deli $$

(Map p194; ☎808-262-2354; www.kalapawaimarket.com; 750 Kailua Rd; dinner mains $14-24; ⏱6am-9pm Mon-Thu, to 9:30pm Fri & Sat, 7am-9pm Sun) A gourmet, self-serve deli by day, after 5pm it transforms into an inviting, eclectic bistro. The eggplant bruschetta and other share dishes are excellent paired with a wine flight (a series of tasting-sized pours). But it's hard to resist the creative, ingredient-driven mains. Dine

Drink and fruit stand, Waiahole (p206)
BRANDON TABIOLO / GETTY IMAGES ©

streetside on the lanai or in the intimate candlelit dining room.

Cinnamon's Restaurant
Breakfast $

(Map p194; ☎808-261-8724; www.cinnamons808.com; Kailua Sq, 315 Uluniu St; mains $7-13; ⏲7am-2pm; 🚹) Locals pack this family cafe decorated like Grandma's house for the airy chiffon pancakes drowning in guava syrup, Portuguese sweet-bread French toast, eggs Benedict mahimahi, curried-chicken-and-papaya salad, and Hawaiian plate lunches. Waits are long on weekends; only the breakfast menu is available Sunday.

Tokuname Sushi Bar & Restaurant
Japanese $$

(Map p194; ☎808-262-8656; www.tokoname hawaii.com; 442 Uluniu St; sushi $5-10, dinner mains $10-16; ⏲4-10pm) Surprisingly good sushi considering the suburban location in Kailua. Daily early-bird and late-night sushi power hour (9pm to 10pm) specials help keep the costs down, too.

Baci Bistro
Italian $$

(Map p194; www.bacibistro.com; 30 Aulike St; mains lunch $10-15, dinner $15-25; ⏲11:30am-2pm & 5:30-10pm Mon-Fri, 5:30-10pm Sat & Sun) Home-grown Italian cooking, where the owner knows most patrons by name. Don't miss the white chocolate mascarpone cheesecake. The ravioli is made fresh daily.

Buzz's
Steak $$$

(Map p194; ☎808-261-4661; http://buzzsoriginalsteakhouse.com; 413 Kawailoa Rd; mains lunch $9-17, dinner $16-38; ⏲11am-3pm & 4:30-9:30pm) Classic mainlander expat territory; beachfront home-owning regulars here definitely get the best service. But the old-school kitschy island decor, surf-and-turf menu (complete with throwback salad bar) and proximity to the beach make it worth the stop. Book ahead, but still expect a wait.

The Best...
Picnic Food To Go

1 **Sweet Home Waimanalo** (p191)

2 **Kalapawai Market** (p200)

3 **Waiahole Poi Factory** (p207)

4 **Whole Foods** (p200)

5 **Tamura's Poke** (p200)

 Drinking

Suburban Kailua does not have a hard-core nightlife. The places we list for drinking are also good for eating.

Lanikai Juice
Cafe

(Map p194; ☎808-262-2383; www.lanikaijuice.com; Kailua Shopping Center, 600 Kailua Rd; ⏲6am-8pm Mon-Sat, 7am-7pm Sun) With fresh fruit gathered from local farmers, this addictive juice bar blends a tantalizing assortment of smoothies with names such as Ginger 'Ono or Kailua Monkey. Early in the morning, local yoga fanatics hang out at sunny sidewalk tables with overflowing bowls of granola topped with acai berries, bananas, blueberries and grated coconut.

Morning Brew Coffee House & Bistro
Cafe

(Map p194; ☎808-262-7770; http://morningbrewhawaii.com; Kailua Shopping Center, 600 Kailua Rd; ⏲6am-8pm Tue-Sat, to 7pm Sun & Mon; 🛜) Baristas at this pleasant cafe cup everything from chai to 'Funky Monkey' mochas with banana syrup. Swing by for an espresso or for bagel breakfasts, hot-pressed panini lunches, and ahi tuna kebabs and wine at dinner.

Kailua Town Pub & Grill
Pub

(Map p194; 808-230-8444; http://kailuatownpub.com; 26 Ho'olai St; 10am-2am Mon-Sat, 7am-2am Sun) This casual Irish pub wannabe has tasty from-scratch Bloody Marys, sports on the TV and a friendly mixed-age crowd. Best burgers in town, too, not to mention the fish and chips.

Shopping

Downtown Kailua has antiques, thrift and island gift stores aplenty, especially around the Macy's on Kailua Rd in the dead center of town. Various art galleries are best visited on the second Sunday afternoon of the month during the **Kailua Art Walk**.

Kailua Shopping Center
Gifts, Books

(Map p194; 600 Kailua Rd) Start your souvenir shopping downtown at this strip mall opposite Macy's department store. Pick up Hawaiiana books and beach reads at **Bookends** (808-261-1996; 9am-8pm Mon-Sat, to 5pm Sun), tropically scented lotions and soaps at **Lanikai Bath and Body** (808-262-3260; http://lanikaibathandbody.

com; 10am-6pm Mon-Fri, to 5pm Sat, to 4pm Sun), or beachy home accents, tote bags and kids' toys at **Sand People** (808-261-8878; www.sandpeople.com; 10am-6pm Mon-Sat, to 5pm Sun).

Mu'umu'u Heaven
Clothing, Homewares

(Map p194; 808-263-3366; www.muumuuheaven.com; 767 Kailua Rd; 10am-6pm Mon-Sat, 11am-4pm Sun) Recycling at its most fabulous: all the fun and funky, tropical-print dresses, skirts, tops and accessories are sewn using at least a little fabric from vintage muumuus. A second set of rooms contains equally colorful and eccentric homewares and original island art, some muumuu-inspired.

Madre Chocolates
Food & Drink

(Map p194; 808-377-6440; http://madrechocolate.com; 20-A Kainehe St; 11am-7pm Tue-Fri, to 6pm Sat) Aficionados will be wowed by these award-winning Hawaiian-made boutique chocolates infused with island flavors – coconut and caramelized ginger, passion fruit, kiawe-smoked sea salt. Kailua is home, but there's a new store in Honolulu's Chinatown.

Hula skirts at a mu'umu'u factory

Island Insights

Offshore in Kaneʻohe Bay, **Moku o Loʻe** (Coconut Island), southeast of Heʻeia State Park, was a royal playground, named for the coconut trees planted there in the mid-19th century by Princess Bernice Pauahi Bishop. During WWII, the US military used it for R&R. Today the Hawaiʻi Institute of Marine Biology occupies much of the island, which you might recognize from the opening scenes of the *Gilligan's Island* TV series.

Lily Lotus — Clothing
(Map p194; ☎808-888-3564; www.lilylotus.com; Suite 102, 609 Kailua Rd; ⏰10am-6pm Mon-Sat, 11am-4pm Sun) Outfit for the yoga lifestyle with breathable and organic clothing from a Honolulu-local designer. You can also buy mats, jewelry and accessories by Lily and other makers.

ℹ Information

Kailua Information Center (☎808-261-2727, 888-261-7997; www.kailuachamber.com; Kailua Shopping Center, 600 Kailua Rd; ⏰10am-4pm Mon-Fri, to 2pm Sat) Retiree-run chamber of commerce center with limited info; good $1 maps. Open occasional Sundays 10am to 1pm.

ℹ Getting There & Around

Outside the morning and evening commutes, it's normally a 30-minute drive between Waikiki and Kailua along the Pali Hwy (Hwy 61), about the same from the airport via the H-3 Fwy.

To/From the Airport

SpeediShuttle (☎877-242-5777; www.speedishuttle.com) Shared-ride shuttle service from Honolulu International Airport.

Bicycle

Avoid parking headaches by cycling around town.

Bike Shop (☎808-261-1553; www.bikeshophawaii.com; 270 Kuʻulei Rd; rentals per day/week from $20/100; ⏰10am-8pm Mon-Fri, 9am-5pm Sat, 10am-5pm Sun) Full-service sales, rental and repair shop. In addition to cruisers, it rents performance street and mountain bikes ($40 to $85 per day).

Hawaii B-Cycle (http://hawaii.bcycle.com; 24hr/30-day pass $5/30; ⏰5am-10pm) Davis Building (767 Kailua Rd); Hahani Plaza (515 Kailua Rd) Kailua's bicycle exchange program was the first in the state. Pay for a pass online or at the kiosk, borrow the shiny-white cruiser bicycle with basket for a quick trip around town, and then return to any B-station.

Bus

Though having a car is most convenient, especially if you're visiting the rest of the Windward Coast, riding buses to, and around, Kailua is possible. Note that stop placement may require more walking than you're used to, and outlying vacation rentals may be difficult or impossible to access. Useful routes:

56 and 57 Honolulu's Ala Moana Center to downtown Kailua (corner Kailua Rd and Oneawa St; 45 to 60 minutes, every 15 minutes); all continue to Waimanalo (25 minutes), some go on to Sea Life Park (30 minutes).

70 Downtown Kailua to Kailua Beach Park (five minutes) and Lanikai (15 minutes), runs only every 90 minutes.

KANEʻOHE BAY AREA

POPULATION 37,070

The state's largest bay and reef-sheltered lagoon, Kaneʻohe Bay stretches from the Mokapu Peninsula north to Kualoa Point. It is largely silted and bad for swimming, although the near-constant tradewinds that sweep across the bay can offer some great sailing opportunities. The extended area has a couple of interesting sights that have day-trip potential. The town

Kailua & Kane'ohe Bay Area

WINDWARD COAST KANE'OHE BAY AREA

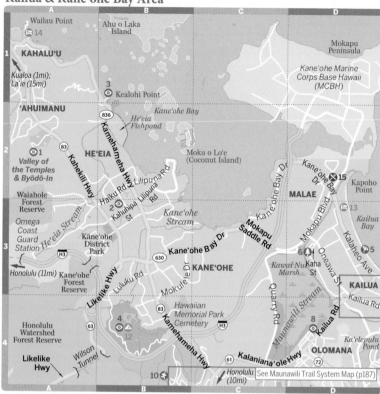

itself is a Marine-base suburb, populated by chain restaurants and stores. It just doesn't pack the eating and sleeping appeal of neighboring town Kailua, which is only 6 miles (15 minutes) south.

◉ Sights & Activities

Valley of the Temples & Byōdō-in   Temple

(Map p204; www.byodo-in.com; 47-200 Kahekili Hwy; temple admission adult/child under 13yr/ senior $3/1/2; ◷9am-5pm) So peaceful and park-like, it might take you a minute to realize Valley of the Temples is an interdenominational cemetery. Up at the base of the Ko'olau Range's verdant fluted cliffs sits Byōdō-in, a replica of a 900-year-old temple in Uji, Japan. The symmetry

is a classic example of Japanese Heian architecture, with rich vermilion walls. The 3-ton brass bell is said to bring peace and good fortune to anyone who rings it.

Ho'omaluhia Botanical Garden   Gardens

(Map p204; ☑808-233-7323; www.honolulu. gov/parks/hbg.html; 45-680 Luluku Rd; ◷9am-4pm) FREE Beneath the dramatic ridged cliffs of the Ko'olau Range, O'ahu's largest botanical garden encompasses 400 acres of trees and shrubs from around the world. Plants are arranged in six regionally themed areas accessible by car. Pick up a map at the small visitor center, located at the far end of Luluku Rd, over 1 mile *mauka* from the Kamehameha Hwy. Call ahead to register for

reef snorkeling and lunch. Free transportation from Waikiki.

Koʻolau Golf Club
Golf

(Map p204; ☎808-236-4653; www.koolau-golfclub.com; 45-550 Kionaole Rd; green fees $55-145) Considered the toughest and one of the most picturesque golf course on Oʻahu. This tournament courses is scenically nestled beneath the Koʻolau Range. For practice, there's a driving range and both chipping and putting greens.

Pali Golf Course
Golf

(☎info 808-266-7612, reservations 808-296-2000; www.honolulu.gov/des/golf/pali.html; 45-050 Kamehameha Hwy; green fees $22-55) This municipal 18-hole hillside course has stunning mountain views, stretching across to Kaneʻohe Bay. Club and handcart rentals are available. Reserve tee times in advance.

🛏 Sleeping

Besides a few noted exceptions below, the nearby town of Kailua is by far a better place to sleep and eat – unless you crave big-name-chain fast food.

free two-hour guided nature walks (10am Saturday and 1pm Sunday).

Heʻeia Pier
Harbor

(Map p204) Just north of, and run in conjunction with, the state park is one of the Windward Coast's only small boat harbors. It's fun just to watch the comings and goings of local boat owners. On weekends they head out to the 'sandbar', a raised spit in the bay that becomes a mooring party place for people to kick back and relax.

Captain Bob's Picnic Sails
Boat Tour

(Map p204; ☎808-942-5077; www.captainbob-picnicsail.com; 4hr cruise $95) Captain Bob's catamaran tour launches at Heʻeia Pier and stops at a sandbar, as well as for

Gyotaku Fish Prints

Gyotaku by Naoki (Map p204; 🖉866-496-8258; http://gyotaku. com; 46-020 Alaloa St, Unit D, Kane'ohe) You'll probably have seen Naoki's magnificent *gyotaku* (Japanese-style fish prints) all over O'ahu in galleries, restaurants and bars, but there's nothing like watching him print up a freshly caught fish in his own studio in Kane'ohe. All the fish he prints are eaten later and the spectacular art on hand is for sale. Call ahead to check the studio is open because Naoki is often out fishing. It's a little hard to find, but well worth the effort.

Ho'omaluhia Botanical Garden
Campground $

(Map p204; Kahua Nui-Makai Campsites; 🖉808-233-7323; https://camping.honolulu.gov; 45-680 Luluku Rd; 3-night campsite permit $32; ☺9am Fri-4pm Mon) The grassy, botanical-garden-surrounded tent sites at the base of the Ko'olau Range are cool and green, fed by frequent mists. With an overnight guard and gates that close, it's among O'ahu's most petty-theft-free campgrounds. Reserve your permit for one of 15 campsites online.

Paradise Bay Resort
Hotel $$

(Map p204; 🖉808-239-6658; http://paradise bayresorthawaii.com; 47-039 Lihikai Dr; studio from $229, 1-/2-bedroom apt incl breakfast $250/280; ✳🛜) The Windward Coast's only resort property is a step above area rentals. Casual, earth-tone contemporary rooms with kitchenettes are just the beginning. Here, bayside breakfasts, a Wednesday Hawaiian-food happy hour, evening mai tais and Hawaiian music, and a Saturday-morning bay cruise are all complimentary. Stand up paddling lessons, kayaking, ecotours and spa services are available, but cost extra.

ℹ️ Getting There & Around

Two highways run north–south through Kane'ohe. The slower but more scenic Kamehameha Hwy (Hwy 836) hugs the coast. Further inland, the Kahekili Hwy (Hwy 83) intersects the Likelike Hwy (Hwy 63) and continues north past the Valley of the Temples. Kane'ohe Marine Corps Base Hawaii (MCBH) occupies the entire Mokapu Peninsula; the H-3 Fwy terminates at its gate. Waikiki is 11 miles (25 minutes) over the *pali*, Kailua is 6 miles (15 minutes) south.

Sights are spread out in the Kane'ohe area, which makes using the bus a challenge, but it does run here.

Route 55 Honolulu's Ala Moana Center to downtown Kane'ohe (one hour, departs every 20 minutes), then continues along Kamehameha Hwy toward Turtle Bay on the North Shore.

Route 56 Connects Kailua and Kane'ohe (20 minutes) every 30 minutes or so.

KAHALU'U & WAIAHOLE

Driving north along the Kamehameha Hwy, you'll cross a bridge near Kahulu'u's Hygienic Store (it's not particularly clean, it just used to be part of Hygienic Dairy). There you'll make a physical and cultural departure from the gravitational pull of Honolulu. Now you've officially crossed into 'the country,' where the highway becomes a two-laner and the ocean shares the shoulder.

◉ Sights

Senator Fong's Plantation & Gardens
Gardens

(Map p188; 🖉808-239-6775; www.fonggar-den.com; 47-285 Pulama Rd, Kahalu'u; adult/child 5-12yr $14.50/9; ☺tours 10:30am & 1pm Sun-Fri) 🌿 A labor of love by Hiram Fong (1907–2004), the first Asian American elected to the US Senate, these flowering gardens aim to preserve Hawaii's plant life for future generations. The lush 700-acre grounds are accessible only on the 1½-hour, 1-mile guided walking tours.

Eating

Mike's Huli Huli Chicken
Food Truck $

(Map p188; ☎808-277-6720; https://sites.google.com/site/mikeshulihulichicken; 47-525 Kamahameha Hwy, Kahalu'u; meals $7-11; ⏰10.30am-7pm) At the convergence of Kamehameha and Kahekili Hwys, a cluster of food trucks have taken up residence. As seen on TV's Food Network, 'Monkey Mike' not only rotisserie roasts birds, but also bakes *kalua* pork and minces *lomilomi* salmon.

Waiahole Poi Factory
Hawaiian $

(Map p188; ☎808-239-2222; http://waiahole-poifactory.com; 48-140 Kamehameha Hwy, Waiahole; meals $7-11; ⏰11am-5pm) 🌿 This family-owned roadside landmark sells *'ono* traditional Hawaiian plate lunches, baked *laulau* and squid, freshly pounded poi and seafood *poke* by the pound, and homemade *haupia* for dessert. Get here early at lunchtime, as food sells out fast.

Ranch, which encompasses most of the area. Coastal He'eia Fishpond is an impressive survivor from the days when stone-walled ponds used for raising fish were common on Hawaiian shores. Boat tours, and other activities, are available both from the ranch and from a local macadamia nut farm.

Beaches

Kualoa Regional Park
Beach

(Map p188; 49-479 Kamehameha Hwy) Family groups gather for weekend picnics on the wide, grassy field that fronts the narrow white-sand beach here. There's good swimming, with a magnificent mountain-scenery backdrop. Stroll south along the beach to **'Apua Pond**, a 3-acre brackish salt marsh on Kualoa Point – a nesting area for the endangered *ae'o* (Hawaiian stilt).

Tours

Tropical Farms
Tour

(Map p188; ☎808-237-1960; www.macnutfarm.com; 49-227 Kamehameha Hwy; tours $20;

KUALOA

Although nowadays there is not a lot of evidence, in ancient times Kualoa was one of the most sacred places on O'ahu. When a chief stood on Kualoa Point, passing canoes lowered their sails in respect. The children of chiefs were brought here to be raised, and it may have been a place of refuge where kapu (taboo) breakers and fallen warriors could seek reprieve from the law. Because of its rich significance to Native Hawaiians, Kualoa is listed in the National Register of Historic Places.

What few sites remain are mostly on, or adjacent to, the omnipresent Kualoa

Ho'omaluhia Botanical Garden
LINDA CHING / GETTY IMAGES ©

⏰9:30am-5pm, tours 11am Mon-Sat) Sure, it's a bit of a kitschy tourist trap, but everything for sale at this family-owned business is homegrown Hawaiian. The open-air store overflows with various flavored macadamia nuts, local jams and sauces, natural remedies and arts and crafts.

Kualoa Ranch   Tour
(Map p188; 📞808-237-7321; www.kualoa.com; 49-560 Kamehameha Hwy; tours adult/child from $27/16; ⏰tours 9am-3pm; 🚼) In the 1800s the Judd family purchased the roughly 4000 acres that make up today's Kualoa Ranch from Kamehameha III and Queen Kalama. It's still O'ahu's largest cattle ranch (with 1500 head), but the family's descendants expanded the business into a slick tourist sight to help support the land.

If you want to see where Hurley built his *Lost* golf course, Godzilla left his footprints and the *Jurassic Park* kids hid from dinosaurs, take the movie tour that covers the many films and TV shows shot in the Ka'a'awa Valley. ATV and horseback rides also mosey along in this busy area. Go a bit more off the beaten trail with the recommended 6WD jungle tour into Hakipu'u Valley's steep slopes covered

with tropical vegetation. Hakipu'u is also where most of the ranch's ancient sites are located; you may have a bit more luck seeing some if you book a private Ali'i tour ($130, four hours). Other options include hula lessons, a guided Hakipu'u hike and a fishpond boat and garden tour. Book all tours at least a couple of days in advance; they fill up. There's a cafe on-site.

Sleeping

Camping is available at the popular (and sometimes noisy) regional park, but most look for vacation rental lodging south in Kailua or further north along the coast.

✖ Eating

Aunty Pat's Café   Cafe $$
(Map p188; www.kualoa.com/amenities/aunty-pats-cafe; 49-560 Kamehameha Hwy; meals $7-15, lunch buffet adult/child 4-11yr $16/11; ⏰7:30am-3pm; 🚼) At Kualoa Ranch's visitor center, this cafeteria lays out a filling midday buffet. Banana pancakes for breakfast and grass-fed beef burgers for lunch are cooked à la carte.

Cyclists, Kualoa Ranch

DANA EDMUNDS / GETTY IMAGES ©

Island Insights

That eye-catching islet you see offshore from Kualoa Regional Park is called Mokoli'i (Little Lizard). In ancient Hawaiian legend, it's said to be the tail of a *mo'o* (lizard spirit) slain by the goddess Hi'iaka and thrown into the ocean. Following the immigration of Chinese laborers to Hawaii, this cone-shaped island also came to be called Chinaman's Hat, a nickname that predominates today, regardless of any political incorrectness.

KA'A'AWA

POPULATION 1325

Here the road tightly hugs the coast and the *pali* move right on in, with barely enough space to squeeze a few houses between the base of the cliffs and the highway. A narrow neighborhood beach used mainly by fishers has a grassy lawn fronted by a shore wall.

⊙ Sights

Crouching Lion   Mountain

(Map p188) The Crouching Lion is a landmark rock formation just north of mile marker 27 on the Kamehameha Hwy. According to legend, the rock is a demigod from Tahiti who was cemented to the mountain during a jealous struggle between the volcano goddess Pele and her sister Hiiaka. When he tried to free himself by crouching, he was turned to stone.

To spot the lion, stand at the Crouching Lion Inn restaurant sign with your back to the ocean and look straight up to the left of the coconut tree at the cliff above.

Eating

Uncle Bobo's   Hawaiian $

(Map p188; ☎808-237-1000; www.unclebobos.com; 51-480 Kamehameha Hwy; mains $5-13; ⊙11am-5pm Tue-Fri, to 6pm Sat & Sun) You don't usually find buns baked from scratch at a Hawaiian BBQ joint, where a local family dishes up smoked brisket and ribs, grills mahimahi tacos and other island faves done right. The cheery yellow dining room is small, but the beach park across the street has ocean-view picnic tables.

KAHANA VALLEY

In ancient times, the islands were divided into *ahupua'a* – pie-shaped land divisions that ran from the mountains to the sea – providing everything Hawaiians needed for subsistence. Modern subdivisions and town boundaries have erased this traditional organization almost everywhere except here, O'ahu's last publicly owned *ahupua'a*.

Before Westerners arrived, the Kahana Valley was planted with wetland taro, which thrived in the rainy climate. Archaeologists have identified the remnants of more than 120 largely inaccessible sites: agricultural terraces and irrigation canals, the remains of a heiau, fishing shrines and numerous *hale* (houses). In the early 20th century the lower valley was planted with sugarcane, which was hauled north to Kahuku via a small railroad. The upper reaches were used during WWII to train soldiers in jungle warfare.

Beaches

Kahana Bay   Beach

(Map p188; www.hawaiistateparks.org; Kamehameha Hwy (Hwy 83)) Although many of Kahana's archaeological sites are inaccessibly deep in the valley, impressive **Huilua Fishpond** (Map p188) is visible from the highway and can be visited simply by walking down to the beach. The beach itself offers mostly safe swimming with a gently sloping sandy bottom. Watch out for the riptide near the bay's southern reef break. There are restrooms, outdoor

209

showers, picnic tables and usually drinking water. Ten roadside campsites (advance state-park camping permit required) don't offer much privacy.

Sights & Activities

Ahupua'a o Kahana State Park
Park

(Map p188; www.hawaiistateparks.org; Kamehameha Hwy (Hwy 83); ☺sunrise-sunset) ✐ FREE In spite of over 40 years of political controversy and failed plans for a living-history village, this park is currently still open to visitors.

Starting near the community center, the gentle, 1.2-mile round-trip **Kapa'ele'ele Trail** runs along a former railbed and visits a fishing shrine and a bay-view lookout, then follows the highway back to the park entrance.

Park before the private residential neighborhood, then walk 0.6 miles further up the valley road to the start of the **Nakoa Trail**, a 3.5-mile rainforest loop that crisscrosses Kahana Stream and bushwhacks through thick vegetation.

Both of these trails can be very slippery and muddy when wet. Don't attempt the Nakoa Trail if any rain is forecast or dark clouds are visible in the sky, due to the danger of flash floods.

The signposted park entrance is a mile north of Crouching Lion Inn. Turn *mauka* past the picnic tables and drive up the valley road to an unstaffed orientation center, where hiking pamphlets with trail maps are available outside by the educational boards.

Island Insights

A *hukilau* was a traditional Hawaiian method of group fishing with drag nets. In the late 1940s, this community celebration was revived for tourists as a local Mormon church fundraiser; this lasted until the early 1960s, when the state started imposing taxes.

PUNALU'U

POPULATION 880

This sleepy seaside community consists of a string of houses and businesses lining the highway.

Beaches

Punalu'u Beach Park
Beach

(Map p188; Kamehameha Hwy (Hwy 83)) At this long, narrow swimming beach, an offshore reef protects the shallow waters in all but stormy weather. Be cautious of strong currents near the mouth of the stream and in the channel leading out from it, especially during high surf. The roadside park has restrooms, outdoor showers and picnic tables.

Sleeping

Check **VRBO** (www.vrbo.com) and other online sites; this part of the coast has some good deals on beachfront vacation rentals.

Pat's at Punalu'u
Condo $$

(Map p188; ☎808-255-9840; 53-567 Kamehameha Hwy; ☺studio/1 bedroom from $100/125; ⊠) An older, seven-story residential condominium complex, Pat's houses spacious, sometimes well-worn, units – all with ocean views. Rentals here are privately owned and listed; some are available through **VRBO** (www.vrbo.com) and through **Paul Comeau Condo Rentals** (☎808-293-2624, 800-467-6215; www.paulspunaluucondos.com).

Eating

Keneke's Grill
Hawaiian $

(Map p188; ☎808-237-1010; www.kenekes.net; 53-138 Kamehameha Hwy; mains $4-10; ☺10am-8pm) Right on the road and with plenty of parking out front, Keneke's comes complete with Christian sayings and quotes on the wall. Hawaiian plate lunches, such as *loco moco* and teriyaki steak, plus burgers and daily specials, fill the menu. Don't miss having shave ice or Dave's ice cream for dessert.

Shrimp Shack
Seafood $$

(Map p188; ☎808-256-5589; http://shrimpshackoahu.com; 53-360 Kamehameha Hwy; meals $10-18; ⏰10am-5pm) The shrimp are fried in garlic and dipped in butter, or you could order mussels or crab legs at this legendary sunny, yellow-painted food truck parked outside Ching's c 1946 general store. You can't miss it roadside – the menu is on a yellow surfboard.

Shopping

Kim Taylor Reece Gallery
Arts

(☎808-293-2000; www.kimtaylorreece.com; 53-866 Kamehameha Hwy; ⏰noon-5pm Mon-Wed, by appointment Thu-Sun) Reece's sepia-toned photographs of traditional Hawaiian *hula kahiko* dancers in motion are widely recognized, but it's his images of Kalaupapa, a place of exile on Moloka'i, that haunt. The artist's gallery inhabits an airy, light-filled two-story house on the *mauka* side of the highway.

HAU'ULA
POPULATION 3470

A small coastal town sitting against a scenic backdrop of hills and majestic Norfolk pines, Hau'ula has a main drag with not much more than a general store, a modern strip mall and a 7-Eleven, but there are hiking possibilities in the area. It is a peaceful, central location on the northeastern coast, 21 miles (40 minutes) from Haleiwa on the North Shore and 24 miles (45 minutes) from Kailua. As you drive by Hau'ula Congregational Church, make sure you look up at the adjacent hill to see the stone ruins of Lanakila Church (c 1853).

Beaches

Hau'ula Beach Park
Beach

(Map p211; Kamehameha Hwy (Hwy 83)) Across the road from the middle of town, this ironwood-shaded beach has a shallow, rocky bottom that isn't too appealing for swimming but does attract snorkelers. It occasionally gets waves big enough for

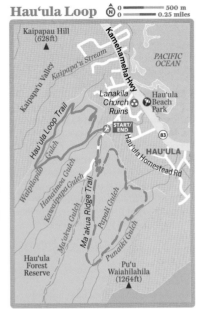

Kaipapau Hill
(628ft)

PACIFIC OCEAN

Kamehameha Hwy

Kaipapau Valley

Kaipapa'u Stream

Lanakila Church Ruins

Hau'ula Beach Park

Hau'ula Loop Trail

START/END

83

HAU'ULA

Hau'ula Homestead Rd

Waipilopilo Gulch

Hanaimoa Gulch

Kawaipapa Gulch

Ma'akua Gulch

Ma'akua Ridge Trail

Papali Gulch

Punaiki Gulch

Hau'ula Forest Reserve

Pu'u Waiahilahila
(1264ft)

local kids to ride. The grassy lawn is popular for family picnics on weekends. The 15 roadside campsites here won't give you a good night's sleep.

Activities

Hau'ula Loop Trail
Hiking

(Map p211; http://hawaiitrails.ehawaii.gov; Ma'akua Rd; ⏰sunrise-sunset) Open to hikers and mountain bikers, the tranquil Hau'ula Loop Trail is a 2.5-mile loop (1½ hours) that clambers through Waipilopilo Gulch onto a ridge over Kaipapa'u Valley. The trail forks off to the right immediately after the road enters the forest reserve, and then rises quickly through a native forest of ohia and hala (screwpine) trees.

Sleeping & Eating

Hale Ko'olau
Apartment $$

(☎808-536-4263, 888-236-0799; www.halekoolau.com; 54-225 Kamehameha Hwy; 1-/2-/3-bedroom apt from $115/205/340; ❄⏰) Beachfronts, lawns, hot tubs and washer-driers are all shared at this wonderfully comfy, slightly timeworn community of bungalows and residential buildings. Prices vary depending on unit size and location (not all have water views); there's even a five-bedroom house (from $370). Hawaiian-family owned and operated.

Papa Ole's Kitchen   Hawaiian $
(808-293-2292; Hau'ula Shopping Center, 54-316 Kamehameha Hwy; mains $5-12; 7am-9pm Thu-Mon, to 3pm Tue) When billing itself as 'da original, with *'ono grinds*,' Papa Ole's doesn't lie. Opt for sauteed veggies or a green salad instead of macaroni and you've made your Hawaiian plate lunch a tiny bit healthier. Dine inside the small cafe, outside at parking-lot picnic tables or take it to-go to the beach park.

LA'IE

POPULATION 4640

Bustling and up-to-date, La'ie is quite a contrast to its rural neighbors. This is the center of the Mormon community in Hawaii, so you are just as likely to see white-collared shirts as board shorts in town. Life here revolves around resident Brigham Young University (BYU) – Hawaii, where scholarship programs recruit students from islands throughout the Pacific. Many students help pay for their living expenses by working as guides at the local Polynesian Cultural Center (PCC), the tourist complex that draws gazillions of visitors each year (second only to Pearl Harbor among O'ahu's attractions).

La'ie is thought to have been the site of an ancient Hawaiian *pu'uhonua* – a place where kapu (taboo) breakers could escape being put to death. And it was a refuge for the Mormon missionaries as well; after an attempt to create a 'City of Joseph' on Lanai failed, the church purchased a 6000-acre plantation here in 1865. In 1919 construction began on a smaller version of the Salt Lake City, UT, temple at the foot of the Ko'olau Range. This dazzling, formal white edifice – open only to practicing Latter Day Saint (LDS, also known as Mormon) church members – stands at the end of a wide boulevard and may be one of the most incongruous sights on O'ahu.

La'ie Beach Park

JULIE THURSTON / GETTY IMAGES ©

Detour:
La'ie Point

Crashing surf, a lava arch and a slice of Hawaiian folk history await at the lookout at La'ie Point. The near-shore island with the hole in it is Kukuiho'olua (Puka Rock). In Hawaiian legend, this island was once part of a giant lizard chopped into pieces by a demigod to stop its deadly attack on O'ahu. From Kamehameha Hwy, head *makai* (seaward) on 'Anemoku St, opposite La'ie Shopping Center, then turn right onto Naupaka St.

Beaches

La'ie Beach Park   Beach
(Map p188; Kamehameha Hwy (Hwy 83)) Located a half-mile south of the main entrance to the Polynesian Cultural Center (PCC), this is an excellent bodysurfing beach, but the shorebreak can be brutal, thus its nickname Pounders Beach. Summer swimming is generally good, but watch for strong winter currents. The area around the old landing is usually the calmest.

Hukilau Beach   Beach
(Map p188; Kamehameha Hwy (Hwy 83)) North of La'ie Shopping Center is a pocket of white sand that's a leisurely place for swimming when summer waters are calm. Just beware any time the surf's up.

◎ Sights & Activities

Polynesian Cultural
Center   Theme Park
(PCC; Map p188; ☑808-293-3333; www.polynesia.com; 55-370 Kamehameha Hwy; adult/child from $40/36; ⏰11.30am-9pm Mon-Sat; ⛹) A nonprofit cultural park owned by the Mormon Church, the PCC revolves around eight Polynesian-themed 'villages' representing Hawaii, Rapa Nui (Easter Island), Samoa, Aotearoa (New Zealand), Fiji, Tahiti and Tonga. The admission price is steep, but this includes frequent village shows and a park-wide boat parade showcasing native dances.

BYU students dressed in native garb demonstrate poi pounding, coconut-frond weaving, handicrafts, music and games. You'll learn a bit more if you add on the Ambassador option, which includes a personal guide. The evening Ali'i Luau show and buffet, another add-on, is one of the island's biggest and best, with some authentic Hawaiian dances and foods. Afterwards you can see Ha: Breath of Life, a Polynesian song-and-dance revue that's partly authentic, partly Bollywood-style extravaganza. Check online for ticket packages; advance discounts are sometimes offered.

Gunstock Ranch   Horseback Riding
(Map p188; ☑808-341-3995; http://gunstock-ranch.com; 56-250 Kamehameha Hwy; trail rides from $89; ⛹) Take a small-group horseback ride across a working ranch at the base of the Ko'olau Range. Options include scenic mosey-alongs, advanced giddy-ups, picnic and moonlight trail rides, plus there's a kiddie experience that includes a 30-minute guide-led ride (ages two to seven, $39).

Eating

La'ie Shopping
Center   Fast Food, Supermarket $
(Map p188; 55-510 Kamehameha Hwy; ⏰most shops closed Sun) Fast-food restaurants, shops and services cluster in this mini-mall, about a half-mile north of the PCC.

Campgrounds

- Waimanalo Bay Beach Park (p191)
- Bellows Field Beach Park (p190)
- Ho'omaluhia Botanical Garden (p206)
- Kualoa Regional Park (p207)
- Friends of Malaekahana (p214)

Foodland supermarket has a takeout deli and bakery, but doesn't sell alcohol and it's closed Sundays (this is Mormon country).

Hukilau Cafe
Hawaiian $

(Map p188; ☏808-293-8616; 55-662 Wahinepe'e St; mains $4-9; ⊙6am-2pm Tue-Fri, 7am-11:30am Sat) In a backstreet in town, this small cafe is the kind of place locals would rather keep to themselves. Local *grinds* – such as Portuguese-sweet-bread French toast and a teriyaki burger lunch – are right on. In case you're wondering, this isn't the restaurant featured in the movie *50 First Dates,* but is said to be the inspiration for it.

MALAEKAHANA STATE RECREATION AREA

You'll feel all sorts of intrepid pride when you discover this wild and rugged coastal area just north of La'ie. A long, narrow strip of sand stretches between Makahoa Point to the north and Kalanai Point to the south with a thick inland barrier of ironwoods.

Beaches

Malaekahana State Recreation Area
Beach

(Map p188; www.hawaiistateparks.org; Kamehameha Hwy; ⊙7am-7:45pm Apr-early Sep, to 6:45pm early Sep-Mar) This long, slightly steep, but relatively uncrowded beach is popular with families. Swimming is generally good here year-round, although there are occasionally strong currents in winter. Bodyboarding, board surfing and windsurfing are also possible. When the tide is low, you can wade over to Moku'auia (Goat Island), a state bird sanctuary about 400yd offshore. It has a small sandy cove with good swimming and snorkeling.

Sleeping

Friends of Malaekahana Campground
Campground $

(Map p188; ☏808-293-1736; www.malaekahana. net; 56-335 Kamehameha Hwy; tent site per person $12, rental units $40-150; ⊙gates open 7am-7pm only; @) ✔ Let the surf be your lullaby and the roosters your wake-up call at Makahoa Point, about 0.7 miles north of the park's main entrance. Here the nonprofit Friends of Malaekahana maintains tent sites by the beach, very rustic 'little grass shacks,' canvas yurts and duplex cabins, providing 24-hour security, outdoor hot showers and internet access at the campground office.

Make reservations at least two weeks in advance; there's usually a two-night minimum stay.

Kalanai Point Campground
Campground $

(Map p188; ☏808-293-1736; www.hawaiistateparks.org; tent sites $18; ⊙8am Fri-8am Wed) Kalanai Point, the main section of the park, is less than a mile north of La'ie. It has picnic tables, BBQ grills, restrooms, showers and good public camping – advance permits are required.

KAHUKU
POPULATION 1780

Kahuku is a former sugar-plantation town. Much of the old sugar mill that operated here until 1996 was knocked down, but the remnants of the smokestack and the old iron gears can be seen behind the post office. The rest of the former mill grounds have been transformed into a small shopping center containing the town's bank, post office, grocery store and eateries. Between here and the start of the North Shore at Turtle Bay Resort (4 miles north), look for roadside markets selling produce, an antique junk shop and craft stands.

◎ Sights

Kahuku Farms   Farm
(Map p188; ☎808-628-0639; www.kahukufarms. com; 56-800 Kamehameha Hwy; tours adult/child 5-12yr $22/15; ⊗11am-4pm Wed-Mon, tours 2pm; 🚹) 🅿 Take a tractor-pulled wagon tour through the taro patch and fruit orchards at this family farm – sampling is included. Then stop in at the gift shop for bath products and foodstuffs made from the farm's bounty. Call for tour reservations.

James Campbell National Wildlife Refuge   Wildlife Reserve
(Map p188; ☎808-637-6330; www.fws.gov/ jamescampbell; off Kamehameha Hwy (Hwy 83); ⊗tours by reservation only) 🅿 **FREE** A few miles northwest of Kahuku town heading toward Turtle Bay, this rare freshwater wetland provides habitat for four of Hawaii's six endangered waterbirds – the 'alae kea (Hawaiian coot), the ae'o (Hawaiian black-necked stilt), the koloa maoli (Hawaiian duck) and the 'alae 'ula (Hawaiian moorhen). During stilt nesting season, which is normally mid-February through mid-October, the refuge is off-limits to visitors.

The rest of the year you may only visit by taking a volunteer-guided tour. Finding the refuge is tricky, so ask for directions when you call ahead for tour reservations.

Kahuku Land Farms   Market
(Map p188; ☎808-232-2202; 56-781 Kamehameha Hwy; ⊗10am-7pm) A number of local farm stands group together just west of the Turtle Bay Resort entrance. Stop here for a fresh-cold coconut water ($3) and to peruse the unexpected selection of fruits, including pitaya (dragonfruit) and pomelo.

Yurt, Malaekahana State Recreation Area

LINDA CHING / GETTY IMAGES ©

✗ Eating

Kahuku is a favorite eating stop on circle-island road trips. Shrimp ponds at the north side of town supply O'ahu's top restaurants, while colorful food trucks that cook up the crustaceans are thick along the highway. Note that not all of these serve shrimp and prawns actually raised locally; some import the crustacean critters from elsewhere. Kahuku's food trucks line up *makai* along Kamehameha Hwy and are usually open from 10am to 6pm or 6:30pm daily (later in summer), depending upon supply and demand. Expect to pay at least $13 per dozen shrimp with two-scoop rice. Wait in line, order your shrimp or prawns the original way – drowning in delicious garlicky butter – or sweet-and-spicy, then chow down at outdoor picnic tables.

Kahuku Grill   Burgers, Seafood $

(Map p188; 📞808-852-0040; http://kahukugrill.com; 55-565 Kamehameha Hwy; mains $8-12; ⏰11am-9pm Mon-Sat; 👪) Serving from a window in one of the old wooden mill buildings near the center of the small town, this outdoor cafe has real aloha spirit. The pancakes are fluffy, the handmade beef burgers juicy and the island-style plates piled high. It's well worth the wait, especially for coconut and macadamia-crusted shrimp with organic Pupukea greens.

Giovanni's   Seafood $$

(Map p188; www.giovannisshrimptruck.com; 56-505 Kamehameha Hwy; plates $13; ⏰10:30am-6:30pm) The original, graffiti-covered shrimp truck that spawned an empire. No longer a lonely little vehicle, Giovanni's is flanked by a covered patio and surrounded by a bevy of other food trucks – serving different meals, smoothies, fro-yo and shave ice.

Romy's Kahuku Prawns & Shrimp   Seafood $$

(Map p188; 📞808-232-2202; www.romyskahuku-prawns.org; 56-781 Kamehameha Hwy; plates $12-17; ⏰10am-6pm) Eat overlooking the aquaculture farm where your giant, and pricey,

Paraglider, Ko'olau Range

Windward Coastal Drive

A day's leisurely drive up the coast to Kahuku – along rocky inlets, under overgrown monkey pod trees, past ancient fishponds and through valleys dotted with small towns and farms – is a must-do on the Windward Coast. Turn north off the Likelike Hwy (Hwy 63) onto Kamehameha Hwy in Kane'ohe. You'll still be in the middle of civilization for a short while, but that way you won't miss sights such as the He'eia Pier and Sunshine Arts Gallery. As you head north from town, the scene quickly turns rural. We list the major sights in this chapter. But take your time, or else you'll miss the smaller treasures – an unattended roadside cart with tropical flowers and an honor jar for payment, a woodcarver's workshop where he turns trees into giant tikis with a chainsaw, tiny beach parks between road and sea, or an orchid nursery where you can stop and ship a gift home. Note that not all the places to eat along the way are worth the stop. We stand by our recommendations.

prawns are raised. Steamed shrimp and whole fish available, too. Try the *pani popo* (Samoan coconut buns) for dessert.

Fumi's Kahuku Shrimp Seafood $$
(Map p188; ☎808-232-8881; 56-777 Kamehameha Hwy; plates $10-13; ⏰10am-7pm) Shrimp is sold from its original truck and just up the road from an added building; both have picnic tables. Alternative eating options include tempura shrimp, fried fish and burgers.

North Shore & Central Oʻahu

Pipeline, Sunset, Waimea… You don't have to be a surfer to have heard of the North Shore; the epic breaks here are known worldwide.

Sure, winter brings giant swells that can reach 15ft to 40ft in height. But there is more to this coast than monster waves. The beaches are gorgeous year-round, perfect for swimming in summer. And there are so many activities besides surfing. Try stand up paddling or kayaking, take a snorkeling or whale-watching tour, go hiking or horseback riding – jump out of an airplane, even.

The laid-back communities here are committed to keeping life low-key and rural – and if that's what you're after, do some exploring among the pineapple and coffee plantations of Central Oʻahu. Slow down. Spend the day cruising, and don't forget to stop at Green World Coffee Farm for a local brew or at Ted's Bakery for chocolate-*haupia* (coconut pudding) pie.

Waimea Bay (p233)

North Shore & Central Oʻahu Highlights

Waimea Bay Beach Park

This picture-perfect beach (p233) at the mouth of the Waimea River has had everyone from Captain Cook's men in 1779 to the Beach Boys singing its praises. Winter brings massive waves that attract surfers and rubber-neckers alike, while in summer the sea can be as tranquil and fl as a lake, perfect for swimming. The lush Waimea Valley offers opportunities for inland explorir

Laniakea Beach

Only 3 miles northeast of Haleʻiwa, Laniakea Beach (p235) is known for its amazing *honu* (green sea turtles). This a basking, not a nesting, location for th *honu*, who seem to have it picked out as a favorite hangout. Volunteers are on hand during the daylight hours to answer questions and to look after the turtles' interests, making sure no one gets too close. Green sea turtle, Laniakea Beach

Stand Up Paddling

Give yourself a good workout, acquire a new skill, have a lot of fun and do some wildlife-watching all at the same time by taking a stand up paddling lesson starting at Haleʻiwa Beach Park (p236). You'll be heading up the Anahulu Stream, a top spot to learn and also a favorite with big green sea turtles (*honu*).

Haleʻiwa

The North Shore's only real town, Haleʻiwa (p235) is the region's de facto surf city and a gauge on wave conditions. If the town is all hustle and bustle, chances are that the ocean is flat. If the swells are breaking, it could take an hour through heavy traffic to make it the 8 miles out to Sunset Beach.

Ted's Bakery

You've got to stop at Ted's (p230), even if it's just for the legendary chocolate-*haupia* (coconut pudding) cream pie that pulls return customers from all over Oʻahu. Ted's is *the* place to eat on the North Shore. This is where surfers load up for breakfast, locals grab a quick snack and holiday-makers dig into plate lunches. You'll be glad you made the trip. Frozen desserts, Ted's Bakery

221

North Shore & Central O'ahu Itineraries

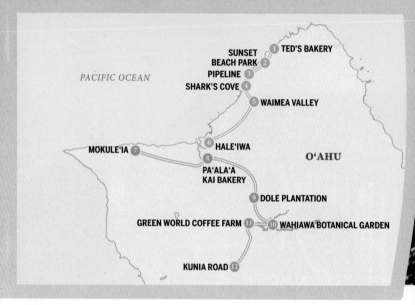

8 MILES

DAY ONE

Grab a late breakfast at ❶**Ted's Bakery** (p230), a classic North Shore eatery. The chocolate-covered glazed doughnuts are sinful, or you could fuel up with a full, hot meal of Spam and eggs. Next head to ❷**Sunset Beach Park** (p228) and cruise down the bike path under the shady trees to nearby sandy Sunset Beach – great for lazing about, sun worshipping and ocean gazing.

Keep heading west. If it's winter and the surf is up, you have to stop at the ❸**Pipeline** (p229) at 'Ehukai Beach Park and see if there are any pro surfers shooting through a barrel. If the water is

calm and the temperature warm, stop for some snorkeling. The reef at ❹**Shark's Cove** (p231) is home to a beautiful array of colorful marine life.

In the afternoon, shake off the sand and head inland to ❺**Waimea Valley** (p234). Wander the trails through the lush tropical foliage of this impressive 1800-acre nature park.

Finish your day by heading to ❻**Hale'iwa** (p235), the only real town on the coast. Check out the shops and galleries before having a meal at one of the many restaurants, such as Cafe Haleiwa.

40 MILES

DAY TWO

Adrenaline junkies should get up early; morning is prime time for skydiving at **7 Mokule'ia** (p242). If you'd prefer someone to actually be steering your flight, take a glider, ultralight or a biplane ride from Dillingham Airfield instead. Afterwards, drive by **8 Pa'ala'a Kai Bakery** (p241) for a 'snow puffy' (flaky chocolate cream puff) to celebrate survival of your adrenaline-filled morning.

For a sticky-sweet overdose of everything pineapple that the kids will love and agriculturally inclined grown-ups are sure to find interesting, head to the **9 Dole Plantation** (p246). Walk it all off with a wander through **10 Wahiawa Botanical Garden** (p247): the chirping of the birds is a peaceful antidote to the pineapple craziness of your last stop.

The perfect place for a caffeine intake, roadside **11 Green World Coffee Farm** (p246) is a coffee extravaganza offering up a great vibe plus free tastings of a wide variety of locally grown beans and flavored brews.

Finish the day with a drive down **12 Kunia Road** (p245), Central O'ahu's most scenic drive. As you head toward the south coast, the island opens up beneath you. Pineapple fields, blue sky and shimmering water fill your field of view.

Maze at Dole Plantation (p246)

Discover North Shore & Central O'ahu

NORTH SHORE

Turtle Bay
POPULATION 410

Idyllic coves and coastal rock beds define the island's northeastern tip, where the North Shore and the Windward Coast meet. Dominating the area is Turtle Bay Resort, with its low-key, view-perfect hotel and restaurants, golf course, condo village and public access to the nearby beaches. So far, it's the only large-scale tourist development on this side of the island, and locals have fought to keep it that way. Massive expansion plans have been scaled back to just 25% of original proposals, but whether even that will go through is still in question.

Beaches

Kuilima Cove   Beach
(Map p226; [icon]) Just east of the Turtle Bay Resort on Kuilima Point is beautiful little Kuilima Cove and its perfect, protected **Bayview Beach**. On the bay's right-hand side is an outer reef that not only knocks down the waves but facilitates great snorkeling in summer – and, in winter, some moderate surf. Rent bodyboards, snorkel sets and beach gear at the resort's on-site Sand Bar.

Kaihalulu Beach   Beach
(Map p226) A mile's walk along the beach east of Kuilima Cove is this beautiful, curved, white-sand beach backed by ironwoods. The rocky bottom makes for poor swimming, but the shoreline attracts morning beachcombers. Continue another mile east, detouring up onto the bluff by the golf course, to reach scenic **Kahuku Point**, where fishers cast throw-nets and pole-fish from the rocks.

Kawela Bay   Beach
(Map p226) West of the Turtle Bay Resort, a 1.5-mile shoreline trail runs over to Kawela Bay. In winter you might spy whales cavorting offshore. After walking round **Protection Point**, named for its WWII bunker, voila, you've found Kawela Bay, with its thicket of banyan trees as seen on

Sunset Beach Park (p228)
TROPICALPIXSINGAPORE/GETTY IMAGES ©

Royal Birthstones

Oʻahu's central uplands were once the domain of royalty, with the area so sacred that commoners were forbidden even to pass through. Kukaniloko, 0.75 miles north of Wahiawa, had unique importance as the *piko* (navel) or central point of the island, a portal to the spirit world. It was at this sacred spot that the divine welcomed chiefly offspring into the world. Consequently it was of great importance that a female *aliʻi* (chief) reach the site in time for a ritual childbirth. Thirty-six chiefs were present to witness the event. The woman needed to lean properly against the backrest stone, named Kukaniloko, while giving birth for her child to be blessed by the gods. If all went according to plan, the child would be taken to a nearby temple and welcomed as a member of royalty. Those born here were of such a high lineage that chiefs from other islands would seek to enhance their prestige by marrying a Kukaniloko-born royal.

The freely accessible **Kukaniloko Birthstones State Historic Site** (www. hawaiistateparks.org) is not much to look at today, but it's one of only two documented birthing places in Hawaii (the other is on Kauaʻi). The royal birth of Kapawa is thought to have been the first to take place here, but genealogical records are inexact, indicating only that his birth was sometime between 1100 and 1400. Experts estimate that the site dates to the 12th century. The stones were still in use during the time of Kamehameha I, who rushed up to Kukaniloko for the birth of his son Liholiho in 1797. Many of the petroglyphs you'll see on the rocks are of recent origin, but the eroded circular patterns are original. The original configuration would have been two rows of 18 stones for the 36 chiefs. Today more than 100 stones lie in a field 0.25 miles west of Kamehameha Hwy (Hwy 99), on the red dirt road opposite Whitmore Ave. Look for them past the pineapple field, among a stand of eucalyptus and coconut trees.

TV's *Lost*. For the best swimming and snorkeling, keep walking to the middle of the bay.

Activities

Turtle Bay Golf
Golf

(☏808-293-8574; www.turtlebayresort. com; Turtle Bay Resort, 57-091 Kamehameha Hwy; green fees $75-185; ⏲by reservation only) Turtle Bay's two top-rated, par-72 courses abound in water views. The more challenging Palmer Course is the site of the PGA Championship Tour. The Fazio Course is host of the LPGA Tour's SBS Open. You can get discounts for hotel guests and twilight play.

Hans Hedemann Surf School
Surfing

(Map p226; ☏808-447-6755; www.hhsurf.com/ hh/en/turtlebay.html) Located in the Turtle Bay Resort, this surfing and SUP school is an extension of Hans Hedemann's well-known Waikiki school. It offers lessons for beginners and intermediates for both disciplines virtually right outside the hotel.

Guidepost
Outdoors

(Map p226; ☏808-293-6020; http://tbrapp. com/activities; Turtle Bay Resort, 57-091 Kamehameha Hwy; 👫) Swimming and snorkeling not exciting enough for you? Guidepost, the Turtle Bay Experience Center, can organize everything from horseback rides to surfing lessons to Segway rentals, plus kayaking, fishing and helicopter tours.

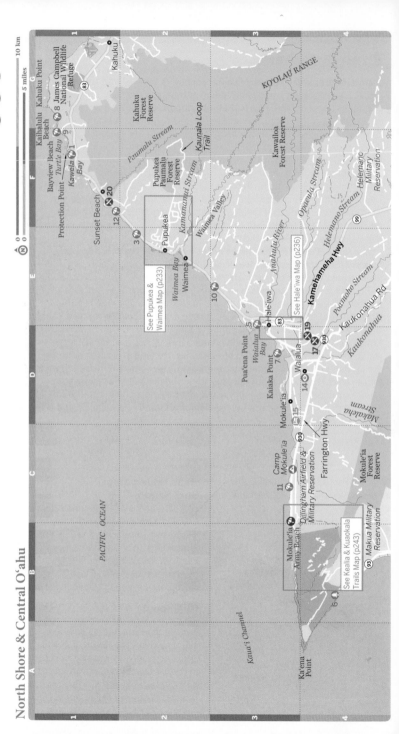

NORTH SHORE & CENTRAL O'AHU

5 miles
10 km

PACIFIC OCEAN

Kaua'i Channel

Ka'ena Point

Makua Military Reservation

See Kealia & Kuaokala Trails Map (p243)

6

Mokule'ia Army Beach

Dillingham Airfield & Military Reservation

11 Camp Mokule'ia

Farrington Hwy

Mokule'ia Forest Reserve

Mokule'ia

15

14

Waialua

Kaiaka Point

Pua'ena Point

Waialua Bay

5

7

19

17

930

Makaleha Stream

Hale'iwa

83

See Hale'iwa Map (p236)

10

Kamehameha Hwy

Anahulu River

Kaukonahua Rd

Kaukonahua

Psamoho Stream

Waimea

Waimea Bay

See Pupukea & Waimea Map (p233)

3

Pupukea

12

20

Sunset Beach

Protection Point

Bayview Beach Beach

Kaihalulu Kahuku Point

8 James Campbell National Wildlife Refuge

9

1

Kawela Bay

Turtle Bay

83

Kahuku

KO'OLAU RANGE

Kahuku Forest Reserve

Pupukea Paumalu Forest Reserve

Kaunala Loop Trail

Kaunala Trail

Paumalu Stream

Kamananui Stream

Waimea Valley

Kawailoa Forest Reserve

Opaeula Stream

Helemano Stream

Helemano Military Reservation

99

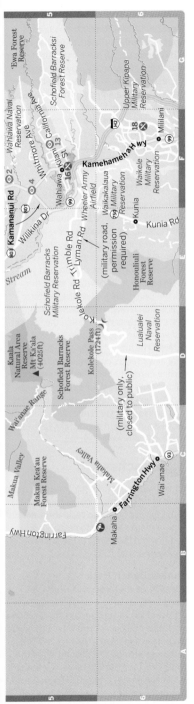

North Shore & Central Oʻahu

🛏 Sleeping

A good number of the privately owned
Turtle Bay area condos are available for
vacation rental on websites such as **VRBO**
(www.vrbo.com) and others. Minimum stays
may apply for all area lodging.

Turtle Bay Resort   Resort $$$
(Map p226; ☎808-293-6000; www.turtle-
bayresort.com; 57-091 Kamehameha Hwy; r/
cottage/villa from $259/659/1090; ❄@🛜❄)
Situated on a dramatic point, Turtle
Bay Resort boasts impressive 800-acre
surrounds. Each of the slightly dated
guest lodgings has an ocean view; deluxe
rooms come with private lanai. Ocean
villas ($550 to $1200) have high ceilings,

Triple Crown of Surfing

During the North Shore's **Triple Crown of Surfing** (http://vanstriplecrownofsurfing.com; ☺Nov-Dec) championships, touring pros compete for pride – and megabucks in prizes. The kick-off is the Reef Hawaiian Pro at Hale'iwa Ali'i Beach Park in mid-November. The competition's second challenge, the Vans World Cup of Surfing (late November to early December), rides at Sunset Beach. The final leg, the Billabong Pipe Masters, happens in early to mid-December at Pipeline.

deep soaking tubs and a villa-guest-only private pool, in addition to sharing the resort's many other amenities. Check for package discounts online.

Eating & Drinking

Ola
Seafood $$

(Map p226; ☎808-293-0801; www.olaislife.com; Turtle Bay Resort, 57-091 Kamehameha Hwy; mains lunch $10-24, dinner $19-58; ☺11am-10pm) Reserve in advance and you might get to dine by torchlight with your toes in the sand. This open-air cabana bar and restaurant stakes out an unparalleled position beachside. The menu is regular surf-and-turf; *pupu* such as *kalua* (cooked in an underground pit) pork nachos and ahi *poke* are a bit more interesting.

Pa'akai
Seafood $$$

(Map p226; ☎808-293-6000; www.turtlebay resort.com; Turtle Bay Resort, 57-091 Kamehameha Hwy; mains $30-75; ☺5.30-10pm) Turtle Bay Resort's top seafood restaurant with a name that means 'sea salt.' The best in local fish, prawns, lobster and scallops as well as steak and lamb from the land. Try the pan-seared *kampachi* for a can't-miss dish. Full bar and nightly live entertainment. Casual wear is fine; reservations recommended.

Surfer, The Bar
Bar

(Map p226; ☎808-293-6000; www.turtlebay resort.com; Turtle Bay Resort, 57-091 Kamehameha Hwy; mains $10-20) Big-name North Shore musicians occasionally play live sets at the resort's Surfer, The Bar, where the stage is set for anything from open-mic nights to surf-film screenings. Happy-hour coconut margaritas and 'lychee-tinis' are a bargain. Plenty of tasty *pupu* and bar-food options (mains $10 to $20).

Sunset Beach

Cruising southwest down the road from Turtle Bay you'll get a brief taste of what this rugged, rural coast was like before the surfers and superstars moved in. After about 4 miles, when an increasing number of homes appear through your windshield, you'll know you've hit the Sunset Beach area. Sure, the western orientation makes these beaches a great place to – guess what? – see the sun set. But way more people come to watch the surfers. The infamous Pipeline breaks here in winter, as do several world-class surfing competitions. The long stretch of golden sand is great for all ocean-lovers, and the laid-back residential community is a good location to rent a place and kick back island-style. A handy bike path leads from here almost to Waimea.

Beaches

For every beach parking lot you see, there are at least four more pedestrian access paths tucked back into residential areas. Trick is there's limited to no parking. Heading out by bicycle is the best way to explore them all.

Sunset Beach Park
Beach

(Map p226; 59-104 Kamehameha Hwy) Like many beaches on the North Shore, Sunset Beach has a split personality. In winter big swells come in for pro wave riders and the posse of followers these rock stars of the sea attract. The second leg of the Triple Crown of Surfing takes place here in late November and early December. In summer, Sunset is a prime place to log beach time. Waves calm down, there's a swimming channel before the reef and trees for shade.

In winter, the tremendous surf activity causes the slope of the beach to become increasingly steep as the season goes on. Though the water looks more inviting in summer, be aware there are still some nasty currents about.

Backyards is a smokin' hot reef break off Sunset Point on the northeastern side of the beach.

'Ehukai Beach Park   Beach
(Map p226; 59-337 Ke Nui Rd) Banzai Pipeline, aka **Pipeline**, aka Pipe – call it whatever you want, this place is known the world over as one of the biggest, heaviest and closest-to-perfect barrels in all of wave riding. When the strong westerly swells kick up in winter, the waves can reach over 15ft before breaking on the ultrashallow reef below. The final leg of the Triple Crown of Surfing is held here in early to mid-December.

For expert board riders who know what they're doing (no, a day of lessons at Waikiki Beach doesn't count), this could be surfing's holy grail. The waves break only a few yards offshore, so spectators are front-row and center. In the summer months everything calms down and there's even some decent snorkeling off this beach.

Activities

Ke Ala Pupukea Bike Path   Cycling
A partly shaded bike path provides an excellent link between the beaches along part of the North Shore. Pie-in-the-sky plans are to expand it from Turtle Bay to Waialua. In the meantime, the trail runs roughly 3 miles on the *makai* side of Kamehameha Hwy, from O'opuola St in Sunset Beach to the northern end of Waimea Bay.

Sleeping

Rentals abound around Sunset Beach, check both the big online sites, such as **VRBO** (www.vrbo.com) and others, plus local ones such as Team Real Estate in Hale'iwa.

O'ahu Family Rental   Apartment $$
(www.oahufamilyrentals.com; studios $90, 1-bedroom apt $150-165; ❋ 🛜) A local surfer family owns several rentals that are an easy bike ride from the beach (cruiser

Surf Movies 101

The North Shore's epic waves have starred, or at least had cameos, in some of the best surf movies ever made. Check these out:

○ *Soul Surfer* (2011) A girl's journey back to competition surfing after a shark attack.

○ *Riding Giants* (2004) This documentary surveys the history and lore of surfing.

○ *The Ride* (2003) A hit on the head sends one wave-rider back to 1911, surfing with the Duke.

○ *Blue Crush* (2002) Can love come between a surfer and the Banzai Pipeline?

○ *North Shore* (1987) A big-wave wannabe braves a summer on the North Shore.

○ *Five Summer Stories* (1972) Eddie Aikau co-stars as a legendary local surfer – himself.

○ *Endless Summer* (1966) The original, existential, life-in-search-of-the-wave epic.

usage included). The smallest studio doesn't have much floor space but is fresh and cheery; a loftlike one bedroom has exposed-beam ceilings and original hula stained glass. Shared laundry facilities; insider beach advice included.

Eating

Ted's Bakery   Hawaiian $

(Map p226; ☑808-638-8207; www.tedsbakery. com; 59-024 Kamehameha Hwy; meals $7-16; ⏱7am-8pm; 🚻) Quintessential North Shore, Ted's is the place surfers load up for breakfast, laid-back locals grab a snack, suntanned vacationers dig into plate lunches – and everybody goes for dessert. The chocolate-*haupia* (coconut) cream pie is legendary across the island. Full-meal favorites include the meat-filled fried rice with eggs at breakfast and melt-in-your-mouth, lightly pan-fried garlic shrimp any other time.

Pupukea

A largely residential area, Pupukea climbs from the coast further into the hills than you may think possible. There are a few services, including a big Foodland grocery store, along the highway. Higher up, hiking opportunities and an ancient Hawaiian site await.

Beaches

Pupukea Beach Park   Beach

(59-727 Kamehameha Hwy) With deep-blue waters, a varied coastline and a mix of lava and white sand, Pupukea, meaning 'white shell,' is a very scenic stretch. The long beach encompasses three areas: Shark's Cove to the north, Old Quarry in the center and Three Tables to the south. The waters off Pupukea Beach are all protected as a marine life conservation district.

The reef formation at **Shark's Cove** provides an excellent habitat for marine life, including sea turtles, and is good for snorkeling. When seas are calm, this is a great area for water exploring, just make sure you always wear shoes to protect from sharp coral. Despite the cove's name, the white-tipped reef sharks aren't usually a problem; just keep your distance and don't provoke them. One of O'ahu's most popular cavern dives is also accessed here. Some of the caves are very deep and labyrinthine, and there have been a number of drownings, so divers should only venture into them with a local expert.

The rock features at **Old Quarry** appear as if they were cut by human hands, but rest assured that they are natural. Coastal tide pools are interesting microhabitats, best explored at low tide during calm summer seas. Be careful, especially if you have kids in tow, because the rocks are razor sharp. There are showers and restrooms in front of Old Quarry; bus 52 stops out front.

The flat ledges rising above the water give **Three Tables** its name. In summer only, the area is good for snorkeling and diving. The best coral and fish, as well as some small caves, lava tubes and arches, are in deeper water further out. Access to Three Tables is just beyond Old Quarry, where there are a few unmarked parking spots.

Sights

Pu'u o Mahuka Heiau State Historic Site
Temple

(www.hawaiistateparks.org; off Pupukea Rd; ⊙ sunrise-sunset) 🌿 FREE A cinematic coastal panorama and a stroll around the grounds of O'ahu's largest temple reward those who venture up to this

231

national historic landmark, perched on a bluff above Waimea Bay. It's a dramatically windswept and lonely site. Though the ruined walls leave a lot to be imagined, it's worth the drive for the commanding views, especially if you get here at sunset.

Pu'u o Mahuka means 'hill of escape' – but this was a *luakini* heiau, where human sacrifices took place. Likely dating from the 17th century, the temple's stacked-stone construction is attributed to the legendary *menehune* (the 'little people' who, according to legend, built many of Hawaii's fishponds, heiau and other stonework), who are said to have completed their work in just one night.

To get here, turn *mauka* onto Pupukea Rd by the Foodland supermarket; the monument turnoff is about 0.5 miles uphill, from where it's another roughshod 0.7 miles to the heiau.

 ## Sleeping

As with much of the North Shore, accommodation options here are mostly vacation rentals.

Backpackers Vacation Inn & Hostel
Hostel $

(808-638-7838; http://backpackers-hawaii.com; 59-788 Kamehameha Hwy; dm $27-30, d $62-85, studio/2br/3br cabin from $120/170/215; @ 🛜) The only budget option on the North Shore. If you care more about money and location than about the odd bit of peeling paint or modest-to-the-point-of-ramshackle furnishings, this friendly, backpacker-style village is for you. Hostel rooms are mostly located in the two large main buildings.

Ke Iki Beach Bungalows
Apartment $$

(808-638-8229, 866-638-8229; http://keikibeach.com; 59-579 Ke Iki Rd; 1-/2-bedroom apt from $205/230; ❄ 🛜) Smartly updated tropical decor adds to the retreat feel of this bungalow community on the white-sand beach just north of Pupukea Beach Park. Grassy lawns and a garden full of tropical trees complete the picture. Kick back on the shared beachfront lanai, nap in a hammock beneath the palm trees or head out for a swim.

 ## Eating

Sharks Cove Grill
Hawaiian $$

(808-638-8300; www.sharkscovegrill.com; 59-712 Kamehameha Hwy; dishes $4-8, meals $11-16; ⏰8:30am-8:30pm) Order your taro burger or ahi skewers from the food-truck window, pull up a rickety covered patio seat and watch the waves as a chicken pecks the ground nearby. The food's OK; the experience is totally North Shore.

Pupukea Grill
Hawaiian $$

(808-779-7943; www.pupukeagrill.com; 59-680 Kamehameha Hwy; meals $9-15; ⏰11am-5pm Tue-Sun) Grilled-fish tacos, panini sandwiches and *poke* bowls aren't typical food-truck fare. Take yours to go; the parking-lot picnic tables aren't appetizing.

Island Insights

The large boulders standing at the end of Kulalua Point, which mark the northernmost end of Pupukea Beach, are said to be followers of Pele, the Hawaiian goddess of fire and volcanoes. To acknowledge their loyalty (or in alternative tellings of the legend, to punish their nosiness for observing the goddess's passage from onshore), Pele made her followers immortal by turning them to stone.

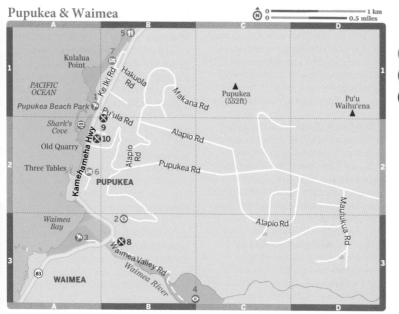

Waimea

An artist couldn't paint a better picture: white sand meets azure water at the mouth of a lushly green river valley. Black outcroppings of lava rock sit offshore a deep arc of beach. The bay is so stunning, in fact, that it's hard not to catch your breath when you round the highway curve and see it. Captain Cook's men, the first Westerners to sail into Waimea Bay, had the same reaction. An entry in the 1779 ship's log noted its uncommon beauty. Back then the valley was heavily settled; the lowlands terraced in taro, the valley walls dotted with house sites and the ridges topped with heiau. Just about every crop grown in Hawaii thrived in this valley, including a rare pink taro favored by aliʻi (royalty). Back then Waimea River emptied into the bay and served as a passage for canoes traveling to upstream villages. Post contact, logging and plantation clearing resulted in a devastating 1894 flood, after which residents abandoned the settlement. Today, the beach park is an immensely popular stop on

Oʻahu itineraries, and you can hike up into the valley to see a few of the original sites.

 Beaches

Waimea Bay Beach Park   Beach
(61-031 Kamehameha Hwy) It may be a beauty, but it's certainly a moody one. Waimea Bay changes dramatically with

233

the seasons: it can be tranquil and as flat as a lake in summer, then savage in winter, with the island's meanest rip currents. Typically, the only time it's calm enough for swimming and snorkeling is from June to September, maybe October. Winter water activities at this beach are *not* for novices – the waves at Waimea can get epically huge.

The beach plays host to the annual Eddie Aikau memorial surf competition Quiksilver between December and February. Eddie Aikau was a legendary waterman and Waimea lifeguard who died trying to save compatriots from a double-hull outrigger-canoe accident en route from Hawaii to Tahiti.

This is the North Shore's most popular beach, so parking is often tight. On weekends, Waimea Valley across the street offers paid parking. Don't park along the highway; police are notorious for towing away dozens of cars at once. Note, too, that jumping off the big rock formation at the southern end of the cove is technically forbidden. Facilities include showers, restrooms and picnic tables, and a lifeguard on duty daily.

◉ Sights

Waimea Valley
Gardens, Park

(☎808-638-7766; www.waimeavalley.net; 59-864 Kamehameha Hwy; adult/child 4-12yr $15/7.50; ⊙9am-5pm; ♿) 🌿 Craving land instead of sea? This 1800-acre Hawaiian cultural and nature park, just inland from Waimea Bay, is a sanctuary of tropical tranquility. Among the junglelike foliage you'll find up to 5000 native and exotic plant species. Wander the numerous paths alongside Kamananui Stream and up to different cultural stations, which may have demonstrations of ancient Hawaiian games and practices.

The valley is home to numerous ancient sites, but few are on the paths. Equally interesting are the replicas of buildings ancient Hawaiians dwelled in and a restored heiau dedicated to Lono, the traditional god of fertility and agriculture. Guided hikes ($10 to $15) lead into otherwise inaccessible parts of the valley and are worth making time for; reservations required.

Waterfall, Waimea

STEVE DUCHESNE/GETTY IMAGES ©

Laniakea Beach

Laniakea Beach
Beach

(Map p226; http://malamanahonu.org; Kamehameha Hwy (Hwy 83)) Between the highway's 3- and 4-mile markers, this narrow spit of sand is visited by basking *honu* (green sea turtles), who migrate here from French Frigate Shoals in the remote Northwestern Hawaiian Islands. Stay back at least 20ft from these endangered sea creatures, which are very sensitive to noise and human disturbance. Volunteers are on hand to answer questions. Most people park alongside the highway opposite the beach, but vehicle break-ins and theft are a risk.

Hale'iwa

POPULATION 2011

Originally a plantation-era supply town in the 1900s, Hale'iwa today is the de facto surf city of the North Shore. It's all about the waves here and everyone knows it. If the town is all hustle and bustle, chances are the ocean is flat. If the swells are breaking, it could take you an hour to travel the 8 miles through rubber-necking traffic to Sunset Beach. Despite being a tourist hub, there's a laid-back ambience to Hale'iwa town that's in perfect concert with the rest of the coast. Old false-front wooden buildings sell shave ice, and eclectic shops intermingle with modern amenities. As the biggest outpost around, this is the place to find a decent meal, pick up a new T-shirt, rent a long-board for the day and then hang around after sunset, wishing you could stay just a little bit longer.

 Beaches

Hale'iwa Ali'i Beach Park
Beach

(66-167 Hale'iwa Rd) Home to some of the best surf on the North Shore, waves here can be huge and the beach is a popular spot for surf contests. In mid-November the Triple Crown of Surfing gets under way on this break. When it's relatively flat, the local kids rip it up with their body-

boards and mere mortals test their skills on the waves. The 20-acre beach park has restrooms, showers, a wide grassy area with picnic tables and lifeguards.

Hale'iwa Beach Park   Beach

(Map p226; 62-449 Kamehameha Hwy) On the northern side of the harbor, this park is protected by a shallow shoal and breakwater so is usually a good choice for swimming. There's little wave action, except for the occasional north swells that ripple into the bay. Although the beach isn't as pretty as others, the 13-acre park has basketball and volleyball courts, an exercise area, a softball field and a large parking lot.

Kaiaka Bay Beach Park   Beach

(Map p226; 66-449 Hale'iwa Rd) Beachside trees a mile or so west of town offer shade, and turtles sometimes show up. But the swimming is better at the other local beaches, so look elsewhere if you're wanting to get wet.

◉ Sights

Lili'uokalani
Protestant Church   Church

(66-090 Kamehameha Hwy) Hale'iwa's historic 1832 church takes its name from Queen Lili'uokalani, who spent summers on the shores of the Anahulu River and attended services here. As late as the 1940s, services were held entirely in Hawaiian.

🏃 Activities

If you're a beginner board rider, the North Shore has a few tame breaks such as **Pua'ena Point**, just north of Hale'iwa Beach Park, and **Chun's Reef**, north of town. Even if you've caught a few waves in Waikiki, it's smart to take a lesson with one of the many freelancing surfers to get an introduction to local underwater hazards. Ask around the beach, where surf school vans rent gear and offer same-day instruction, or book ahead for surf or stand up paddling lessons. Expect to pay from $75 to $90 for two-hour group lessons, $100 to $180 for a private lesson and $30 to $45 to rent a board for the day ($60 with paddle).

Hale'iwa

Whale-watching season is December through May, and snorkeling season runs June through September.

Rainbow Watersports   SUP

(📞808-372-9304; www.rainbowwatersports. com; ⊙by reservation only) The local stand up paddling specialist offers calm-water classes, lessons for braving the waves, and four-hour coastal paddle tours (from $189), with snorkeling and lunch included. Rentals available, too. These guys wrote the Stand Up Paddle Book.

Surf 'n' Sea   Water Sports

(📞808-637-9887; www.surfnsea.com; 62-595 Kamehameha Hwy; ⊙9am-7pm) The big daddy of all surf shops, this colorful wooden building by the sea rents most any kind of water gear you can think of: surfboards, paddleboard set-ups, wetsuits, car racks,

Hale'iwa

snorkel sets, kayaks, beach umbrellas and chairs... Lessons, tours and bicycle rental, too.

North Shore Surf Girls Surfing
(☏808-637-2977; www.northshoresurfgirls.com; ⏰by reservation only) Some of the instructors here were featured in the movie *Blue Crush,* and they're all especially great teaching kids and other women to bodyboard, surf and stand up paddle. Packages include a sunset Hawaiian-BBQ surfing tour.

Sunset Surratt Surf Academy Surfing, SUP
(☏783-8657; www.surfnorthshore.com) 'Uncle Bryan,' born and raised on the North Shore, has been coaching pro surfers for decades. He and his staff teach all levels from beginner to advanced, and stand up paddlers. Rentals offered.

Deep Ecology Diving
(☏808-637-7946; www.deepecologyhawaii.com; 66-456 Kamehameha Hwy; dives from $95)
If you're keen to get under the waves, the folks at Deep Ecology can help. Summer shore dives explore Shark's Cove and Three Tables, while offshore lava tubes, coral reefs, arches and cathedrals await boat divers. With a strong ecological bent, these divers are conscious about the ocean and create ecodive boat trips with that in mind.

North Shore Shark Adventures Adventure Sports
(☏808-228-5900; http://sharktourshawaii.com; Hale'iwa Small Boat Harbor; 2hr tour adult/child $120/60) Submerge in a cage surrounded by sharks about 3 miles offshore. Shark sightings guaranteed. Return transport for a fee from Waikiki.

⊙ Tours

Deep Ecology dive outfitters offer excellent boat tours as well.

Historic Hale'iwa Tour Walking Tour
(☏808-637-4558; www.gonorthshore.org; 66-434 Kamehameha Hwy; tour $10; ⏰3pm Wed & 9:30am Sat) Reserve in advance for the 90-minute walking tours that take in the scattered historic buildings of town. The visitor center also sells illustrated tour maps ($2) that describe all the old structures and can be followed at your own pace.

North Shore Ecotours Hiking
(☏877-521-4453; www.northshoreecotours.com; hiking tour adult/child $90/60, driving tour $65/45) Native Hawaiian guides lead three different, easy to difficult hikes on private land. All begin with a ride to the trailhead in a Swiss military off-road vehicle; taking a tour in the Pinzgauer is also possible.

Festivals & Events

The Hale'iwa Farmers Market has special festival-like theme weekends throughout the year.

Hale'iwa Arts Festival   Arts
(www.haleiwaartsfestival.org; ⏲Jul) More than 100 artists gather at Hale'iwa one weekend in July to sell their wares. Music, food, cultural tours and hands-on demonstrations are also scheduled.

Sleeping

Hale'iwa has no hotels, but there are a number of vacation rentals in the area.

Kaiaka Bay Beach Park   Campground $
(Map p226; https://camping.honolulu.gov; 66-449 Hale'iwa Rd; 5-night campsite permit $52; ⏲8am Fri-8am Wed) Advance permits are required for the seven tent sites at Hale'iwa's only campground. The park has restrooms, outdoor showers and picnic tables.

Team Real Estate   Accommodation Services $$
(☎808-637-3507; www.teamrealestate.com; North Shore Marketplace, 66-250 Kamehameha Hwy; studio from $60, 1-/2-/3-/4-bedroom from $95/150/165/250) This local real-estate agency handles a dozen or so vacation rentals along the North Shore. Options run the gamut from studio apartments and condos to multibedroom beachfront luxury homes.

Eating

Matsumoto's Shave Ice   Sweets $
(☎808-637-4827; www.matsumotoshaveice.com; 66-087 Kamehameha Hwy; snacks $3-5; ⏲9am-6pm; 🚗) O'ahu's classic circle-island drive just isn't complete without stopping for shave ice at this legendary tin-roofed 1920s general store, locally known as Matsumoto's. Some families drive from Honolulu to the North Shore with one goal in mind: to stand in line here for a cone drenched with island flavors, such as *liliko'i,* banana, mango and pineapple.

Beet Box Cafe   Health Food $
(☎808-637-3000; www.thebeetboxcafe.com; Celestial Natural Foods, 66-443 Kamehameha Hwy; mains $7-10; ⏲9am-5pm Mon-Sat, to 4pm Sun; 🚗) 🌱 At the back of the town's karmically cool health-food store hides a popular vegetarian-friendly deli. Breakfast is served all day, lunch is hot plates, sandwiches or salads.

Waialua Bakery & Juice Bar   Bakery, Deli $
(☎808-341-2838; 66-200 Kamehameha Hwy; items $1-8; ⏲10am-5pm Mon-Sat; 🚗) Many of the ingredients for the smoothies here come from the owners' farm in Waialua. Breads for the

Hale'iwa Art Gallery (p240)

piled-high sandwiches, cookies and treats are all made from scratch.

Haleʻiwa Farmers Market   Market $

(www.haleiwafarmersmarket.com; Waimea Valley, 59-864 Kamehameha Hwy; ⏱3-7pm Thu; 🅿🚶) So much more than produce; here 40 vendors sell artisan crafts and organic, seasonal edibles. At the time of writing, the market was being held at Waimea Valley, but intentions are to move back to Haleʻiwa.

Grass Skirt Grill   Hawaiian $

(📞808-637-4852; 66-214 Kamehameha Hwy; mains $6-13; ⏱11am-6pm) Retro surf decor covers every square inch! The names of the island-style plate lunches seem familiar – teriyaki chicken, *ono* (a type of mackerel) burgers – but the results are way above average, using brown rice, local greens and homemade sauces. These are great takeout meals when you're beach bound. Cash only.

Kono's Restaurant   Hawaiian $

(📞808-637-9211; www.kaluapork.com; 66-250 Kamehameha Hwy; mains $6-12; ⏱7am-2.30pm Mon-Sat, 8am-3pm Sun) If you like pork, this is as good as it gets – legendary Kalua pork cooked daily for over 15 hours! The Triple Crown Sandwich ($15) features three kinds of pork, but we think the Pork Rice Bowl ($8.99) with Kalua pig, rice and guava BBQ sauce tops the selection.

Kono's is right on the main road. Look for the logo of a pig on a surfboard!

Cafe Haleiwa   Breakfast $$

(📞808-637-5516; 66-460 Kamehameha Hwy; mains breakfast & lunch $5-12, dinner $18-30; ⏱7am-2pm daily, plus 6-10pm Wed-Sat; 🚶) Locals have been fueling up at this laid-back surf-style diner since the 1980s. A daily menu of fresh preparations focuses on local ingredients and may feature mains such as lamb or mahimahi. Here even the side-dish vegetables are stars. Grab a bottle of wine from Bonzers Wine Shop next door.

The Best...
Summer Swimming

1 Bayview Beach (p224)

2 Waimea Bay Beach Park (p233)

3 Haleʻiwa Beach Park (p236)

4 Sunset Beach Park (p228)

Banzai Sushi Bar   Japanese $$

(📞808-637-4404; http://banzaisushibarhawaii.com; 66-246 Kamehameha Hwy, North Shore Marketplace; mains $10-20; ⏱noon-9:30pm) It's all about the atmosphere at Banzai Sushi Bar. This open-air sushi bar has surf films scrolling on the walls and live bands jamming on Saturday evenings. We like its mantra – keep it real, keep it raw.

Haleiwa Joe's   Seafood $$$

(📞808-637-8005; www.haleiwajoes.com; 66-011 Kamehameha Hwy; mains lunch $11-19, dinner $19-40; ⏱11:30am-9:30pm) With a superb location overlooking the marina, Joe's is the place for romantic dinners. Lunches are just so-so; we much prefer the inventive *pupu,* discounted at happy hour.

Drinking

Lanikai Juice   Juice Bar

(📞808-637-7774; www.lanikaijuice.com; 66-215 Kamehameha Hwy; snacks & drinks $4-8; ⏱8am-7pm) Kailua's favorite smoothie and fresh-juice bar has branched out. You can expect the same commitment to fresh ingredients and creative combos.

Coffee Gallery   Cafe

(📞808-637-5571; www.roastmaster.com; North Shore Marketplace, 66-250 Kamehameha Hwy; snacks & drinks $2-6; ⏱6:30am-8pm; 🛜) Coffee lovers rejoice over the house-roast beans and brews here.

Mobile Meals

Though we prefer the original Kahuku shrimp trucks, which are only 15 miles away on the Windward Coast, there are a number of food trucks around Hale'iwa town. Expect to pay between $8 and $14 a plate, between 10am and 6pm only. Look for **Blue Water Shrimp** by Gas Station 76 in the center of town; **Giovanni's** sits in a parking lot with several other food trucks across from the intersection with Pa'ala'a Rd; and **Macky's** is near the roundabout at the far southern end of town.

 Shopping

From trendy to quirky, you will find most of the North Shore's boutiques and galleries in Hale'iwa. The central shopping hub is in the North Shore Marketplace, which is across from Achui Lane in the center of town. There are T-shirt and surfwear shops everywhere.

Hale'iwa Art Gallery   Arts, Crafts
(www.haleiwaartgallery.com; North Shore Marketplace, 66-250 Kamehameha Hwy; ☉10am-6pm) Featuring works by 20-plus local and regional painters, photographers, sculptors, glass-blowers and mixed-media artists.

Guava   Clothing
(www.guavahawaii.com; Hale'iwa Town Center, 66-165 Kamehameha Hwy; ☉10am-6pm) A chic, upscale boutique for beachy women's apparel such as gauzy sundresses and strappy sandals.

Kai Ku Hale   Homewares, Gifts
(http://kaikuhale.com; Hale'iwa Town Center, 66-145 Kamehameha Hwy; ☉10am-7pm) Bring island style home with Hawaiian art, wood wall carvings, homewares and jewelry.

Growing Keiki   Clothing, Children
(http://thegrowingkeiki.com; 66-051 Kamehameha Hwy; ☉10am-6pm; 👶) This kids' shop has gear for junior surf grommets and budding beach bunnies, including mini aloha shirts, trunks and toys.

Ukulele Site   Music
(☎808-622-8000; www.theukulelesite.com; 66-560 Kamehameha Hwy; ☉11am-6pm Mon-Sat, to 5pm Sun) The North Shore's top ukulele store, this place also has a top online site and ships all over the world. Head to the store to see and try out a mind-boggling array of ukuleles.

ℹ **Getting There & Around**

From Honolulu International Airport to Hale'iwa is 27 miles, normally 40 minutes via the H-1, H-2 and Kamehameha Hwy. Because the North Shore basically only has one long road, it's time consuming, but possible to get around by bus. Route 52 (Circle Island Wahiawa) runs from the Ala Moana Center in Honolulu to Hale'iwa in 1¾ hours, making stops in town and at beaches all the way to Turtle Bay.

Waialua

POPULATION 2465

If you find the relatively slow pace of life on the North Shore just too hectic, head over to Waialua. This sugar-mill town ground to a halt in 1996, when production ended. Since then, creative locals have transformed the old mill into a crafty, island-born shopping complex. The surrounding area is filled with small-scale farms, nurseries and a few McMansions claiming ag-exempt tax status. Beach access is difficult here, but they aren't the North Shore's best anyway.

Sights

Waialua Sugar Mill   Historic Site

(Map p226; www.sugarmillhawaii.com; 67-106 Kealohanui St; ⏱9am-5pm Mon-Sat, 10am-5pm Sun) The now-defunct sugar mill that was the genesis of the town in the 1900s has been redeveloped to house a number of shops and businesses. You can still see the old smoke stack and plenty of history. The rambling **Waialua Coffee – Island X Hawaii** warehouse is stuffed full of everything from vintage aloha shirts to wooden handicrafts and pieces of original art.

In addition to buying its Waialua-local, estate-grown coffee as beans or grounds, you can pick up a hot cuppa joe (or shave ice) from a little **coffee stand** in the corner.

The **North Shore Soap Factory** features sugar-mill history displays. While you're there, peek through the glass and watch the soap makers craft the all-natural bars they sell, made with local ingredients such as *kukui* (candlenut tree) nuts and coconut cream.

On Saturday and Wednesday mornings, the **Waialua Farmers Market** sets up in the sugar-mill parking lot. Surfboard-makers and craft vendors keep this market lively.

 Eating

Pa'ala'a Kai Bakery   Bakery $

(Map p226; ☎808-637-9795; www.pkbsweets. com; 66-945 Kaukonahua Rd; snacks & pastries $2-4; ⏱5:30am-7pm) Take a detour down a country road to find this family-run bakery, a pilgrimage for anyone craving a 'snow puffy' (flaky chocolate cream puff dusted with powdered sugar) or hot *malasada* (Portuguese-style doughnuts).

Scoop of Paradise Ice Cream Factory   Ice Cream $

(Map p226; ☎808-637-3020; www.facebook. com/scoopofparadisefactory; 66-935 Kaukona-hua Rd; ⏱9am-6pm) Exquisite homemade ice cream, coffees, cakes and smoothies in an old building next to Pa'ala'a Kai Bakery. After careful research, we recommend the chocolate and macadamia nut ice cream. It also has a shop in Haleiwa, but this is the factory.

Coffee Gallery (p239)

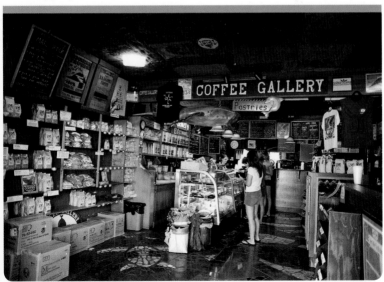

ANN CECIL/GETTY IMAGES ©

Mokule'ia to Ka'ena Point

POPULATION 1839

The further down the road you go, the fewer signs of habitation you'll see in this desolate corner of the island. Farrington Hwy finally dead ends into a rocky, un-developed patch short of the island's edge. Few visitors make it this far, but there are a string of striking beaches, and numerous aviation adventures from Dillingham Airfield, for those who do.

 Beaches

Mokule'ia Beach Park   Beach

(Map p226; 68-919 Farrington Hwy) The beach itself is a nice sandy stretch, but the rocky seabed makes for poor swimming. When waters are calm and flat in summer, snor-kelers swim out along the shallow reef. Keen windsurfers often congregate on this stretch of shore, taking advantage of the consistent winds. The park has a large grassy area with picnic tables, restrooms and outdoor showers; but there aren't any lifeguards.

Army Beach   Beach

(Farrington Hwy (Hwy 930)) Opposite the western end of Dillingham Airfield, this is the widest stretch of sand on the Mokule'ia shore, although it's not maintained and there are no facilities. The beach also has very strong rip currents, especially during high winter surf. If the beach looks familiar, it might be because it appeared in the pilot of the hit TV drama *Lost*.

Ka'ena Point State Park   Beach

(www.hawaiistateparks.org; Farrington Hwy (Hwy 930); ☼sunrise-sunset) From Army Beach you can drive further down the road, passing still more white-sand beaches with aqua-blue waters. The bit of sand off the pull-out just beyond the first Ka'ena State Park sign has a small rock-free swimming area accessible in calm surf. The large parking area is not only desolate but can also be a bit trashed. Car break-ins are commonplace.

 Activities

Skydiving, hang gliding and biplane and glider rides all take off from **Dillingham Airfield** (68-760 Farrington Hwy). Call ahead, as flights are weather dependent.

Honolulu Soaring   Scenic Flights

(☎808-637-0207; www.honolulusoaring.com; Dillingham Airfield, Farrington Hwy (Hwy 930); rides from $79; ☼10am-5:30pm) Plenty of great options. Take a scenic tour over the North Shore; go for an aerobatic thrill ride; or have a mini-lesson in a glider plane. Return transport from Waikiki to Dillingham Airfield costs $40.

Pacific Skydiving Center   Skydiving

(☎808-637-7472; www.pacificskydivinghonolulu. com; Dillingham Airfield, 68-760 Farrington Hwy (Hwy 930); tandem jumps from $139; ☼7.30am-2.30pm) Want to jump out of a perfectly good airplane? Tandem jumps attached to an instructor range from the relatively sedentary 10,000ft jump with 15 to 20 seconds of freefall right up to 'the Chal-lenge,' a monster jump from 24,000ft with more than 100 seconds of freefall. Your budget may well choose your jump for you! Jumps include free Waikiki pickup.

Paradise Air   Gliding

(☎808-497-6033; www.paradiseairhawaii.com; Dillingham Airfield, Farrington Hwy (Hwy 930); flights from $175; ☼by reservation only) Soar

---

Not Lost After All

Does Army Beach look familiar? It appeared in the pilot of the hit TV drama *Lost*. When *Lost* first started filming here, tourists driving along the highway would see the smoking wreckage of a crashed plane sitting on the beach. Needless to say, a burned-out jetliner is an alarming site, and many called 911 to mistakenly report an emergency.

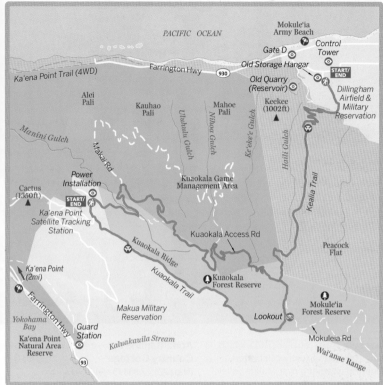

like a bird in an ultralight powered hang-glider called a trike, accompanied by an instructor who may even let you pilot.

Stearman Biplane Rides
Scenic Flights

(☎808-637-4461; www.stearmanbiplanerides. com; Hangar B6, Dillingham Airfield, Farrington Hwy (Hwy 930); flights from $175; ☾by reservation only) Loop-de-loop on an aerobatic flight, take a short scenic tour (20 minutes) or retrace the route the Japanese took to Pearl Harbor (40 minutes) – all in a restored 1941 Boeing biplane.

Kaʻena Point Trail
Mountain Biking, Hiking

(www.hawaiistateparks.org; ☾sunrise-sunset) A mountain-bike-friendly hiking path leads from the end of Farrington Hwy along the remaining 2.5 miles out to Kaʻena Point. The terrain is scrubland reaching up to the base of the Waiʻanae Range, while the shoreline is wild and windswept. From December to May you may be able to spot whales from this area.

We recommend doing the full hike from the other side of the point, on the Waiʻanae Coast.

Kealia & Kuaokala Trails
Hiking

(http://hawaiitrails.ehawaii.gov) Beyond the Gate D entrance above Dillingham Airfield, the 2.5-mile, one-way **Kealia Trail** switchbacks steeply up (1660ft elevation change) through exposed country with ocean views along the way. It connects to the 2.5-mile, one-way

Kuaokala Trail (see also p161), which brings hikers to a justly celebrated ridge-top viewpoint over Makua Valley and the Wai'anae Range.

Hawaii Polo Horseback Riding
(☎808-220-5153; www.hawaii-polo.org; 68-539 Farrington Hwy (Hwy 930); rides from $85; ⊗by reservation only) When the polo ponies aren't playing, you can take a ride around their 100-acre stomping grounds at the polo club. Sunset beach rides recommended. You can even take a polo lesson!

 Sleeping

Surprisingly, even out here in the middle of nowhere, there are some vacation rentals available. In addition to the usual rental agencies, **Solikai** (www.solikai.com) lists a few colorful, oceanfront beach cottages.

**Anna Banana's
Country Cottage** Cottage $
(Map p226; ☎808-754-6461; www.vrbo.com/425288; cottage per night $95) Want a secluded, quiet place to stay for two in Mokule'ia just back from the beach? Then Anna Banana's Country Cottage is the place to go. If there are more of you, opt for **Carly's Country Cottage** (www.vrbo.com/422422, per night $115) on the same site. There's a three-night minimum stay, but you may want to stay for weeks.

Camp Mokule'ia Campground $
(Map p226; ☎808-637-6241; www.campmokuleia.com; 68-729 Farrington Hwy; campsites per person $18; ⊗office 8:30am-5pm Mon-Fri, 10am-5pm Sat) Looking for solace and solitude? This church-run seaside camp is open to travelers – by reservation only – as long as there isn't a prebooked group. Amenities are ultrabasic, with outdoor showers and chemical toilets. It also has well-worn lodge rooms, cabins and tent cabins.

CENTRAL O'AHU

Central O'ahu is the island's forgotten backwater. Squeezed by enormous military bases, the area is frequented by camo-painted Humvees and Black Hawk choppers. A few highways head north to Wahiawa, the region's central town: the H-2 Fwy is the fastest option, while Kunia Road (Hwy 750), the furthest west, is the most scenic.

Kunia Road (Hwy 750)

Three routes head north from the H-1 to Wahiawa, the region's central town. The H-2 Fwy is the fastest route. But if you're not in a hurry (and why would you be?), you should take the scenic, slightly longer Kunia Road through the center of the island. The drive starts in sprawling suburbia but soon breaks free into an expansive landscape with 360-degree views. As you gain altitude, views of Honolulu and Diamond Head emerge below you; be sure to pull off somewhere and look back at the landscape. Corn-fields gradually give way to enormous pineapple plantations, all hemmed in by the mountains to the west.

If you want to see what a current-day plantation village looks like, turn west off Hwy 750 onto Kunia Dr, about 5.5 miles north of H-1. The little town of **Kunia**, in the midst of the pineapple fields, is home to the workers employed by Del Monte. Rows of gray-green wooden houses with corrugated-tin roofs stand on low stilts. Residents take pride in their little yards, with bougainvillea and birds of paradise adding a splash of brightness despite the wash of red dust that blows in from the surrounding pineapple farms.

The rural landscape continues until you pass Schofield Barracks Military

Reservation. This massive army base is the largest on the island and is a hive of activity – it's not uncommon to be passed on the highway by camo-painted Humvees while Black Hawk choppers hover overhead. Onward from Wahiawa, two routes – rural Kaukonahua Rd (Hwy 803) and busy Kamehameha Hwy (Hwy 99) – lead through pineapple-plantation country to the North Shore.

Wahiawa

POPULATION 16,714

On first inspection Wahiawa, with its numerous fast-food joints and pawn shops, doesn't tend to inspire. It's just a residential town near Hawaii's largest army base. But the land around Wahiawa was long considered sacred; this was the summer home of royalty. The cooler temperatures made for serene living when the mercury climbed.

Later the area was found to be well suited to agricultural purposes and plantations sprung up. Not much is left of the ancient temples and sites that once occupied the area, but you can pay tribute to the pineapple at Dole Plantation.

 Sights

Dole Plantation

Theme Park

(Map p226; 808-621-8408; www.dole-plantation.com; 64-1550 Kamehameha Hwy; visitor center admission free, adult/child 4-12yr maze $6/4, train ride $8.50/6.50, walking tour $5/4.25; 9:30am-5.30pm;) Expect a sticky-sweet overdose of everything *ananas* (pineapple) at Dole Plantation's visitor-center gift shop. Watch fruit-cutting demonstrations and buy pineapple potato chips and fruity trinkets, then take your pineapple ice-cream sundae outside for more pineapple educational fun.

Green World Coffee Farm

Farm

(Map p226; 808-622-2326; http://greenworldcoffeefarm.com; 71-101 N Kamehameha Hwy; 6am-6pm Mon-Fri, 7am-6.30pm Sat & Sun) A must for coffee nuts, these guys roast all their coffee on-site with home-grown beans and beans from throughout the Hawaiian islands. There is free sampling, free wi-fi and a great vibe in this roadside coffee extravaganza. They ship all over the world with a huge range of products including a huge variety of flavored coffee.

Wahiawa Botanical Gardens

Gardens

(Map p226; 808-522-7064; www.honolulu.gov/parks/hbg; 1396 California Ave; 9am-4pm,

Tasty Pineapple Tidbits

○ In 1901 James Dole planted O'ahu's first pineapple patch in Wahiawa.

○ Dole's original 12-acre Wahiawa plot has since grown to 8000 acres.

○ Each acre of a pineapple field supports about 6500 plants.

○ The commercial pineapple variety grown in Hawaii is smooth cayenne.

○ It takes nearly two years for a pineapple plant to reach maturity.

○ Each plant produces just two pineapples, one in its second year and one in its third year.

○ Pineapples are harvested year-round, but the long, sunny days of summer produce the sweetest fruit.

○ The average pineapple weighs 5lb.

closed Dec 25 & Jan 1) 🏷 **FREE** Started 80 years ago as an experiment by the local sugarcane farmers, the unstaffed 27-acre garden has evolved to showcase plants that thrive in a cool and moist climate. There's a mix of the manicured, with lawns and pruned ornamental plants, and the wild, with a gully of towering hardwoods, tropical ferns and forests of bamboo. Paths, some wheelchair friendly, weave their way through the garden. It's located 1 mile east of Kamehameha Hwy (Hwy 99).

🍴 Eating

Wahiawa is recommended as a day trip from, or a stopover en route to, the North Shore, which has better eating options. In town there are a number of small Asian eateries and fast-food joints.

Maui Mike's Barbecue, Fast Food **$**
(Map p226; ☎808-622-5900; http://maui-mikes.com; 96 S Kamehameha Hwy; meals $6-9; ⏰10:30am-8:30pm; 🅿) At Mike's you have the choice of chicken, chicken or chicken – all free range, fire roasted and super fresh. Even the Cajun-spiced fries are 100% natural and trans-fat free.

Poke Stop Seafood **$**
(Map p226; http://poke-stop.com; 95-1840 Meheula Pkwy, Mi'ilani; meals $8-14; ⏰8am-8:30pm Mon-Sat, to 7pm Sun) This excellent fisherman-owned seafood outlet is 5 miles south of Wahiawa, off the H-2. Load up here for a picnic of incredible *poke* or a gourmet plate lunch of blackened fish and garlic shrimp. You can also eat in.

Wahiawa Botanical Gardens

SPRADA/GETTY IMAGES ©

101. Surf Ba... ...aiian Islands.

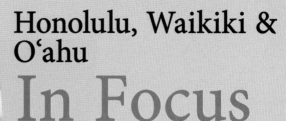

Honolulu, Waikiki & O'ahu

In Focus

Vintage postcard among lei
LINDA CHING LINDA CHING / GETTY IMAGES ©

O'ahu Today

Surfers, O'ahu

> O'ahu is a mosaic of cultures, both East and West, but underneath it all beats a Hawaiian heart.

belief systems
(% of population)

66 None or unaffiliated
24 Christian
10 Other

if O'ahu were 100 people

43 would be Asian
19 White Non-Hispanic
19 Two or more races
9 Native Hawaiian and Other Pacific Islander
8 Hispanic or Latino
2 Black Non-Hispanic

population per sq km

🛉 ≈ 30 people

O'AHU   JAPAN   USA

The Hawaiian Renaissance

In the 1970s, Hawaiian culture, battered by colonization, commodified and peddled to tourists, was ready for a revival; it just needed the spark. In 1976 a replica of the ancient Polynesian sailing canoe *Hokule'a* sailed to Tahiti using only the sun, stars, wind and waves for a compass, bringing a burst of cultural pride. That same year a group of Hawaiian activists occupied Kaho'olawe, which the US government had used for bombing practice since WWII. A Native Hawaiian rights movement soon emerged.

When the state of Hawaii held its landmark Constitutional Convention in 1978, it passed a number of amendments, such as making Hawaiian an official state language (along with English) and mandating that Hawaiian culture be taught in public schools. In the community, traditional arts such as *lauhala* (pandanus leaf weaving), *kapa* (bark cloth) making, wood carving, hula and *la'au lapa'au* (plant medicine) experienced a revival. Heiau (temples) and fishponds started being restored as well.

NOEL HENDRICKSON/GETTY IMAGES ©

Today, O'ahu is a mosaic of cultures, both East and West, but underneath it all beats a Hawaiian heart. Traditional Hawaiian culture remains an important part of island life and identity, reflected in ways both large and small – in spontaneous hula dancing on an airplane, an *oli* (chant) sung before political ceremonies in Honolulu or a *lomilomi* massage at a healing spa.

Seeking a Sustainable Balance

Hawaii is almost wholly dependent on the outside world. The majority of the state's consumer goods, including 85% of its food, are imported. The state spends $6 billion a year on oil and coal, all of it imported. Despite a wealth of natural-energy sources, over 90% of Hawaii's power still comes from carbon-based fuels. As the state's population swells to nearly 1.4 million – and 70% of those people reside on O'ahu – new housing developments sprawl, stressing water resources, transportation systems, public schools and landfills.

After losing sugar and pineapple to cheaper developing-world imports, Hawaii's economic eggs were left in one basket: tourism. When recession tanked the US economy in 2008, tourism to Hawaii went downhill with it. The immediate reaction was severe budget cuts, but most politicians agree that diversifying Hawaii's economy, while striving for energy independence and agricultural self-sufficiency, is a better solution.

Tourism will likely be Hawaii's bread and butter for the foreseeable future, even though it comes at a price. It brings in seven million visitors annually – around five times the state population – crowding roads, beaches and surf breaks, and driving up the price of real estate, not to mention fueling resistance to development. Some locals feel inundated by O'ahu's 'unofficial residents,' having mixed feelings about tourism and the US military, which controls vast tracts of land.

Many acknowledge that O'ahu's economic model is both unstable and unsustainable and that the island stands at a crossroads – Hawaii can either move toward securing a more homegrown future or it can suffer the worsening side effects of its addiction to tourism, imported goods and fossil fuels. Here's one reason for hope: both the modern sovereignty movement and antidevelopment activism are rooted in *aloha 'aina* (literally, 'respect for the land'), a traditional Hawaiian value that is deeply felt by almost everyone who lives here.

History

Dancers, Polynesian Cultural Center (p213), La'ie

Dancers, Polynesian Cultural Center (p213), La'ie

HOLGER LEUE/LOOK-FOTO/GETTY IM

More than 2000 miles from the US mainland, Hawaii can feel like another country – that's because it once was. Polynesians in canoes first colonized this tropical archipelago more than a millennium before Western explorers, whalers, missionaries and entrepreneurs arrived on ships. The tumultuous 19th century stirred a melting pot of immigrants from Asia, America and Europe even as it ended the Hawaiian kingdom founded by Kamehameha the Great.

Ancient Hawai'i

Almost nothing is known about the first wave of Polynesians (likely from the Marquesas Islands) who landed on this archipelago between AD 300 and 600. A second wave of Polynesians from the Tahitian Islands began arriving around AD 1000, and they conquered the first peoples and obliterated nearly all traces of their history and culture. Legends of the *menehune* – an ancient race of little people

10 million BC

Lava from an underwater volcano breaks the ocean's surface and O'ahu emerges as an island.

who built temples and great stoneworks overnight – may refer to these original inhabitants.

Although the discovery of Hawaii may have been accidental, subsequent journeys were not. Tahitians were highly skilled seafarers, navigating more than 2400 miles of open ocean without maps, and with only the sun, stars, wind and waves to guide them. In their double-hulled canoes, they imported to the islands their religious beliefs, social structures and over two dozen food plants and domestic animals. What they didn't possess is equally remarkable: no metals, no wheels, no alphabet or written language, and no clay to make pottery.

After trans-Pacific voyaging stopped completely around 1300 (for reasons unknown today), Hawaiian culture evolved in isolation. Nevertheless it retained a family resemblance to other Polynesian cultures. Ancient Hawaii's highly stratified society was run by chiefs (ali'i) whose right to rule was based on their hereditary lineage to the gods. Clan loyalties trumped expressions of individuality, elaborate traditions of gifting and feasting conferred prestige, and a humanlike pantheon of gods inhabited the natural world.

Several layers of ali'i ruled each island, and life was marked by warring battles as they jockeyed for power and status. The basic political subdivision was the ahupua'a, a wedge-shaped slice of land from the mountains to the sea that contained all the resources each chiefdom needed. Below the chiefs were the kahuna (experts or masters), who included both the priests and the guild masters – canoe makers, healers, navigators and so on. Maka'ainana (commoners) did most of the physical labor, and were obligated to support the ali'i through taxes. Below all was a small class of outcasts (kaua).

Ancient Hawaii's culture of mutuality and reciprocity infused what otherwise resembled a feudal agricultural society: chiefs were custodians of their people, and humans custodians of nature, all of which was sacred – the living expression (or mana, spiritual essence) of the universe's soul. Everyone played their part, through work and ritual, to maintain the health of the community and its relationship to the gods. In practice, a strict code of ritualized behavior – the kapu system – governed every

IN FOCUS HISTORY

The Best...
Hawaiian Temples & Sacred Sites

1 Kane'aki Heiau (p159)

2 Pu'u o Mahuka Heiau State Historic Site (p231)

3 Kea'iwa Heiau State Recreation Area (p147)

4 Ulupo Heiau State Monument (p195)

5 Waimea Valley (p234)

6 Kukaniloko Birthstones (p225)

AD 300–600
The first wave of Polynesians voyage by canoe to the Hawaiian Islands.

1000
Sailing from Tahiti, a second wave of Polynesian voyagers arrives in Hawaii.

1778–79
Captain Cook visits Hawaii twice, the first Westerner to arrive in Hawaii.

Polynesian Wayfaring

In 1976, a double-hulled canoe and her crew set off to recreate the journey of Hawaii's earliest settlers and also to do what no one had done in more than 600 years: sail 4800 miles round-trip to Tahiti without benefit of radar or compass, satellites or sextant.

Launched by the **Polynesian Voyaging Society** (http://pvs.kcc.hawaii.edu/), this modern-day reproduction of an ancient Hawaiian seafaring double-hulled canoe was named *Hokule'a* (Star of Gladness). The *Hokule'a* successfully sailed to Tahiti and back using only traditional Polynesian wayfaring navigational methods of observing stars, wave patterns, seabirds and clouds.

The *Hokule'a's* Micronesian navigator, Mau Piailug, wasn't without tools. He knew how to use horizon or zenith stars – those that always rose over known islands – as a guide, then evaluate currents, winds, landmarks and time in a complex system of dead reckoning to stay on course. In the mind's eye, the trick is to hold the canoe still in relation to the stars while the island sails toward you.

Academic skeptics had long questioned whether Hawaii's early settlers really were capable of journeying back and forth across such vast, empty ocean. After 33 days at sea, *Hokule'a* proved those so-called experts wrong by reaching its destination, where it was greeted by 20,000 Tahitians.

This historic achievement inspired a new appreciation for and interest in Polynesian and Hawaiian cultures. Today, the *Hokule'a* is undertaking an ambitious five-year (2013-17) project to circle the globe. Keep up with progress at www.hokulea.com.

---

aspect of daily life; violating the *kapu* could mean death. Hawaiians also enjoyed life immensely, cultivating rich traditions in music, dance and athletic sports.

The First Westerners

British explorer Captain James Cook spent a decade traversing the Pacific Ocean over the course of three voyages. His ostensible goal was to locate a fabled 'northwest passage' between the Pacific and Atlantic Oceans. However, his were also self-conscious voyages of discovery, and he sailed with a full complement of scientists and artists to document the places, plants and peoples they found. In 1778, and quite by accident, Cook chanced upon the Hawaiian Islands. He dubbed the archipelago the Sandwich Islands in honor of his patron, the Earl of Sandwich.

1795
Kamehameha the Great conquers O'ahu, nearly completing the unification of the Hawaiian kingdom.

1819
Kamehameha II (Liholiho) abolishes the ancient *kapu* (taboo) system; heiau (temples) are destroyed.

1820
The first Christian missionaries are permitted by the Hawaiian monarchy to land on O'ahu.

Cook's arrival ended nearly 500 years of isolation, and it's impossible to overstate the impact of this, or even to appreciate now what his unexpected appearance meant to Hawaiians. Cook's arrival at Kealakekua Bay on the Big Island of Hawai'i happened to coincide with the *makahiki,* an annual harvest festival in honor of the god Lono. Cook's ships were greeted by a thousand canoes, and Hawaiian chiefs and priests honored Cook with feasting, religious rituals and deference suggesting they perhaps considered him to be an earthly manifestation of the god.

When Cook set sail some weeks later, he encountered storms that damaged his ships and forced him to return. Suddenly, the islanders' mood had changed: no canoes rowed out to meet the ships, and mistrust replaced welcome. A series of small conflicts escalated into an angry confrontation on the beach, and Cook, in an ill-advised fit of pique, shot to death a Hawaiian while surrounded by thousands of natives, who immediately descended on Cook, killing him in return.

Kamehameha the Great

In the years following Cook's death, a small, steady number of trading ships sought out Hawaii as a mid-Pacific supply point, and increasingly the thing that Hawaiian chiefs traded for most was firearms. Bolstered with muskets and cannons, Kamehameha, one of the chiefs on the Big Island, began a tremendous military campaign in 1790 to conquer all the Hawaiian Islands. Other chiefs had tried this and failed, but Kamehameha not only had guns, he was prophesied to succeed and possessed an unyielding, charismatic determination.

Within five bloody years Kamehameha had conquered all the main islands but Kaua'i (which eventually joined peacefully). The bloody campaign on O'ahu started with a fleet of war canoes landing on the shores of Waikiki in 1795. Kamehameha then led his warriors up Nu'uanu Valley to meet the entrenched O'auhuan defenders. The O'ahuans, who were prepared for spear-and-stone warfare, panicked when they realized Kamehameha had brought in a handful of Western sharpshooters with modern firearms. Fleeing up the cliffs in retreat, they were forced to make a doomed last stand (see the box, p177).

Kamehameha was a singular figure whose reign established the most peaceful era in Hawaiian history. A shrewd politician, he configured multi-island governance to mute competition among the *ali'i.* A savvy businessman, he created a highly profitable monopoly on the sandalwood trade in 1810 while trying to protect *'iliahi* trees from overharvest. Most of all, Kamehameha successfully absorbed growing foreign influences while fastidiously honoring ancient religious customs, despite creeping doubts among his people about Hawai'i's native gods.

Traders, Whalers & Soul Savers

After Cook's expedition sailed back to Britain, news of his 'discovery' of Hawaii soon spread throughout Europe and the Americas, opening the floodgates to Western

1826
Missionaries create an alphabet for the Hawaiian language and set up the first printing press.

1843
British naval officer George Paulet seizes O'ahu for five months; his illegal actions are disavowed by the British government.

1845
Kamehameha III, Hawaii's first Christian king, moves the capital of the kingdom from Maui to Honolulu.

The Best...
Honolulu Historical Buildings

explorers, traders and missionaries. By the 1820s, whaling ships began pulling into Honolulu for fresh water and food, supplies, liquor and women. To meet their needs, ever more shops, taverns and brothels sprang up around the harbor. By the 1840s, Hawaii had become the whaling capital of the Pacific.

To the ire of dirty-devil whalers, Hawaii's first Christian missionary ship sailed into Honolulu on April 14, 1820, carrying staunch Calvinists who were set on saving the Hawaiians from their 'heathen ways.' Their timing could not have been more opportune, as Hawaii's traditional religion had been abolished the year before following the death of Kamehameha the Great. Both missionaries and the whalers hailed from New England, but soon were at odds: missionaries were intent on saving souls, while to many sailors there was 'no God west of the Horn.'

The missionaries' zeal to save pagan souls was matched only by their disdain of nearly every aspect of Hawaiian culture. They worked tirelessly to stamp out public nakedness, 'lewd' hula dancing, polygamy, gambling, drunkenness and fornication with sailors. To them, all kahuna were witch doctors, and Hawaiians hopelessly lazy. Converts to Christianity came, since the missionaries' god was clearly powerful, but these conversions were not usually deeply felt. Hawaiians often quickly abandoned the church's teachings, reverting to their traditional lifestyle.

However, the missionaries gained enough influence with Hawaiian royalty to have laws enacted against drunkenness and prostitution. Most whaling boats then abandoned Honolulu, preferring to land at licentious Lahaina on Maui. By the mid-19th century, sons of O'ahu's original missionary families had become citizens of Hawaii and even more importantly, the island's new political and economic powerbrokers. Downtown Honolulu became the headquarters of their plantation-era corporations, whose board members today read much like a roster from the first mission ships.

Losing the Land

Born and raised in Hawaii after Western contact, Kamehameha III struggled to keep traditional Hawaiian society alive while evolving the political system to better suit foreign, and frequently American, tastes. In 1848 foreign missionaries convinced the king to pass a sweeping land-reform act called the Great Mahele. It permanently altered the

1848
King Kamehameha III institutes the Great Mahele, which allows commoners and foreigners to own land.

1866
The first group of patients with Hansen's disease (leprosy) are exiled from O'ahu to Moloka'i.

1885
Captain John Kidwell plants pineapples, today the state's biggest cash crop, in Honolulu's Manoa Valley.

Hawaiian concept of land rights: for the first time, land became a capitalist commodity that could be bought and sold.

The hope was that the Great Mahele would create a nation of small freeholder farmers, but instead it was an utter disaster – for Hawaiians, at least. Confusion reigned over boundaries and surveys. Unused to the concept of private land, and sometimes unable to pay the tax, many Hawaiians simply failed to follow through on the paperwork to claim their titles. Many of those who did – perhaps feeling that life as a taro farmer simply wasn't the attraction it once was – immediately cashed out, selling their land to eager and acquisitive foreigners.

Many missionaries ended up with sizable tracts of land, and more than a few left the church to devote themselves to their new estates. Honolulu's already prominent foreign community, composed largely of US and British expats, also opened businesses and schools, started newspapers and, most importantly, landed powerful government positions as ministry officials and consuls to the king, steadily wresting control over island affairs away from the Hawaiian monarchy.

Royal insignia on the gates of 'Iolani Palace (p41)

1893
Queen Lili'uokalani is overthrown. The son of an American missionary announces a new provisional government.

1901
Waikiki's first tourist hotel opens for Matson Navigation Company luxury-liner passengers.

1912
Champion Waikiki surfer Duke Kahanamoku wins his first gold medal for swimming at the Olympics.

King Sugar & the Plantation Era

Ko (sugarcane) arrived in Hawaii with the early Polynesian settlers. In 1835 Bostonian William Hooper saw a business opportunity to establish Hawaii's first sugar plantation. Hooper persuaded Honolulu investors to put up the money for his venture and then worked out a deal with Kamehameha III to lease agricultural land on Kaua'i. The next order of business was finding an abundant supply of low-cost labor, which was necessary to make sugar plantations profitable.

The natural first choice for plantation workers was Native Hawaiians, but even when willing, they were not enough. Due to introduced diseases such as typhoid, influenza, smallpox and syphilis, the Native Hawaiian population had steadily and precipitously declined. An estimated 800,000 indigenous people lived in the islands before Western contact, but by 1800, the Native Hawaiian population had dropped by two-thirds, to around 250,000. By 1860, Native Hawaiians numbered fewer than 70,000.

Wealthy plantation owners began to look overseas for a labor supply of immigrants accustomed to working long days in hot weather, and for whom the low wages would seem like an opportunity. In the 1850s, wealthy sugar-plantation owners began recruiting laborers from China, then Japan and Portugal. Many immigrants came intending to stay for a short time and return home rich, but ended up settling here instead and never leaving the islands, let alone getting rich.

During the US Civil War, sugar exports to Union states on the mainland soared, making plantation owners wealthier and more powerful. After annexing Hawaii in 1898, the US restricted Chinese and Japanese immigration, which made O'ahu's plantation owners turn to Puerto Rico, Korea and the Philippines for laborers. All of these different immigrant groups, along with the shared pidgin language they developed and the uniquely mixed culture of plantation life itself, transformed Hawaii into the multicultural, multiethnic society it is today.

Fall of the Monarchy

As much as any other monarch, King David Kalakaua, who reigned from 1874 to 1891, fought to restore Hawaiian culture and native pride. With robust joy, he resurrected hula and its attendant arts from near extinction – earning himself the nickname 'the Merrie Monarch' – much to the dismay of missionaries. He cared not a whit about placating the plantation oligarchy either. The king spent money lavishly and piled up massive debt. Wanting Hawaii's monarchy to be equal to any in the world, he built Honolulu's 'Iolani Palace, holding an extravagant coronation ceremony in 1883. Foreign businessmen considered these actions to be egotistical follies.

Kalakaua was a mercurial decision-maker given to summarily replacing his entire cabinet on a whim. A secret, antimonarchy group of mostly non–Native Hawaiian residents calling themselves the Hawaiian League formed, and in 1887 they forced Kalakaua to sign a new 'bayonet' constitution that stripped the monarchy of most of its powers, and changed the voting laws to include only those who met certain income

1936

Pan American airlines flies the first passenger planes from the US mainland to Hawaii.

1941

Japan stages a surprise attack on Pearl Harbor, catapulting the USA into WWII.

1959

Hawaii becomes the 50th state; Japanese American WWII veteran Daniel Inouye elected to US Congress.

and property requirements – effectively disenfranchising all but wealthy, mostly Caucasian business owners. To ensure economic profitability, the Hawaiian League was ready to sacrifice Hawaiian sovereignty.

When King Kalakaua died in 1891, his sister and heir, Princess Lili'uokalani, ascended the throne. The queen fought against foreign intervention and control as she secretly drafted a new constitution to restore Native Hawaiian voting rights and the monarchy's powers. In 1893, before Lili'uokalani could present this constitution to Hawaii's people, a hastily formed 'Committee of Safety' put into violent motion the Hawaiian League's long-brewing plans to overthrow the Hawaiian government. Without an army to defend her and opting to avoid bloodshed, the queen stepped down.

After the coup, the new provisional government immediately requested annexation by the US. However, much to their surprise, President Grover Cleveland reviewed the situation and refused: he condemned the coup as illegal, conducted under a false pretext and against the will of the Hawaiian people, and he requested Lili'uokalani be reinstated. Miffed but unbowed, the Committee of Safety instead established their own government, the Republic of Hawaii.

Annexation, War & Statehood

For five years, Queen Lili'uokalani pressed her case (for a time while under house arrest at 'Iolani Palace) – even collecting an antiannexation petition signed by the vast majority of Native Hawaiians – to no avail. In 1898, spurred by President McKinley, the US approved a resolution for annexing the Republic of Hawaii as a US territory.

In part, the US justified this colonialism because the ongoing Spanish-American War had highlighted the strategic importance of the islands as a Pacific military base. Indeed, some Americans feared that if the US didn't take Hawaii, another Pacific Rim power (such as Japan) just might. The US Navy quickly established its Pacific headquarters at Pearl Harbor and built Schofield Barracks, at that time the largest US army base in the world, in central O'ahu.

On December 7, 1941, a wave of Japanese bombers attacked Pearl Harbor (see p140), a devastating surprise attack that instantly propelled the USA into WWII. In Hawaii the US Army took control of the islands, martial law was declared, and civil rights were suspended. Japanese immigrants and Hawaii residents of Japanese ancestry suffered intense racial discrimination and deep suspicions over their loyalties, and around 1250 people were unjustly detained in internment camps on O'ahu.

The end of WWII brought Hawaii closer to the center stage of American culture and politics. Three decades had already passed since Prince Jonah Kuhio Kalaniana'ole, Hawaii's first delegate to the US Congress, introduced a Hawaii statehood bill in 1919, but it received a cool reception in Washington DC. Even after WWII, Hawaii was seen as too much of a racial melting pot for many US politicians to support statehood. Not until August 21, 1959, with more than 90% of the islanders voting for statehood, did Hawaii finally become the USA's 50th state.

1993
President Clinton signs 'Apology Resolution,' recognizing the illegal overthrow of the Hawaiian kingdom in 1893.

2008
Barack Obama, who was born and grew up in Honolulu, becomes the 44th US President.

2012
US President Barack Obama is re-elected. Just as in 2008, Obama wins over 70% of the vote in Hawaii, more than in any other state.

People of Oʻahu

Schoolchildren in Honolulu

ERIC WHEATER / GETTY IMAGE

Everything you imagine when you hear the name Hawaii is probably true. Whatever your postcard idyll might be – a paradise of white sandy beaches, emerald cliffs and azure seas; of falsetto-voiced ukulele strummers, lithesome hula dancers and sun-bronzed surfers – it exists somewhere on the islands. But beyond the frame of that magical postcard is a startlingly different version of Hawaii, a real place where everyday people live.

Slow Down, This Ain't the Mainland

Oʻahu is a Polynesian island, yes. But one with shopping malls, landfills, industrial parks, cookie-cutter housing developments, military bases and ramshackle small towns. In many ways, it's much like the rest of the US, and a first-time visitor stepping off the plane may be surprised to find a place where interstate highways and McDonald's look pretty much the same as back on 'da mainland.'

Underneath the veneer of an imported consumer culture is a different world, a world defined by – and proud of – its cultural separateness, its geographical isolation, its unique mix of Polynesian, Asian and Western traditions. While those cultures don't always blend seamlessly, there are very few places in the world today where so many different ethnicities, with no one group commanding a substantial majority, get along.

Perhaps it's because they live on a tiny island in the middle of an ocean that O'ahu residents strive to treat one another with aloha, act polite and respectful, and 'no make waves' (ie be cool). As Native Hawaiians say, 'We're all in the same canoe.' No matter their race or background, everyone shares the common awareness of living in one of the earth's most extraordinary spots.

The Best...
Local Cultural Experiences

1 Prince Lot Hula Festival (p65)

2 Nā Mea Hawai'i (p64)

3 Waikiki Community Center (p109)

4 Na Lima Mili Hulu No'eau (see the box text, p128)

5 'I Love Kailua' Town Party (p197)

Island Identity

Honolulu is 'the city,' not only for those who live on O'ahu but for all of Hawaii. Far slower paced than New York City or Los Angeles, Hawaii's capital can still be surprisingly cosmopolitan, technologically savvy and fashion conscious. Right or wrong, Honoluluans see themselves at the center of every-thing; they deal with the traffic jams and high-rises because along with them come better-paying jobs, vibrant arts and cultural scenes, trendy shops and (relatively tame) nightlife. Ritzy suburbs sprawl along the coast east of Waikiki, while military bases are found around Pearl Harbor to 'Ewa in the west and Wahiawa in the island's center.

If it weren't for the occasional ride into the city to pick up supplies, the lifestyle of rural O'ahuans is as 'small town' as you'll find anywhere else in Hawaii. O'ahu's Windward Coast, North Shore and Leeward Coast are considered 'the country.' (Though in a landscape as compressed as this island, 'country' is relative: rural areas are not too far from the urban or suburban, and there are no vast swaths of uninterrupted wilderness like on the mainland.) Here status often isn't measured by a Lexus but by a monster truck.

'Ohana (extended family and friends) is important everywhere, but in small towns it's often the center of life. Even in Honolulu, when locals first meet, they don't ask 'What do you do?' but 'Where you wen' grad?' (Where did you go to high school?). Like ancient Hawaiians comparing genealogies, locals define themselves in part by the communities to which they belong: extended family, island, town, high school. And when two locals happen to meet outside Hawaii, there's an automatic bond, often based on mutual homesickness. But wherever they go, they're still part of Hawaii's extended 'ohana.

Multiculturalism

During the 2008 US presidential election, Barack Obama, who spent much of his boy-hood in Honolulu, was lauded by locals because of his calm demeanor and his respect for diversity. He also displayed true devotion to his 'ohana by suspending his cam-paign and visiting his sick grandmother in Honolulu. She died days before the election. To locals, these are the things that count. What didn't matter to Hawaii is what the rest of the nation seemed fixated on: his race.

That Obama is mixed race was barely worth mentioning. Of course he's mixed race – who in Hawaii isn't? One legacy of the plantation era is Hawaii's unself-conscious and inclusive mixing of ethnicities; cultural differences are freely

261

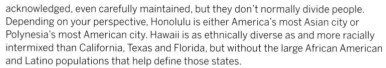

acknowledged, even carefully maintained, but they don't normally divide people. Depending on your perspective, Honolulu is either America's most Asian city or Polynesia's most American city. Hawaii is as ethnically diverse as and more racially intermixed than California, Texas and Florida, but without the large African American and Latino populations that help define those states.

Among older locals, plantation-era stereotypes still inform social hierarchies and interactions. During plantation days, whites were the wealthy plantation owners, and for years after people would half-seriously joke about the privileges that came with being a haole (Caucasian) 'boss.' Hawaii's youth often dismiss racial distinctions even as they continue to speak plantation-born pidgin. With intermarriage, it's not uncommon to meet locals who can rattle off several different ethnicities in their ancestry – for example, Native Hawaiian, Chinese, Portuguese and haole.

Lifestyle

The values of tolerance and acceptance extend beyond race – they apply also to religion and sexual orientation. While for many years Hawaii was politically behind the curve in its treatment of gay, lesbian and transgender people, especially in some tight-knit rural communities, today the right to same-sex civil unions is guaranteed by state law.

Politically, most voters are middle-of-the-road Democrats who vote along party, racial, ethnic, seniority and local/nonlocal lines. In everyday life, most people don't jump into a controversial topic just to argue the point. At community meetings and activist rallies, the most vocal liberals are often mainland transplants. Yet as more mainlanders settle on O'ahu, especially around Kailua and Kane'ohe on the Windward Coast, traditional stereotypes are fading.

Native Hawaiians still struggle with the colonial legacy that has marginalized them in their own homeland. Hawaiians constitute a disproportionate number of those homeless (about a third) and impoverished. Native Hawaiian schoolchildren, on average, are below state averages in reading and math and are more likely to drop out of school. Hawaiian charter schools were created in part to address this problem. However, many Native Hawaiians feel that some form of sovereignty is necessary to correct these deeply entrenched inequities.

Who Are You?

Haole White person (except local Portuguese). Can be insulting or playful, depending on context.

Hapa Person of mixed ancestry, usually hapa haole (literally, 'half white').

Hawaiian Person of Native Hawaiian ancestry. Don't use the term 'Hawaiian' as a catchall for island residents; Native Hawaiians are the indigenous race.

Kama'aina Person who is native to a particular place (literally, 'child of the land'). Commonly, 'kama'aina discounts' apply to any island resident (ie anyone with a state driver's license).

Local Person who grew up in Hawaii. To call a transplant 'almost local' is a compliment, despite its emphasis on the insider/outsider mentality.

Transplant Person who moves to Hawaii as an adult; can never be 'local.'

Honolulu's Chinatown still has its seedy edges, just like in the 19th-century whaling days, with skid rows of drug addicts, prostitutes and panhandlers. The use of 'ice' (methamphetamine, aka crystal meth) became rampant in the 1990s, in both urban and rural communities, where it's an ongoing social and law-enforcement challenge. Homelessness and a lack of affordable housing are also serious social and political issues, with hundreds of O'ahuans encamped semipermanently at public beaches, especially on the Wai'anae Coast (see p155).

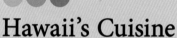

Hawaii's Cuisine

Forget about pineapple upside-down cake and tiki-bar cocktails. 'Dis is seriously broke da mout!' That's the ultimate compliment you'll hear if you hang around locals long enough. It means something is so delicious it breaks the mouth. And that's no exaggeration. Here in the islands, people go crazy over food, especially in Honolulu. So, be brave and eat everything in sight. It's all 'ono grinds (good eats).

The Island 'Diet'

Before human contact, the only indigenous edibles in Hawaii were ferns and ʻohelo berries. The first Polynesians to journey to this archipelago from far across the Pacific brought with them *kalo* (taro), *ʻulu* (breadfruit), *ʻuala* (sweet potato), *maiʻa* (banana), *ko* (sugarcane) and *niu* (coconut), plus chickens, pigs and dogs for meat – and they enjoyed an abundance of seafood.

Western explorers dropped off cattle and horses, and later missionaries and settlers planted exotic fruits such as pineapple and guava. When the sugar industry peaked in the late 19th century, bringing waves of immigrant laborers from Asia and Europe, Hawaii's cuisine developed a taste and identity all its own. It took plantation imports, including rice, *shōyu* (soy sauce), ginger and chili pepper, but never abandoned Native Hawaiian staples like *kalua* pork and poi (pounded taro root).

Today, Hawaii's food traditions are multiethnic. Local *grinds* (food), like saimin noodle soup and Spam *musubi* (rice balls), are island renditions of comfort food from other countries, often Asia. This tasty culinary mishmash has turned locals into adventurous and passionate eaters who are always hungry for that next knockout mouthful of *'ono kine grinds* (good food), maybe from a food truck near you.

Hawaiian Traditions

With rich, earthy flavors and indigenous Polynesian ingredients, Hawaiian cooking is unique. *Kalua* pig (traditionally roasted in an underground pit layered with hot stones and banana and *ti* leaves) and starchy poi (a purplish paste pounded from taro, often fermented and sour-tasting) are Hawaii's endemic 'meat and potatoes'. Locals describe the consistency of poi as one-, two- or three-finger, indicating how many fingers are required to scoop it from bowl to mouth.

Poi is nutritious and easily digestible but tastes relatively bland – its purpose is to balance the stronger flavors of other dishes, such as *lomilomi* salmon (minced salted fish with diced tomato and green onion) or *laulau* (a bundle of pork, chicken or fish wrapped in taro and *ti* leaves and steamed). Other savory Hawaiian dishes include baked *'ulu, limu* (seaweed), *'opihi* (tiny limpet shells picked off reefs at low tide) and *pipi kaula* (beef jerky). Sweet *haupia* pudding is made of coconut cream traditionally thickened with arrowroot.

Local Food

Sticky white rice is more than a side dish in Hawaii. It's a culinary building block, an integral partner in everyday meals. Without rice, Spam *musubi* would just be a slice of canned meat. The *loco moco* would be nothing more than an egg-covered hamburger. Just FYI, rice almost always means sticky white rice. Not fluffy rice. Not wild rice. And *definitely* not instant rice.

Cheap, filling and tasty, a local 'mixed plate lunch' includes two-scoop rice, a scoop of mayonnaise-laden macaroni salad and a hot, hearty main dish, such as Korean–style *kalbi* short ribs, Filipino pork *adobo,* batter-fried *mochiko* (Japanese rice-flour) chicken or *furikake*-encrusted mahimahi. Islanders on a healthy kick will ask for brown rice and tossed salad greens instead of the usual sides.

Another local favorite is *poke,* which is bite-sized cubes of raw fish typically marinated in *shōyu*, oil, chili peppers, green onions and seaweed, though you'll find all kinds of flavor profiles. Saimin is an island-style soup of chewy egg noodles and Japanese broth, garnished with green onion, dried nori or perhaps *kamaboko* (pureed, steamed fish cake) or an egg. *Manapua,* the local version of Chinese *bao* (steamed or baked buns), have a variety of fillings, from *char siu* (barbecued pork) to black sugar.

On a hot day, nothing beats a mound of snowy shave ice, packed into a cup and drenched with sweet syrups in an eye-popping rainbow of hues. Purists stick with only ice but, for added decadence, ask for sweet azuki beans, *mochi* (sticky, sweet Japanese pounded-rice cakes) or ice cream underneath, or maybe *haupia* cream or a dusting of *li hing mui* (dried, salted plums) powder on top.

Hawaii Regional Cuisine & Locavarianism

In the early 1990s, island chefs including Alan Wong, Roy Yamaguchi and Sam Choy started partnering with local farmers, ranchers and fishers. Dubbed Hawaii Regional cuisine (HRC), this culinary movement was hallmarked by its Asian and Pacific Rim fusion tastes such as Peking duck in ginger-*liliko'i* (passion fruit) sauce or grilled butterfish glazed with Japanese miso (fermented soybean paste). But Hawaii Regional cuisine remained upscale, usually only found at destination beach-resort restaurants and celebrity chefs' kitchens.

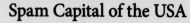

Spam Capital of the USA

Hawaii may be the only place in the nation where you can eat canned Spam with pride. While US food maker Hormel's Spam, a pork-based luncheon meat, is the butt of jokes almost everywhere, there's little stigma in Hawaii. Here locals consume nearly seven million cans per year!

Of course, Spam looks and tastes different in Hawaii. It is always eaten cooked (typically sautéed to a light crispiness in sweetened *shōyu*), not straight from the can, and is served as a tasty breakfast dish – Spam and eggs, Spam and rice, etc.

Spam was first canned in 1937 and introduced to Hawaii during WWII, when the Hawaiian Islands were considered a war zone. During that period fresh meat imports were replaced by this standard GI ration. By the time the war ended, Hawaiians had developed an affinity for the fatty canned stuff.

The most-common preparation is Spam *musubi:* a block of rice with a slice of fried Spam on top (or in the middle), wrapped with a strip of black sushi nori. Created in the 1960s, it has become a classic, and thousands of *musubi* are sold daily at grocers, lunch counters and convenience stores.

For Spam trivia, recipes and games, go to www.spam.com. Or plan your trip around the **Waikiki Spam Jam** (p110), a huge street festival in late April.

Today, Hawaii's locavarian cuisine focuses on seasonally fresh, sustainable, often organic ingredients, such as Nalo greens or grass-fed beef from North Shore free-range cattle. It's as popular at food trucks and farmers' markets as gourmet dining rooms. Meanwhile, small-scale farmers are slowly shifting island agriculture away from corporate-scale, industrialized monocropping (eg pineapples) enabled by chemical fertilizers, pesticides and herbicides. With more than 85% of Hawaii's food having to be shipped in, the locavarian food movement is about not just taste but also economic self-sufficiency.

Island Drinks

Fruit trees thrive in Hawaii, so you'd expect to find fresh juices everywhere. Wrong. Only syrupy fruit drinks like POG (passion fruit, orange and guava) are readily found at supermarkets. For more pure, often organic and locally harvested juices, check out farmers' markets, natural-foods stores and **Lanikai Juice** (p201). Two traditional Hawaiian tonics made from island-grown plants are 'awa (kava), a mild sedative and intoxicant, and *noni* (Indian mulberry), which some consider a cure-all. Both are pungent in smell and taste.

Every beach-hotel bar mixes zany tropical cocktails topped with a fruit garnish and a little toothpick umbrella. The legendary mai tai is a mix of rum, grenadine, orange curaçao, orgeat syrup and orange, lemon, lime and/or pineapple juices. The state's best-known microbrewer is the **Kona Brewing Co** (http://konabrewingco.com), which has an outpost in Hawai'i Kai (p174). A few local brewpubs have also popped up in Honolulu (see p77).

Hawaii is the only state in the USA to grow coffee. The finest coffee beans come from the Big Island, where 100% Kona coffee has gourmet cachet. **Green World Coffee Farm** (p246), near Wahiawa in Central O'ahu, is a must for coffee enthusiasts and offers up a range of free tasters. **Waialua Soda Works** (www.waialuasodaworks.com) bottles old-fashioned soda pop that's naturally flavored by tropical fruit such as *liliko'i*.

Celebrating with Food

Throughout Hawaii, to celebrate is to feast. Whether a 300-guest wedding or a birthday party for *'ohana* (extended family and friends), a massive spread is mandatory. Most gatherings happen outdoors at parks, beaches and backyards, featuring a potluck buffet of homemade dishes. If you're invited to someone's home for a meal, show up on time, remove your shoes at the door and bring dessert (eg a local bakery cake).

In ancient Hawaii, a luau was held to commemorate auspicious occasions such as births and war victories. Luau are still commonplace in contemporary island life, for example, to celebrate a baby's first birthday or a wedding. Commercial luau offer the elaborate feast and hip-shaking, grass-skirted Polynesian dancing that many tourists expect, and an all-you-can-eat buffet with a typically mediocre sampling of traditional Hawaiian dishes.

Annual events such as the **Hawaii Food & Wine Festival** (p66) showcases the island's bounty. Honolulu's **Pan-Pacific Festival** (p65) and **Aloha Festivals** (p111) also feature *ho'olaule'a* (block parties) with local chefs and food vendors. Weekly farmers' markets held all around O'ahu share the same festive atmosphere year-round.

IN FOCUS HAWAII'S CUISINE

The Best...
Local Plate Lunches

1 Poke Stop (p247)

2 Ted's Bakery (p230)

3 Haili's Hawaiian Foods (p121)

4 Me's BBQ (p118)

5 Rainbow Drive-In (p121)

6 Waiahole Poi Factory (p207)

Dining Out & Self-Catering

Informal dining is Hawaii's forte. For local food and rock-bottom prices, swing by retro drive-ins and diners with Formica tables, open from morning till night, or Japanese–style *okazuya* (takeout delicatessens), which are sold out by early afternoon. Portion sizes can be gigantic, so feel free to split a meal or take home leftovers, like locals do.

For gourmet cuisine by Hawaii's star chefs, explore Honolulu. Hawaii's cutting-edge foodie trends, such as *izakaya* (Japanese pubs serving food), all start in the capital city, too. Outside Honolulu and Waikiki, restaurants close early in the evening (see p309 for typical opening hours and see p311 for prices). Open from *pau hana* (happy hour) until late, most bars serve tasty *pupu* (appetizers or small shared plates) like *poke,* shrimp tempura or edamame (fresh soybeans in the pod).

The casual Hawaii dress code means T-shirts and flip-flops are ubiquitous, except at Honolulu's most upscale restaurants and at Waikiki's luxury resort hotels. The older generation of locals tends toward neat, modest attire, which for men usually just means an aloha shirt and slacks. Smoking is not allowed inside restaurants. For tips on eating out with kids, see p278.

For groceries, head to farmers' markets and locally owned supermarkets. In Hawaii, most groceries are imported. The everyday price of food averages 30% more than on the US mainland, so you may not save much money by cooking your own meals.

Food Glossary

If someone offers you a *broke da mout malasada* or *'ono kine poke,* would you try it? Don't miss out because you're stumped by the lingo.

adobo – Filipino chicken or pork cooked in vinegar, *shōyu,* garlic and spices

'awa – kava, a Polynesian plant used to make an intoxicating drink

bentō – Japanese–style box lunch

broke da mout – delicious; literally 'broke the mouth'

char siu – Chinese barbecued pork

chirashizushi – assorted sushi and/or sashimi served over rice

crack seed – Chinese preserved fruit; a salty, sweet and/or sour snack

donburi – Japanese–style large bowl of rice topped with a protein (eg chicken cutlet)

furikake – Japanese seasoning or condiment, usually dry and sprinkled atop rice; in Hawaii, often mixed into *poke*

grind – to eat

grinds – food (usually local)

guava – green-yellow fruit with moist, pink flesh and lots of edible seeds

gyōza – Japanese grilled or steamed dumplings, usually containing minced pork or shrimp

haupia – coconut-cream pudding dessert

Child eating shave ice
LINDA CHING/GETTY IMAGES ©

hijiki – Japanese seaweed

hulihuli chicken – rotisserie-cooked chicken with island-style barbecue sauce

ikura – salmon roe

imu – underground earthen oven used to cook *kalua* pig and other luau food

'inamona – roasted ground *kukui* (candlenuts), used to flavor dishes such as *poke*

izakaya – Japanese pub serving food

kaiseki ryōri – formal Japanese cuisine consisting of a series of small, seasonally inspired dishes

kalbi – Korean–style grilled dishes, often marinated short ribs

kalo – taro, often pounded into poi

kalua – traditional Hawaiian method of cooking pork and other luau food in an underground pit

kamaboko – pureed, steamed fish cake

katsu – deep-fried cutlets, usually pork or chicken; see *tonkatsu*

kaukau – food

ko – sugarcane

laulau – a bundle made of pork or chicken and salted butterfish, wrapped in taro and *ti* leaves and steamed

li hing mui – sweet-salty preserved plum; also a flavor of crack seed

liliko'i – passion fruit

loco moco – dish of rice, fried egg and hamburger patty topped with gravy or other condiments

lomilomi salmon – minced, salted salmon with diced tomato and green onion

The Best...
Island Sweets

1 Leonard's (p120)

2 Matsumoto's Shave Ice (p238)

3 Crack Seed Store (p77)

4 Waiola Shave Ice (p120)

5 Liliha Bakery (p77)

6 Bubbie's (p174)

IN FOCUS HAWAII'S CUISINE

Crack Seed

Forget candy bars. Hawaii's most popular snack is crack seed, sold prepackaged in supermarkets and convenience stores or by the pound at candy shops. It's an addictive, mouth-watering Chinese invention that can be sweet, sour, salty, spicy or some combination of all four (umm, *umami*). Like Coca-Cola or curry, the various flavors of crack seed are impossible to describe. Just one taste and you'll be hooked.

Crack seed is usually made from dried fruit such as plums, cherries, mangoes or lemons. The most popular flavor – which is also the most overwhelming to the uninitiated – is *li hing mui*. These days powdered *li hing mui* – sour enough to pucker the most stoic of faces – is used to spice up just about everything, from shave ice to fresh-fruit margaritas.

The Best...
Star Chefs' Kitchens

IN FOCUS HAWAII'S CUISINE

luau – Hawaiian feast

mai tai – tiki-bar drink typically containing rum and tropical fruit juices

malasada – sugar-coated Portuguese fried doughnut (no hole), often with a custard filling

manapua – island version of *bao* (Chinese–style steamed or baked bun) with sweet or savory filling

miso – Japanese fermented soybean paste, usually red or white

mochi – sticky, sweet Japanese pounded-rice cake

musubi – island version of Japanese *onigiri* (rice ball)

nabemono – Japanese clay-pot soup or stew made with meat and/or vegetables

nigiri – hand-molded Japanese sushi atop oval-shaped rice

niu – coconut

noni – Indian mulberry with smelly, yellow-green fruit, used medicinally in Hawaii

nori – Japanese seaweed, usually dried

ogo – crunchy, salty seaweed, often added to *poke; limu* in Hawaiian

okazuya – Japanese takeout deli, often specializing in home-style island cooking

'ono – delicious

'ono kine grinds – good food

'opihi – edible limpet

pau hana – happy hour; literally 'stop work'

pho – Vietnamese soup, typically beef broth, noodles and fresh herbs

pipi kaula – Hawaiian beef jerky

poha – cape gooseberry

poi – staple Hawaiian starch made of mashed taro, often fermented until sour

poke – cubed raw fish mixed with *shōyu,* sesame oil, salt, chili pepper, *furikake, 'inamona* or other condiments

ponzu – Japanese citrus sauce

pupu – bar snack or appetizer

saimin – local-style noodle soup, similar to Japanese *rāmen*

shave ice – cup of finely shaved ice, sweetened with colorful syrup

shōyu – Japanese soy sauce

soba – thin Japanese buckwheat-flour noodles

star fruit – translucent yellow-green fruit with five ribs like the points of a star and sweet, juicy pulp

taro – plant with edible starchy corm used to make poi; called *kalo* in Hawaiian

teppanyaki – Japanese style of cooking with an iron grill

tonkatsu – breaded and fried pork cutlets, also prepared as chicken *katsu*

tsukemono – Japanese pickled vegetables

udon – thick Japanese wheat-flour noodles

'ulu – breadfruit, a staple Hawaiian starch prepared much like a potato

ume – Japanese pickled plum

uni – sea urchin, often served as *nigiri* sushi

wagyū – Japanese marbled beef, usually served as steak

Name That Fish

In Hawaii, most fish go by Hawaiian and/or Japanese names. For sustainable seafood and sushi choices, download the free Hawaii pocket guide from **Monterey Bay Seafood Watch** (www.seafoodwatch.org).

'ahi – yellowfin or bigeye tuna; red flesh, served raw or rare

aku – skipjack tuna; red flesh, strong flavor; *katsuo* in Japanese

'ama'ama – mullet; delicate white flesh

awa – milkfish; tender white flesh

kajiki – Pacific blue marlin; *a'u* in Hawaiian

mahimahi – 'dolphin' fish; firm pink flesh

moi – threadfish; flaky white flesh, rich flavor; traditionally reserved for *ali'i* (Hawaiian royalty)

monchong – pomfret; mild flavor, firm pinkish-white flesh

'o'io – bonefish; rarely eaten outside of Hawaii

onaga – ruby snapper; soft and moist; *'ula'ula* in Hawaiian

ono – a white-fleshed, flaky mackerel; also called wahoo

opah – moonfish; firm and rich

'opakapaka – pink snapper; delicate flavor

'opelu – mackerel scad; usually pan-fried

papio – jackfish; also called *ulua*

shutome – broadbill swordfish; succulent and meaty

tako – octopus; chewy texture; *he'e* in Hawaiian

tombo – albacore tuna; light flesh, mild flavor, silky texture

unagi – freshwater eel; usually grilled or served raw as sushi

Hawaii's Arts & Crafts

Man playing slack key guitar

The islands' arts are all around you. Any night in Waikiki you might catch a slack key guitar great in concert. But you also may overhear an impromptu ukulele performance at a rural beach park or happen upon a hula halau (school) performing at a farmers' market. Keep your eyes and ears open, the local music, hula, native crafts and storytelling are a great way to experience Hawaiian culture.

Music

Tune your rental-car radio to a Hawaiian station and you'll hear everything from contemporary Hawaiian folk rock to reggae-inspired 'Jawaiian' sounds. Traditional Hawaiian music is rooted in ancient chants and missionary hymns. As arriving immigrants introduced new melodies and instruments, those were then incorpor-ated and adapted to create a unique local style. The sound usually includes *leo ki'eki'e* (falsetto, or high voice) vocals, sometimes just referred to as 'soprano' for women, that employs a *ha'i* (vocal break, or split-note) style, with a singer moving abruptly from one register to another. Traditional instruments used are the steel guitar, slack key guitar and ukulele.

Both the ukulele and the steel guitar contribute to the lighthearted hapa haole Hawaiian tunes with English lyrics that were popularized in Hawaii after the 1930s, of which

'My Little Grass Shack' is a classic example. The *Hawaii Calls* radio show was broadcast worldwide for 40 years from Waikiki's Moana Hotel, making this music instantly recognizable. Don Ho further popularized the genre. The modern slack key era was launched with legendary Gabby Pahinui's first recording, 'Hi'ilawe', in 1946.

The most famous traditional Hawaiian musician today is probably still the late Israel (IZ) Kamakawiwo'ole, whose *Facing Future* is Hawaii's all-time bestselling album. Among women, the unquestioned master was the late Aunty Genoa Keawe, whose impossibly long-held notes in the song 'Alika' set the standard (and set it high). Her O'ahu-born '*ohana* (family) still performs as a group in Waikiki. Also look for albums by Keali'i Reichel, Amy Hanalali'i Gillom and Raiatea Helm. The slack key tradition lives on in Keola Beamer, Led Kaapana and Cyril and Martin Pahinui, among others. Dennis and David Kamakahi combine their talents on slack key guitar and ukulele, respectively.

In Honolulu, for classic and contemporary Hawaiian music tune into KINE Radio (105.1 FM). You can browse for recordings online at **Mountain Apple Company** (www.mountainapplecompany.com) or **Mele** (www.mele.com). Also check out recent winners of the **Na Hoku Hanohano Awards** (www.nahokuhanohano.org), Hawaii's version of the Grammies.

The Best...
Live Acts

1 Brothers Cazimero

2 Martin Pahinui

3 Jerry Santos & Friends

4 Kelly Boy De Lima with Kapena

5 Henry Kapono

6 Natural Vibrations

Hula

In ancient Hawaii hula was both a solemn ritual and entertainment. Dancers used hand gestures, facial expressions and synchronized movement, accompanied by rhythmic beats and *mele* (chants), as an offering to the gods or to celebrate the accomplishments of *ali'i* (chiefs). Hula contained the oral history for the ancient Hawaiians, who had no written language.

When Christian missionaries arrived, they viewed hula dancing as licentious and condemned the practice. The tradition might have been lost forever if King Kalakaua, the Merrie Monarch, had not revived it in the late-19th century. Today serious students still join a hula *halau*, where they study under a *kumu hula* (hula teacher). Schools teach both *kahiko* (ancient) and '*auana* (modern) hula styles. *Kahiko* performances are raw and elemental, accompanied only by chanting and thunderous gourd drums. Western-influenced '*auana* is the more mainstream contemporary style, using English lyrics, harmonious singing, stringed instruments, modern island-style clothing and sinuous arm movements. Big commercial productions with vigorously shaking hips and Vegas showgirl–style headdresses might be entertaining, but they're more related to Tahitian dance than hula. (Ancient dancers here wore pounded-bark cloth, or *kapa*, skirts or wraps – not grass skirts.)

Waikiki is the best place to reliably catch hula performances. Bars, restaurants and hotels often include hula in their evening entertainment, and the Kuhio Beach Torch Lighting & Hula Show is free. Another way to experience hula is to attend a luau; the Polynesian Cultural Center on the Windward Coast has the most authentic performances. You never know, you may also be lucky enough to see a *halau* performing at a local festival; always check event calendars. For more on hula see p191.

Want to learn yourself? Island resorts often have an introductory hula lesson in their activity schedule, as does Waikiki Community Center.

Hawaiian Art & Crafts

Ancient Hawaiian skills still contribute to many of the beautiful artisan products produced today. Some of the most prized items are native-wood bowls, often made of beautifully grained tropical hardwoods such as koa and milo. Hawaiian bowls are not decorated or ornate, but are shaped to bring out the natural beauty of the wood. The thinner and lighter the bowl, the finer the artistry and the greater the value. Don't be fooled by cheap monkeypod bowls imported from the Philippines.

The Art of the Lei

Lei making may be Hawaii's most transitory art form. Fragrant and ephemeral, lei embody the beauty of nature and the embrace of the community, freely given and freely shared. In the islands' ancient past, lei makers wound, braided or strung together feathers, nuts, shells, seeds, seaweed, vines, leaves and fruit, in addition to the fragrant tropical flowers more common today. Lei were part of sacred hula dances, given as special gifts to loved ones, used as healing medicine for the sick and as offerings to the gods. So powerful a symbol were they that on ancient Hawaii's battlefields, the right lei could bring peace to warring armies.

Today, locals continue to honor loved ones with lei at weddings, birthdays, anniversaries, graduations and public ceremonies. For visitors to Hawaii, the tradition of giving and receiving lei dates back to the 20th-century steamships; disembarking passengers were greeted by local vendors who would toss garlands around their necks.

In 1927, the poet Don Blanding called for making a holiday to celebrate lei. Leonard and Ruth Hawk later composed the popular tune 'May Day is Lei Day in Hawaii'. Today, May 1, Lei Day, is celebrated across the islands with Hawaiian music, hula dancing, parades, lei-making workshops and contests.

A typical Hawaiian lei costs anywhere from $10 for a single strand of orchids or frangipani to thousands of dollars for a 100% genuine Ni'ihau shell lei necklace. Be aware that most *kukui* (candlenut) lei are cheap imports, thus the low prices. Freshly made flower lei are available near the airport and in Chinatown among other places, including some supermarkets. For intricately crafted feather lei, drop by Na Lima Mili Hulu No'eau in Waikiki. Services such as **Lei Greeting** (www.leigreeting.com) can arrange to meet your party at the airport with a suitable floral welcome.

LEI ETIQUETTE

○ Never refuse a lei or take one off in the presence of the giver. It's considered rude as the giving is a sign of affection or regard.

○ Resist the temptation to wear a lei intended for someone else. It's thought to be bad luck.

○ Don't give a closed lei to a pregnant woman, as many believe it can bring bad luck to the unborn child; choose an open (untied) lei or *haku* (head) lei instead.

○ Ideally, you should not throw a lei in the trash, as it could be taken as a sign you are throwing the giver's love away. If possible instead, untie the string and return the lei's natural elements to the earth (eg scatter flowers in the sea, bury seeds or nuts).

Protestant missionaries introduced quilting to Hawaii in the early-19th century, but the vibrant colors and natural patterns are based on indigenous *kapa* (pounded-bark cloth) designs. Traditional quilts typically have one solid colored fabric, which has been folded into fourths or eighths and cut into a repeating pattern (remember making snowflakes in school?). These are then appliquéd onto neutral foundation cloth. Each part of a traditional quilt has meaning and each design was once thought to contain the very spirit of the crafter. For example, an *'ulu* (breadfruit) design symbolizes abundance, pineapple represents the warmth and welcome of an aloha, and *kalo* (taro) embodies strength. If you want to buy a hand-sewn, island-made treasure, expect to pay thousands of dollars at galleries. If prices are low, such as at the Aloha Swap Meet in Pearl Harbor, the quilts were likely made in the Philippines. The Mission House at the Polynesian Cultural Center on the Windward Coast sells works made by Mormon volunteers.

Try your own hand at it by learning from experienced Hawaiian quilters during day classes often organized by island resorts. Area museums sometimes also have classes. Noted quilt makers and designers like Althea Poakalani Serrao and family (www.poakalani.net), Elizabeth Root (www.quiltshawaii.com), Nalani Gourd (http://hawaiianquilting.net) have websites that are excellent tools.

Many modern painters, printmakers, photographers and graphic and textile artists draw inspiration from Hawaii's cultural heritage, as showcased at the multimedia Hawai'i State Art Museum in downtown Honolulu. Also check out the contemporary island art galleries in nearby Chinatown. Arts and crafts fairs take place island wide throughout the year. The Honolulu **Made in Hawaii Festival** (www.madeinhawaiifestival.com) happens during a weekend in August; check out the **Island Craft Bulletin** (http://icb-web.net) for other events.

Traditional *kapa* (pounded bark cloth)
HIMANI/GETTY IMAGES ©

On-Screen Art

Academy Award–winning film *The Descendants,* based on Kaui Hart Hemmings' novel, caused quite the buzz on Oʻahu where it originated. The story is about Matt King (George Clooney), a man descended from Hawaiian royal and missionary ancestors who manages a family land trust on Kauaʻi.

He has to learn to be a father to his daughters after his wife is involved in a critical accident and he discovers she was having an affair. The movie producers spent a month preparing for the film by living in Lanikai and 11 weeks of filming there. Locals have noted how surprisingly accurate the portrayal of the island and its people is compared to other movies. Numerous scenes were shot locally on Waikiki Beach and around Honolulu. The gorgeous island-style homes featured actually increased interest in the local real-estate market. Look for Hemmings in a cameo as King's secretary, and with family members in the party scene at the Outrigger Canoe Club below Diamond Head.

For more island-based films, see p25.

Literature

Hawaii's early literary canon has long been dominated by foreign writers. Authors such as Mark Twain and Isabella Bird wrote the earliest travelogues about the islands. Later James Michener's historical saga *Hawaii* became a classic tome. More recently, Hawaii-based historical fiction has included *The Last Aloha* by Gaellen Quinn, *Honolulu* by Alan Brennert, and *Bird of Another Heaven* by James Houston.

Contemporary literature by local writers doesn't exoticize Hawaii as it examines the everyday complexities of island life – today and in the past. Honolulu-born Kiana Davenport's works are well recommended: *Song of Exile* follows two fictional families from WWII through US statehood. Kaui Hart Hemmings, also Oʻahu-born, made a splash when her first novel, *The Descendants,* was made into a movie. Lois-Ann Yamanaka, author of the award-winning anthology *Saturday Night at the Pahala Theatre,* caused controversy with the gritty depictions of local life in her novels and poetry. To read about up-and-coming authors, check out the biannual journal published by **Bamboo Ridge Press** (www.bambooridge.com), which has launched many local writers' careers. For more suggested reads, see p27.

Family Travel

Family kayaking at Kailua Beach Park (p193)

With so much surf and sand, O'ahu's coastline could be likened to a giant, free water park. But there are also plenty of outdoor activities and a few good museums and sights to keep kids of all ages occupied when they tire of swimming. Traveling families have been coming to the island for decades; local resorts, hotels and restaurants are well prepared. So stop for a shave ice and relax; keiki (children) are most welcome here.

Sights & Activities

Beaches line the entire island, so families really can't go wrong on O'ahu. All sides have opportunities to swim, snorkel, bodyboard and beachcomb at some time during the year.

Since the largest number of kid-catering resorts and restaurants are concentrated in the 20-block area of Waikiki, it's a top choice for families. At the beach teens and tweens can learn to surf – and everybody loves the outrigger-canoe rides. Nearby are the Waikiki Aquarium, with its learning-oriented fun, and the Honolulu Zoo. Whale watching and other boat excursions base locally. From Waikiki it's a short drive to greater Honolulu sights such as the interactive Bishop Museum, where the little ones get to walk through a 'volcano', and to Manoa Valley with its hikes and gardens.

If you like your family trip a little more low-key, Kailua on the Windward Coast is also

Need to Know

Changing facilities Available in shopping malls, big hotels and at sights

Cribs (cots) Usually available, check ahead with hotel

Diapers (nappies) Sold island-wide at grocery, drug and convenience stores

Health Doctors most accessible in Honolulu

Highchairs Usually available

Kids' menus Widely available

Strollers Bring your own, or rent online and have delivered to your hotel

Transport Reserve car seats with rental agencies in advance

a great base. Several good beaches are nearby and older kids and adults can learn to kayak or stand-up paddle at the town beach park. Hikes are possible in the area, and north up the coast is the Polynesian Cultural Center, one of the island's biggest attractions. Southeast O'ahu's highlights, including the fabulous and family-friendly snorkeling at Hanauma Bay and Makapu'u Lighthouse, are a short jaunt south. For that matter, Honolulu is less than 30 minutes over the *pali* (cliffs).

Discount admission to sights is usually available for children aged between four and 12; little ones under four are often free.

The surf is the main attraction at the North Shore, which has some treacherous winter waves. Swimming in summer is usually safe, but there's little beyond the beach to entertain kids.

Those staying out at Disney's Aulani resort in leeward O'ahu are a solid 40 minutes (without traffic) from Honolulu. The Lagoons (the coves at Ko Olina) offer some of the island's most child-friendly swimming. And the coast has a few other attractions – boat cruises, another swimming beach, a water park – but it *is* isolated.

For more sight and activity suggestions, see the Honolulu for Children (p48), Waikiki for Children (p107) and the Best for Kids (p169) boxed texts.

Children's Programs

Area botanical gardens host occasional children's programs, especially on weekends, as do the larger museums and animal parks.

Sleeping & Eating with Kids

Children under 18 often stay for free when sharing a hotel room with their parents, if they use existing bedding. Cribs (cots) and roll-away beds are usually available on request (sometimes for a surcharge) at hotels and resorts, but it's best to check in advance. Vacation rentals may have these, or an extra futon for the little ones to flop down on. The bigger the resort, the more likely it is to have extensive family-oriented services such as kids activities and clubs, game rooms or arcades, wading and other playful pool features. Hotel concierges are usually a good resource for finding babysitting services, or you can contact Nannies Hawaii (http://nannieshawaii.com).

Don't be scared away from dining out on O'ahu; even fancy places like Roy's or Alan Wong's welcome well-behaved little ones. Many restaurants have children's menus (eg grilled cheese sandwiches, chicken fingers) at significantly lower prices, and high chairs are usually available. Food trucks and other outdoor eateries are family faves, as they're super casual and the location may provide space for kids to roam. Many beach parks have picnic tables. Sandwiches and meals to-go are readily available at cafes, drive-ins and grocery stores. Look for baby food, infant formula, soy and cow's milk at any supermarket or convenience store. Note that most women choose to be discreet about breastfeeding in public.

Restaurants, lodgings and sights that especially cater to families, with good facilities for children, are marked with a family icon (👪) throughout this book.

Getting Around

Most car-hire companies rent child-safety seats from $10 per day. Online services such as Paradise Baby (www.paradisebabyco.com) and Baby's Away (www.babysaway.com) deliver rented car seats, strollers, playpens and cribs and more right to your door.

Many public women's restrooms have changing tables. Separate, gender-neutral 'family' facilities are sometimes available at airports, museums and other sights. For valuable tips on traveling, consult Lonely Planet's *Travel with Children,* which is also full of interesting anecdotes.

The Best...
Family Fun

1 Hanauma Bay (p175)

2 Waikiki Aquarium (p102)

3 Bishop Museum (p57)

4 Polynesian Cultural Center (p213)

5 Manoa Valley sights (p55)

Hawaiian monk seal, Waikiki Aquarium (p102)

LINDA CHING/GETTY IMAGES ©

Green Oʻahu

Hawaiian green sea turtle

M.M.SWEET/GETTY IMAG

Oʻahu is a Polynesian paradise possessing varied natural environments — from mountain to sea, lushly verdant to dismally dry. It's also a high-profile test case of whether humans can achieve a sustainable relationship with nature. Conservation efforts, both state-funded and grassroots, are gaining strength. From marine biologists and wildlife conservationists to Hawaiian artists and rural land-loving locals, aloha ʻaina (love or respect for the land) runs deep.

Environmental Issues

Though Oʻahu lags a little behind some of her sisters, an environmental consciousness has taken root on what is the most densely populated and heavily touristed of the Hawaiian Islands. A wide coalition of scientists, activists and residents has made conservation efforts a slow but steady success. For the latest environmental issues facing the island, check out **Environment Hawaii** (www. environment-hawaii.org).

Conservation

Hawaii's ecosystem is fragile – in fact, 25% of all the endangered species in the US are endemic to the Hawaiian Islands. Vast tracts of native forest were long ago cleared to make way for the monocrop industries of sugarcane and pineapple. In the 1960s the advent of mass tourism posed new challenges to the environment with the rampant development of land-hungry resorts and water-thirsty golf courses, which now number more than 40. Additionally, the large military presence has come into question for its environmental practices. Just the sheer number of visitors to the island puts immense pressure on the ecosystem.

That said, some notable progress has been made. There is a strong local belief in 'Keeping the Country, Country', a sentiment you may see on bumper stickers, T-shirts or homemade yard signs. Legal action has successfully been used to halt development in rural areas such as the Windward Coast and the North Shore.

The waters around the island have been made part of the Hawaiian Islands Humpback Whale National Marine Sanctuary; approaching within 100yd of a whale is illegal. Overfishing is still a problem, but the killing of sea turtles by the longline industry has been banned and there's an effort afoot to restrict the laying of gillnets.

Though invasive species still threaten endemic ones, a recently proposed bill contains measures meant to help quarantine any brown tree snakes that stowaway aboard aircraft. This species poses a severe threat to the island's bird populations.

Some local conservation groups have gotten together to work toward restoring habitats in their neighborhoods. For example, a Maunalua Bay project removed more than three million pounds of invasive algae by organizing community *huli* (pull) parties.

Recycle & Reuse

Recycling bins are not common on the street, but you'll find them at beaches, public parks and some museums and tourist attractions. Local hotels are lagging a bit behind in the recycling stakes. Thankfully, a good number of local restaurants now provide compostable and biodegradable to-go containers. Some businesses even make recycling an art: Mu'umu'u Heaven, in Kailua on the Windward Coast, turns old Hawaiian dresses into chic new ensembles. And local surfboard makers are experimenting with soy- and sugar-based foam forms.

Transportation

Being on the dry and less-windy side of the island, Honolulu occasionally sees increased levels of vehicle-related smog. After decades of controversy, O'ahuans are looking forward to a light-rail commuter transit system becoming a reality in 2018. The elevated train will connect Kapolei, via the airport, with Honolulu. Further development is intended to stretch through to Waikiki.

Honolulu's public transportation system, TheBus, has a 'Going Green!' program and has new hybrid vehicles in service and plans to introduce more. Future proposals include the purchase of 'clean' biodiesel buses. Recycling has already been implemented system-wide, and only low volatile organic compound (VOC) paints and petroleum-free, part-cleaning solvents are used.

Sustainable Icon

It seems like everyone's going green these days, but all ecotourism outfits are not created equal. Throughout the guide, the sustainable icon (🍃) indicates listings that we are highlighting because they contribute to sustainable tourism. Many are involved in conservation, others support a locavore lifestyle, and some maintain and preserve Hawaiian identity and culture.

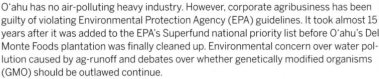

Pollution

O'ahu has no air-polluting heavy industry. However, corporate agribusiness has been guilty of violating Environmental Protection Agency (EPA) guidelines. It took almost 15 years after it was added to the EPA's Superfund national priority list before O'ahu's Del Monte Foods plantation was finally cleaned up. Environmental concern over water pollution caused by ag-runoff and debates over whether genetically modified organisms (GMO) should be outlawed continue.

Plastic pollution can be an issue on and offshore. Like other Hawaiian islands, O'ahu has moved to ban plastic store bags from July 2015. Plastic bags and other plastic items can be mistaken as jellyfish and eaten by endangered sea turtles. Further out in the ocean around O'ahu, the density of floating debris is ever increasing. Some scientists estimate that the 'great Pacific garbage patch' may be larger than Texas and reach 90ft deep. A local Honolulu company is pioneering efforts to develop monitoring vessels and systems, which could protect the island's shores from the mass.

Sustainable Travel

More than 4.5 million visitors land on O'ahu's shores every year – outnumbering residents more than three to one. Tourism, either directly or indirectly, provides one out of every three jobs in Hawaii. Pressures from tourism can be intense, as corporations seek to build more condos and hotels, to irrigate golf courses and to, well, sprawl. Sustainable travel practices can help ensure the island stays a paradise in the years to come.

Eat Locally

Every food product not made on O'ahu has been imported. The great distances and amount of fuel used makes the 'locavore' or 'eat local' movement sound even more appetizing. More and more restaurant menus these days sound like agricultural report cards. Creative island chefs love featuring island-grown produce such as Nalo greens, North Shore grass-fed beef and locally caught seafood – and telling you so.

Farmers markets, too, are booming on O'ahu. Search for a comprehensive list of locations and times at www.hawaii.gov. Even farms themselves have gotten in on the trend. Waialua on the North Shore is known for its small orchards and taro patches. The organizers of noteworthy Hale'iwa Farmers Market have gotten several of these growers together to participate in Oahu Agri-Tours (http://oahuagritours.com), which take you on a variety of farm and Hawaiian cultural practice tours from Waikiki. Around Kahuku on the Windward Coast, numerous fresh fruit and vegetable stands sit roadside, and one farm has opened its fields to visitors on weekends. Further south, planters in Waimanalo turn out incredible produce. Slow Food O'ahu (www.slowfoodoahu.org) also sponsors agro tours and organizes social events.

Support Ecofriendly Businesses

How ecofriendly a company really is can be hard to determine. Look for our sustainable icon throughout the text or contact local watch groups when in doubt.

Alternative Hawaii (www.alternative-hawaii.com) Focuses on Hawaii's natural and cultural beauty, with hundreds of tourism listings – and some advertorial.

Dolphin Smart (http://sanctuaries.noaa.gov/dolphinsmart) NOAA certifies boat tour businesses that use prescribed dolphin-safe practices.

Hawaii Ecotourism Association (www.hawaiiecotourism.org) Has an ecotour certification program and honors noteworthy outfitters, hotels and other local businesses.

Hawai'i 2050 Initiative

Even the government has gotten into the green swing of things, creating the Hawai'i 2050 (www.hawaii2050.org) sustainability plan. This evolving statewide program combines community input with a governmental task force to formulate economic, social and environmental policies that focus on renewable energy, living sustainably within the bounds of the islands' natural resources and striking a balance between profitable tourism and Hawaiian cultural preservation. A tall order, but as the plan itself states, this is 'not an academic or political exercise; it is a matter of the survival of Hawai'i as we know it.'

Tread Lightly

Every step we take has an impact, but we can minimize the effect by being aware of our surrounds. Staying on trails helps preserve plant life. Riding ATVs can cause erosion damage even when keeping to one track. Coral is a living creature: touching it, standing on it, bumping into it or stirring up sand that settles on top of it can kill the delicate polyps.

Seeds caught in the soles of shoes or bugs hiding out in the bottom of backpacks potentially pose a threat. Cleaning thoroughly before arrival helps fight the introduction of invasive species.

As mentioned, plastics are a problem. The tap water on the island is completely safe and drinkable. Buying a refillable bottle from a local business or sight can help reduce waste (and it's a cool souvenir). Local reusable grocery bags are also available at every drugstore and supermarket for just a dollar or two. Pick up one with a tropical design – or a funny illustrated diagram of a *poke* (cubed raw fish) bowl – and you'll get a minivacation every time you shop at home.

Offset Carbon

Waikiki and greater Honolulu have a comprehensive bus network; parking is such a hassle there that staying without a rental car alleviates a lot of aggravation.

Further afield, a car becomes more necessity than luxury. But it's still possible to keep it parked and cycle around the North Shore and Kailua on the Windward Coast. Kailua town has started B-Cycle, a low-cost bicycle-swap program with two station locations at present.

Smart Cars and some hybrid vehicles are available as rentals in Waikiki. Climate Care (www.climatecare.org) runs a flight carbon-offset donation program.

Volunteering on Vacation

If you want to give something back during your trip, you can help out by volunteering even a few spare hours. Whether you're helping to pul up invasive plants, count migratory whales, restore ancient Hawaiian archaeological sites or rebuild hiking trails, there's no better way to connect with locals and their *aloha 'aina* tradition.

The free tabloid *Honolulu Weekly* (www.honoluluweekly.com/calendar) lists volunteering opportunities.

Check out the following volunteering organizations for other possible projects.

Hawai'i Nature Center (www.hawaiinaturecenter.org) Volunteering-tourism opportunities in Honolulu to help the environment and encourage community development.

Hawaiian Islands Humpback Whale National Marine Sanctuary (http://hawaiihumpbackwhale. noaa.gov) Join in one of three annual whale counts.

Hui o Ko'olaupoko (www.huihawaii.org) Restores the *'aina;* projects include replanting wetlands like He'eai Stream on the Windward Coast.

Kahea (www.kahea.org) This environmental alliance preserves sensitive shorelines and Native Hawaiian cultural sites.

Malama Hawai'i (www.malamahawaii.org) A volunteer-oriented network of community and environmental groups with volunteer listings and conservation projects for *na keiki* (kids).

Mālama Maunalua (http://malamamaunalua.org) Opportunities to help restore Maunalua Bay in southeast O'ahu.

Nature Conservancy (www.nature.org/hawaii) Protects Hawaii's rarest ecosystems by buying up tracts of land; it also sometimes has volunteer opportunities.

Preserve Hawai'i (www.preservehawaii.org) A local volunteer-opportunity clearing house that uses social media to post events.

Sierra Club (www.hi.sierraclub.org/oahu) Activities range from political activism to trail maintenance and environmental clean-up.

Surfrider Foundation (www.surfrider.org/oahu) Grassroots group dedicated to oceans and beaches; holds regular weekend beach clean-ups.

Campground, Ho'omaluhia Botanical Garden (p206)
LINDA CHING/GETTY IMAGES ©

Land & Sea

With a total land area of 597 sq miles, O'ahu is the third-largest Hawaiian island. Though it accounts for less than 10% of Hawaii's total land mass, roughly 70% of state residents call 'the gathering place' home. The City and County of Honolulu incorporates the entire island, as well as the Northwestern Hawaiian Islands – dozens of small, unpopulated islands and atolls stretching more than 1200 miles across the Pacific.

Geography

The island of O'ahu is really two separate shield volcanoes that arose two to three million years ago and formed two mountain ranges: Wai'anae in the northwest (and Ko'olau in the southeast. O'ahu's last gasp of volcanic activity occurred between 10,000 and one million years ago, creating the tuff cone of Diamond Head, southeast O'ahu's most famous geographical landmark. The forces of erosion – wind, rain and waves – subsequently added more geologic character, cutting valleys, creating beaches and turning a mound of lava into paradise. O'ahu's highest point, Mt Ka'ala (4020ft), is in the central Wai'anae Range.

All of this oceanic plate tectonic activity can really shake things up. Small earthquakes are not uncommon here but Honolulu tends to be safely distant from the epicenter and feels only minor shocks. A tsunami could hit the island, although this has not happened recently.

An Evolving Ecosystem

It has been said that if Darwin had arrived in Hawaii first, he would have developed his theory of evolution in a period of weeks instead of years. Almost all the plants and animals carried by wind and waves across the vast ocean adapted so uniquely to these remote volcanic islands that they evolved into new species endemic to Hawaii. For example, the 56 known species of the honeycreeper bird all descended from a single type of finch. Unfortunately, only 18 of those species survive, and six are on the endangered list. Having evolved with limited competition and few predators, native species fare poorly among more aggressive introduced flora and fauna and foreign-borne diseases.

Prior to human contact, the Hawaiian Islands had no native mammals, save for monk seals and 'ope'ape'a (hoary bats), which are rarely seen on O'ahu. When Polynesians arrived, they introduced pigs, chickens, rats, coconuts, bananas, taro and about two dozen other plants... not to mention people. The pace of alien-species introduction escalated with the arrival of Europeans, who brought cattle, goats, mongooses, mosquitoes, foreign song birds and more. Nearly every species introduced has been detrimental to the local environment. Today, Hawaii is the 'extinction capital of the USA,' accounting for 75% of the nation's documented extinctions. Most environmentalists agree that the next big threat on O'ahu is from the brown tree snake, which has led to the extinction of all native birds on the Pacific island of Guam.

The Best...
Natural Preserves

1 Ka'ena Point State Park (p242)

2 Diamond Head State Monument (p169)

3 Waimea Valley (p234)

4 Ho'omaluhia Botanical Garden (p204)

5 Lyon Arboretum (p56)

6 Hanauma Bay Nature Preserve (p175)

Dolphin Swims

Signing up for a dolphin 'encounter' deserves careful consideration. According to many marine biologists, human interaction tires wild dolphins, potentially leaving them without critical energy to feed or defend themselves. Repeated contact has driven some dolphins out of their natural habitats into less-safe resting places.

In captivity, dolphins are trained to perform using techniques ranging from positive behavioral modification to food deprivation. Some have had to undergo surgery to repair damaged fins after participating in dolphin-swim programs; all can be exposed to human-borne illnesses and bacteria. The 2008 Oscar-winning documentary *The Cove* (www.thecovemovie.com), featuring an ex-dolphin trainer turned activist, looks at the 'dolphinarium' biz.

Animals

Marine Life

Up to 10,000 migrating North Pacific humpback whales come to Hawaiian waters for calving each winter; whale watching is a major highlight. The world's fifth-largest whale, the endangered humpback can reach lengths of 45ft and weigh up to 40 tons. Other whales (such as rarely seen blue and fin whales) also migrate through.

O'ahu waters are home to a number of dolphins, the most notable of which is the spinner dolphin, which likes the western waters off leeward O'ahu. These acrobats are nocturnal feeders that come into sheltered bays during the day to rest. They are sensitive to human disturbance, and federal guidelines recommend that swimmers do not approach closer than within 50yd.

One of the Pacific's most endangered marine creatures is the Hawaiian monk seal, named both for the monastic cowl-like fold of skin at its neck and for its solitary habits. The Hawaiian name for the animal is 'ilio holo i ka uaua, meaning 'the dog that runs in rough water.' Adults are more than 7ft long and 400lb of toughness, some with the scars to prove they can withstand shark attacks. Once nearly driven to extinction, they now number around 1300. Although monk seals breed primarily in the remote Northwestern Hawaiian Islands, they have begun hauling out on the northwestern beaches and may be spotted at Ka'ena Point in leeward O'ahu. For their wellbeing, keep at least 150ft from these endangered creatures, limit your observation time to 30 minutes, and never get between a mother and her pup.

Native Hawaiians traditionally revere the green sea turtle, which they call *honu*. Often considered a personal *'aumakua* (protective deity), a *honu* frequently appears in petroglyphs (and today in tattoos). For ancient Hawaiians they were a prized source of food, caught in accordance with religious and traditional codes. Adults can grow more than 3ft long and weigh more than 200lb. Young turtles are omnivorous, but adults (unique among sea turtles) become strict vegetarians. This turns their fat green – hence their name. Green sea turtles can be seen along the North Shore. Note that they are endangered and protected by federal law. Keeping a distance of 50ft is advised.

O'ahu's near-shore waters also harbor hundreds of tropical fish, including rainbow-colored parrotfish, moray eels and ballooning puffer fish, to name just a few.

Feathered Friends

Most of the islets off Oʻahu's Windward Coast are sanctuaries for seabirds, including terns, noddies, shearwaters, Laysan albatrosses and boobies.

Plants

Oʻahu blooms year-round. The classic hibiscus is native to Hawaii, but many of the hundreds of varieties growing here have been introduced. Other exotic tropical flowers commonly seen include blood-red anthurium, brilliant orange bird-of-paradise, showy bougainvillea and numerous varieties of heliconia. Strangely enough, while Hawaii's climate is ideal for orchids, there are only three native species. Most of the agricultural plants associated with the island, such as the pineapple, were introduced. Other endemic species you might see include the following:

ʻilima The island's official flower, a native groundcover with delicate yellow blossoms often strung into lei.

koa trees Tall, upland tree with flat, mature crescent-shaped leaves; wood is used to make canoes, ukuleles and exquisite bowls.

naupaka A common shrub with oval green leaves and a small pinkish-white, five-petal flower. It's said that the mountain variety and beach variety were once a young male and female, separated and turned into plants because of Pele's jealousy of their love.

ʻohia lehua A native shrub or tree with bright-red, tufted pompom flowers; thought to be sacred to the goddess Pele.

National, State & County Parks

Oʻahu has no national parks, but the federal government manages Valor in the Pacific National Monument at Pearl Harbor, as well as the James Campbell National Wildlife Refuge on the edge of the North Shore. About 25% of the island's land is protected, although some tension exists between the government and a few rural communities that want more land for affordable housing and farming. From Diamond Head near Waikiki to Kaʻena Point on the remote northwestern tip of the island, a rich system of state parks and forest reserves is loaded with outdoor opportunities, especially hiking. Dozens of county beach parks offer all kinds of aquatic adventures. The state's Department of Land & Natural Resources (www.hawaii.gov/dlnr) has useful online information about hiking, history and aquatic safety.

Outdoor Activities & Adventures

Snorkeling above a Hawaiian coral reef

ROBINSON ED/GETTY IMAG

O'ahu is a dream destination for those keen to get outside, whether you're searching for action and adventure or just a leisurely stroll. Here you can hike the sandy beachside, or climb up into the mountains for a forest trek. Go for a simple snorkel or an all-day scuba dive. Island-wide opportunities for swimming, kayaking, stand-up paddling and more abound. Oh, and did we mention there's some pretty decent surfing?

Water Sports

If you want to get wet, O'ahu is the place for you. The island is ringed with beautiful white-sand beaches, ranging from crowded resorts to quiet, hidden coves. All of the beaches on the island are public, though a few have park gates that close during specified hours. Most of the more than 50 beach parks have restrooms and showers; about half are patrolled by lifeguards.

Swimming

O'ahu has distinct coastal areas, each with its own peculiar seasonal water conditions. As a general rule, the best places to swim in winter are in the south, and in summer, to the north. The southern stretch from Barbers Point in leeward O'ahu to Kailua Beach in windward Oʻahu encompasses some of the most popular beaches on the island. This includes the legendary Waikiki Beach. Small summer swells here pick up from May through to September, making it a tad rougher for swimming. A word of warning: approximately 10 days after a full moon, box jellyfish swim into the shallow waters, especially around Waikiki, and stay for a day or two; check www.to-hawaii.com/jellyfishcalendar.html for predicted arrivals.

The North Shore has epic waves in winter; swimming is not advisable from at least late October through to early May. During summer, the ocean can be as calm as a lake. The exception is Bayview Beach in Turtle Bay, which is well protected year-round. The Waiʻanae Coast in leeward Oʻahu typically has similar swimming conditions to those of the North Shore, with incredible surf in winter and more swimmable conditions in summer. But you'll find sheltered year-round swimming at Ko Olina and Pokaʻi Bay Beach Park.

Snorkeling

There really isn't much of an excuse to not go snorkeling on Oʻahu. The water is warm, the currents are generally gentle and the underwater visibility is awesome. Shallow reefs and nearshore waters are awash with fish and colorful corals. You can expect to spy large rainbow-colored parrotfish munching coral on the sea floor, schools of silver needlefish glimmering near the surface, brilliant yellow tangs, odd-shaped filefish and ballooning puffer fish.

As activities go, this is about as cheap as it gets, with mask and snorkel rentals available nearly everywhere for around $15 a day. If you're staying at a vacation rental or condo, one or two sets are usually free for guest use.

The year-round snorkeling mecca is scenic Hanauma Bay Nature Preserve in southeast Oʻahu, which has a protected bay. When summer waters are calm on the North Shore, Waimea Bay and Shark's Cove in Pupukea provide top-notch snorkeling in pristine conditions, and far less human activity than at Hanauma. Sans Souci Beach Park and Queen's Surf Beach are smaller snorkel sites in Waikiki.

Bodysurfing & Bodyboarding

Bodysurfing is a great way to catch some waves, sans equipment. There's a bit of a knack to it, but once you've found the groove, it's good times ahead. The ideal locations are sandy shorebreaks where the inevitable wipeouts aren't that painful.

If you're just getting started, Waimanalo Bay and Bellows Field Beach Parks in windward Oʻahu have gentle shorebreaks. If you're someone who knows your way around the surf, head to Sandy and Makapuʻu Beach Parks in southeast Oʻahu. Other challenging shorebreaks are at Waimea Bay Beach Park on the North Shore, and at Kailua's Kalama Beach and Laʻie's Pounders Beach on the Windward Coast.

Bodyboarding is the bridge between bodysurfing and surfing – with that in mind, you're spoilt for break choices. If you want to see and be seen, the island's most popular bodyboarding site is Kapahulu Groin in Waikiki. Otherwise, if you're keen for shorebreaks, try the aforementioned bodysurfing waves. If you want something a bit bigger, have a look at the surfing spots below.

Surfing

Oʻahu is known the world over for surfing – and rightfully so. The island boasts 594 defined surfing sites, nearly twice as many as any other Hawaiian island. Whether you're a seasoned board rider or brand new to the sport, you'll find the appropriate break for your taste here. See p294 for more information on popular surf beaches.

Beginner surfing lessons are available in Waikiki, in Honolulu and in Kailua on the Windward Coast. On the North Shore, lessons are available out of Haleʻiwa, but there

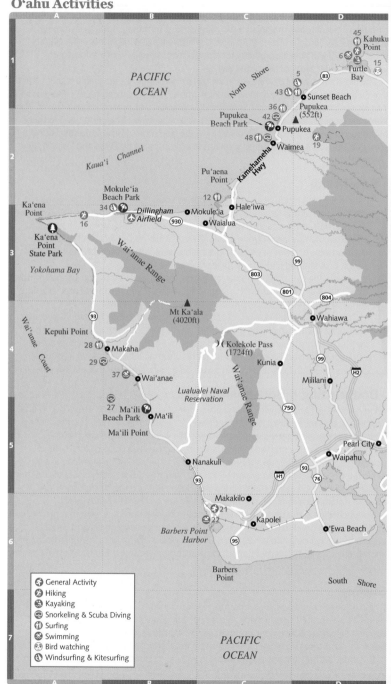

PACIFIC
OCEAN

North Shore

45 Kahuku
Point
6
Turtle
15 Bay

5

43 Sunset Beach

36 Pupukea
42 (552ft)
Pupukea
Beach Park
Pupukea

48 Waimea

19

Kaua'i Channel

Pu'aena
Point

Mokule'ia
Beach Park
34
Dillingham
Airfield 12 Hale'iwa
16 Mokule'ia
Waialua

Ka'ena
Point 930

Ka'ena
Point
State Park

Yokohama Bay

Wai'anae Range

99

803

801

804

93

Mt Ka'ala
(4020ft)

Wahiawa

Kepuhi Point

Kolekole Pass
(1724ft)

28 Makaha Kunia

29

99

H2

37 Wai'anae

Mililani

Lualualei Naval
Reservation

Wai'anae Range

27 Ma'ili
Beach Park
Ma'ili

750

Ma'ili Point

Pearl City

Waipahu

Nanakuli

H1 93

93
76

Makakilo

21
22 Kapolei

'Ewa Beach

Barbers Point
Harbor

95

Barbers
Point

South Shore

General Activity
Hiking
Kayaking
Snorkeling & Scuba Diving
Surfing
Swimming
Bird watching
Windsurfing & Kitesurfing

PACIFIC
OCEAN

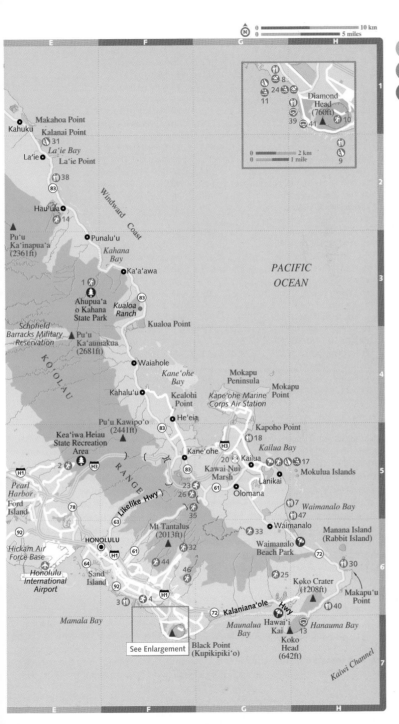

PACIFIC
OCEAN

Makahoa Point
Kahuku
Kalanai Point
La'ie Bay
La'ie
La'ie Point
Hau'ula
Pu'u
Ka'inapua'a
(2361ft)
Punalu'u
Kahana
Bay
Ka'a'awa
Ahupua'a
o Kahana
State Park
Kualoa
Ranch
Kualoa Point
Schofield
Barracks Military
Reservation
Pu'u
Ka'aumakua
(2681ft)
Waiahole
Kane'ohe
Bay
Mokapu
Peninsula
Mokapu
Point
Kahalu'u
Kealohi
Point
Kane'ohe Marine
Corps Air Station
Pu'u Kawipo'o
(2441ft)
He'eia
Kea'iwa Heiau
State Recreation
Area
Kapoho Point
Kane'ohe
Kailua Bay
Kailua
Kawai Nui
Marsh
Lanikai
Mokulua Islands
Pearl
Harbor
Ford
Island
Olomana
Waimanalo Bay
Hickam Air
Force Base
Mt Tantalus
(2013ft)
Waimanalo
Manana Island
(Rabbit Island)
HONOLULU
Waimanalo
Beach Park
Honolulu
International
Airport
Sand
Island
Koko Crater
(1208ft)
Makapu'u
Point
Mamala Bay
Kalaniana'ole Hwy
See Enlargement
Black Point
(Kupikipiki'o)
Maunalua
Bay
Hawai'i
Kai
Hanauma Bay
Koko
Head
(642ft)
Kaiwi Channel

Windward Coast

KO'OLAU

RANGE

Likelike Hwy

Diamond
Head
(760ft)

0 ————— 10 km
0 ————— 5 miles

0 ——— 2 km
0 ——— 1 mile

O'ahu Activities

are only two small, beginner breaks there. Most North Shore waves are pro-level advanced. Even if you're experienced, you should take a lesson from one of the local experts to learn about the conditions. Daily board rentals ($35 to $45) are available at surf shops in the above-mentioned areas, plus in Wai'anae on the Leeward Coast. The colorful **Franko's O'ahu Surf Map** (www.frankosmaps.com), available at souvenir and sport shops islandwide, lists every beach and break, with a short description.

Wahine (women) looking for a more intensive experience should sign up for one of the week-long surf camps (about $2200) that operate here. Along with daily lessons and accommodation, packages usually include meals, yoga or massage, and other activities. Check out: **Sunset Suzy's Surf Camp** (☎780-6963; www.sunsetsuzy.com), retreats at **Surf into Yoga** (☎638-8137; http://surfintoyoga.com), **Kelea Surf Spa** (☎949-492-7263; www.keleasurfspa.com) and Surf HNL Girls Who Surf (p62).

Stand-Up Paddling

The latest craze in board riding has taken the O'ahu scene by storm. Stand-up paddling, or stand-up paddle boarding, is a derivative of surfing where the rider stands on the board and uses a long paddle instead of stroking with his or her arms. It can be done on flat water and, for those who know what they're doing, in the surf. Beginners love it as there is little risk (the water is calm), and it's easily learned by a variety of ages and athletic abilities – besides, it's just plain fun. For more about the sport see the box, p235.

You can take lessons in Waikiki, Honolulu, Kailua on the Windward Coast, and in Hale'iwa and Turtle Bay on the North Shore. Guided tours are sometimes also available. Equipment rentals (about $60 per day) are widely available from the island's water-sports outfitters.

Kayaking

Who says you need an engine to get around the sea? Kayaking is an enjoyable way to explore the turquoise waters. Rentals run from about $35 to $55 per day. The top kayaking destination is undoubtedly Kailua Beach on the Windward Coast, which has three uninhabited islands within the reef to which you can paddle. Landings are allowed on two of the islands: Moku Nui, which has a beautiful beach good for sunbathing and snorkeling; and Popoi'a Island (Flat Island), where there are some inviting walking trails. You can reserve ahead for rentals, or some may be available at the beach. Contact outfitters directly for rental.

Guided kayak tours (four hours, approximately $125) are available from Kailua and from the nearby Kane'ohe Bay area, plus up at Turtle Bay on the North Shore. Waikiki doesn't have the same *Robinson Crusoe* feel to it, but kayak rentals are also available at Fort DeRussy Beach, plus you can rent in Hale'iwa on the North Shore.

Kitesurfing & Windsurfing

Kite- and windsurfing action on O'ahu centers on Kailua along the Windward Coast, where you'll find the vast majority of rentals and lessons. Kailua Beach has persistent year-round tradewinds and superb conditions for all levels, from beginner to pro, in different sections of the bay. It's never a slacker, but the very best winds typically occur in summer, when east-to-northeast trades run at eight to 15 knots. And when high-pressure systems come in, they can easily double that, which makes for awesome speed.

Men in a Hawaiian outrigger canoe
LIYSA/GETTY IMAGES ©

O'ahu Surf Beaches & Breaks *Jake Howard*

Hawaiian for 'the gathering place', O'ahu has become a hub for the islands' surf economy. Because O'ahu has some of the most diverse surf breaks in the islands, boarders of all skill levels can find what they're looking for.

In Waikiki, slow and mellow combers (long, curling waves) provide the perfect training ground for beginners. Board rentals abound on central **Waikiki Beach** and local beachboys are always on hand for lessons at spots like mellow **Queens**, mushy left- and right-handed **Canoes**, gentle but often crowded **Populars** and ever-popular **Publics**. In Honolulu proper, **Ala Moana** offers a heavy tubing wave – it's *not* a learning locale. Waves in this area are best during summer, when south swells arrive from New Zealand and Tahiti.

Reckon yourself a serious surfer? A pilgrimage to the famed North Shore is mandatory. In winter, when the waves can reach heights of more than 30ft, spots like **Waimea Bay**, **Pipeline** (at 'Ehukai Beach Park) and **Sunset Beach** beckon to the planet's best professional surfers.

While home to some great waves, the **Wai'anae Coast** in leeward O'ahu has turf issues; the locals who live and surf here cherish this area and are trying to hold onto its last vestiges of Hawaiian culture and community. In winter, large west swells can make for big surf at places like **Makaha Beach Park**, but tread lightly: the locals know each other here, so there will be no question that you're from out of town.

If you're looking for a multipurpose wave, **Diamond Head Beach** in Honolulu is friendly to short-boarders, long-boarders, windsurfers and kitesurfers. And for a good day of bodysurfing, **Sandy Beach Park** and **Makapu'u**, in southeast O'ahu, are ideal. If you go out here, do so with caution: the pounding waves and shallow bottom have caused some serious neck and back injuries.

For surf reports, call **Surf News Network** (☎596-7873; www.surfnewsnetwork.com), a recorded surf-condition telephone line that reports winds, wave heights and tide information, or check out **Wavewatch** (www.wavewatch.com) or **Surfline** (www.surfline.com) online.

JAKE HOWARD IS A WRITER FOR ESPN.COM AND THE SURFER'S JOURNAL, AND PREVIOUSLY WROTE FOR SURFER MAGAZINE.

Just a few years ago, nobody had heard of kitesurfing (also sometimes called kiteboarding). Fast-forward to today and, when it's windy, you'll see more kites over the water than over the land. Combine a wakeboard with a small parachute and add water, stir in the mentality of a windsurfer and the water knowledge of a surfer, and you have kitesurfing. It's amazing to watch and hard to master – if you're keen to learn on O'ahu, the place to try your hand is Kailua. The same top-notch outfitters there teach both kitesurfing and windsurfing, and have rental gear for both. Hawaiian Watersports in Waikiki will provide transport to Kailua free with a lesson. In general, kitesurfing lessons cost about $250 for three hours, windsurfing $130 for two. Rentals run $30 to $45 per day for a windsurfing rig or just a kite board; a full kitesurfing set up is about $260 for three hours and requires supervision.

In addition to Kailua, the speed and jumps at Diamond Head in southeast O'ahu are also popular with local kite- and windsurfers. If you have your own equipment, other recommended spots include Malaekahana State Recreation Area in windward O'ahu for open-water cruising; Mokule'ia Beach Park for consistent North Shore winds; and Backyards, off Sunset Beach on the North Shore, with the island's highest sailable waves. In Waikiki, Fort DeRussy Beach offers good conditions, but you have to contend with catamarans and crowds.

Outrigger Canoeing

There's not much in Hawaii that's more traditional then outrigger canoeing. First popularized by Native Hawaiians as a means to get around the Pacific, it has since become an activity popular with tourists, hard-core water sportspeople and recreational ocean goers. The best place to give it a crack is Kuhio Beach Park in Waikiki, where you can ride right from the sand and surf the waves back in. The round trip will cost around $25 and is very popular with kids.

Diving

Whether you're an old pro or a beginner, O'ahu has plenty to offer under the sea: lessons, boat dives, shore dives, night dives, reef dives, cave dives and wreck dives. The water temperatures are perfect for diving, with yearly averages from 72°F to 80°F. Even better than the bathwater temperatures is the visibility, which is usually perfect for seeing the plethora of fish, coral and other sea creatures. Because of its volcanic origins, the island also has some cool underwater caves and caverns.

Two-tank boat dives average about $120 to $150 and include all gear. Several dive operators offer a beginners' 'discover scuba' option, an introductory course that includes brief instruction, and possibly swimming-pool practice, followed by a shallow beach or boat dive. The cost is generally $130 to $180, depending on the operation and whether a boat is used. Full, open-water PADI certification courses can be completed in as little as three days and cost around $500.

O'ahu's top summer dive spots include the caves and ledges at Three Tables and Shark's Cove on the North Shore, and the Makaha Caverns off Makaha Beach in leeward O'ahu. For wreck diving, the sunken 165ft ship *Mahi*, also off Makaha Beach, is a prize. Numerous spots between Honolulu and Hanauma Bay on southeast O'ahu provide good winter diving. Diving outfitters operate out of Waikiki, Hawai'i Kai in southeast O'ahu, Kailua on the Windward Coast, Hale'iwa on the North Shore and Wai'anae and Kapolei/Ko Olina in leeward O'ahu. In Kapolei, snuba (modified scuba diving where you remain attached via oxygen line to the boat) is also available.

Franko's O'ahu Dive Map (www.frankosmaps.com), a full-color illustrated map available around the island, lists dive sites and descriptions. **Divers Alert Network** (www.diversalertnetwork.org) provides advice on diving insurance, emergencies, decompression services, illness and injury.

The Best...
Diving & Snorkeling Spots

1 Hanauma Bay (p175)

2 Shark's Cove (p231)

3 Offshore at Makaha (p157)

4 Three Tables (p231)

5 Ko Olina lagoons (p151)

IN FOCUS OUTDOOR ACTIVITIES & ADVENTURES

Responsible Diving & Snorkeling

Of the 700 fish species that live in Hawaiian waters, nearly one-third are found nowhere else in the world. Divers can also often see spinner dolphins, green sea turtles and manta rays. The waters hold hard and soft corals, anemones, unusual sponges and a variety of shellfish. The popularity of underwater exploration is placing immense pressure on many sites. Please consider the following tips when diving to help preserve the ecology and beauty of reefs.

Don't touch the turtles Minimize your disturbance of marine animals. It is illegal to approach endangered marine species too closely; these include whales, dolphins, sea turtles and the Hawaiian monk seal. In particular, do not ride on the backs of turtles, as this causes them great anxiety.

Please don't feed the fish Doing so disturbs their normal eating habits and can encourage aggressive behavior; besides, you might feed them food that is detrimental to their health.

Be conscious of the coral Take care not to touch coral with your body (never stand on it) or drag equipment across the reef. Polyps can be damaged by even the gentlest contact. If you must hold on, only touch exposed rock. Be conscious of your fins; even without contact, the surge from heavy strokes near the reef can damage delicate organisms. When treading water in shallow reef areas, take care not to kick up clouds of sand. Settling sand can easily smother delicate reef organisms.

Take only pictures Resist the temptation to collect coral or shells from the seabed. Buy an underwater camera and take pictures instead.

Pack it out Ensure that you remove all your trash and any other litter you may find. Plastics in particular are a serious threat to marine life. Turtles can mistake plastic for jellyfish and eat it.

Practice proper buoyancy Major damage can be done by divers descending too fast and colliding with the reef. Make sure you are correctly weighted and that your weight belt is positioned so that you stay horizontal. Be aware that buoyancy can change over an extended trip.

Care for caves Spend as little time in underwater caves as possible; your air bubbles may be caught within the roof and thereby leave previously submerged organisms high and dry.

Boating

Catamaran sunset cruises out of Waikiki and Honolulu may not be particularly active, unless you count drinking as sport, but there are other boating options around the island.

Whale Watching

Catching a view of a whale on Oʻahu isn't a fluke. Between December and May, humpback whales and their newly birthed offspring visit the harbors of northern and western Oʻahu. Hawaiian spinner dolphins are year-round residents of the Waiʻanae

Coast in leeward O'ahu. Whale- and dolphin-watching boat trips depart from Honolulu, Hale'iwa on the North Shore, and from Kapolei, Ko Olina and Wai'anae on the Leeward Coast. (For cautions about swimming with dolphins, see p286.)

Learn more about Hawaii's humpback whales and find out how to volunteer to participate in one of three annual whale counts at the **Hawaiian Islands Humpback Whale National Marine Sanctuary** (http://hawaiihumpbackwhale.noaa.gov). Note that you don't always need a boat; look for whale sightings from land along the North Shore at Turtle Bay or from Ka'ena Point, and from Makapu'u Lighthouse in southeast O'ahu.

Fishing

Why order dinner when you can catch it? There are a number of sport-fishing operations around the island that'll take you out on the sea for the day and help you land the big one. Do respect the ocean, respect marine preserves and practice catch-and-release. There are outfitters operating out of Kewalo Basin in Honolulu, out of Hawai'i Kai in southeast O'ahu and from Wai'anae Small Boat Harbor in leeward O'ahu.

The Best...

Beaches for *Keiki* (Kids)

1 Ko Olina lagoons (p151)

2 Hanauma Bay (p175)

3 Kuhio Beach Park, Waikiki (p100)

4 Bayview Beach (p224)

5 Poka'i Bay Beach Park (p154)

Hiking

Even though O'ahu is Hawaii's most populous island, nature sits right outside Waikiki's door. About 25% of the island is protected natural areas. The entire coastline is dotted with beaches, while the lush mountainous interior is carved by hiking trails.

Trails

Even if you don't have a lot of time, there are plenty of hikes that can be accessed near Waikiki. The island's classic hike, and its most popular, is the short but steep trail to the city overlook at the crater's summit in Diamond Head State Monument in southeast O'ahu. It's easily reached from Waikiki and ends with a panoramic city view. Also in the island's southeast corner, investigate the Kuli'ou'ou Ridge Trail: the views are worth the sturdy climb.

In Honolulu, the less-trodden Manoa Falls Trail is another steep but rewarding excursion. Two miles further is the Nu'uanu Pali Lookout, which has a similar flavor and makes for a good double shot. Also only a few miles from downtown Honolulu, the forested Tantalus and Makiki Valley area has extensive trail network, with fine overlooks of Honolulu and surrounding valleys. Wa'ahila Ridge Trail provides a different perspective on the area and good bird watching possibilities.

Just to the west of Honolulu in the Pearl Harbor area, 'Aiea Loop Trail is popular with both hikers and mountain bikers. It's contained within Kea'iwa Heiau State Recreation Area, which also allows an opportunity for an ancient temple visit.

Traveling a bit further afield to the Windward Coast, the Maunawili Trail System in Kailua provides a varied walk that covers a lot of different territory, including a waterfall, along with up to 10 miles of travel. Outside Kailua, a short, tree-shaded climb will take you to lesser-known Likeke Falls. For an excellent beach stroll, take to the sands outlining Kailua Bay. North up the coast, there are several quiet upland hikes in Ahupua'a o Kahana State Park and above Hau'ula; all take you deep into the forest and are worth exploring.

On the North Shore, the mixed sand-and-rock coastline at Turtle Bay makes for a pleasant trek. Further west, above Pupukea, Kaunala Loop Trail was considered sacred by Hawaiian royalty – it's no wonder, since the view is awesome.

Far from anywhere else, one of the most stunning of the island's hikes starts in Ka'ena Point State Park at the northwestern edge of leeward O'ahu. The trail hugs the coastline, as blue ocean crashes against dark volcanic rocks below and craggy cliffs rise above. Expect to see shorebirds, and maybe monk seals, in the windswept natural reserve on the uninhabited tip of the island.

Note that other ridge climbs and more challenging trails exist; ours is not meant to be a comprehensive list. Search the excellent website administered by **Na Ala Hele Trail & Access System** (☏587-0062; http://hawaiitrails.ehawaii.gov) for trails, printable topo maps and announcements of recently developed or reopened paths. Maps by the **US Geological Survey** (www.usgs.gov) are available in some island bookstores and can be ordered, or downloaded free online. Pay attention to the map dates, as some may have been drawn decades ago.

Camping on O'ahu

O'ahu has no full-service campgrounds with swimming pools and wi-fi as on the US mainland, but you can pitch a tent at many county and some state parks around the island. Expect basic facilities: restrooms, open-air showers and some picnic tables or grills. The Windward Coast contains the best camping option. Two beach parks down in Waimanalo are well recommended; you can camp in the shadow of the majestic Ko'olau Range at a botanical garden in the Kane'ohe Bay area; and Malaekahana State Recreation Area has both a public and a private campground. On the North Shore, camping options are extremely limited, but there is a church camp in Mokule'ia that accepts campers when it's not group-booked. We don't recommend camping on the Wai'anae Coast in leeward O'ahu, where some homeless islanders have set up permanent tent cities. There are no suitable campgrounds near Waikiki.

Note that all county- and state-park campgrounds on O'ahu are closed Wednesday and Thursday nights (from 8am Wednesday to 8am Friday) and some are only open on weekends. Permits are required for all; you must apply in advance from one of the following.

City and County of Honolulu (☏768-3440; https://camping.honolulu.gov; tent sites free; ⊙8am-4pm Mon-Fri). Administers beach parks and their campgrounds across O'ahu. Apply for your free permit online, no sooner than two Fridays prior to the requested date.

Division of State Parks (☏587-0300; www.hawaiistateparks.org; Room 131, 1151 Punchbowl St, Honolulu; tent sites $18; ⊙8am-3:30pm Mon-Fri) Administers state parks and recreation areas. You can apply for the required permits in person or online up to 30 days in advance.

Guided Hikes

Local guided hikes provide entry onto otherwise inaccessible private land in the valleys of Kualoa Ranch on the Windward Coast, and out of Hale'iwa and in Waimea Valley on the North Shore. The latter is highly recommended. Hawai'i Nature Center in the Makiki Forest Recreation Area, near Honolulu, leads family-oriented hikes by reservation. Island-wide, clubs arrange group hikes that you can meet and join up with; no transportation provided. Outfitters offer guided hiking tours, the main advantage being that bus transport from Waikiki is included. On tours, it's always a good idea to ask what, if any, food or water is provided. Group hikes are also listed in the *Honolulu Weekly* (http://honoluluweekly.com) calendar; alternatively, contact one of the following.

Hawaiian Trail & Mountain Club (http://htmclub.org; group hike per person $3) Volunteer community group that organizes informal hikes every weekend.

Sierra Club (www.sierraclubhawaii.com; group hike per person $5) Organizes weekend hikes around O'ahu; provides volunteer opportunities to rebuild trails and restore native plants.

O'ahu Nature Tours (☏924-2473; www.oahunaturetours.com; tours $30–55) Hiking-oriented options include two waterfall treks and a Diamond Head crater climb.

Hawaiian Escapades (☏366-0400; www.hawaiianescapades.com; tours $65–120) Wander through a botanical garden or hike Manoa Valley with these tours.

Hiking Hawaii (☏855-808-4453; http://hikinghawaii808.com; tours $40-165) These guys operate all over the island.

Hiking Preparation & Safety

It's advisable to hike with at least one other person; at the very least, tell a reliable individual where you are going and when you are expected back. Pack four pints of water per person for a full-day hike, carry a whistle to alert rescuers should the need arise,

wear sunscreen and, above all, start out early. Sturdy footwear with good traction is a must here, where it often gets muddy.

Overall, O'ahu is a very safe place to go for a hike. You won't find any poison oak, snakes, poison ivy or many wild animals to contend with. There is the rare chance you might encounter a wild boar – as exciting and death defying as that sounds, unless cornered they are rarely a problem. However, flash floods (see p314) and the following are potential hazards:

Landslides Be alert to the possibility of landslides and falling rocks. Swimming under non-maintained waterfalls can be dangerous, as rocks may dislodge from the top. Be careful on cliff edges as rocks here tend to be crumbly.

Nightfall Darkness falls fast once the sun sets, and ridge-top trails are no place to be caught unprepared at night. Always carry a flashlight just in case.

Cycling & Mountain Biking

Though challenging, it's possible to cycle around O'ahu; for more see p318.

Mountain biking is still an emerging sport on the island and opportunities to rent the appropriate off-road bikes are limited to Kailua on the Windward Coast and Honolulu. Having said that, there are some trails worth seeking out. In Hau'ula, the loop trail is a fun track (if only it were a little bit longer!); Maunawili Trail System is a scenic 10-mile ride that connects the mountain Nu'uanu Pali Lookout with sea level in Waimanalo – both are on the Windward Coast. In southeast O'ahu check out the Kuli'ou'ou Ridge Trail for great views and a staunch climb, and in Pearl Harbor there's the 'Aiea Loop Trail that is part of Kea'iwa Heiau State Recreation Area.

Hawaii Bicycling League (📞735-5756; www.hbl.org; group rides free) Local bicycle club holds group road-cycling rides most weekends, from 10-mile jaunts to 60-mile travails.

Cyclists at Sunset Beach Park (p228)
ANN CECIL/GETTY IMAGES ©

Bike Hawaii (📞734-4214; www.bikehawaii.com; tours $60–120) Tours offered by this adventure outfitter include mountain biking alone, and in conjunction with hiking, snorkeling and kayaking. A 5-mile rainforest road ride cruises downhill on pavement.

Horseback Riding

Saddle up, pardner. There are several opportunities for exploring rural parts of the island by horseback. Ride through a valley ranch in Kualoa or La'ie on the Windward Coast, or trot beachside at the polo club in Mokule'ia, canter the coast at Turtle Bay or plod along the mountainside above Pupukea on the North Shore. A 1½-hour trail ride costs between $60 and $90.

Golf

Some say that a round of golf is the perfect way to ruin a good walk, but if you disagree, O'ahu could very well be paradise. With more than 40 courses to choose from you're spoiled for golfing choice. You'll find PGA-level courses with the atmosphere of a private club, resort courses, and municipal greens with lower fees, a relaxed atmosphere and similarly spectacular surrounds.

The most highly rated courses include Ko'olau Golf Club (p205) in Kane'ohe on the Windward Coast; Ko Olina Golf Club (p152) in leeward O'ahu; and at Turtle Bay Golf (p225) on the North Shore. For a full list of O'ahu courses, log on to www.islandgolf. com. Green fees run from about $85 to $185 for 18 holes. Discounted rates are often available if you don't mind teeing off in the afternoon or reserve in advance online.

City and County of Honolulu (📞 296-2000 golf reservations; www.honolulu.gov/des/golf. html; green fees $50) runs six 18-hole municipal golf courses. Reservations for out-of-state visitors are accepted up to three days in advance, and can be made online.

Yoga & Massage

The outdoorsy lifestyle of O'ahu is an ideal setting for rejuvenation. Yoga classes are offered all over the island. Look for sessions in Waimanalo and Kailua on the Windward Coast and in Hale'iwa and Waialua on the North Shore, among other towns.

Therapeutic massages can also be had in a number of locations, including Kailua and Hale'iwa.

Alternative Adventures

Sick of swimming and surfing? Though we don't see how you could be, there are other adrenaline-fueled options. Hawai'i Kai in southeast O'ahu is alternative water sports central: parasail, waterski, ride a banana boat...even journey below the sea in a submersible scooter and above it with a water-borne jetpack (a la Buzz Lightyear).

Prefer sky to sea? Head up to Dillingham Airfield, in Mokule'ia on the North Shore. From there you can take a glider ride, fly in a biplane, help operate a powered hang glider or simply jump out of a plane (tandem, with a chute).

Bird Watching

Most islets off O'ahu's Windward Coast are sanctuaries for seabirds, including terns, noddies, shearwaters, Laysan albatrosses, boobies and 'iwa (great frigate birds). Moku Manu (Bird Island), off the Mokapu Peninsula near Kane'ohe, has the greatest variety of species, including a colony of 'ewa'ewa (sooty terns) that lays its eggs in ground scrapes. Although visitors are not allowed on Moku Manu, bird watchers can visit Moku'auia (Goat Island), offshore from Malaekahana State Recreation Area on the Windward Coast. In Kailua, the Kawai Nui Marsh is another place to see Hawaiian waterbirds in their natural habitat.

On the edge of the North Shore, James Campbell National Wildlife Refuge encompasses a native wetland habitat protecting some rare and endangered waterbird species.

Hikers who tackle O'ahu's many forest-reserve trails, especially around Mt Tantalus, can expect to see the 'elepaio (Hawaiian monarch flycatcher), a brownish bird with a white rump, and the 'amakihi, a yellow-green honeycreeper, the most common endemic forest birds on O'ahu. The 'apapane, a bright-red honeycreeper, and the 'i'iwi, a scarlet honeycreeper, are rarer.

For birding checklists and group field trips, contact the **Hawaii Audubon Society** (☏528-1432; www.hawaiiaudubon.com). **O'ahu Nature Tours** (☏924-2473; www.oahunaturetours.com) offers custom bird watching tours.

'I'iwi (scarlet honeycreeper)
SAMI SARKIS/GETTY IMAGES ©

Running

In the early hours of the morning you'll see joggers aplenty in parks, on footpaths and on beaches all around the island. Running on O'ahu is huge. Kapi'olani Park and the Ala Wai Canal are favorite jogging spots in Waikiki.

O'ahu has about 75 road races each year, from 1-mile fun runs and 5-mile jogs to competitive marathons, biathlons and triathlons. For an annual schedule of running events, check out the **Running Room** (www.runningroomhawaii.com) and click on 'Races.'

The island's best-known race is the Honolulu Marathon, which has mushroomed from 167 runners in 1973 into one of the largest in the US. Held in mid-December, it's an open-entry event, with an estimated half of the roughly 25,000 entrants running in their first marathon. For information, contact the **Honolulu Marathon Association** (www.honolulumarathon.org).

Tennis

O'ahu has 181 public tennis courts at county parks throughout the island; for locations, log on to www.honolulu.gov/rep/site/dpr/dpr_docs/tenniscourts.pdf. If you're staying in Waikiki, the most convenient locations are the courts at the Diamond Head Tennis Center in Kapi'olani Park; and at the Kapi'olani Park Tennis Courts, opposite the Wai-kiki Aquarium. The courts at Ala Moana Beach Park in Honolulu are also close.

Joggers, Ala Moana Beach Park (p40)
JON HICKS/GETTY IMAGES ©

Lei

CORNWELL DAVID/GETTY IMAGE

Fragrant and ephemeral, lei embody the beauty of nature and the embrace of the community, freely given and freely shared. Greetings. Honor. Respect. Peace. Love. Celebration. Spirituality. Good luck. Farewell. These beautiful garlands, handcrafted from fresh tropical flora, can signify all of these meanings, and more.

The Art of the Lei

Lei making is a sensuous and transitory art form. In choosing their materials, lei makers tell a story – since flowers and plants embody place and myth – and express emotions. They may use feathers, nuts, shells, seeds, seaweed, vines, leaves and fruit, in addition to the more familiar fragrant tropical flowers. Handmade lei are typically created by knotting, braiding, winding, stringing or sewing the raw natural materials together.

Worn daily, lei were integral to ancient Hawaiian society. In the islands' Polynesian past, lei were made part of sacred hula dances and given as special gifts to loved ones, as healing medicine to the sick and as offerings to the gods, all practices that continue in Hawaii today. So powerful a symbol were they that on ancient Hawaii's battlefields, the right lei could bring peace to warring armies.

Today, locals continue to wear lei for special events, such as weddings, birthdays, anniversaries, graduations and public ceremonies. In general, it's no longer common to make one's own lei, unless you're a devoted member of a *hula halau* (hula school). For ceremonial hula (as opposed to popular competitions or shows for entertainment), performers are often required to make their own lei, even gathering the raw materials by hand.

Modern Celebrations

For visitors to Hawaii, the tradition of giving and receiving lei can be dated back to the 19th-century steamships that first brought tourists to the islands. At the height of cruise-ship tourism, passengers would be greeted upon disembarking by local vendors who would throw garlands around the necks of the *malihini* (newcomers, or foreigners).

The tradition of giving a kiss with a lei began during WWII, allegedly when a hula dancer at a USO club was dared by her friends to give a military serviceman a peck on the cheek when she placed a flower lei over his head.

In 1927 the poet Don Blanding and Honolulu journalist Grace Tower Warren called for making May 1 a holiday to celebrate lei. The next year, Leonard and Ruth Hawk composed the popular tune 'May Day is Lei Day in Hawaii,' a song that later became a hula *mele* (song). Today, Lei Day is celebrated across the islands with Hawaiian music, hula dancing, parades, lei-making workshops and contests, and more fun.

Lei in Print

Ka Lei: The Leis of Hawaii (Ku Pa'a Publishing, 1995) Written by Marie McDonald, a recognized *kapuna* (elder), this is an in-depth look at the art of Hawaiian lei making both before Western contact and during contemporary times.

Na Lei Makamae: The Treasured Lei (University of Hawai'i Press, 2003) This artful, beautiful blend of botany and culture by Marie McDonald and Paul Weissich surveys the Hawaiian flowers traditionally used in lei and their meaning and mythology.

Lei Etiquette

⦿ Don't wear a lei hanging directly down around your neck. Instead, drape a closed (circular) lei over your shoulders, making sure that equal lengths are hanging over your front and back.

⦿ When traditionally presenting a lei, bow your head slightly and raise the lei above your heart. Don't drape it with your own hands over the head of the recipient, as this isn't respectful. Let them do it themselves.

⦿ Don't give a closed lei to a pregnant woman, as it may bring bad luck to the unborn child; choose an open (untied) lei or *haku* (head) lei instead.

⦿ Resist the temptation to wear a lei intended for someone else. It's bad luck.

⦿ Never refuse a lei, and don't take one off in the presence of the giver.

⦿ When you stop wearing your lei, don't throw it in the trash. Untie the string and return the lei's natural elements to the earth (eg scatter flowers in the sea, bury seeds or nuts) instead.

Shopping for Lei

A typical Hawaiian lei costs anywhere from $10 for a single strand of orchids or plumeria to thousands of dollars for a 100% genuine Ni'ihau shell lei necklace. Beware that some *kukui* (candlenut) and *puka* shell lei are just cheap (even plastic) imports.

When shopping for a lei, ask the florist or shopkeeper for advice about the most appropriate lei for the occasion and indicate if you're giving the lei to a man or a woman.

You can buy fresh lei in Chinatown at Cindy's Lei Shoppe (p86) or at a number of other specialists on Maunakea St. For intricately crafted feather lei, drop by Na Lima Mili Hulu No'eau on Kapahulu Ave near Waikiki. Freshly made flower lei are available near the airport, and services such as Lei Greeting (www.leigreeting. com) can arrange to meet your party with a suitable floral welcome.

Lei Overboard

When you're leaving the islands, it's tradition to cast a lei into the ocean; if it returns to the beach, it's said you will one day return to Hawaii. But don't throw your lei into the water without first removing the string and the bow.

King Kamehameha the Great Statue (p47), draped in lei
JAMES RANDKLEV/GETTY IMAGES ©

Survival
Guide

Nu'uanu Pali (p186)
JOHN ELK III/GETTY IMAGES ©

Directory

Accommodations

RATES

In this guide, unless otherwise stated, reviews indicate high-season rates for a double-occupancy room:

$	under $100
$$	$100 to $250
$$$	over $250

Quoted rates generally don't include taxes of almost 14%. Unless noted, breakfast is *not* included and bathrooms are private.

RESERVATIONS

A reservation guarantees your room, but most reservations require a deposit, after which, if you change your mind, the establishment may not refund your money. Note cancellation policies and other restrictions before making a deposit.

SEASONS

◦ During high season – mid-December through late March or mid-April, and to a lesser degree, June through August – lodgings are more expensive and in demand.

◦ Certain holidays and major events command premium prices, and for these, lodgings can book up a year in advance.

◦ In low or shoulder seasons, expect significant discounts and easier booking.

AMENITIES

◦ Accommodations offering online computer terminals for guests are designated with the internet icon (@); an hourly fee may apply.

◦ In-room internet access is often wired (not wireless); a daily fee may apply.

◦ When wireless internet access is offered, the wi-fi icon (📶) appears. Look for free wi-fi hot spots in common areas (eg hotel lobby, poolside).

◦ Where an indoor or outdoor pool is available, the swimming icon (🏊) appears.

◦ Air-conditioning (❄) is a standard amenity at most hotels and resorts and some condos. At many hostels and some condos, B&Bs and vacation rentals, only fans may be provided.

◦ For more icons and abbreviations used with reviews in this book, see How to Use This Book.

B&BS & VACATION RENTALS

B&B accommodations on O'ahu are usually spare bedrooms at residential homes. With restrictive local regulations that make it impossible to license new businesses, the majority of B&Bs and vacation rentals are technically illegal. Officials know this, and usually turn a blind eye unless there's a complaint. A recent statewide crackdown did result in closures and forfeited guest reservations, so this de facto policy of acceptance is subject to change at any time.

Contrary to their name, most B&Bs do not offer a full breakfast; they provide supplies – coffee, juices, fruits and breads or pastries, usually – stocked in the unit's refrigerator. Unless they have a state-approved restaurant kitchen, they can be fined if caught making hot meals for guests.

Because B&Bs and vacation rentals discourage unannounced drop-ins, they sometimes do not appear on maps in this book. Same-day reservations are hard to get – always try to book B&Bs in advance, especially since they tend to fill up weeks or months ahead of time. Many B&Bs have minimum-stay requirements of a few nights, though some will waive this if you pay a surcharge.

Typically, a vacation rental means renting an entire

Book Your Stay Online

For more accommodations reviews by Lonely Planet authors, check out http://www.lonelyplanet.com/hotels. You'll find independent reviews, as well as recommendations on the best places to stay. Best of all, you can book online.

apartment, duplex, condo or house (with no on-site manager and no breakfast provided), but many B&Bs also rent stand-alone cottages. Often all these kinds of properties, which typically have kitchens, are handled by the same rental agencies. Ask about added cleaning fees, commonly for stays of less than five nights.

Most B&Bs and vacation rentals are found in Kailua, as well as elsewhere along the Windward Coast and on the North Shore. This book reviews B&Bs and vacation rentals that can be reserved directly through the owners or through local real estate agencies listed in the destination chapters earlier. Also try:

Affordable Paradise Bed & Breakfast (www.affordable-paradise.com)

Bed & Breakfast Hawaii (www.bandb-hawaii.com)

Air B&B (www.airbnb.com)

Craigslist (http://honolulu.craigslist.org)

Hawaii Beach Homes (http://hawaii-beachhomes.com)

Hawaii's Best Bed & Breakfast (www.bestbnb.com)

HomeAway (www.homeaway.com)

Vacation Rental by Owner (www.vrbo.com)

CAMPING & CABINS

For public and private campgrounds, camping permits and cabin reservations, see p298.

Practicalities

o **Electricity** 110/120V, 50/60Hz

o **Magazines** Monthly *Honolulu Magazine* (www.honolulumagazine.com) is a glossy lifestyle mag, while *Ka Wai Ola* (www.oha.org/kwo) covers Native Hawaiian issues.

o **Newspapers** *Honolulu Star-Advertiser* (www.staradvertiser.com, www.honolulupulse.com) is Hawaii's major daily. *Honolulu Weekly* (http://honoluluweekly.com) is a free alternative tabloid.

o **Radio** O'ahu has more than 45 radio stations; for Honolulu, see p88.

o **Smoking** Prohibited in enclosed public spaces, including airports, bars, restaurants, shops and hotels (where smoking rooms are rarely available).

o **Time** Hawaii-Aleutian Standard Time (HAST) is GMT-10. Hawaii doesn't observe Daylight Saving Time (DST). The euphemism 'island time' means taking things at a slower pace, or occasionally being late.

o **TV** All major US networks and cable channels available, plus 24-hour tourist information.

o **Video Systems** NTSC standard (incompatible with PAL or SECAM systems); DVDs coded region 1 (US and Canada only).

o **Weights & Measures** Imperial (to convert between metric and imperial, see the inside front cover).

Business Hours

Unless there are variances of more than a half-hour in either direction, the following standard opening hours apply throughout this book:

Banks	8:30am-4pm Mon-Fri, some to 6pm Fri & 9am-noon or 1pm Sat
Bars & clubs	to midnight daily, some to 2am Thu-Sat
Businesses	8:30am-4:30pm Mon-Fri; some post offices 9am-noon Sat
Restaurants	breakfast 6-10am, lunch 11:30am-2pm, dinner 5-9:30pm
Shops	9am-5pm Mon-Sat, some also noon-5pm Sun; major shopping centers keep extended hours

Climate

Hale'iwa

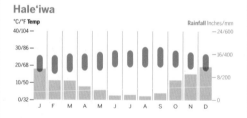

Windward O'ahu

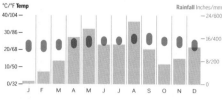

Honolulu

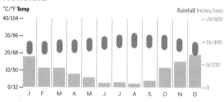

Courses

Hawaiian language, arts-and-crafts and cultural classes are most plentiful in Honolulu (p64) and Waikiki (p109). To learn how to surf, windsurf, kitesurf (kiteboard), stand-up paddle or scuba dive, browse the Activities listings in the destination chapters of this book.

Road Scholar (☎ 800-454-5768; www.roadscholar.org) Top-notch educational programs for those aged 50 or over focusing on Hawaii's people and culture and the natural environment. One- to two-week programs cost from $1600 to $3300, including accommodations, meals, classes and activities, but not airfare to/from Hawaii.

Customs Regulations

Currently, each international visitor is allowed to bring into the USA duty-free:

○ 1L of liquor (if you're over 21 years old)

○ 200 cigarettes (one carton) or 50 (non-Cuban) cigars (if you're over 18)

○ Amounts higher than $10,000 in cash, traveler's checks, money orders and other cash equivalents must be declared. For more information, check with **US Customs and Border Protection** (www.cbp.gov).

○ Most fresh fruits and plants are restricted from entry into Hawaii (to prevent the spread of invasive species). At Honolulu's airport, customs officials strictly enforce both import and export regulations (see p317). Because Hawaii is a rabies-free state, pet quarantine laws are draconian. Questions? Contact the **Hawaiian Department of Agriculture** (http://hawaii.gov/hdoa).

Electricity

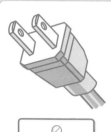

120V/60Hz

120V/60Hz

Food

In this book, restaurant prices usually refer to an average main course at dinner (lunch is often cheaper, sometimes half-price):

$	mains under $12
$$	most mains $12-30
$$$	mains over $30

These prices don't include drinks, appetizers, desserts, taxes or tip (see p313).

Lunch is generally served between 11:30am and 2:30pm, and dinner between 5:30pm and 9pm daily, though some restaurants close later, especially on Friday and Saturday nights. If breakfast is served, it's usually between 6am and 10am, with weekend brunch until 2pm.

For more about Hawaii's cuisine, see p264.

Gay & Lesbian Travelers

The state of Hawaii has strong minority protections and a constitutional guarantee of privacy that extends to sexual behavior between consenting adults. As of December 2013, same-sex marriage is legal in Hawaii. But showing affection toward a same-sex partner in public isn't common.

Waikiki is without question the epicenter of O'ahu's LGBTQ nightlife (see p124), but this laid-back 'scene' is muted by US mainland standards. **Honolulu Pride** (www.honolulupride.org), in early June, celebrates with a parade from Ala Moana's Magic Island to Waikiki's Kapi'olani Beach Park.

The monthly magazines **Odyssey** (www.odysseyhawaii.com) and **eXpression!** (www.expression808.com), both distributed free at LGBTQ-friendly businesses in Waikiki, cover O'ahu's gay scene. The national monthly magazine **OutTraveler** (www.outtraveler.com) archives gay-oriented Hawaii travel articles online.

Helpful DIY resources include the website **Gay Hawaii** (www.gayhawaii.com) and **Purple Roofs** (www.purpleroofs.com/usa/hawaii/oahu.html), an online accommodations directory. **Pacific Ocean Holidays** (http://gayhawaiivacations.com) arranges package vacations.

Insurance

Getting travel insurance to cover theft, loss and medical problems is highly recommended. Some policies do not cover 'risky' activities such as scuba diving and motorcycling, so read the fine print. Make sure your policy at least covers hospital stays and an emergency flight home.

Paying for your airline ticket or rental car with a credit card may provide limited travel accident insurance. If you already have private US health insurance or a homeowner's or renter's policy, find out what those policies cover and only get supplemental insurance. If you have prepaid a large portion of your vacation, trip cancellation insurance may be a worthwhile expense.

Worldwide travel insurance is available at www.lonelyplanet.com/travel_services. You can buy, extend and claim online anytime – even if you're already on the road.

For car-rental insurance, see p320.

Internet Access

o In this book, the @ symbol indicates an internet terminal is available, while the 🛜 symbol indicates a wi-fi hot spot; either may be free or fee-based.

o Most hotels and resorts, and many coffee shops, bars and other businesses, offer public wi-fi (sometimes free only for paying customers).

International Visitors

ENTERING HAWAII

○ Visa and passport requirements change often; double-check *before* you come.

○ For current info, check the visa section of the **US Department of State** (http://travel.state.gov) and the **US Customs & Border Protection** (www.cbp.gov/travel).

○ Upon arrival, most foreign visitors must register with the **US-Visit program** (www.dhs.gov/us-visit), which entails having electronic (inkless) fingerprints and a digital photo taken; the process usually takes less than a minute.

PASSPORTS

○ A machine-readable passport is required for all foreign citizens to enter Hawaii.

○ Passports must be valid for six months beyond expected dates of stay in the USA.

○ Any passport issued or renewed after October 26, 2006, must be an 'e-passport' with a digital photo and an integrated biometric data chip.

VISAS

○ Currently, under the US Visa Waiver Program (VWP), visas are not required for citizens of 36 countries for stays of up to 90 days (no extensions).

○ Under the VWP you must have a return ticket (or onward ticket to any foreign destination) that is nonrefundable in the USA.

○ All VWP travelers must register online at least 72 hours before arrival with the **Electronic System for Travel Authorization** (https://esta.cbp.dhs.gov/esta/), which currently costs $14. Registration is valid for two years.

○ Travelers who don't qualify for the VWP must apply for a tourist visa. The process is not free, involves a personal interview and can take several weeks, so apply early.

CONSULATES

O'ahu has no foreign embassies. Honolulu has only a few consulates, including:

Australia (☎ 529-8100; Penthouse, 1000 Bishop St)

Japan (☎ 543-3111; 1742 Nu'uanu Ave)

Korea (☎ 595-6109; 2756 Pali Hwy)

Netherlands (☎ 531-6897; ste 702, 745 Fort St Mall)

New Zealand (☎ 595-2200; 3929 Old Pali Rd)

MONEY

○ All prices in this book are quoted in US dollars. See p31 for exchange rates.

○ Foreign currency can be exchanged for US dollars at larger banks only in Honolulu or Waikiki; airport exchange booths are convenient but expensive.

○ Most ATMs are connected to international networks and have OK exchange rates.

○ Large hotels, restaurants and stores accept US-dollar traveler's checks as if they're cash, although smaller businesses and fast-food chains may refuse them.

Honolulu, Waikiki and a few island towns have cybercafes or business centers with pay-as-you-go internet terminals (typically $6 to $12 per hour) and sometimes wi-fi.

Hawaii's **public libraries** (www.librarieshawaii.org) provide free internet access via their online computer terminals, but you will need a temporary nonresident library card ($10). A few library branches now offer free wi-fi (no card required).

Language

Hawaii has two official languages: English and Hawaiian. There's also an unofficial vernacular, pidgin, which has a laid-back, lilting accent and a colorful vocabulary that permeates the official tongues. While Hawaiian's multisyllabic, vowel-heavy words may seem daunting, the pronunciation is actually quite straightforward.

Legal Matters

If you are arrested, you have the right to an attorney; if you can't afford one, a public defender will be provided free. The **Hawaii State Bar Association** (☎ 537-9140; http://hsba.org) can make attorney referrals.

- If you are stopped by the police while driving, be courteous. Don't get out of the car unless asked.

- It's illegal to have open containers of alcohol (even empty ones) in motor vehicles; unless containers are still sealed and have never been

opened, store them in the trunk.

- Bars, nightclubs and stores may required photo ID to prove you're of legal age (21 years) to buy or consume alcohol.

- Drinking alcohol in public anywhere besides a licensed premises (eg bar, restaurant), including at beaches and parks, is illegal.

- In Hawaii, anyone caught driving with a blood alcohol level of 0.08% or greater is guilty of driving under the influence (DUI), a serious offense that may incur heavy fines, a suspended driver's license, jail time and other stiff penalties.

- The possession of marijuana and nonprescription narcotics is illegal. Foreigners convicted of a drug offense face immediate deportation.

- Public nudity (as at beaches) and hitchhiking are illegal, but sometimes police ignore them.

Money

- Major banks, such as the **Bank of Hawaii** (www.boh.com) and **First Hawaiian Bank** (www.fhb.com), have extensive ATM networks throughout O'ahu.

- Some B&Bs, condominiums and vacation-rental agencies will not accept credit cards, instead requiring cash, traveler's checks or personal checks drawn on US bank accounts.

- Hawaii has a 4.17% state sales tax tacked onto virtually everything, including meals,

groceries and car rentals. Accommodations taxes total nearly 14%.

TIPPING

In Hawaii, tipping practices are the same as on the US mainland, roughly:

Airport and hotel porters $2 per bag, minimum of $5 per cart.

Bartenders 15% to 20% per round, minimum of $1 per drink.

Hotel maids $2 to $4 per night, left under the card provided; more if you're messy.

Parking valets At least $2 when your keys are returned.

Restaurant servers 18% to 20%, unless a service charge is already on the bill.

Taxi drivers 15% of the metered fare, rounded up to the next dollar.

Post

The **US Postal Service** (USPS; ☎ 800-275-8777; www.usps.com) is inexpensive and reliable. Mail delivery to/from Hawaii usually takes slightly longer than on the US mainland.

Public Holidays

On the following holidays, banks, schools and government offices (including post offices) close, and transportation and museums operate on a Sunday schedule. Holidays falling on a weekend are usually observed the following Monday. For major annual festivals and events, see p28.

New Year's Day January 1

Martin Luther King Jr Day Third Monday in January

Presidents' Day Third Monday in February

Easter March or April

Prince Kuhio Day March 26

Memorial Day Last Monday in May

King Kamehameha Day June 11

Independence Day July 4

Statehood Day Third Friday in August

Labor Day First Monday in September

Columbus Day Second Monday in October

Veterans Day November 11

Thanksgiving Fourth Thursday in November

Christmas Day December 25

Safe Travel

In general, Hawaii is a safe place to visit. Because tourism is so important, state officials have established the **Visitor Aloha Society of Hawaii** (VASH; ☎ 926-8274; www.visitoralohasocietyof

hawaii.org), which provides non-monetary emergency aid to short-stay visitors who become the victims of accidents or crimes.

THEFT & VIOLENCE

O'ahu is notorious for thefts from parked cars, both locals' and tourist rentals. Thieves can pop open a trunk or pull out a door-lock assembly in seconds. They strike not only at remote trailheads when you've gone for a hike but also in crowded beach parking lots where you'd expect safety in numbers.

Try not to leave anything of value in your car anytime you walk away from it. If you must, pack things well out of sight *before* pulling up to park; thieves watch and wait to see what you put in your trunk. Some locals always leave their cars unlocked with the windows rolled down to avoid paying for broken windows.

Stay attuned to the vibe on any beaches at night, even in Waikiki where police patrol, and in places like campgrounds and roadside county parks where drunks, drug users and gang members hang out. In rural areas, there may be pockets of resentment against tourists, particularly on the Wai'anae Coast, where homeless encampments have taken over a few beaches (see p155).

FLASH FLOODS & WATERFALLS

No matter how dry a streambed looks, or how sunny the sky above is, a sudden rainstorm miles away can cause a flash flood in minutes, sending down a huge surge of debris-filled water that

sweeps away everything in its path. Always check the weather report before starting a hike; this is crucial if you're planning on hiking in valleys or swimming in natural pools or waterfalls. Swimming underneath waterfalls is always risky due to the danger of falling rocks.

Tell-tale signs of an impending flash flood include sudden changes in water clarity (eg it becomes muddy), rising water levels and/or floating debris, and a rush of wind, the sound of thunder or a low, rumbling roar. If you notice any of these signs, immediately get to higher ground (even a few feet could save your life). Don't run downstream – you can't beat a flash flood!

TSUNAMI

On average, tsunamis (incorrectly called tidal waves – the Japanese term *tsunami* means 'harbor wave') occur only about once a decade in Hawaii, but they have killed more people statewide than all other natural disasters combined. The tsunami warning system is tested on the first working day of every month at 11:45am for less than one minute, using the yellow speakers mounted on telephone poles around the island. If you hear a tsunami warning siren at any other time, head for higher ground immediately; telephone books have maps of evacuation zones. Turn on the radio or TV for news bulletins. For more information, visit the **Pacific Disaster Center** (www.pdc. org) and **Hawaii State Civil Defense** (www.scd.hawaii.gov) online.

Telephone

CELL (MOBILE) PHONES

Check with your service provider about using your phone in Hawaii. Among US providers, Verizon has the most extensive network; AT&T, Cingular and Sprint get decent reception. Cell coverage may be spotty or nonexistent in rural areas, on hiking trails and at remote beaches.

International travelers need a multiband GSM phone in order to make calls in the USA. With an unlocked multiband phone, getting a US prepaid rechargeable SIM card is usually cheaper than using your own network. SIM cards are available at major telecommunications or electronics stores, which also sell inexpensive prepaid phones.

DIALING CODES

⊙ All Hawaii phone numbers consist of a three-digit area code (☎808) followed by a seven-digit local number.

⊙ To call long-distance from one Hawaiian island to another, dial ☎1-808 + local number.

⊙ Always dial '1' before toll-free numbers (☎800, 888 etc). Some toll-free numbers only work within Hawaii or from the US mainland (and possibly Canada).

⊙ To call Canada from Hawaii, dial ☎1 + area code + local number (international rates apply).

⊙ For all other international calls, dial ☎011 + country code + area code + local number.

⊙ To call Hawaii from abroad, the international country code for the USA is ☎1.

USEFUL NUMBERS

⊙ Emergency (police, fire, ambulance) ☎911

⊙ Local directory assistance ☎411

⊙ Long-distance directory assistance ☎1-(area code)-555-1212

⊙ Toll-free directory assistance ☎1-800-555-1212

⊙ Operator ☎0

Tourist Information

In the arrivals area at the airport there are tourist-information desks with helpful staff. While you're waiting for your bags to appear on the carousel, you can leaf through racks of tourist brochures and magazines, such as **101 Things to Do** (www.101thingstodo.com), **This Week** (http://thisweekmaga zines.com) and **Spotlight's O'ahu Gold** (www.spotlight hawaii.com), which are packed with discount coupons. For pre-trip planning, browse the information-packed website of the **Hawaii Visitors & Convention Bureau** (☎ 800-464-2924; www. gohawaii.com), which has a business office in Waikiki.

Tours

If you're short on time, the following tours give a quick overview of island highlights. For more local tours, anything from historical walks to organic farm visits, see the destination chapters earlier in this book, especially Honolulu (p64), the North Shore (p219) and the Windward Coast (p181). For guided hikes, see p299. For older-adult learning vacations, see p310.

Hawaiian Escapades (☎ 888-331-3668; www. hawaiianescapades.com; tours $65-120) Waterfall walks, circle-island adventures and, most popularly, *Hawaii 5-0* and *Lost* TV location tours that pick up and drop off in Waikiki.

E Noa Tours (☎ 591-2561, 800-824-8804; www.enoa.com) O'ahu-based tour company utilizes smaller buses and knowledgeable local guides, with standard circle-island tours (adult/child from $73/60) that include Waikiki hotel pick-ups/drop-offs.

Roberts Hawaii (☎ 539-9400, 800-831-5541; www.robertshawaii.com) Conventional bus and van sightseeing tours of O'ahu, such as marathon full-day 'Circle Island' trips (adult/child from $53/29) that include Waikiki hotel pick-ups/drop-offs.

Travelers with Disabilities

⊙ Bigger, newer hotels and resorts in Hawaii have elevators, TDD-capable phones and wheelchair-accessible rooms (reserve these well in advance).

⊙ Telephone companies provide relay operators (dial ☎711) for hearing impaired.

⊙ Many banks provide ATM instructions in Braille.

○ Traffic intersections have dropped curbs and audible crossing signals in cities and some towns, as well as all along Waikiki's beachfront.

○ Honolulu's **Department of Parks and Recreation** (📞768-3027; www.honolulu. gov/parks/dprbeachaccess. html) provides all-terrain beach mats and wheelchairs for free (call ahead to make arrangements) at several beaches, including Ala Moana, Hanauma Bay, Sans Souci, Kailua, Kualoa and Poka'i Bay.

○ Guide dogs and service animals are not subject to the same quarantine requirements as pets; contact the Department of Agriculture's **Animal Quarantine Station** (📞808-483-7151; http://hawaii.gov/hdoa/) before arrival.

TRANSPORTATION

○ All public buses on O'ahu are wheelchair-accessible and will 'kneel' if you're unable to use the steps – just let the driver know that you need the lift or ramp.

○ If you have a disability parking placard from home, bring it with you and hang it from your rental car's rearview mirror when using designated disabled-parking spaces.

○ Some major car-rental agencies offer hand-controlled vehicles and vans with wheelchair lifts. You'll need to reserve these well in advance.

USEFUL RESOURCES

Access Aloha Travel (📞545-1143, 800-480-1143; www.accessalohatravel.com)

Local travel agency can help book wheelchair-accessible accommodations, rental vans and sightseeing tours.

Disability & Communication Access Board (www.hawaii.gov/health/dcab/travel) Online 'Traveler Tips' brochures provide info about airports, accessible transportation, sightseeing, and medical and other support services.

●●●

Volunteering

For volunteering opportunities on O'ahu, see p283.

Transport

●●●

Getting There & Away

 AIR

Most visitors to O'ahu arrive by air. Honolulu is a major Pacific hub and intermediate stop on many flights between the US mainland and Asia, Australia, New Zealand and the South Pacific. Flights can be booked online at www.lonelyplanet.com/bookings.

AIRPORTS

US mainland, interisland and international flights arrive at **Honolulu International Airport** (HNL; Map p38; http://hawaii.gov/hnl), a modern facility with all the usual amenities such as currency-exchange booths, duty-free shops and fast-food eateries, as well as flower lei stands. You'll find visitor information desks, car-rental counters and courtesy phones in the baggage claim area. Free **Wiki-Wiki shuttle buses** (🕓6am-10pm) connect the airport's public terminals.

To get through airport security checkpoints, you'll need a boarding pass and photo ID. Airport security measures restrict many common items (eg pocket knives, any liquids or gels over 3oz) from being carried on planes. These regulations often change, so get the latest information from the **Transportation Security Administration** (TSA; 📞866-289-9673; www.tsa.gov).

TICKETS

Air fares to Honolulu vary tremendously, depending on the season and day of the week you fly. Competition is highest among airlines flying from major US mainland cities, especially with **Hawaiian Airlines** (www.hawaiianair.com) and **Alaska Airlines** (www.alaskaair.com). Generally speaking, return fares from the US mainland to Hawaii cost from $400 (in low season from the West Coast) to $800 or more (in high season from the East Coast).

Agricultural Inspection

All checked and carry-on bags leaving Hawaii for the US mainland must be checked by an agricultural inspector using an X-ray machine. You cannot take out gardenia, jade vine or Mauna Loa anthurium, even in lei, although most other fresh flowers and foliage are permitted. With the exceptions of pineapples and coconuts, most fresh fruit and vegetables are banned. Also not allowed to enter mainland states are plants in soil, fresh coffee berries (roasted beans OK), cactus and sugarcane. For more information, contact the **USDA Honolulu office** (☎ 861-8490) or go online to http://hawaii.gov/hdoa.

Offered by major airlines and online travel booking sites, vacation packages that include airfare, accommodations and possibly car rental, tours and/ or activities may cost less than booking everything separately. **Pleasant Holidays** (☎ 800-742-9244; www. pleasantholidays.com) offers competitive vacation packages from the US mainland.

Within Hawaii

Fast, frequent flights connect Honolulu with the Neighbor Islands. Interisland fares vary wildly; expect to pay from $60 to $180 one way. Round-trip fares are usually double the one-way fare with no additional discounts. The earlier you book your interisland ticket, the more likely you are to find a cheaper fare. Buy tickets on airline websites, which often post online-only deals.

◦ Of the two main interisland carriers, **Mokulele Airlines** (www.mokuleleairlines.com) tends to be cheaper, but **Hawaiian Airlines** (www. hawaiianair.com) has far more flights and reliable service.

◦ **Island Air** (www.islandair. com) uses smaller smaller turboprop aircraft that almost double as sightseeing planes – tons of fun!

●●●

Getting Around

O'ahu is a relatively easy island to get around, whether you're traveling by car or public bus. Compared with US mainland cities, island traffic is fairly manageable, although traffic into, out of and through Honolulu jams up during weekday morning and afternoon rush hours.

TO/FROM THE AIRPORT

Honolulu International Airport is on the western outskirts of the metro area, approximately 10 miles from Waikiki via Ala Moana Blvd/Nimitz Hwy (Hwy 92) or the H-1 (Lunalilo) Fwy. An airport taxi to Waikiki costs approximately $35 to $45, depending on where your hotel is exactly. Major car-rental agencies have booths or courtesy phones in the arrivals baggage-claim area.

AIRPORT SHUTTLE

Of a few door-to-door airport shuttle companies, **Roberts Hawaii** (☎ 441-7800, 800-831-5541; www.airportwaikik-ishuttle.com) operates buses to Waikiki hotels around the clock. Shuttles depart frequently from the roadside median on the airport's ground level outside baggage claim. Reservations for airport pick-ups are helpful but not always required; for the return trip to the airport, you must call 48 hours in advance. The ride to/ from Waikiki averages 45 minutes, depending on how many stops the shuttle makes. The one-way/round-trip fare is $15/28, with surcharges for bicycles, surfboards, golf clubs, strollers and other oversized or excess baggage.

BUS

Buses 19 and 20 travel to downtown Honolulu, Ala Moana and Waikiki, taking anywhere from 45 to 80 minutes. Buses stop at the roadside median on the airport's second level, upstairs from baggage claim and outside the airline check-in counters. Buses fill up fast, so catch them at the first stop outside the interisland terminal; the next stops are outside the main terminal's Lobby 4 and Lobby 7. Buses run every 20 minutes from 6am to 11pm daily; the regular one-way adult fare is $2.50. Luggage is restricted to what you can hold on your lap or stow under the seat (maximum size: 22in × 14in x 9in). In Waikiki, buses stop on Kalia Rd, Saratoga Rd and every couple of blocks along Kuhio Ave.

Climate Change & Travel

Every form of transport that relies on carbon-based fuel generates CO_2, the main cause of human-induced climate change. Modern travel is dependent on airplanes, which might use less fuel per mile per person than most cars but travel much greater distances. The altitude at which aircraft emit gases (including CO_2) and particles also contributes to their climate change impact. Many websites offer 'carbon calculators' that allow people to estimate the carbon emissions generated by their journey and, for those who wish to do so, to offset the impact of the greenhouse gases emitted with contributions to portfolios of climate-friendly initiatives throughout the world. Lonely Planet offsets the carbon footprint of all staff and author travel.

CAR

The easiest driving route to Waikiki is via Hwy 92, which starts out as the Nimitz Fwy and turns into Ala Moana Blvd. Although this route hits local traffic, it's hard to get lost. For the fast lane, take the H-1 Fwy eastbound, then follow signs 'To Waikiki.' Returning to the airport, beware of the poorly marked interchange where H-1 and Hwy 78 split; if you're not in the right-hand lane at that point, you could easily end up on Hwy 78 by mistake. It takes about 25 minutes – if you don't hit heavy traffic – to drive from Waikiki to the airport via H-1, but give yourself at least 45 minutes during weekday morning and afternoon rush hours.

BICYCLE

Cycling around O'ahu is a great, nonpolluting way to travel. Realistically, as a primary mode of transportation, cycling can be a challenge. Bicycles are prohibited on freeways, so take the bus (p328) to get beyond Honolulu's metro-area traffic. Every public bus is equipped with a rack that can carry two bicycles. Let the driver know that you'll be loading your bike, then secure your bicycle onto the fold-down rack, hop aboard and pay the regular fare (no bicycle surcharge). Hawaii's **Department of Transportation** (http://hidot.hawaii.gov/highways/bike-map-oahu) publishes a *Bike O'ahu* route map, available free online and at local bike shops.

RENTAL

- Rental rates start at $20 to $40 per day (up to $85 for high-tech road or mountain bikes); multiday and weekly discounts may be available. A hefty credit-card deposit is usually required.

- You can easily rent beach cruisers and hybrid commuter bikes in Waikiki (see p131), Kailua (p203) and Wai'anae (p156).

- For high-end road and mountain bikes, visit specialty bike shops, including in Honolulu (p62) and Kailua (p203).

- Some B&Bs, guesthouses and hostels rent or loan bicycles to guests.

ROAD RULES

- Generally, bicycles are required to follow the same state laws and rules of the road as cars. Bicycles are prohibited on freeways and sidewalks.

- State law requires all cyclists under age 16 to wear helmets.

- Any bicycle used from 30 minutes after sunset until 30 minutes before sunrise must have a forward-facing headlight and at least one red rear reflector.

BUS

O'ahu's extensive public bus system, **TheBus** (848-5555; www.thebus.org; infoline 5:30am-10pm), is convenient and easy to use, but you can't set your watch by it. Besides not getting hung up on schedules, buses sometimes bottleneck, with one packed bus after another passing right by crowded bus stops (you can't just flag a bus down anywhere along its route).

As long as you don't try to cut your travel time too close or schedule too much in one day, the bus is a great deal. All buses are wheelchair-accessible and have two front-loading, fold-down bicycle racks (let the driver know before using them). One caveat: with arctic blasts of air-con, a public bus in Honolulu is probably the coldest place on O'ahu, regardless of the season.

FARES & PASSES

○ The regular one-way fare is $2.50/1 for adults/children aged six to 17.

○ Pay upon boarding with coins or $1 bills; bus drivers don't give change.

○ For each paid fare, one free transfer (two-hour time limit) is available from the driver.

○ A $35 visitor pass valid for unlimited rides during four consecutive days is sold at Waikiki's ubiquitous ABC Stores and TheBus Pass Office (☏848-4444; 811 Middle St; ⏱7:30am-4pm Mon-Fri), far west of downtown Honolulu.

○ A monthly bus pass ($60), valid for unlimited rides during a calendar month (not just any 30-day period), is sold at TheBus Pass Office, 7-Eleven convenience stores, UH Manoa Campus Center and Foodland and Times supermarkets.

○ Seniors (65 years and older) and anyone with a documented physical disability can buy a $10 discount ID card at TheBus Pass Office, which entitles you to pay $1 per one-way fare, or $5/30 for a pass valid for unlimited rides during one calendar month/year.

ROUTES & SCHEDULES

More than 100 bus routes collectively cover most of O'ahu, but leave some popular viewpoints, parks and hiking trails beyond reach. Most routes run fairly frequently throughout the day from around 6am until 8pm (or later in Honolulu and Waikiki), with reduced night and weekend schedules. The Ala Moana Center shopping mall is Honolulu's central transfer point.

Confusingly, the same numbered bus route can have different destinations, even though buses generally keep the same number when inbound and outbound. For instance, bus 8 can take you into the heart of Waikiki or away from it toward Ala Moana, so take note of both the number and the written destination before jumping on. If in doubt, ask the driver.

For a table of useful bus routes to/from Waikiki, see p131; for Honolulu, see p88.

CAR

Most visitors on O'ahu rent their own vehicles, but if you're just staying in Waikiki and Honolulu, a car may be more of an expensive hindrance than a help. Free parking is usually plentiful, except in Honolulu and Waikiki. When parking on city streets, bring change for the meters, beware of color-coded curbs and read all posted restrictions to avoid being ticketed and possibly towed.

AUTOMOBILE ASSOCIATIONS

AAA has reciprocal agreements with some international automobile associations (eg Canada's CAA), but bring your membership card from home.

American Automobile Association (AAA; ☏593-2221; www.hawaii.aaa.com; 1130 N Nimitz Hwy, Honolulu; ⏱9am-5pm Mon-Fri, to 2pm Sat) Members are entitled to discounts on select car rentals, hotels, sightseeing and attractions, as well as free road maps and travel-agency services. For emergency roadside assistance and towing, members can call ☏800-222-4357.

DRIVER'S LICENSE

○ Foreign visitors can legally drive in Hawaii with a valid driver's license issued by their home country.

○ Car-rental companies will generally accept foreign driver's licenses, but usually only if they're written in English. Otherwise, be prepared

Don't Get Lost

Directions on O'ahu are often given by using landmarks. If someone tells you to 'go 'Ewa' (an area west of Honolulu) or 'go Diamond Head' (east of Waikiki), it simply means to head in that direction. Two other commonly used directional terms are *makai* (toward the ocean) and *mauka* (toward the mountain, or inland).

Street addresses on some island highways may seem random, but there's a pattern. For hyphenated numbers, such as 4-734 Kuhio Hwy, the first part of the number identifies the post office district and the second part identifies the street address. Thus, it's possible for 4-736 to be followed by 5-002; you've just entered a new district, that's all.

to present an International Driving Permit (IDP) along with your home license.

RENTAL

Agencies

Avis, Budget, Enterprise, National and Hertz have rental cars at Honolulu International Airport. Alamo, Dollar and Thrifty operate a mile outside the airport off Nimitz Hwy (free courtesy shuttles provided). All things being equal, try to rent from a company with its lot inside the airport. On the drive back to the airport, all highway signs lead to on-site rental car returns, and looking for a lot outside the airport when you're trying to catch a flight can be stressful.

Rental cars are also available at agency branch offices in Waikiki (see p132), although rates may be higher than at the airport. Independent car-rental agencies in Waikiki are more likely to rent to younger drivers under age 25 (surcharges may apply) and/or offer one-day deals on 4WD vehicles. When you pick up your vehicle, most agencies will request the name and phone number of the place where you're staying. Some agencies are reluctant to rent to anyone who lists a campground as their address; a few specifically add 'No Camping Permitted' to rental contracts. Alternatively, **Hawaii Campers** (☏ 222-2547; www.hawaiicampers.net) rents pop-top VW camper vans, equipped with kitchens, (from $125 to $155 per day, weekly discounts available).

Major car-rental agencies on O'ahu, some of which offer 'green' hybrid models:

Advantage (☏ 800-777-5500; www.advantage.com)

Alamo (☏ 877-222-9075; www.alamo.com)

Avis (☏ 800-331-1212; www.avis.com)

Budget (☏ 800-527-0700; www.budget.com)

Dollar (☏ 800-800-3665; www.dollar.com)

Enterprise (☏ 800-261-7331; www.enterprise.com)

Hertz (☏ 800-654-3131; www.hertz.com)

National (☏ 877-222-9058; www.nationalcar.com)

Thrifty (☏ 800-847-4389; www.thrifty.com)

Rates

- The daily rate for renting a compact car usually ranges from $35 to $75, while typical weekly rates are $150 to $300.

- When getting quotes, always ask for the full rate *including taxes, fees and surcharges*, which can easily add more than $10 a day.

- Rental rates usually include unlimited mileage, but ask first.

- If you belong to an automobile club or a frequent-flyer program, you may be eligible for discounts. Also check **Discount Hawaii Car Rental** (www.discounthawaiicarrental.com).

Insurance

- Required by law, liability insurance covers any people or property that you might hit.

- For damage to the rental vehicle, a collision damage

Driving Distances & Times

DESTINATION	MILES TO/ FROM WAIKIKI	AVERAGE DRIVING TIME
Diamond Head	3	10min
Hale'iwa	37	55min
Hanauma Bay	11	25min
Honolulu Airport	10	25min
Ka'ena Point State Park	49	70min
Kailua	17	30min
Ko Olina	31	45min
La'ie	38	65min
Nu'uanu Pali Lookout	11	20min
Pearl Harbor	15	30min
Sunset Beach	43	65min
Waimanalo	20	35min

waiver (CDW) costs an extra $15 to $20 a day.

○ If you decline CDW, you will be held liable for any damage up to the full value of the car.

○ Even with CDW, you may be required to pay the first $100 to $500 for repairs; some agencies also charge you for the rental cost of the car during the entire time it takes to be repaired.

○ If you have collision coverage on your vehicle at home, it might cover damage to car rentals; ask your insurance agent before your trip.

○ Some credit cards offer reimbursement coverage for collision damage if you rent the car with that card; check before you leave home.

○ Most credit-card coverage isn't valid for rentals over 15 days or for 'exotic' models (eg convertibles, 4WD Jeeps).

Reservations

Always make reservations in advance. With most car-rental companies there's little or no cancellation penalty if you change your mind before arrival. Walking up to the counter without a reservation will subject you to higher rates, and during busy periods it's not uncommon for all cars to be rented out (no kidding). If you need a child-safety seat ($10 per day, maximum $50),

reserve one when booking your car.

ROAD RULES

Slow, courteous driving is the rule on O'ahu, not the exception. Locals don't honk (unless they're about to crash), don't follow too closely (eg tailgate), and let other drivers pass. Do the same, and you may get an appreciative *shaka* (Hawaiian hand greeting sign) in return.

○ Talking or texting on a cell phone or mobile device while driving is illegal.

○ Driving under the influence (DUI) of alcohol or drugs is a criminal offense (see p313).

○ The use of seat belts is required for the driver, front-seat passengers and all children under age 18.

○ Child safety seats are mandatory for children aged three and younger; children aged four to seven who are under 4ft 9in tall must ride in a booster seat or be secured by a lap-only belt in the back seat.

MOPED & MOTORCYCLE

Surprisingly, a moped or motorcycle can be more expensive to rent than a car. Mopeds cost from $40/175 per day/week, while motorcycles start around $125/500 per day/week (hefty credit-card deposit usually required). Both are rented in Waikiki (see

p132), but you'll have to contend with heavy urban traffic.

ROAD RULES

○ You can legally drive a moped in Hawaii with a valid driver's license issued by your home state or country. Motorcyclists need a specially endorsed motorcycle license.

○ The minimum age for renting a moped is 16; for a motorcycle it's 21.

○ Helmets are not legally required, but rental agencies often provide them free – use 'em.

○ By law, mopeds must be ridden by one person only and always driven single file at speeds of 30mph or less. They're prohibited on sidewalks and freeways.

TAXI

Taxis have meters and charge a flag-down fee of $3.10, plus another $3.60 per mile and 50¢ per suitcase or backpack. Taxis are readily available at the airport, resort hotels and shopping malls, but otherwise you'll probably need to call for one. In Honolulu and Waikiki, try:

Charley's (☎ 233-3333, from payphones 877-531-1333; www.charleystaxi.com)
City Taxi (☎ 524-2121; www.citytaxihonolulu.com)
TheCab (☎ 422-2222; www.thecabhawaii.com)

Glossary

'a'a – type of lava that is rough and jagged

ae'o – Hawaiian black-necked stilt

'ahinahina – silversword plant with pointed silver leaves

ahu – stone cairns used to mark a trail; an altar or shrine

ahupua'a – traditional land division, usually in a wedge shape that extends from the mountains to the sea (smaller than a *moku*)

'aina – land

'akala – Hawaiian raspberry or thimbleberry

'akohekohe – Maui parrotbill

'alae ke'oke'o – Hawaiian coot

'alae 'ula – Hawaiian moorhen

'alauahio – Maui creeper

ali'i – chief, royalty

ali'i nui – high chiefs, kingly class

aloha – the traditional greeting meaning love, welcome, good-bye

aloha 'aina – love of the land

'amakihi – small, yellow-green honeycreeper; one of the more common native birds

anchialine pool – contains a mixture of seawater and freshwater

'apapane – bright red native Hawaiian honeycreeper

a'u – swordfish, marlin

'aumakua – protective deity or guardian spirit, deified ancestor

'awa – see *kava*

'awa'awa – bitter

azuki bean – often served as a sweetened paste, eg as a topping for shave ice

braguinha – a Portuguese stringed instrument introduced to Hawaii in the late 19th century from which the ukulele is derived

e komo mai – welcome

'elepaio – Hawaiian flycatcher; a brownish native bird with a white rump

hã – breath

ha'i – voiced register-break technique used by women singers

haku – head

hala – pandanus tree; the leaves *(lau)* are used in weaving mats and baskets

hale – house

Haloa – the stillborn son of Papa and Wakea, Hawaiian earth mother and sky father deities

haole – Caucasian; literally, 'without breath'

hapa – portion or fragment; person of mixed blood

hapa haole – Hawaiian music with predominantly English lyrics

hapu'u – tree fern

hau – indigenous lowland hibiscus tree whose wood is often used for making canoe outriggers (stabilizing arms that jut out from the hull)

he'e nalu – wave sliding, or surfing

heiau – ancient stone temple; a place of worship in Hawaii

holua – sled or sled course

honi – to share breath

honu – turtle

ho'okipa – hospitality

ho'okupu – offering

ho'olaule'a – celebration, party

ho'onanea – to pass the time in ease, peace and pleasure

hukilau – fishing with a *seine*, involving a group of people who pull in the net

hula – Hawaiian dance form, either traditional or modern

hula 'auana – modern hula, developed after the introduction of Western music

hula halau – hula school or troupe

hula kahiko – traditional and sacred hula

'i'iwi – scarlet Hawaiian honeycreeper with a curved, salmon-colored beak

'iliahi – Hawaiian sandalwood

'ilima – native plant, a ground cover with delicate yellow-orange flowers; O'ahu's official flower

'ilio holo kai – 'the dog that runs in the sea'; Hawaiian monk seal

'io – Hawaiian hawk

ipo – sweetheart

ipu – spherical, narrow-necked gourd used as a hula implement

issei – first-generation immigrants to Hawaii who were born in Japan

kahili – a feathered standard, used as a symbol of royalty

kahuna – knowledgeable person in any field; commonly a priest, healer or sorcerer

kahuna lapa'au – healer

kahuna nui – high priest(ess) or royal co-regent

kalo lo'i – taro fields

kama'aina – person born and raised, or a longtime resident, in Hawaii; literally, 'child of the land'

kane/Kane – man; if capitalized, the name of one of four main Hawaiian gods

kapa – see *tapa*

kapu – taboo, part of strict ancient Hawaiian social and religious system

kapuna – elders

kaua – ancient Hawaiian lower class, outcasts

kaunaoa – a yellowish-orange vine used in Lana'i lei

kava – a mildly narcotic drink ('awa in Hawaiian) made from the roots of *Piper methysticum*, a pepper shrub

keiki – child

ki – see *ti*

ki ho'alu – slack key

kiawe – a relative of the mesquite tree introduced to Hawaii in the 1820s, now very common; its branches are covered with sharp thorns

kika kila – Hawaiian steel guitar

ki'i – see *tiki*

ki'i akua – temple images, often carved wooden idols

kilau – a stiff, weedy fern

kipuka – an area of land spared when lava flows around it; an oasis

ko – sugarcane

koa – native hardwood tree often used in making Native Hawaiian crafts and canoes

koki'o ke'oke'o – native Hawaiian white hibiscus tree

kokua – help, cooperation

koloa maoli – Hawaiian duck

kona – leeward side; a leeward wind

konane – a strategy game similar to checkers

konohiki – caretakers of *ahupua'a*

ko'olau – windward side

Ku – Polynesian god of many manifestations, including god of war, farming and fishing (husband of Hina)

kukui – candlenut, the official state tree; its oily nuts were once burned in lamps

kuleana – rights

kumu hula – hula teacher

Kumulipo – Native Hawaiian creation story or chant

kupuna – grandparent, elder

ku'ula/Ku'ula – a stone idol placed at fishing sites, believed to attract fish; if capitalized, the god of fishers

la'au lapa'au – plant medicine

lanai – veranda; balcony

lau – leaf

lauhala – leaves of the *hala* plant, used in weaving

lei – garland, usually of flowers, but also of leaves, vines, shells or nuts

leptospirosis – a disease acquired by exposure to water contaminated by the urine of infected animals, especially livestock

limu – seaweed

lokelani – pink damask rose, or 'rose of heaven'; Maui's official flower

loko i'a – fishpond

loko wai – freshwater pond

lolo – stupid, feeble-minded, crazy

lomi – to rub or soften

lomilomi – traditional Hawaiian massage; known as 'loving touch'

Lono – Polynesian god of harvest, agriculture, fertility and peace

loulu – native fan palms

luakini – a type of *heiau* dedicated to the war god Ku and used for human sacrifices

luau – traditional Hawaiian feast

luna – supervisor or plantation boss

mahalo – thank you

mahele – to divide; usually refers to the Great Mahele land reform act of 1848

mahu – a transgendered or cross-dressing male

mai ho'oka'awale – leprosy (Hansen's disease); literally, 'the separating sickness'

mai'a – banana

maile – native plant with twining habit and fragrant leaves; often used for lei

maka'ainana – commoners; literally, 'people who tend the land'

makaha – a sluice gate, used to regulate the level of water in a fishpond

makahiki – traditional annual wet-season winter festival dedicated to the agricultural god Lono

makai – toward the sea; seaward

make – to die

malihini – newcomer, visitor

mamo – a yellow-feathered bird, now extinct

mana – spiritual power

mauka – toward the mountains; inland

mele – song, chant

menehune – 'little people' who, according to legend, built many of Hawaii's fishponds, heiau and other stonework

milo – a native shade tree with beautiful hardwood

moa – jungle fowl

mokihana – a tree with leathery berries that faintly smell of licorice, used in *lei*

moku – wedge-shaped areas of land running from the ridge of the mountains to the sea

mokupuni – low, flat island or atoll

mo'i – king

mo'o – water spirit, water lizard or dragon

muumuu – a long, loose-fitting dress introduced by the missionaries

na keiki – children

na'u – fragrant Hawaiian gardenia

naupaka – a native shrub with delicate white flowers

Neighbor Islands – the term used to refer to the main Hawaiian Islands except for O'ahu

nene – a native goose; Hawaii's state bird

nisei – second-generation Japanese immigrants

niu – coconut palm

no ka 'oi – the best

'ohana – family, extended family; close-knit group

'ohi'a lehua – native Hawaiian tree with tufted, feathery, pom-pom-like flowers

'olelo Hawai'i – the Hawaiian language

oli – chant

olona – a native shrub

'ope'ape'a – Hawaiian hoary bat

'opihi – an edible limpet

pahoehoe – type of lava that is quick and smooth- flowing

pakalolo – marijuana; literally, 'crazy smoke'

palaka – Hawaiian-style plaid shirt made from sturdy cotton

pali – cliff

paniolo – cowboy

Papa – earth mother

pau – finished, no more

pa'u – traditional horse riding, in which lei-bedecked women in flowing dresses ride for show (eg in a parade)

pau hana – 'stop work'; happy hour

Pele – goddess of fire and volcanoes; her home is in Kilauea Caldera

pidgin – distinct local language and dialect, originating from Hawaii's multiethnic plantation immigrants

pikake – jasmine flowers

piko – navel, umbilical cord

pili – a bunchgrass, commonly used for thatching traditional *hale* and *heiau*

pohaku – rock

pohuehue – beach morning glory (a flowering plant)

pono – righteous, respectful and proper

pua aloalo – yellow hibiscus

pua'a waewae loloa – 'long-legged pigs,' an ancient Hawaiian euphemism for human sacrificial victims

pueo – Hawaiian owl

puka – any kind of hole or opening; puka shells are small, white and strung into necklaces

pukiawe – native plant with red and white berries and evergreen leaves

pule – prayer, blessing, incantation or spell

pulu – the silken clusters encasing the stems of tree ferns

pupu – snack or appetizer; also a type of shell

pu'u – hill, cinder cone

pu'uhonua – place of refuge

raku – a style of Japanese pottery characterized by a rough, handmade appearance

rubbah slippah – flip-flops

sansei – third-generation Japanese immigrants

shaka – hand gesture used in Hawaii as a greeting or sign of local pride

shōji – translucent paper-covered wooden sliding doors
stink-eye – dirty look

taiko – Japanese drumming
talk story – to strike up a conversation, make small talk
tapa – cloth made by pounding the bark of paper mulberry, used for Native Hawaiian clothing (*kapa* in Hawaiian)
ti – common native plant; its long shiny leaves are used for wrapping food and making hula skirts (*ki* in Hawaiian)

tiki – wood- or stone-carved statue, usually depicting a deity (*ki'i* in Hawaiian)
tutu – grandmother or grandfather; also term of respect for any member of that generation

'ua'u – dark-rumped petrel
ukulele – a stringed musical instrument derived from the *braguinha*, which was introduced to Hawaii in the 1800s by Portuguese immigrants
'uli'uli – gourd rattle containing seeds and decorated with feathers, used as a hula implement

'ulu – breadfruit
'ulu maika – ancient Hawaiian stone bowling game
wahi pana – sacred or legendary place
Wakea – sky father
warabi – bracken fern
wauke – paper mulberry, used to make *tapa*
wiliwili – the lightest of the native woods

zendo – communal Zen meditation hall

Behind the Scenes

Author Thanks
Craig McLachlan

A huge thanks to my on-the-road assistant and exceptionally beautiful wife, Yuriko! And cheers to Paul & Nezia, Phil & Liwei and everyone else who helped us out.

Acknowledgments

Climate map data adapted from Peel MC, Finlayson BL & McMahon TA (2007) 'Updated World Map of the Köppen-Geiger Climate Classification', Hydrology and Earth System Sciences, 11, 163344.

Cover photographs
Front: Waikiki Beach, Bob Pool/Corbis
Back: Sailboat near Diamond Head and Waikiki, Tomas del Amo/Corbis

This Book

This 2nd edition of Lonely Planet's *Discover Honolulu, Waikiki & O'ahu* was written by Craig McLachlan. The previous edition was written by Sara Benson and Lisa Dunford. This guidebook was produced by the following:

Destination Editor Alexander Howard
Product Editors Briohny Hooper, Elizabeth Jones, Kate Mathews
Senior Cartographer Anthony Phelan
Book Designer Jessica Rose
Assisting Editors Susan Paterson, Kirsten Rawlings, Saralinda Turner
Assisting Cartographer Gabriel Lindquist
Cover Researcher Naomi Parker
Thanks to Sasha Baskett, Kate Chapman, Brendan Dempsey, Ryan Evans, Anna Harris, Kate James, Martine Power, Diana Saengkham, Lyahna Spencer, Tony Wheeler.

Index

See also separate subindexes for Activities (p331), Beaches (p333) & Sights (p333).

000 Map pages

Activities

....

Beaches

....

Sights

000 Map pages

How to Use This Book

These symbols give you the vital information for each listing:

☑	Telephone Numbers	☎	Wi-Fi Access	☒	Bus
⊙	Opening Hours	≋	Swimming Pool	☒	Ferry
P	Parking	☒	Vegetarian Selection	M	Metro
⊖	Nonsmoking	☒	English-Language Menu	S	Subway
❋	Air-Conditioning	☒	Family-Friendly	☒	London Tube
@	Internet Access	☒	Pet-Friendly	☒	Tram

Look out for these icons:

 No payment required

✐ A green or sustainable option

Our authors have nominated these places as demonstrating a strong commitment to sustainability – for example by supporting local communities and producers, operating in an environmentally friendly way, or supporting conservation projects.

All reviews are ordered in our authors' preference, starting with their most preferred option. Additionally:

Sights are arranged in the geographic order that we suggest you visit them, and within this order, by author preference.

Eating and Sleeping reviews are ordered by price range (budget, mid-range, top end) and within these ranges, by author preference.

Map Legend

Note: Not all symbols displayed appear on the maps in this book

Sights
- ☺ Beach
- ☺ Bird Sanctuary
- ☺ Buddhist
- ☺ Castle/Palace
- ☺ Christian
- ☺ Confucian
- ☺ Hindu
- ☺ Islamic
- ☺ Jain
- ☺ Jewish
- ☺ Monument
- ☺ Museum/Gallery/ Historic Building
- ☺ Ruin
- ☺ Shinto
- ☺ Sikh
- ☺ Taoist
- ☺ Winery/Vineyard
- ☺ Zoo/Wildlife Sanctuary
- ☺ Other Sight

Activities, Courses & Tours
- ☺ Bodysurfing
- ☺ Diving
- ☺ Canoeing/Kayaking
- • Course/Tour
- ☺ Sento Hot Baths/Onsen
- ☺ Skiing
- ☺ Snorkeling
- ☺ Surfing
- ☺ Swimming/Pool
- ☺ Walking
- ☺ Windsurfing
- ☺ Other Activity

Sleeping
- ☺ Sleeping
- ☺ Camping

Eating
- ☒ Eating

Drinking & Nightlife
- ☺ Drinking & Nightlife
- ☺ Cafe

Entertainment
- ☺ Entertainment

Shopping
- ☺ Shopping

Transport
- ☺ Airport
- ☺ BART station
- ☺ Border crossing
- ☺ Boston T station
- ☺ Bus
- ☺ Cable car/Funicular
- ☺ Cycling
- ☺ Ferry
- M Metro station
- ☺ Monorail
- P Parking
- ☺ Petrol station
- ☺ Subway/SkyTrain station
- ☺ Taxi
- ☺ Train station/Railway
- ☺ Tram
- Ⓤ Underground station
- • Other Transport

Information
- ☺ Bank
- ☺ Embassy/Consulate
- ☺ Hospital/Medical
- @ Internet
- ☺ Police
- ☺ Post Office
- ☺ Telephone
- ☺ Toilet
- ☺ Tourist Information
- • Other Information

Geographic
- ☺ Beach
- ☺ Lighthouse
- ☺ Lookout
- ▲ Mountain/Volcano
- ☺ Oasis
- ☺ Park
-)(Pass
- ☺ Picnic Area
- ☺ Waterfall

Population
- ☺ Capital (National)
- ◉ Capital (State/Province)
- ● City/Large Town
- ● Town/Village

Boundaries
- International
- State/Province
- Disputed
- Regional/Suburb
- Marine Park
- Cliff/Wall

Routes
- Tollway
- Freeway
- Primary
- Secondary
- Tertiary
- Lane
- Unsealed road
- Plaza/Mall
- Steps
-)= Tunnel
- Pedestrian overpass
- Walking Tour
- Walking Tour detour
- Path/Walking Trail

Hydrography
- River, Creek
- Intermittent River
- Canal
- Water
- Dry/Salt Lake
- Reef

Areas
- Airport/Runway
- Beach/Desert
- Cemetery (Christian)
- Cemetery (Other)
- Glacier
- Mudflat
- Park/Forest
- Sight (Building)
- Sportsground
- Swamp

Our Story

A beat-up old car, a few dollars in the pocket and a sense of adventure. In 1972 that's all Tony and Maureen Wheeler needed for the trip of a lifetime – across Europe and Asia overland to Australia. It took several months, and at the end – broke but inspired – they sat at their kitchen table writing and stapling together their first travel guide, *Across Asia on the Cheap*. Within a week they'd sold 1500 copies. Lonely Planet was born.

Today, Lonely Planet has offices in Franklin, London, Melbourne, Oakland, Beijing and Delhi, with more than 600 staff and writers. We share Tony's belief that 'a great guidebook should do three things: inform, educate and amuse'.

Our Writer

CRAIG MCLACHLAN

A Kiwi from the southern end of the Polynesian triangle, Craig is a regular on O'ahu and has an MBA from the University of Hawai'i at Manoa. He has covered many other destinations for Lonely Planet, including Greece, Japan and Tonga. Craig considers himself a 'freelance anything' and past jobs have included pilot, karate instructor, photographer, tour leader, hiking guide, novelist and Japanese interpreter. He once set the record for climbing Japan's 100 Famous Mountains!
See www.craigmclachlan.com.

Read more about Craig at:
http://auth.lonelyplanet.com/profiles/craigmclachlan

Published by Lonely Planet Publications Pty Ltd
ABN 36 005 607 983
2nd edition – September 2015
ISBN 978 1 74321 458 9
© Lonely Planet 2015   Photographs © as indicated 2015
10 9 8 7 6 5 4 3 2 1
Printed in China